MW00979597

JUSTICES ON THE BALLOT

Justices on the Ballot addresses two central questions in the study of judicial elections: How have state supreme court elections changed since World War II? And, what explains the changes that have occurred? To answer these questions, Herbert M. Kritzer takes the broadest scope of any study to date, investigating every state supreme court election between 1946 and 2013. Through an analysis of voting returns, campaign contributions and expenditures, television advertising, and illustrative case studies, he shows that elections have become less politicized than commonly believed. Rather, the changes that have occurred reflect broader trends in American politics, as well as increased involvement of state supreme courts in hot-button issues.

Herbert M. Kritzer is the Marvin J. Sonosky Chair of Law and Public Policy at the University of Minnesota Law School. Over the last thirty-five years he has conducted research on the American civil justice system relating to contingency fee legal practice, scientific evidence, and alternative forms of representation, among many other topics. He is the author of six books, including most recently *Risks, Reputations, and Rewards: Contingency Fee Legal Practice in the United States* (2004).

Justices on the Ballot

CONTINUITY AND CHANGE IN STATE SUPREME COURT ELECTIONS

HERBERT M. KRITZER
University of Minnesota Law School

CAMBRIDGE
UNIVERSITY PRESS

32 Avenue of the Americas, New York, NY 10013-2473, USA

Cambridge University Press is part of the University of Cambridge.

It furthers the University's mission by disseminating knowledge in the pursuit of education, learning, and research at the highest international levels of excellence.

www.cambridge.org
Information on this title: www.cambridge.org/9781107090866

First published 2015

A catalog record for this publication is available from the British Library.

Library of Congress Cataloging in Publication Data
Kritzer, Herbert M., 1947– author.
Justices on the ballot : continuity and change in state supreme court elections / Herbert M. Kritzer.
pages cm
Includes bibliographical references and index.
ISBN 978-1-107-09086-6 (hardback)
1. Judges – United States – States – Election. 2. Courts of last resort – United States – States. I. Title.
KF8776.K75 2015
347.73′3–dc23 2015003332

ISBN 978-1-107-09086-6 Hardback

Contents

Tables

Figures

Preface and Acknowledgments

Soon after I started teaching at the University of Wisconsin in 1977, I began tracking state supreme court elections in Wisconsin. In particular I tracked the partisan patterns in voting in those elections using the method of correlating the county-level vote for supreme court candidates with the county-level vote for governor, a method that was an important part of Philip Dubois' 1980 book, *From Bench to Ballot: Judicial Elections and the Quest for Accountability*. I was attracted to this method in part because it resembled an approach I had seen used by the late Frank Munger, with whom I studied as a graduate student in political science at the University of North Carolina at Chapel Hill; Frank's interest was in political parties, and he used county-level correlations across consecutive gubernatorial elections as a means for identifying when state-level shifts in partisan alignments had occurred. My own purpose in tracking partisan patterns in Wisconsin supreme court elections was primarily as a basis for discussing supreme court elections in a course on the American judicial system that I regularly taught during my thirty-year tenure at the University of Wisconsin.

The idea of moving beyond Wisconsin arose when I was invited by Steve Landsman to present a paper at the 2006 Clifford Symposium on Tort Law and Social Policy. The theme of the 2006 symposium was "Is the Rule of Law Waning in America." I proposed to prepare a paper on judicial selection ("Law Is the Mere Continuation of Politics by Different Means: American Judicial Selection in the Twenty-First Century"), a large part of which focused on state supreme court elections. For that paper I assembled county-level data for eight states in addition to Wisconsin going back to 1946. After completing that paper, I decided to extend the project to include all states using partisan, nonpartisan, or hybrid elections for the state's supreme court (what in New York is called the Court of Appeals) at any time starting from 1946, and I began assembling county-level data for all statewide general elections and certain primary elections. I eventually decided to include retention elections as well, and because only two states, California and Missouri, had state supreme court retention elections prior to 1946, I included all such elections starting with the first one in California in 1936.

While assembling the Wisconsin data had been easy because the county-level election returns were (and are) always published in the *Wisconsin Blue Book*, assembling the data for the analysis presented in this book, covering all states using elections for their state supreme courts between 1946 and 2013, proved to be a significant, and at times frustrating, undertaking. For many states the information is readily available online or in published form (e.g., in state "blue books," "legislative manuals," and the like); however, for others the information is to be found only in archives or in local newspapers that could be obtained only on microfilm via interlibrary loan.

I received tremendous assistance in this endeavor from reference librarians and interlibrary loan staff at the University of Wisconsin Law Library, the William Mitchell College of Law Library, and the University of Minnesota Law Library (particularly Suzanne Thorpe and Mary Rumsey). A number of individuals in state election offices were extremely helpful and responsive, as were a number of scholars who provided me with data from their states and/or answered questions about possible sources for their states.

Historical data on gubernatorial elections through 1990 were obtained from the Interuniversity Consortium for Political and Social Research (ICPSR Studies No. 1 and No. 13). Gubernatorial election data from later years came either from election websites maintained by the various states or from the *CQ Press Voting and Elections Collection*.

Many people assisted over the decade I worked on this project. I would particularly like to thank Jess Clayton, who worked as a project assistant for me at the University of Wisconsin in the early stages of this research, and Elise Larson and SungGeun Kim, who provided research assistance in the latter stages of the project at the University of Minnesota Law School.

Melinda Gann Hall and Larry Aspin generously provided me information on state supreme court retention elections; the Judicial Elections Data Initiative based at Washington University St. Louis (Andrew Martin, Principal Investigator) was also a source of information on retention elections. As noted above, I received assistance from scholars in several states in obtaining election data for those states: Anne Bloom (California), Richard Brisbin (West Virginia), Charles Bullock (Georgia), Kevin McGuire (North Carolina), and Nancy Reichman (Colorado).

Adam Skaggs at the Brennan Center provided me with spreadsheets containing data on advertising in 2006, 2008, and 2010; Melinda Gann Hall made available similar data from 2002 and 2004 (Melinda also generously shared with me draft chapters of her book, *Going Negative*); Eeva Moore at Justice at Stake made available data for 1999, 2003, 2007, and 2009; Ken Goldstein made available video of some advertisements from the files of CMAG; Travis Rideout shared materials obtained by the Wisconsin Advertising Project for the 2000, 2002, and 2010 elections.

Denise Roth Barber at the National Institute on Money in State Politics provided me with candidate-level data on contributions to those running for state supreme court. David Rottman at the National Center for State Courts made available public opinion survey data collected for the National Center in 1999 and 2009. Peter Knapp at William Mitchell College of Law shared with me information he had compiled on decision patterns for the Minnesota Supreme Court.

Many others generously took the time to answer questions; these persons include Kathleen Barber, Larry Baum, William Blake, Chris Bonneau, Walter Borges, Paul Brace, Brad Canon, Anthony Champagne, John Culver, Philip Dubois, James Ely, Charles Epp, James Gibson, Gwladys Gilleron, Daniel Guenther, Robert Howard, Steve Landsman, Stefanie Lindquist, Yann Marguet, David Neubauer, Malia Reddick, John Scheb, and John Voelker. I am sure there are others and to those I offer my thanks and my apologies for not listing them here.

A decision by the then editors of *Law & Society Review*, Jon Goldberg-Hiller and David Johnson, to reject a paper due to its length led me to realize that it was time to turn the materials I had gathered and the papers I had written into a book. Without their decision I would probably still be trying to spin out articles rather than turning the materials into what I hope readers find to be a coherent whole.

I received helpful comments at a number of conferences where I presented parts of the analyses that became elements of the book. Melinda Gann Hall read and commented on many of the draft chapters, and then read the entire completed manuscript, providing many insightful comments. Charles Myers, the director of the University Press of Kansas, read portions of the manuscript even though the book was not under consideration at the Press, and made some very helpful suggestions for revisions. Many helpful suggestions also came from the reviewers from Cambridge University Press. John Berger, my editor at Cambridge, has been very helpful during the revision process. My friend Carolyn Fuller proofread the entire draft manuscript prior to submission for review.

I want to also acknowledge support I received over a period of many years from the University of Wisconsin Graduate School, the University of

Wisconsin Political Science Department, William Mitchell College of Law, the University of Minnesota Law School, and the family of Marvin J. Sonosky whose generosity to the University of Minnesota Law School endowed the chair that I currently hold.

Finally . . . "Once in love with Amy, always in love with Amy . . ." My beloved wife of forty-five years, Amelia Howe Kritzer, has been my joy and support as I've worked on this project, and the many other projects I've undertaken during my forty-plus years as a member of the academy.

Introduction

The United States is all but unique in using popular elections to choose and/or retain judges. Not all states use elections, and the states that do vary widely in the specifics of their electoral arrangements. Moreover, the use of elections has been controversial from the start. Judges are supposed to be independent, and elections are the archetypical method of making public officials accountable. Ironically, the initial adoption of popular elections was at least in part intended to *increase* judicial independence, in this case independence from the elected officials who selected judges (Hall 1984a; Shugerman 2012). However, it quickly became apparent that elections introduced their own tensions in the independence versus accountability equation.

What role should politics play in the selection and retention of judges? In her concurring opinion in *Republican Party of Minnesota v. White*,[1] Justice Sandra Day O'Connor observed, "Minnesota has chosen to select its judges through contested popular elections … If the State has a problem with judicial impartiality, it is largely one the State brought upon itself by continuing the practice of popularly electing judges." Since stepping down from the Supreme Court, Justice O'Connor has been a prominent advocate for abandoning both partisan and nonpartisan elections as methods for selecting and retaining state judge (see, for example, O'Connor 2010).

At least since 2000, there has been a sharp increase in political activity surrounding some elections for state supreme court justices (Glaberson 2000a; Sample et al. 2010b).[2] The amount of money being raised by candidates in

1 536 U.S. 765, 792 (2002).

2 There is much less focus on lower level state courts. However, recent analyses of elections for intermediate courts of appeals at the state level (Frederick and Streb 2008; Streb et al. 2007) suggest that there has not been any significant change, nor does there appear to have been an increase, in contestation in elections for trial court judgeships (Nelson 2011).

some elections has skyrocketed. Television advertising has increased. Interest groups have been active players both as direct contributors and through independent advertising and activities. In one of the most extreme examples, an election for a seat on the Supreme Court of Appeals of West Virginia led to a 5-4 U.S. Supreme Court ruling that it is a violation of due process for a justice to sit on a case involving a major contributor to his or her campaign.[3] Whether the increased political activity, and the use of judicial elections more generally, is a positive or a negative for the courts is a matter of debate (Bonneau and Hall 2009; Brandenburg and Caufield 2009; Geyh 2003; Gibson 2008a, 2009; Gibson et al. 2011; Hall 2011).

While I will discuss the implications of the changes that have occurred for judicial elections and judicial selection more generally, that is not the primary focus of this book. Rather, the central questions are:

- What has changed?
- Where have those changes occurred and where have they not occurred?

What explains why change has occurred in some places but not others? To answer these questions, I examine the patterns in state supreme court elections across the United States. Unlike most contemporary studies of supreme court elections that have focused on the last 20–30 years, most of my analysis covers the entire period since the end of World War II, and for some discussions traces judicial elections in particular states back to their beginning in order to better understand contemporary patterns and the nature of change, or lack or change, that has occurred.

Central to the story that I tell here is that changes have occurred in some states but not in others – at least not yet. This leads to the question of what explains the changes that have occurred? My answer to this question is twofold. First, what we are seeing in state supreme court elections is part of larger changes that have occurred in American politics: the demise of the one-party Democratic South (Cohn 2014), the broad increase in political polarization (Hare and Poole 2014), and sharp increases in spending on elections by ideological and economic interest groups. However, these factors do not account for why change has occurred in some places and not in others, and this leads to the second part of my answer: when courts become involved in highly

[3] *Caperton v. A.T. Massey Coal Co.*, 556 U.S. 868 (2009). The election involved the defeat of an incumbent by a candidate who had received an "extraordinary amount from, and through the efforts of, the board chairman and principal officer" (Justice Kennedy's phrase) of Massey Coal. At the time, Massey was appealing a $50 million judgment for "fraudulent misrepresentation, concealment, and tortious interference with existing contractual relations," and while the case was not yet before the Supreme Court of Appeals, it was clearly headed that way.

controversial issues or issues impacting major economic interests, it should not be surprising that there is a strong political response that gets played out in the arena of judicial selection and retention. Importantly, as observed by Alan Tarr, there has been an "increasing involvement of courts, particularly in recent decades, in addressing issues with far-reaching policy consequences" (Tarr 2003:6).

In Chapter 1 I present the contrasting cases of Minnesota and Wisconsin which serve to illustrate both the presence and absence of change and the key factor accounting for that presence and absence. While early in the first third of the twentieth century Minnesota had a period of sharp conflict in elections for the state supreme court, the period since World War II has seen little conflict or rancor in those elections. Wisconsin is almost the mirror image. Until the mid- to late 1990s, Wisconsin was the archetypical nonpartisan state with regard to its supreme court, both in terms of electoral politics (Adamany and Dubois 1976) and decision patterns (Adamany 1969). In recent years Wisconsin has become the poster child for conflict and rancor both in the court itself and at the polls (Basting 2008; Corriher 2013; Sample et al. 2010b:32–33). I argue that the difference between the two states reflects the Wisconsin court deciding controversial issues related to tort (injury) law while the Minnesota court has avoided deciding, or not been placed in the position of having to decide, the kinds of issues that have led to a political backlash against a state supreme court or its justices.

In Chapter 2 I discuss the history of the use of elections to select and retain supreme court justices. I reiterate the findings of scholarship that, ironically, the shift from executive appointment to election was motivated in significant part by a desire to *reduce* the influence of politics and increase judicial independence. This happened at a time before voters were asked to complete an official ballot, what is known as the Australian ballot; the result was to give great power to parties in most states. This power flowed from the absence of primary elections as a means of choosing a party's candidates for office and from the absence of official ballots. Each party would choose its candidates and then print ballots listing those candidates, including judicial candidates, which the party's supporters would then deposit in the ballot box. As Chapter 1 discusses, this practice was not universal in judicial elections; Wisconsin structured its judicial elections in a way that served to limit party influence, and those elections developed a strong tradition of nonpartisanship. The adoption of the Australian ballot made possible the development of formally nonpartisan elections which began to be adopted in the early part of the twentieth century, and still later states began to adopt a system employing retention elections in which voters essentially give a thumbs up or a thumbs down as to whether a judge should continue in office. The second part of Chapter 2 provides a detailed discussion of the myriad variations in the election systems used for state supreme courts.

Chapter 3 answers the question of why we should care about how state supreme court justices are selected. That is, does the method of selection matter, and if so how? I consider three broad questions in this chapter, drawing heavily on extant studies but also adding several original analyses. The first question is whether the method of selection affects the public's view of their state supreme court. A subsidiary question is whether the election process, particularly the presence of negative advertising , has negative consequences for public support of the court. The second question is whether the method of selection has any direct or indirect effects on the decisions state supreme courts make; for this discussion I focus on the kinds of issues that seem to mobilize voters and interest groups: capital punishment and crime more generally, abortion, same-sex marriage, and torts. The third question examined is whether the need for candidates in judicial elections to raise money to run their campaigns has an impact on the decisions they make on the court; specifically, is there any evidence that campaign contributions lead justices, consciously or unconsciously, to favor parties and interests who were the source of those contributions? Importantly, this does not mean simply that justices vote in a way their contributors would favor because the causal relationship may run from voting (or expected voting) to contributions rather than from contributions to voting; sorting out the causal direction is both crucial and extremely difficult, and as I will show we lack a good answer one way or the other.

The next four chapters are the core of my original analysis. Chapter 4 looks at whether since 1946 state supreme court elections have increased in the likelihood of being contested and in the degree of competitiveness; the chapter includes retention elections focusing on the percentage voting in favor of retention. Chapter 5 examines changes in spending and television advertising; this chapter covers a more limited period due to the absence of systematic data prior to 1990 regarding contributions and prior to1999 regarding television advertising. Chapters 6 and 7 look at whether state supreme court elections have become more "political" in the sense of whether voting patterns fall along a partisan (party) dimension. Chapter 6 looks at this for statewide elections since 1946, both those conducted on a partisan basis and elections that do not explicitly identify candidates with a political party, and Chapter 7 examines voting patterns in all statewide retention elections, going back to the first such election in California in 1936. Chapters 6 and 7 include a combination of statistical analysis and discussion of specific elections that illustrate the underlying factors driving particular patterns.

As noted, the core data for the analysis in the following chapters cover all state supreme court elections since 1946 in states using partisan, nonpartisan, and what I label hybrid (party nominates but general election ballot is nonpartisan) elections, plus all state supreme court retention elections since the first such election in California in 1936. For both statewide and district elections, I have compiled information on the vote totals for both primary and general elections, including runoffs where they occurred. For statewide elections, I have compiled county-level vote totals for virtually all contested general elections and for nonpartisan primaries in the several states where a candidate winning a majority in the primary does not have to stand in the subsequent general election.[4] These data have been compiled from published state reports, state archives, and online sources.[5] As noted previously, the data money and advertising employed in Chapter 5 cover a shorter period; the data used in that chapter were assembled from a variety of sources that are detailed in the chapter.

In the final chapter I reprise the main findings of my analyses and reiterate my argument that much of the change that has occurred in state supreme court elections either reflects broader political changes or flows from the kinds of issues that contemporary state supreme courts have to confront. I then turn to a consideration of what changes might be considered in our systems for selecting and retaining state supreme court justices. Rather than limiting my discussion to the various systems now in use among the states, I look beyond the United States and describe two systems used for selecting judges in many other countries. Using elements of what other countries do, I go on to propose several changes that would preserve some role for the electorate, but potentially improve the selection process; I do not argue that these changes would eliminate politics from selection or retention, but some might serve to tamp down some aspects of politics as currently played out in judicial elections. I conclude with a bit of pessimism about the prospects that any of the changes I suggest will come about, and argue that a possible change that could serve to reduce some of the current patterns decried by critics of judicial elections is a return to partisan elections, although with some specific limitations – there

4 For two elections, the county-level information is lost to history; I have also omitted a third election which was conducted entirely on a write-in basis.

5 The original sources in some cases presented problems because the county-level figures occasionally did not add to the statewide totals. In some cases, there was what appeared to be a clear error in a county-level figure which when modified summed to the total. More often, it was not possible to resolve the inconsistency, and I retained the reported county-level figures for any analysis involving the county-level data and retained the state-level totals for analysis involving state-level data.

is some evidence, albeit very limited, that citizens would prefer partisan elections of judges over any of the other systems currently in use!

A NOTE ON THE GRAPHS

The story and analysis that I present in this book is told in significant part through the use of graphs showing changing patterns over time. Ideally the graphs would all appear in color. Alas, the world of publishing is not yet ideal and economic realities dictated that the graphs be published in black and white. However, I have prepared color versions of all of the statistical graphs and have made those available electronically at http://z.umn.edu/sscelections. My hope is to also include on that website versions of many of those graphs updated to include later elections; versions covering elections through 2014 should be available at the time this book appears in print.[6]

[6] Some of the updated graphs for Chapters 6 and 7 will show slight differences for 2014 from the version of the graphs based on the book. Those differences reflect the recomputation of some correlations that in the updated version could use the average of 2010 and 2014 gubernatorial election patterns.

1

A Tale of Two States

The kinds of changes in state supreme court elections that have been described by those who would change current systems of selection and retention are far from a universal development. This is clearly illustrated by the two neighboring states of Wisconsin and Minnesota: while Wisconsin has seen substantial changes, Minnesota has not. These two states have important similarities in terms of political culture, largely sharing what Daniel Elazar labeled a "moralistic political culture" (Elazar 1966:89–92, 97). They are two of the Midwestern states that have had generally liberal politics over the last fifty years, with Minnesota supporting the Republican presidential candidate only one time in the fourteen elections between 1960 and 2012, and Wisconsin supporting the Republican candidate five times in those same fourteen elections. One difference between the two states is in their economies; both have strong agricultural sectors, but Minnesota's industrial base has been more technology-oriented while Wisconsin was more dependent on heavy manufacturing. As a result, Wisconsin has been more affected by the exit of heavy industry to nonunion states and to overseas locations. However, it is unclear why this economic difference would be reflected in the different patterns found in elections for the two states' supreme courts. Thus, an intriguing puzzle is why these two neighbors have taken such different paths vis-à-vis state supreme court elections over the last fifteen to twenty years. The answer to that puzzle, I argue, is found in significant part in the kinds of decisions the courts have been called on to make, or were expected to make, in recent years. Thus, the stories of Wisconsin and Minnesota that follow illustrate the phenomena that this book addresses.

THE WISCONSIN STORY

The Battle of 2011

The winter of 2011 was a time of political turmoil in Madison, Wisconsin. In the 2010 election, Wisconsin voters had given the Republican Party control of both houses of the state legislature and also elected a Republican to be governor. Governor Scott Walker and the Republican majorities in the legislature set out to make major changes in how the state did business, and sharply reducing the power of government employees was at or near the top of their agenda. A bill to limit the rights of government employee unions to bargain on behalf of their members led the Democrats in the state senate to flee the state in order to deprive the Republican majority of the quorum needed to vote on budget-related matters. After almost three weeks of inaction, the Republican majority hurriedly pushed through a bill in the absence of the Democrats that imposed many of the restrictions but which they claimed did not fall into the category of a budget issue and hence had a lesser requirement for a quorum in the state senate. Several lawsuits followed in an effort to block the bill on grounds that its passage violated procedural requirements. A trial judge hearing one of the suits issued an injunction to prevent the bill from going into effect until the courts had decided the issue.[1]

All of this was taking place as the time for the spring nonpartisan elections in Wisconsin was approaching. The spring elections are when Wisconsin voters elect local government officials, school boards, and judges, all on nonpartisan ballots. In April 2011, Wisconsin Supreme Court justice David Prosser was running for reelection. Justice Prosser had been appointed to the Wisconsin Supreme Court in 1998 by Republican governor Tommy Thompson to fill a vacancy created by the resignation of Justice Janine Geske (a previous Thompson appointee). At the time of his appointment to the court, David Prosser was a well-known political figure in the state. He was a member of the state assembly from 1979 to 1996, serving as minority leader for six of those years and assembly speaker for two years. He relinquished his seat in the assembly in 1996 to run unsuccessfully for the U.S. House of Representatives. A month after Prosser lost the 1996 election, Governor Thompson appointed him to the Wisconsin Tax Appeals Commission, where he was serving at the time of his appointment to the Wisconsin Supreme Court.

1 The Wisconsin Supreme Court later voted 4-3 to reverse the trial court's injunction order; *State of Wisconsin ex rel. Ismael R. Ozanne v. Jeff Fitzgerald et al.*, 798 N.W.2d 436 (Wis. 2011). Three years later, in July 2014, the court upheld the validity of the law in a 5-2 vote; *Madison Teachers, Inc., et al. v. Scott Walker et al.*, 2014 WI 99.

Wisconsin justices serve ten-year terms, and when someone is appointed by the governor to fill a mid-term vacancy,[2] the new justice is required to stand for election for a full ten-year term at the next April election in which no other election for the court, either a justice completing a ten-year term standing for reelection or an open seat election, is to take place.[3] Because of other supreme court elections,[4] Justice Prosser did not come before the voters until 2001, more than two years after his initial appointment; in that election he was unopposed. Going into the 2011 election, the expectation was that Justice Prosser would be easily reelected regardless of what opposition he faced. Three people decided to challenge Prosser, which necessitated a primary election in February.[5] Of the approximately 420,000 voters casting ballots in the supreme court primary, 55 percent voted for Justice Prosser; his closest competitor in the primary received only 25 percent of the vote. However, unlike some states with nonpartisan supreme court elections (e.g., Washington and Oregon), in Wisconsin winning an absolute majority in the primary does not end the contest; consequently Prosser had to face the runner-up from the primary, longtime assistant state attorney general JoAnne Kloppenburg, in April.[6]

Just two days after the February 15 primary election, the Democrats in the state senate decamped to Illinois. Protesters opposed to the Republican plan to limit the bargaining rights of state employees filled the streets in Madison.

[2] Between 1946 and 2013, 21 of the 36 justices who joined the court were appointed to fill vacancies; throughout the history of the court (starting in 1853 when the modern court came into operation), 47 of 76 justices were initially appointed (three of the 29 elected justices were the initial members of the court).

[3] If the vacancy occurs between December 1 and the April election the next spring, the appointee does not stand for election until the following April or later. For example, if the vacancy occurs on December 15, 2015, and there is no other justice standing for election in April 2016, the appointee would not stand for election until at least April 2017 (and it could be several years later).

[4] There is never more than one seat on the Wisconsin Supreme Court on the ballot in an election.

[5] Candidates for the April election had to file nominating petitions by January 4, 2011, well before the controversy over state employee bargaining rights had heated up. There was some speculation that the interest in challenging Prosser came from the fact that there had been significant interpersonal conflict on the court (see http://www.wuwm.com/programs/news/view_news.php?articleid=7770, last visited May 11, 2011). In fact, during the spring election cycle, it was revealed that in one particularly heated conference (during the discussion of whether to discipline a member of the court for actions during that member's election campaign), Justice Prosser called Chief Justice Shirley Abrahamson a "bitch" and threatened "to destroy" her (http://www.jsonline.com/news/statepolitics/118310479.html, last visited May 11, 2011).

[6] The other two candidates in the primary were a Madison attorney, Joel Winnig, and Marla Stephens, who was the director of the appellate division in the state public defender's office. Having a primary in a supreme court election where an incumbent was running was unusual, as was having four candidates running in the primary (although there have been as many as seven candidates when the election was for an open seat).

Anger at the Republican legislature and governor mounted. Even before the legislation was passed and the court challenges were filed, opponents of Governor Walker and the Republican legislative majorities were looking for ways to express their outrage. David Prosser – sitting justice, member of the conservative majority on the state supreme court,[7] former Republican legislator, and presumed ally of Governor Walker – was an obvious target given the approaching April election. Moreover, the Wisconsin Supreme Court had what many saw as a 4-3 division between conservatives and liberals, and defeating Prosser would flip the majority to the liberal side, which could be important in challenges to the bills pending in the legislature.[8]

Not surprisingly, the election campaign was intense. Both candidates opted for public funding, and each received about $400,000. However, it was the outside groups that spent the big bucks, more than $3.5 million.[9] The advertising was extensive, with a total of almost 11,000 airings, 58.5 percent of which were attack ads.[10] The campaigns and their supporters also spent substantial amounts in time and effort to get voters to the polls.

Turnout for the election broke all records for a state supreme court election, exceeding even those that had coincided with a presidential primary. About 1.5 million Wisconsinites voted despite the absence of any other statewide offices on the ballot; the previous two elections, one of which had also been contentious, had turnouts of 800,000 and 830,000. What in January was expected to be a walk in the park for Justice Prosser turned out to be a very close election. Initial results indicated that Justice Prosser had lost by less than 250 votes, but the discovery of a large number of unreported votes in one heavily Republican county gave him a victory by more than 7,000 votes; a recount confirmed Justice Prosser's reelection. Moreover, as shown in Figure 1.1,[11] the

7 That conservative majority came into existence in 2008 when Circuit Court judge Michael Gableman defeated Justice Louis Butler (the first African American to serve on the court, who had been appointed to the court in 2004 by Democratic governor James Doyle).

8 Two members of the court, Chief Justice Shirley Abrahamson and Justice Ann Walsh Bradley, were clearly on the liberal side; however, the third member associated with the liberal side, Justice Patrick Crooks, was less clearly a part of the liberal bloc. In fact, in the ultimate decision on the validity of the law limiting government employee unions, known as Act 10, Justice Crooks sided with the conservatives, producing a 5-2 vote; *Madison Teachers, Inc., et al. v. Scott Walker et al.*, 2014 WI 99.

9 See http://www.brennancenter.org/content/resource/judicial_public_financing_in_wisconsin_2011 (last visited August 23, 2012).

10 It is worth noting that the number of ad airings in Wisconsin was even higher in the 2008 election in which Michael Gableman defeated incumbent Louis Butler. In that election there were almost 12,000 airings, 58.1 percent of which were attack ads.

11 Color versions of this and all other figures (except Figure 2.2) can be accessed at http://z.umn.edu/sscelections. Versions of the figures updated for later elections can also be found on that site.

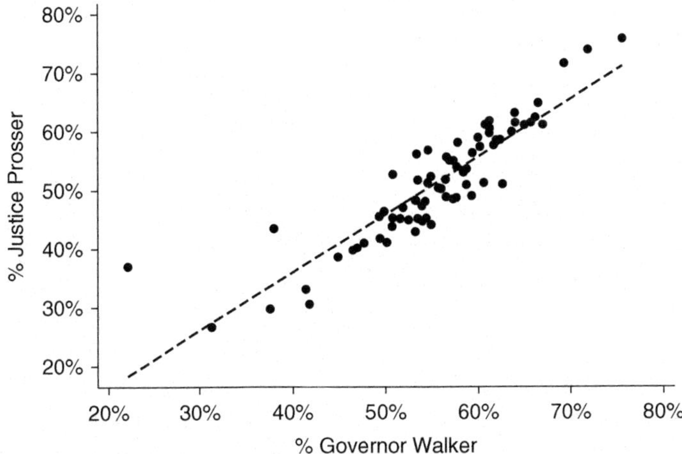

Note: Each data point represents the vote percentages for one county.

FIGURE 1.1. Partisan Pattern in 2011 Wisconsin Supreme Court Election.

voting pattern was extremely partisan. Counties that had been strong backers of Governor Walker were strong backers of Justice Prosser; counties that had gone for Walker's Democratic opponent in November 2010 went strongly for JoAnne Kloppenburg. The correlation between the county percentage for Walker in November 2010 and the county percentage for Justice Prosser in April 2011 was .89.[12] I label correlations computed in this way "partisan correlations," and one has to go back to 1863 to find a Wisconsin Supreme Court election that produced a higher partisan correlation (.926).[13]

The 2011 election reflected a culmination of developments. The 2010 election constituted a sharp shift in political control in Wisconsin, putting in place a Republican legislative majority and a Republican governor that sought to adopt what critics labeled a radical conservative agenda. More important for the discussion here is that the Wisconsin Supreme Court had developed strong factions, and conservative interests were prepared to mount campaigns to ensure a conservative majority on the court. As the next section discusses,

12 While the April 2011 election did mobilize many people and undoubtedly strengthened the partisan pattern, there was also a strong partisan pattern in the February 2011 primary, with a .71. partisan correlation between the vote for Prosser in that primary and for Walker the previous November.

13 As discussed in the next section, the 1863 election occurred at a time when there was no such thing as a nonpartisan election because there were no official ballots; voters simply indicated their preferences on a piece of paper which was deposited in the voting box, and it was common for the political parties to help their supporters by providing preprinted ballots which their supporters then deposited into the ballot box.

this represented a sharp break for a court and a judicial selection system that had a long tradition of nonpartisanship.

Wisconsin's Nonpartisan Tradition

The tradition of nonpartisanship in elections for the Wisconsin Supreme Court dates to the state's first constitution adopted when Wisconsin became a state in 1848. That first constitution required that judges be "elected by the people" but with the proviso that judicial elections could not occur within thirty days of elections for other state officers.[14] In the first few years of statehood, judicial elections were held in September, but by the 1860s those elections had been moved to April. Through the mid-1860s the elections were regularly contested, and the voting patterns evidenced moderate to strong partisanship. The most partisan election occurred in 1863 when the correlation between the voting pattern in the supreme court election and the voting pattern in the gubernatorial election was .93. From 1865 through 1889, only five of seventeen elections were contested.[15] Beginning in 1891, contests became common again, but the partisanship of those elections dropped off sharply, as shown in Figure 1.2. This figure shows the partisan correlation, computed in the manner used for the 2011 election depicted in Figure 1.1, for every contested Wisconsin Supreme Court election; the small open circles along the bottom indicate an uncontested election. From 1891 through 1996, only four elections had partisan correlations greater than .40.

The low partisanship that started in 1891 was due in part to the adoption of what is called the Australian ballot, a change that swept through the United States in the last fifteen years of the nineteenth century. The Australian ballot is a system in which election officials produce an official ballot that is given to the voter at the polling place; the voter marks the ballot in secret and deposits it in the ballot box in such a way that the voter's choices remain secret unless the voter chooses to reveal them. Most states that adopted the Australian ballot included the party of each declared candidate on the ballot. While Wisconsin state law did not explicitly forbid party labels on judicial ballots until 1913,[16] no such labels appeared in the years immediately following Wisconsin's adoption

14 Other states have tried separating the judicial elections by scheduling them at times apart from other elections, but at least some of those efforts were short-lived due to cost and lack of participation (Hall 1984a:352–53). As discussed in Chapter 2, in addition to Wisconsin's holding judicial elections in the spring, a number of other states hold their judicial elections at times separated from the even-year general elections.

15 See Keyes (1895) for a brief review of the first 40 years of elections for the Wisconsin Supreme Court.

16 1913 Wis. Sess. Laws 558.

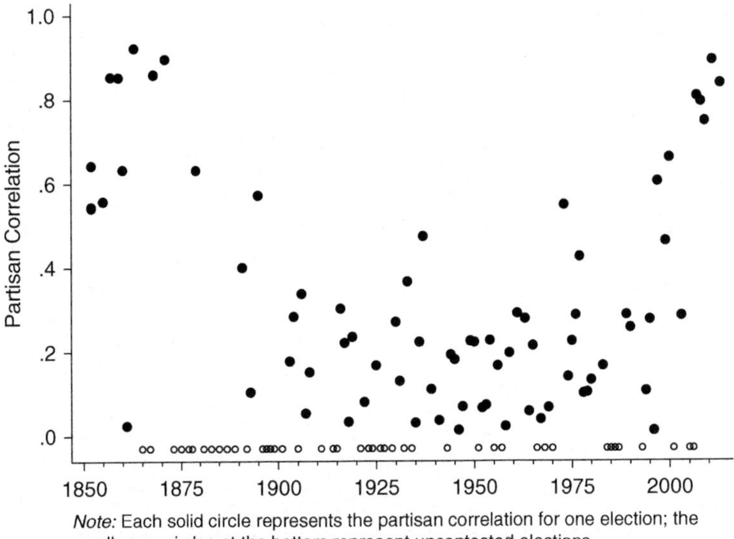

Note: Each solid circle represents the partisan correlation for one election; the small open circles at the bottom represent uncontested elections.

FIGURE 1.2. Partisan Correlations in Wisconsin, 1852–2013.

of the Australian ballot in 1889. Prior to 1913, the statute governing Wisconsin Supreme Court elections read, "No party designation shall be printed on the ballot for any school or judicial officer, except where party nominations are made".[17] Through 1982 the names of judicial candidates were almost invariably followed by the tagline "a nonpartisan judiciary";[18] this language was on sample ballots included in the statute books throughout most of the twentieth century. That tagline was discontinued starting in 1983, and now the ballot simply shows the names of the candidates.

A striking example of the norm of nonpartisanship is the 1983 election for an open seat on Wisconsin's Supreme Court. Three candidates ran in the 1983 primary, including William Bablitch, who had just relinquished his position as Democratic majority leader in the state senate, having been a member of that body for more than ten years. Bablitch, who was well known around the state, won slightly more than 50 percent in the February primary, and then won the April election with 59 percent of the vote against Circuit (trial) Court judge Gordon Myse. The nonpartisan nature of voting in this election is evident in Figure 1.3. The absolute value of the partisan correlation between

17 Wis. Stat. Ch. 5, §38, 1911. Given that the language refers to school or judicial officers, it is possible that the exception was generally understood to apply only to school-related elections.

18 I found one candidate in 1893 whose tagline was "independent."

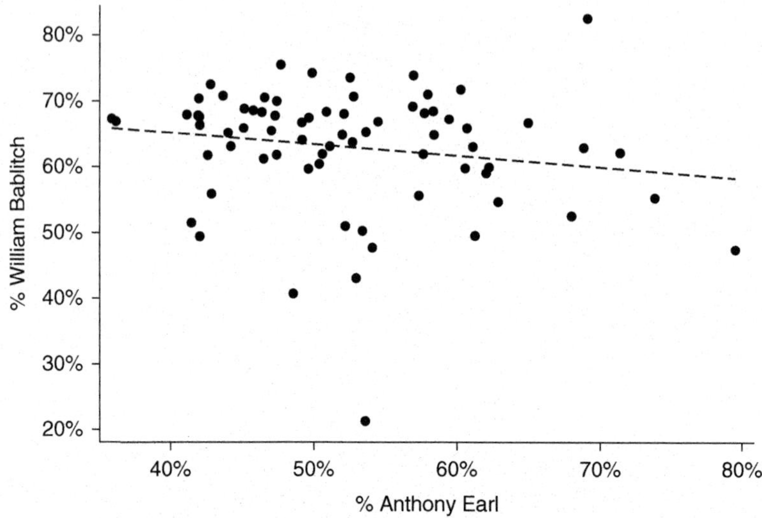

Note: Each data point represents the vote percentages for one county.

FIGURE 1.3. Partisan Pattern in 1983 Wisconsin Supreme Court Election.

the percentage voting for William Bablitch and the percentage voting the previous November for the Democratic gubernatorial was .17, which effectively indicates that there was probably no partisan pattern. Actually, the partisan correlation was negative (−.17) which is why the line in Figure 1.3 slopes slightly downward; this means that counties that had supported Democrat Anthony Earl for governor the previous November were if anything less supportive of Bablitch than were counties that had supported the Republican gubernatorial candidate in 1982. The correlation is slightly depressed by the presence of the two outliers which were the home counties of the two candidates; if these counties are omitted, the correlation is −.26 and the line shown in the figure becomes slightly steeper.

More generally, in a study of state supreme court elections between 1948 and 1974, Dubois (1980:75) found a mean partisan correlation of .18 between county-level voting patterns for governor and state supreme court in Wisconsin; extending his analysis to cover the period 1946–1996 results in a mean of the absolute value of the partisan correlation of .17.[19] Extending the period back to 1891, the mean partisan correlation is .19. The low partisan correlation in elections for the Wisconsin Supreme Court that existed through the late 1990s reflected the strong nonpartisan tradition that existed with regard to those elections.

19 My method differs slightly from the method used by Dubois; I explain this in Chapter 6.

Nonpartisanship went beyond the elections to the Wisconsin Supreme Court. The decisions of the court also reflected nonpartisanship. Studies from the 1960s and 1970s showed strong partisan patterns in state supreme court decision-making in Pennsylvania, Michigan, and California (Beiser and Silberman 1969; Feeley 1971; Schubert 1959b:134–42; Ulmer 1962, 1966). Pennsylvania employed a formally partisan selection system. Michigan employed (and still employs) a system where nominations were typically made by party conventions, but no party labels appeared on the ballot presented to voters in November. California relied on gubernatorial appointments and retention elections. Studies of decision-making by the Wisconsin Supreme Court (Adamany 1969; Dubois 1980:195–200) found no evidence of a partisan pattern even though a majority of judges on the court initially obtained their positions by gubernatorial appointments made to fill vacancies.

This is not to say that there was never conflict on the court or that the court never became involved in controversies that had electoral consequences. One of the original members of the Wisconsin Supreme Court, elected in 1852, was Samuel Crawford. In 1855, he became the first Wisconsin Supreme Court justice to be defeated in a bid for reelection. His defeat came in response to his dissent in a case related to the Fugitive Slave Act in which he took the position that federal law and decisions of the U.S. Supreme Court took precedence over decisions of state courts, including the Wisconsin Supreme Court (Winslow 1912:85–95). His defeat was probably in part a result of his association with the Democratic Party, while his opponent, Orasmas Cole, was supported by persons and newspapers associated with the rapidly growing Republican Party as well as abolitionists opposed to the Fugitive Slave Act. The most prominent abolitionist newspaper in the state charged, "to vote for Judge Crawford is to vote for the constitutionality of the Fugitive Slave Act" (Winslow 1912:87). The partisan correlation in the 1855 election was .57, substantially below the correlations for three of the next four contested elections.

The supreme court election in 1863 was the most partisan in Wisconsin's history, exceeding even the 2011 election. The partisan correlation for that election was .93. Luther Dixon had been appointed chief justice in 1859, replacing Edward Whiton, who had died. As required by Wisconsin law, Dixon stood for election in April of the following year (1860) for the remainder of the late chief justice's term, and secured election with the support of Democratic votes (Winslow 1912:202); the partisan correlation in the 1859 election was .63. Dixon had held an office previously as a Democrat, and one of his early decisions as a Wisconsin Supreme Court justice echoed Crawford's position that federal law was supreme, and that the state courts had to defer to federal law. When it came time to run for reelection during the height of the Civil War in 1863, Dixon had not sought endorsement from any political convention. His name was placed in nomination at the Democratic Party's convention, but ultimately the convention wanted a stronger Democrat and nominated M. M. Cothren on a vote of 88 for Cothren and 73 for Dixon.[20] The opposition to Dixon in part reflected his position on the question of whether the legislature had the power to provide relief to farmers burdened by mortgages on their farms; Dixon had joined the court majority striking down an 1861 law granting such relief. While there was no nomination or endorsement from a Republican Party convention, the Republican legislative caucus came out in support of Dixon, and he received the backing of a significant majority of Republican newspapers (Winslow 1912:202–17). The election was very close, and ultimately was decided by soldiers casting what we would today call absentee ballots; Dixon won with a majority of less than 4,000 votes, having obtained a majority of almost 7,700 votes from the soldiers.

Two more recent examples of heated supreme court elections occurred in the 1960s although neither were particularly partisan in their voting patterns. In 1964 Horace Wilkie, who had been appointed to the court in 1962, ran for election as required for recent appointees. At the time of his appointment, Wilkie had been serving his second four-year term as a Democrat in the Wisconsin Senate representing the city of Madison. He had been active in the revitalization of the state's Democratic Party, and had run unsuccessfully three times as a Democratic candidate for the U.S. House of Representatives. In the 1964 elections, Wilkie was vigorously challenged by Howard Boyle, who had a reputation as a right-wing conservative. Boyle had run unsuccessfully in the 1956 Republican Party primary for U.S. Senate, and ran as an independent in the special election to fill the Senate seat left vacant by the death of Senator Joseph R. McCarthy. However, despite the strong partisan base for the two candidates, the partisan correlation with the gubernatorial election the following fall was only .32 (Adamany and Dubois 1976:758; see also Ladinsky and Silver 1967:167–68).

Three years later, the sitting chief justice of the Wisconsin Supreme Court, George Currie, was defeated by Milwaukee County Circuit (trial) judge Robert Hansen. The outcome was at least in part a result of Currie's joining the majority in the Court's 4-2 decision in *Wisconsin v. Milwaukee Braves, Inc.*,[21] holding that the Milwaukee Braves' move to Atlanta did not violate Wisconsin's antitrust statutes (Koehler 2001:223). The defeat occurred

20 Cothren had previously run unsuccessfully for chief justice as the Democratic candidate opposing Chief Justice Edward Whiton in 1857 (partisan correlation, .85), and he was to run for the court unsuccessfully again in 1879 against Orasmas Cole (partisan correlation, .63).

21 144 N.W.2d 1 (Wis. 1966).

despite the fact that the chief justice had the endorsement of "nearly every Wisconsin newspaper" and was rated as qualified by 97.8 percent of those participating in the Milwaukee County Bar Association's judicial qualification poll (p. 234), compared to 75.6 percent rating the challenger as qualified. The challenger attacked the court's decision in the Braves case, "[w]hat happened in the Braves' case was a judicial abdication of our state's rights to enforce its antitrust laws against a violator" (p. 235), and former Braves' star player Eddie Matthews, join by another former player, campaigned for the challenger and formed the *Braves for Judge Bob Hansen Committee* (p. 237). The result was Currie's defeat by a margin of more than 100,000 votes out of 857,000 cast (p. 238). Despite the controversy in this election, the partisanship was nil, producing a partisan correlation with the previous fall's gubernatorial election of .03 (Dubois 1978:153).

Roots of Change in Wisconsin

Through the first two-thirds of the 1990s, partisanship did not appear to be a factor in Wisconsin Supreme Court elections even when one might have expected it. For example, in 1989, Justice Shirley Abrahamson was opposed by Ralph Adam Fine, a Milwaukee trial judge who touted his tough on crime position while attacking Justice Abrahamson as being soft on crime. Justice Abrahamson won with 55 percent of the vote; the partisan correlation was modestly above the average for the 1946–74 period at .29. The next year, appeals court judge Richard Brown challenged Justice Donald Steinmetz in what some characterized as a "nasty" race; Brown had strong backing from plaintiffs' lawyers, who charged that Steinmetz was biased in favor of the insurance industry (Romenesko 1990). Steinmetz retained his seat on the court with 52 percent of the vote; the partisan correlation was .26. There were also contested elections in 1994, 1995, and 1996; the partisan correlations remained low at .11, .28, and .01.

The election of 1997 appears to mark a break. The election that year was between incumbent Jon Wilcox, who was running for the first time, having been appointed to fill a vacancy in 1992 by Republican governor Tommy Thompson,[22] and Walt Kelly, a Milwaukee lawyer who was known as a civil rights and labor advocate who had handled cases for the American Civil Liberties Union and for abortion rights groups. The partisan correlation in that election was .60. Between 1997 and 2013, nine of twelve elections for the Wisconsin Supreme

[22] Wilcox had served three terms as a Republican member of the state assembly from 1969 to 1975, and then as a circuit court judge for 13 years immediately prior to his appointment to the Wisconsin Supreme Court.

Court were contested, and in only one of those contested elections was the partisan correlation less than .45,[23] while six of the partisan correlations exceeded .65.

What accounts for this change? One earlier development that is noteworthy, but probably does not explain the change in election patterns, is the creation of the Wisconsin Court of Appeals in 1977.[24] With this change, the Wisconsin Supreme Court obtained control over its docket, and the nature of cases being decided by the court changed. No longer was the court handling routine appeals. Prior to 1978, justices were assigned randomly to write the court opinions, and would write majority opinions even in cases in which they were dissenting. In the roughly fifteen-year period (1965–1979), dissent on the court was relatively rare, occurring in an average of 6.7 percent of cases each year; in the period from 1980 through 1996 the dissent rate increased to an average of 17.6 percent of cases each year. From 1997 through 2004, the average was 27.3 percent of cases each year, and from 2004–05 to 2012–13 the dissent rate averaged 55.5 percent.[25] The increase in dissent after the creation of the Court of Appeals would be expected both because the kinds of cases being decided would have changed and the justices would have more time to produce dissenting opinions. There are two factors that might explain the increased dissent starting around 1997: further changes in the kinds of cases being decided and/or changes in court personnel.

One development that occurred soon after the 1996 election, which was an open seat election to fill the position being vacated by retiring chief justice Roland Day, was the ascension of Justice Shirley Abrahamson to the chief's position. In Wisconsin, the chief justice is the member of the court who has served the longest. Abrahamson was appointed to the court in 1976 by Democratic governor Patrick Lucey, becoming the first woman to serve on the court.[26]

[23] The 2003 election between Ed Bruner and Patricia Roggensack produced a partisan correlation of .29. However, this election followed a three-candidate primary in which one candidate was Paul Higginbotham, an African American circuit judge in Madison. The partisan correlation for Higginbotham in the primary was .52; for the combination of Higginbotham plus Bruner (versus Roggensack) it was .42.

[24] The new intermediate appellate courts began operation in 1978.

[25] The figures for the two earlier periods are based on data compiled by Stefanie Lindquist. For the latest period the average is based on data at http://www.scowstats.com/ (last visited June 8, 2014); that source also has data for 1999–2000 through 2003–04, and the mean dissent rate for those five terms is 44.6 percent. In an earlier study, Glick and Pruet (1986:202) found dissent in less than 10 percent of Wisconsin Supreme Court decisions for selected years prior to 1980; after the creation of the Court of Appeals, dissent started to become more common, rising to 15 percent in 1980–81.

[26] Justice Abrahamson remained the sole woman on the court for about 15 years; a second woman, Janine Geske, joined her on the court in 1993, and as of 2014, four of seven members of the court are women.

In recent years, the members of the Wisconsin Supreme Court have routinely been described as forming separate blocs of conservatives and liberals, with Abrahamson being a central member of the liberal bloc.

Abrahamson's tenure as chief justice has been marked by conflict on the court that is not simply ideological. When Abrahamson ran for reelection in 1999, four members of the court, including Democrat William Bablitch, publicly endorsed her opponent; Abrahamson handily won reelection with 63.5 percent of the vote (partisan correlation .46) in an election that was the most expensive up until that time (Bonneau and Hall 2004:187) . The opposition to Abrahamson came in the wake of several incidents dealing with administrative matters: she had ordered that games be removed from computers used by court members and staff, she had authorized the use of the supreme court's chambers for an aerobics class which some justices argued demeaned the court, and she awarded substantial grants to outside groups without obtaining the consent of her colleagues on the court.

In the wake of the highly contentious 2008 election in which Circuit Court judge Michael Gableman defeated incumbent Louis Butler, the first and only African American to have served on the Wisconsin Supreme Court,[27] the court had to consider charges that some of the advertisements run by Gableman constituted a violation of judicial ethics rules. During the Supreme Court's consideration of those charges, Justice Prosser called Abrahamson a "bitch" and threatened to "destroy her" (Marley 2011).[28] The tensions on the court through this time were palpable. In defending himself with regard to the "bitch" remark, Justice Prosser described Abrahamson and Associate Justice Ann Walsh Bradley as "masters at deliberately goading people into perhaps incautious statements. This is bullying and abuse of very, very long standing." Soon after Prosser's reelection in 2011, the Supreme Court decided one of the challenges to the Republican anti-union legislation (Davey 2011a). Subsequently it was reported that Justice Prosser physically attacked Justice Ann Walsh Bradley, one of the dissenters in the union bargaining case, during a heated discussion in Justice Bradley's office the day before the decision

[27] Justice Butler had been appointed to the court by Democratic governor James Doyle in 2004; under Wisconsin's rule that only one supreme court seat at a time can be up for election, he did not stand for election until 2008 because other justices' terms expired in the intervening years.

[28] The court split three to three ("liberals" vs. "conservatives") over whether Justice Gableman should be disciplined in some way, which meant that no discipline was imposed. This was not the first disciplinary case dealing with a newly elected justice; earlier in 2008, the supreme court reprimanded Justice Annette Ziegler, who was elected the previous year, for violating the judicial ethics code by presiding in cases as a trial judge that involved a bank where her husband was a member of the board of directors (Marley 2011).

was released; Prosser claimed he was acting in self-defense (Davey 2011b; Stephenson et al. 2011).[29]

Through this time the Wisconsin Supreme Court was called upon to decide some cases that were politically sensitive. The abolition of the death penalty in Wisconsin in 1853 and the adoption in 2006 of a constitutional amendment banning same-sex marriage has kept those issues off the court's docket, and the court has not been presented with any abortion cases. The area of controversy for the court has been tort law, and some of the decisions the court has made have served to activate conservative business interests. One prominent tort case was a challenge to a $350,000 limit on non-economic damages in medical malpractice cases. In 2005, the Wisconsin Supreme Court struck down this specific cap on a 4-3 vote.[30] Justices voting to strike down the cap were Abrahamson, Bradley, Butler, and Crooks; those who voted to uphold it were Prosser, Wilcox, and Roggensack. That same year the court issued a ruling that made it easier for victims of lead paint poisoning to sue paint manufacturers even if they could not identify which manufacturers' paint they had been exposed to.[31] The vote in this case was similar but with Justice Roggensack not participating; the majority opinion was written by Justice Butler. At least part of the motivation for the challenge to Justice Butler in 2008 was his votes in these two cases, including his majority opinion in the latter case, although the negative campaign to defeat him relied heavily on attacks regarding his work as a public defender years earlier. One important point here is that the "controversial" decisions I have listed are those that were decided in what would typically

[29] The alleged attack was referred to the Dane County District Attorney's office, but ultimately no charges were filed given the conflicting accounts by the other justices who witnessed the event.

[30] *Ferdon v. Wisconsin Patients Compensation Fund*, 701 N.W.2d 440 (Wis. 2005). This decision did not say that caps were per se a violation of the state constitution; it pointed to the relatively low value of the cap and the fact that there was no provision to adjust the cap for inflation.

[31] *Thomas ex rel. Gramling v. Mallet*, 701 N.W.2d 523 (Wis. 2005). One of the first acts of the Republican-controlled legislature that took office in 2011 was to pass a tort reform measure that reversed this decision. That statute also imposed a cap on most punitive damage awards, raised the standard for the admission of expert testimony (essentially adopting the *Daubert* standard (see *Daubert v. Merrell Dow Pharmaceuticals, Inc.*, 509 U.S. 579 [1993]) – something the Supreme Court could have done itself, but had failed to do), adopted a reasonable alternative design standard (in place of the more liberal consumer expectations test) for defective design products liability claims, and imposed penalties for claims filed in bad faith or without a reasonable legal basis (see http://www.michaelbest.com/pubs/pubDetailMB.aspx?xpST=PubDetail&pub=2776, last visited August 25, 2012). It is worth noting that in 2009, a unanimous court found that the inclusion of lead in paint did not constitute a design defect (*Godoy v. E.I. DuPont*, 768 N.W.2d 674 [Wis. 2009]), although the conservative and liberal blocs split with regard to the rationale for the decision with liberals relying on the Restatement (Second) of Torts and the conservatives wanting to move to the Restatement (Third)'s requirement of a "reasonable alternative design" as required by the 2011 legislation.

be labeled a "liberal" direction. There have been a larger number of divided decisions on controversial issues in tort law that went in a conservative direction that apparently did not produce political reactions from liberal interests.[32]

Looking at events of the last fifteen years, it is not surprising that supreme court elections in Wisconsin have become heated affairs. The court has been the scene of substantial conflict, both substantive and personal. While the court has not been called on to decide cases dealing with some of the most controversial issues other courts have had to deal with – abortion, same-sex marriage, the death penalty – it has had to deal with issues that are of substantial concern to conservative business interests, and these interests along with their opponents have played a substantial role in funding justices' election campaigns and mounting major independent advertising efforts. Every one of the seven contested supreme court elections in Wisconsin since 1999 (the first year for which data are available) has seen television advertising and all seven included at least some attack ads. Over this same period in Minnesota there have been ten contested elections (four additional elections were uncontested); in not one of these elections were any television ads aired. Why is Minnesota so different from Wisconsin?

MINNESOTA

Judicial Elections in Minnesota

In Minnesota, judicial elections for all courts have been conducted on a nonpartisan basis since 1912. Between 1890 and 1910, Minnesota's official ballots listed the party of judicial candidates; prior to the use of official ballots, parties were free to nominate candidates and to supply preprinted ballots. Throughout Minnesota's history, judicial elections have taken place in November concurrently with other elections, and since 1884 they occur in even-numbered years when there are other statewide and national elections. Prior to 1950, candidates ran for undesignated seats (other than chief justice); if two seats were to be filled in the election, each voter could cast two votes and the top two candidates won those seats. Starting in 1912, if there were more than twice the number of candidates running as there were seats to be elected, an open (i.e., nonparty) primary election was held. In 1949, the legislature changed to a system where candidates ran for specific seats, retaining primaries for elections in which more than two candidates sought a specific seat. The 1949 legislation also allowed incumbents to be so designated on the ballot (i.e., an incumbent's name on the ballot is followed by the word "incumbent"). A final

[32] See http://www.wiscivilјusticecouncil.org/wwcms/wp-content/uploads/2011/01/WCJC_2011-Guide-Wisconsin-Supreme-Court.pdf (last visited August 25, 2012).

significant change was made in a 1956 constitutional amendment that permitted the legislature to require justices to retire at an age set by the legislature; today that age is seventy – a justice must retire no later than the last day of the month when the justice turns seventy.[33] Minnesota justices serve six-year terms, but if a justice would become eligible for retirement based on years of service within three years of the conclusion of a six-year term, the justice may ask the governor to extend the term until the justice becomes eligible to retire (Minn. Const., Art. VI §9).[34] A justice appointed to fill a vacancy must stand for election in the first general election (i.e., even-year election) that occurs more than one year after the justice was appointed.[35]

The addition of the incumbency indicator starting in 1950 appears to have had a significant impact on both whether incumbents face opposition and whether contested elections are competitive. Between 1912 when elections became nonpartisan and 1948, incumbents were unopposed in only three of the 33 (15 percent) elections in which incumbents ran;[36] since 1950, 34 of 81 (42 percent) incumbents have faced no opposition. During those same two periods, the degree of competitiveness also differed; between 1912 and 1948, in 30 percent (11 of 37) of the contested elections the successful candidate had 55 percent or less compared to less than 10 percent (4 of 43) starting in 1950. It is worth noting that the shift to nonpartisan elections itself did not affect whether contested elections were competitive; between 1857 and 1910, 31 percent (9 of 29) of contested elections were competitive.[37] Moreover, since the system became nonpartisan in 1912, only three incumbents, all three of whom were running in their first election after being appointed, have lost their seats;[38] only six elections have been for open seats and four of those occurred prior to 1946.[39]

In contrast to Wisconsin, Minnesota Supreme Court elections have in recent years continued to be relatively quiet affairs, and have not generated particularly partisan patterns. Figure 1.4 shows the partisan correlations over

33 This discussion is based largely on material in Hedin (2010:2–8).

34 This provision has to do with the formula for computing retirement benefits; it does not affect the requirement that judges retire no later than the last day of the month when they turn 70.

35 Prior to that time, appointees were required by the state constitution to run "at the first annual election that occurs more than thirty days after the vacancy shall have happened" (Art. 6, §10 [1857]).

36 I have omitted from this count the 1912 election for chief justice when a sitting associate justice ran for chief justice.

37 The adoption of the Australian ballot did not affect the competitiveness of elections.

38 George Bunn, who had been appointed in 1911, lost in 1912, but was reappointed to a vacant seat in January 1913. Justice Albert Schaler, who had been appointed in 1915, came in third in the 1916 primary for a single seat. Justice William C. Christianson, who had been appointed in March 1946, came in third in a two-seat election that following November.

39 This count does include the 1912 election for chief justice.

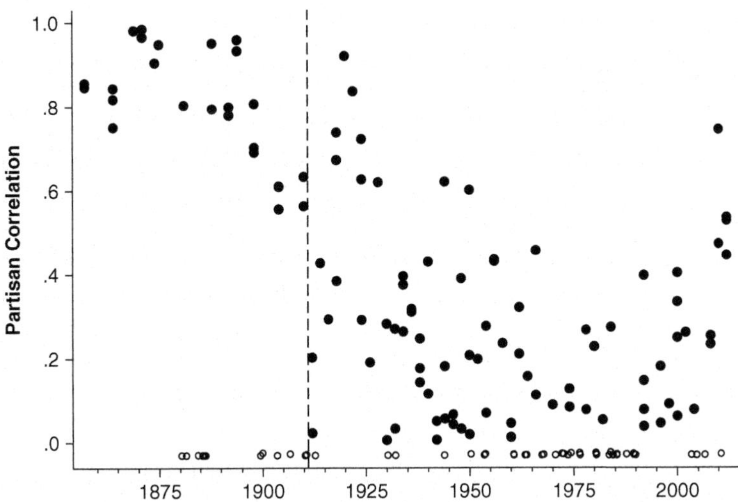

Note: Each solid circle represents the partisan correlation for one election; the small open circles at the bottom represent uncontested elections. The dashed vertical line demarcates the switch from partisan to nonpartisan elections.

FIGURE 1.4. Partisan Correlations in Minnesota, 1857–2012.

the history of elections for the Minnesota Supreme Court;[40] as in Figure 1.2 the small open circles along the bottom indicate uncontested elections. Unsurprisingly, there was significant partisanship prior to 1912 when Minnesota elections became nonpartisan (the broken vertical line in Figure 1.4 demarcates the beginning of nonpartisan elections), and this was true both before and after the adoption of the Australian ballot in 1889 (Slater 2013:371). In the 1920s there were again a number of elections with strong partisan patterns in voting that reflected the rise of the Farmer-Labor Party which merged with the Democrats in 1944 to become the modern Democratic-Farmer-Labor Party. The Farmer-Labor Party actively endorsed candidates for the Minnesota Supreme Court in the 1920s and '30s,[41] but never during this period succeeded

[40] Figure 1.4 omits two contested elections for associate justice, one in 1875 and a second in 1878, because I was unable to locate county-level returns for those elections.

[41] The first endorsements may have come in the 1918 election. The correlations shown in Figure 1.4 focus on the vote for the Farmer-Labor Party gubernatorial candidate starting with 1918 (Democratic-Farmer-Labor starting in 1944 when the DFL came into existence). In 1918, there was no formal Farmer-Labor Party, but the Farmer-Labor label was adopted by the candidate of a coalition of groups that were the forerunner of the actual Farmer-Labor Party (this was necessary due to a ruling by the state attorney general that all candidates on the ballot had to be identified with a party). In 1920 the candidate that would be associated with the Farmer-Labor Party, Henrik Shipstead, was listed as an "Independent" (in computing the correlations, I have treated him as the Farmer-Labor candidate). See Folwell (1969:547–49) for a discussion of Minnesota politics during this period.

in defeating an incumbent. The partisan voting pattern tapered off in the 1930s, perhaps as a result of an agreement among justices that those running for reelection in a given year would campaign together regardless of their political sympathies (Moos 1941:71–72).

Since 1930, there have been only three elections in which the partisan correlation was .60 or greater, as was true for most elections prior to 1912 and for several elections in the 1920s. The first of these post-1930 elections was in 1944 when three seats were up for reelection, including a rare open seat because only two incumbents were running. One of the candidates in the election, Leroy Matson, appears to have generated a partisan voting pattern, particularly when paired against Allan Johnson.[42] Why this should be the case is not clear because neither Matson nor Johnson had previously run for statewide office.

There is a fairly straightforward explanation of the partisan pattern in the second of these elections, which occurred in 1950. In that election incumbent Justice Theodore Christianson, who had been appointed to the office the previous May by the Republican governor, faced Mark Nolan. Nolan was a former state legislator and a Democratic Party activist; Theodore Christianson bore the name of his father, who was the Republican governor of Minnesota from 1925 to 1931. Presumably the citizens of Minnesota recognized the party pedigrees of one or both candidates, and that influenced some of their vote choices producing a partisan correlation of .602.[43]

In the fall of 2010, there were two elections to the court which pitted challengers against incumbents, one who had been on the court for eighteen years and a second who had been a justice for eight years; the partisan correlations in these two elections were .47 and .74. Both challengers had previously run for the court against sitting justices (one having run three times before), producing partisan correlations of .40, .08, and .25.[44] One difference in 2010 was that both challengers had obtained the endorsement of the Republican

[42] As I will explain in more detail in Chapter 6, in multi-seat elections (i.e., elections where candidates did not run for a specific seat), I adopted the practice of pairing the candidates with the highest and lowest votes, followed by the candidates with the second highest and second lowest, and so on. That convention paired Matson and Johnson, and the resulting correlation was .62; correlating Matson's percentage of the total vote with the DFL percentage produces a correlation of −.55; Johnson's percentage of the total vote produces a correlation of +.26.

[43] Dubois (1980:90) mistakenly identified Christianson the judicial candidate as his father the governor of the same name some 20 years earlier.

[44] Only three correlations are listed because the candidate who had run three times, Greg Wersal, had lost the 1998 primary as discussed later. Actually, Wersal has run four times, but withdrew before the 1996 primary for reasons we will discuss.

Party convention.[45] The fact that one race resulted in a higher partisan correlation than the other almost certainly reflected the fact that the challenger in the race with the lower correlation (who had run twice before, once against the same incumbent) was running against Justice Alan Page, a former star player with the Minnesota Vikings, and one of the most successful vote-getters in recent Minnesota politics. Justice Page, who had attended law school at the University of Minnesota while an active professional football player and then worked for a Minnesota law firm during the off-season after graduating, obtained his position by winning a rare open-seat election in 1992. That same candidate, Tim Tingelstad, ran for a fourth time in 2012, this time against incumbent David Stras who had been appointed by Republican governor Tim Pawlenty in 2010, and who had strong conservative credentials, having served as a law clerk for U.S. Supreme Court Justice Clarence Thomas and having had an affiliation with the conservative Federalist Society; in the 2012 election the partisan correlation was essentially nil (.15), which is not surprising given that Tingelstad has presented himself as a conservative.[46]

The 1992 election that placed Alan Page on the Minnesota Supreme Court is one of the very few elections in the period since 1946 that has garnered substantial media attention, in part because of Page's prior career and in part because of some peculiarities of that election.[47] As noted earlier, the

45 In an earlier period (the 1930s), the forerunner of the modern Democratic-Farmer-Labor (DFL) Party in Minnesota sought to influence supreme court elections by endorsing candidates, but as previously noted the justices running for reelection resisted that move by campaigning together regardless of endorsement (see Moos 1941: 71–72).

46 Neither political party endorsed candidates for the Minnesota Supreme Court in 2012; in 2014 the Minnesota Republican Party did endorse one of the candidates for the Minnesota Supreme Court, Michelle MacDonald, who opposed Justice David Lillehaug, who was appointed in 2013 by Democratic governor Mark Dayton. Lillihaug was not endorsed by the DFL, but has a long-standing affiliation with that party, having been appointed U.S. Attorney by President Bill Clinton, and having run for both Minnesota Attorney General and U.S. Senate, failing both times to secure the DFL nomination. MacDonald's endorsement proved to be an embarrassment to the Minnesota Republican Party when it was discovered, after the endorsement, that she was facing drunk driving and resisting arrest charges with a trial scheduled in September (Simons 2014a, 2014b), and was then convicted on some of the charges at that trial (Simons 2014c). The partisan correlations in 2014 (not shown in Figure 1.4) were .57 for the Lillehaug-MacDonald election and .68 for the the election between Wilhelmina Wright and John Hancock. Wright, only the second African American to serve on the Minnesota Supreme Court, had been appointed to the court in 2012 by Governor Dayton; unlike MacDonald, Hancock did not seek an endorsement from the Republican Party. Both incumbents retained their seats on the court.

47 Page, who was serving as an assistant attorney general, had intended to run in 1990 for the seat held by Glen Kelley, who would be forced to retire in April 1991; however, immediately after Page's plans became known, Kelley, who had been expected to run despite his imminent forced retirement, announced his retirement due to health problems and the governor subsequently appointed a replacement, thus canceling the expected election (Wilson 1990).

Minnesota statute concerning retirement of justices contains a provision that allows the governor to extend the term of a state judge, including supreme court justices, for up to three years (or until the date of the judge's mandatory retirement, whichever comes first) in order for the justice to be eligible for "full" retirement benefits. Justice Lawrence Yetka, who had been on the court since 1973, applied to the governor to extend his term through October 31, 1994, when he would turn seventy and the mandatory retirement provision would force him to leave the bench, in order that he could receive "enhanced" pension benefits; the term extension would mean he did not have to run for reelection in 1992. At the time Page sought to file papers to run for the position, but those papers were rejected by the secretary of state after the governor granted Justice Yetka's request for an extension. Page then brought an original jurisdiction action to the Minnesota Supreme Court challenging the extension on the grounds that Justice Yetka was already eligible for retirement benefits; essentially the issue was whether the legislature could tie the extension to the nature of the retirement benefits a judge would receive or to simply whether the judge was eligible for retirement benefits. All sitting members of the state supreme court recused themselves due to the potential conflict of interest, and an acting court consisting of retired justices heard the case. The court ruled that the term extension was invalid on the grounds that the relevant constitutional language referred only to retirement eligibility, not to the nature of the retirement benefits that might be received, and Justice Yetka was eligible to retire without any term extension.[48] Justice Yetka opted not to run for another term. Page faced two other candidates in the primary, winning 59 percent of the vote, and then winning the general election against Kevin Johnson with 62 percent of the vote. The absolute value of the partisan correlation in the Page-Johnson election was .40, with the percentage for Johnson increasing as the percentage voting for the DFL gubernatorial candidate increased; thus, like the Bablitch election in Wisconsin previously described, the pattern ran in the opposite direction one might expect given that Johnson had previously run as a Republican candidate opposing DFL candidate Hubert Humphrey in the 1960 election for state attorney general, and Page was (and is) a well-known African American.

One other election that produced a modicum of media attention occurred in 1998 when challenger Greg Wersal ran in the primary election for the supreme court. Wersal had initiated a run for the court in 1996, and as part of his campaign he distributed literature critical of some decisions by the then current court. An ethics complaint was filed against him; the Minnesota

48 *Page v. Carlson*, 488 N.W.2d 274 (Minn. 1992).

Lawyers Professional Responsibility Board dismissed the complaint, expressing some doubt whether the clause under which the complaint was brought was enforceable. Despite the dismissal, Wersal withdrew from the election, fearing that further complaints might be filed which could put his license to practice at risk. In 1998, he ran again, and this time went to federal court to have limits on what candidates in judicial elections could say struck down. This case eventually became *Republican Party of Minnesota v. White*,[49] the decision which struck down the "announce" clause in Minnesota's judicial ethics code; the announce clause made it unethical for a judicial candidate to announce his or her position on issues that might come before the court for which the candidate was running. In the 1998 primary, Wersal came in a distant third behind incumbent Alan Page and Roger Peterson (who had run unsuccessfully in two previous elections); he ran again in 2010 as one of the candidates endorsed by the Republican Party, and it was that contest that produced the strongest partisan correlation since the elections involving Farmer-Labor candidates in the 1920s.

The low temperature of Minnesota Supreme Court elections over the last dozen years is further indicated by the absence of any television advertising in those elections. This stands in sharp contrast to Wisconsin, where all of the contested elections since at least 1999 have involved television advertising, and as discussed, that advertising has on some occasions been extensive and quite nasty.

Why Has There Been a Lack of Partisanship in Minnesota Supreme Court Elections?

There are two factors that likely explain the failure of a partisan pattern to develop in Minnesota. The first is the designation of incumbents on the ballot, reinforcing the apparently strong norm of reelecting incumbents. The second is the absence from the Minnesota Supreme Court's docket of any of the kinds of issues that have provoked partisan response or strong interest group involvement. Like Wisconsin, Minnesota does not have a death penalty. Unlike Wisconsin, the Minnesota legislature has not imposed caps on any types of tort damages; hence, the Minnesota Supreme Court has not been called on to assess whether such caps are valid under the state constitution. While Minnesota does not have a constitutional amendment on same-sex marriage, it did have a statute limiting marriage to heterosexual couples; however, no challenge to that statute had come to the Minnesota Supreme Court,

[49] 536 U.S. 765 (2002).

and in 2013 the state legislature legalized same-sex marriage.[50] Perhaps the closest of the issues that has motivated proponents of tort reform that has come before both courts concerns expert testimony. The Wisconsin Supreme Court had retained its own standard that turned on relevancy[51] rather than adopting what would be the more defendant-friendly *Daubert* standard.[52] While the Minnesota Supreme Court has declined to adopt the *Daubert* standard, it had earlier modified the *Frye*[53] standard in a way that the current standard, referred to as the *Frye/Mack* standard, has some similarities to the *Daubert* standard.[54]

The Minnesota Supreme Court appears to have made some effort to avoid partisan controversy. For example, in both 2008 and 2010, the court was called on to make decisions about recounts for a statewide office. In both cases the court's unanimous decisions effectively ending the election challenges favored the Democratic candidate, even though most members of the court were appointees of Republican governors. In 2012 the court divided in a conflict between the Republican-controlled state legislature and the Democratic secretary of state on ballot wording for constitutional amendments concerning voter ID and same-sex marriage, with the divided court favoring the Republicans. However, given that one of the dissenters was also a Republican appointee and the second was the sole member of the court who was initially elected, one cannot say that the court divided in a partisan way.

MOVING BEYOND MINNESOTA AND WISCONSIN

Minnesota and Wisconsin present a sharp and fascinating contrast. One state has seen change, while the other has continued along the pattern that emerged at least sixty and possibly eighty years ago. In Wisconsin, elections have become nasty and partisan. In Minnesota they continue as low-key affairs

[50] The same-sex marriage story in Minnesota is a bit more complicated than described here. In 1971 the Minnesota Supreme Court actually decided the first case challenging limits on such marriages, ruling that state law prohibited such marriages and that prohibition did not violate the federal constitution (*Baker v. Nelson* 191 N.W.2d 185 [Minn. 1971]); the U.S. Supreme Court dismissed an appeal of that decision "for want of a substantial federal question" (409 U.S. 810 [1972]). In 1997, the Minnesota legislature passed a state Defense of Marriage Act (*Laws of Minnesota* 1997, chapter 203, article 10). A challenge to this statute in 2011 was dismissed by the trial court which cited *Baker v. Nelson*; in 2012 the Minnesota Court of Appeals overturned the dismissal and returned the case to the trial court (*Benson et al. v. Alverson*, 2012 WL 171399) but before a trial occurred, the state legislature legalized same-sex marriage.

[51] *State v. Walstad*, 351 N.W.2d 469 (Wis. 1984).

[52] One of the actions of Wisconsin's Republican legislature elected in 2010 was to adopt the *Daubert* standard by statute.

[53] *Frye v. United States*, 293 F. 1013 (D.C. Cir. 1923).

[54] *State v. Mack*, 292 N.W.2d 764 (Minn. 1980).

with little partisanship apparent in most elections. I have suggested one potentially generalizable explanation for this difference: the kinds of cases the two courts have been called on to decide and how they have decided them. Do Minnesota and Wisconsin represent larger patterns of stability and change? What do we see if we expand the analysis to cover all states over the period since 1946? The next two chapters consider some preliminary matters, and then in Chapters 4 through I present analyses of what has and has not changed across the country, along with discussions of what best explains the changes that have occurred.

2

Judicial Elections Then and Now

JUDICIAL ELECTIONS, JUDICIAL INDEPENDENCE, AND JUDICIAL ACCOUNTABILITY

The all but unique use of elections for judicial selection by the American states reflects the broader mania for elections in the United States.[1] In the American states, the voters have elected officials ranging from the president down to the commissioners of sewer districts (Colorado among others), park districts (Illinois), library boards (Minnesota), mosquito control boards (Florida), inspector of hides and animals (in Texas until 2007), and there is even at least one community where the epithet, "he couldn't be elected dog-catcher," refers to an actual elective office, although the position goes by the modern title of "animal control officer" (Ireland 2013). Many of the more obscure elected offices in the United States involve agencies with the authority to levy taxes, which suggests that part of the devotion to elections reflects the heritage of "no taxation without representation," traceable to the 1750s

[1] The only other countries that use popular elections in any way are Japan (O'Brien 2006:359), Switzerland (Bedford 1961:240; Wipf 2002:1569), and Boliva, which began using elections under a new constitution ratified in 2009 (Driscoll and Nelson 2012, 2013).

Japan requires that judges of its supreme court stand in a retention-type election after a period of service. Judges up for retention are listed on the ballot and voters are asked to mark an X next to any judge they want to have dismissed (O'Brien 2006:359). One American observer described this system as "removal by popular vote in the event of dissatisfaction with services" (Stason 1958:139). Removing a judge requires that a majority of all people voting in the election vote no; those not voting on the judge count as voting yes. No judge has ever been removed, and few judges stand for election more than one time due to the mandatory retirement age for judges in Japan.

In Switzerland, 18 cantons (the rough equivalent of states in the United States) use direct election by the citizens to select and retain judges of the first instance courts. How many of these elections are truly competitive is not clear (they do not appear to be so in Geneva according to one report I received, and in at least two of the smaller cantons, the elections resemble town meetings and I have no information on whether there are frequently, or even ever, multiple candidates).

and 1760s, and associated with the original "tea party" of the 1770s. However, there is more than taxation driving the desire to elect public officials, and clearly that concern would not apply to judges.

Initial Adoption of Judicial Elections

Elections for at least some judgeships can be found in the earliest years of American independence. Vermont's 1777 constitution called for the "freemen in each county" to choose judges for many of the nascent state's courts (Friedman 1973:111). Georgia provided for the election of some judges in 1812, followed in 1816 by Indiana. However, the popular election of state judges was largely a development of the mid-nineteenth century (Tarr 2012:41–46). Prior to that time, most state judges were appointed usually by the executive and sometimes with the confirmation of one or both houses of the state legislature.

Because judicial elections began to be adopted during the period associated with Jacksonian democracy, some historians have suggested that the move to elections was intended to increase the accountability of judges. The shift to elections was, in the words of Willard Hurst (1950:140), "one phase of the general swing toward broadened suffrage and broader popular control of public office which Jacksonian democracy built on the foundations laid by Jefferson." In this view, a central goal in moving from appointment to elections was to increase the accountability of judges to the electorate.

Selecting judges through election puts front and center the tension between judicial independence and judicial accountability (Geyh 2008). It seems logical to view the goal of the shift to elections, coming in the wake of the height of Jacksonian democracy, to be to shift the balance toward accountability (Carbon and Berkson 1980:1). However, as noted at the beginning of the Introduction, Shugerman (2012; see also Tarr 2012:46–51) argues that the move to elections reflected a goal of *increasing* judicial independence, although the independence that was sought was from politicians rather than from voters. According to Shugerman, the discontent leading to the adoption of elections was that judges essentially did the bidding of the elected officials who appointed them. The reformers believed that elections would separate judges from the other elected officials because the judges would have their own constituency, and that constituency would reward judges for acting independently.

Because of the need to keep the courts operating, it was not possible to completely eliminate appointments. It became common for an elected official, usually the governor, to be empowered to fill judicial vacancies, with the appointee holding office until the next election. Not surprisingly, judges appointed to fill vacancies usually would then run for the office they had been appointed to fill on a temporary basis. Regardless of whether an election involved a previously elected incumbent, an incumbent appointed to fill a vacancy that had occurred since the previous election, or an open seat, the candidates were generally highly dependent on the party leaders who played a central role in mid-nineteenth century elections.

Until the last two decades of the nineteenth century, elections looked very different from what contemporary voters have come to expect. There was no such thing as a voting machine. More important, there were no "official" ballots listing previously nominated candidates. Voters typically indicated their choices on plain pieces of paper and placed those ballots into a ballot box sitting out in public. Because of the number of offices to be filled, voters then (and now) often did not know much about many of the candidates for office. In the absence of official ballots, there were no cues such as party labels for the voters. To insure that party supporters voted for the party's candidates, party leaders would prepare preprinted ballots listing the candidates chosen by the party. These ballots were distributed to party supporters who could then simply deposit the preprinted ballots in the ballot box.[2] If there were judicial offices to be filled, the party's candidates for those offices would be included on the ballot. In some places the parties went one step further, printing their ballots on a specific color of paper so that party officials could observe the color of the ballot their supporters deposited in the ballot box. Party bosses would bring their supporters to the polls, distribute the preprinted ballots, and march their voters to the ballot box while the voters held the colored ballots aloft (Ayres 2000:49). With this device, the bosses knew whom to reward for party loyalty and whom to punish for defection. Significantly, this was also before the development of party primaries, which meant that nomination of candidates was substantially controlled by party leaders. Thus, the party leaders, who were often also the elected officials who would choose whom to appoint as interim judges or who would have appointed judges prior to the shift to elections, had substantial control of who was a candidate for judicial office.

Most judicial elections then and now are conducted simultaneously with elections for other offices. Some states tried to reduce the influence of political parties by scheduling judicial elections at times apart from other elections (Tarr 2012:51). At least some of those efforts were short-lived due to cost and lack of participation (Hall 1984a:352–53). As discussed in Chapter 1, one state

[2] A preprinted ballot would also deal with problems of illiteracy. Some states employed an "oral ballot" where the voter orally announced his choice which was then recorded by the election official, a system which also would deal with voters who were unable to write their choices.

that has done this throughout its existence is Wisconsin; that separation was required under the state's first constitution, with judicial elections initially held in September and subsequently moved to April. In some states, the term of office for judgeships was an odd number of years (e.g., seven years) which meant the terms for some judges expired in odd-numbered years; however, this practice did not necessarily separate judicial elections from elections for governor because some states also held elections for governor and other state offices in odd-numbered years, a system that persists in a small number of states. One state that continues to hold most, if not all, of its statewide judicial elections in odd-numbered years is Pennsylvania.

In Chapter 1 I discussed the arrival of the Australian ballot. Initially, the use of a preprinted official ballot reduced the control of party leaders. For the most part those leaders still had control of nominations, and ballots carried party designations. However, voters now marked their ballots in private, and election laws prevented party representatives from seeing how an individual had marked his, or eventually her, ballot. Moreover, it was now easy for voters to split their votes among candidates of different parties, or alternatively to choose not to vote for some offices on the ballot. Some states created an option on the ballot to vote a "straight ticket" by marking a single box at the top of the ballot. Even with this, there was no way for party leaders to monitor the action of individual voters as had been possible prior to the Australian ballot. However, the process of making official nominations to place candidates on the ballot gave parties a formal role in the election process unlike what they had previously possessed. As shown in Chapter 1, at least in Minnesota the kinds of partisan patterns that existed prior to the Australian ballot continued with the new ballots until the adoption of a nonpartisan system for selecting judges.

The Move to Nonpartisan Elections

The ability to have a system of nonpartisan elections was one of the major impacts of the Australian ballot. While prior to the use of official ballot, states could try to dampen the role of parties by devices such as temporal separation, parties played a key role in most elections, particularly statewide elections. The presence of party designations on the official ballot combined with parties as entities that made nominations formalized the parties' role. However, with the official ballot, the option was now available to make elections at least formally nonpartisan by listing candidates on the official ballot without party designations. This did not necessarily eliminate the parties' role as nominators, or as active participants in the election campaign. It did, however, generally dampen partisan patterns in voting.

In the early years of the twentieth century, states began adopting nonpartisan elections for a range of offices including the judiciary. The first state to formally make this change for the judiciary was North Dakota, with eight others following by 1920 (Tarr 2012:64). By 1945 fourteen states, all in the Midwest and West, had adopted nonpartisan elections for the members of their state supreme courts.[3] The goal of adopting nonpartisan judicial elections was to increase the independence of judges from capture by "ideology and special interests" (see also Hall 1983:341; Shugerman 2012:167). While the use of nonpartisan elections did dampen partisanship, it quickly became evident that the proponents of nonpartisan elections held an overly optimistic view of the electorate which had lost its single most important voting cue.

In the absence of party labels on the ballot, voters sought out cues based on the candidates' names. This was clearly evident in the quirky nature of some election results where voters relied on mistaken name recognition. A clear example of this occurred in Washington in 1990 when Chief Justice Keith Callow ran for reelection to the Washington Supreme Court. An unknown local lawyer, believing that no election should go uncontested, entered the contest. Much to the challenger's surprise, to say nothing of the incumbent's shock and the surprise of the legal establishment in Washington, the challenger won (London 1990). The unknown lawyer who defeated Justice Callow was named Charles W. Johnson. There were at the time three relatively well-known Charles Johnsons in the state: a Tacoma television news anchor, a superior court judge, and a former sergeant-at-arms in the state senate. Presumably, many voters mistook Charles W. Johnson for one of these other Charles Johnsons.[4]

Ohio is an interesting state to look at given the name recognition issue in the absence of partisan labels on the ballot. In Ohio, candidates for the state supreme court seek nominations through party primaries, but no party labels appear on the general election ballot. Also in Ohio, there are some family names that have, or at one time did have, strong partisan linkages. The most prominent such name is "Taft"; one might almost say that t-a-f-t is an alternate spelling for Republican in Ohio. Even in the absence of party labels, if a Taft

[3] Three (Ohio, Michigan, and Arizona) of those 14 states had hybrid systems where parties retained a formal role in the nominating process, either through primaries or conventions, but no party labels appeared on the general election ballot. In addition, Pennsylvania shifted from partisan to nonpartisan elections in 1913, but reverted back to partisan elections 8 years later (Goodman and Marks 2007:428n16).

[4] One possible element here is that Washington had until 2014 a system whereby there is a primary even if there are only two candidates, and if a candidate in the primary wins a majority (which will always be true with only two candidates unless there is a tie), that winner is elected and there is no contest at the general election. In 1990, Charles Johnson won at the primary.

is running for the state supreme court, one observes strong partisan patterns. "There is at least one example in Ohio of how name recognition without party labels on the ballot can cause confusion. A second name that at one time had a strong association with the Republican Party was "Brown."[5] In 1970, *Democrat* Allen Brown ran against *Republican* J.J.P. Corrigan; Corrigan was a name moderately associated with the Democratic Party (presumably because of its Irish origins). The partisan correlation in this election was −.419 indicating that there was a moderate tendency for normally Democratic counties to have unusually high percentages for the Republican Corrigan and for normally Republican counties to have unusually high percentages for Democrat Brown.

The search of alternate cues and the resulting name confusion was not the only result that can be associated with the adoption of nonpartisan elections. Voter participation declined (Tarr 2012:64), fewer incumbents were turned out of office, and independence did increase but not necessarily in the way reformers had hoped. However, as incumbents became more secure, an increasing number of judges initially obtained their offices by appointment because governors in most states were empowered to fill vacancies. Not surprisingly, governors regularly used these positions as a source of patronage, filling vacancies with supporters who were likely to reflect the policy preferences of the governors who appointed them.

While it was states in the Midwest and West that adopted nonpartisan elections in the first quarter of the twentieth century, judicial elections in most southern states were effectively nonpartisan. Nine of the eleven states that were part of the Confederacy employed formally partisan elections into at least the 1970s.[6] As described by V. O. Key in his classic work, *Southern Politics* (1949), for the most part the Democratic Party was the only game in town for state and local politics. Most elections, including judicial elections, were decided in the Democratic Party primary. This meant that nonpartisan elections for state and local offices, including judgeships, effectively existed in most areas of the southern states because the Democratic primary, sometimes with a runoff, determined the election outcome. Hall (1984b:251) argues that the effect of the southern one-party system was to increase the independence of the appellate judiciary in the South, consequently decreasing its accountability to the electorate.

5 Clarence J. Brown, father and son, were longtime Republican members of the U.S. House of Representatives from a district in central Ohio (together they served from 1939 to 1983). Clarence J. Brown, Sr., had previously served as both lieutenant governor and secretary of state.

6 The two exceptions were Virginia and South Carolina. In addition, several border states – Oklahoma, Kentucky, Maryland, and West Virginia – used partisan elections, although they are best described as having a one-party tendency rather than being thoroughly dominated by the Democratic Party.

The one-party system also produced one of the most dramatic examples of name confusion. In 1976 there was an open-seat election for the Texas Supreme Court. At this time judicial elections in Texas were still one-party affairs that were settled in the Democratic primary. The establishment candidate in the election was a well-regarded Court of Civil Appeals judge from San Antonio, Charles Barrow; Barrow was challenged in the primary by an unknown Houston lawyer named Don Yarbrough. Yarbrough had made an election bid the prior year, but that was the limit of his political experience. Yarbrough stunned the Texas establishment by winning the primary with about 60 percent of the vote (Holder 1980). Clearly what had happened was that voters thought they were voting for Don Yarborough (note the two "O's") who had sought the governor's office three times in the 1960s.[7]

After Yarbrough donned the judicial robes, he asked the people of Texas for their prayers, and announced that God had told him to run for the Texas Supreme Court.[8] This statement prompted a political cartoon showing a caricature of Yarbrough and a thought bubble emerging from a cloud, "But I thought it was the **other** Don Yarbrough" (see Figure 2.1). In the wake of the election of Yarbrough to the state supreme court, it came out that he was facing disbarment proceedings for allegedly committing a host of violations of professional ethics. Over the early months he served on the court, the number of charges mushroomed. More important, in May and June of 1977, Yarbrough was caught on tape plotting to kill a former business associate, and making a variety of incriminating statements. On July 15, Yarbrough tendered his resignation.[9] Yarbrough was subsequently tried and convicted on perjury charges and sentenced to prison. He appealed unsuccessfully to the Texas Court of Criminal Appeals, and when it was time for him to appear to begin his sentence, he failed to do so, refusing to return to the United States from the island of Grenada where he had gone with the court's permission to study medicine. Finally, in 1983, while attending classes on St. Vincent, a country with which the United States has an extradition treaty, Yarbrough was arrested, flown immediately to St. Thomas (a U.S. territory), and then back to Texas (on a jet made available by Ross Perot); upon landing, Yarbrough told reporters waiting for his arrival, "It's good to be back, fellas." In July 1983, Yarbrough was sentenced to seven years for bail-jumping, with the sentence to run concurrently

7 Some voters may have confused the supreme court candidate Yarbrough with Ralph Yarborough, a Democrat who had for many years represented Texas in the U.S. Senate.

8 Yarbrough told reporters, "It got to the point where it was so plain and so clear it was like – it wasn't a normal voice – but the longer it went, the plainer it got, and it got down to, 'You run for the Supreme Court'" (Holder 1980:187).

9 The governor of Texas promptly announced that he would appoint Charles Barrow, the man Yarbrough defeated in the primary, to the now vacant seat on the Texas Supreme Court.

FIGURE 2.1. That's Yarbrough Spelled with One O.

with the two-year sentence he had received for perjury; he was later convicted of bribery in federal court and sentenced to six years on that charge.

The Development and Adoption of Retention Elections

Even with the elimination of political parties as major players in judicial elections, advocates for an independent judiciary sought to further limit the role of elections in judicial selection and retention. The ideal solution for many proponents of further change would have been to move to a "short ballot" system whereby only a small number of offices would be filled by election, with judgeships and other offices filled by appointment. However, popular sentiment favored elections. In an attempt to solve the problem of retaining a role for the electorate, Albert Kales, a professor of law at Northwestern University and the director of research at the nascent American Judicature Society, devised a plan that included what we today call retention elections. Under Kales's plan, which appeared in a 1914 book (Kales 1914:245–51), the state's chief justice would be the only judge directly elected. Nominations for other judgeships would be made by a judicial council consisting of presiding judges, presumably based solely on the judicial council's assessment of the candidates' professional qualifications. The elected chief justice would then make appointments from among the persons nominated by the judicial council. After a probationary period of two or three years, the judge would stand in a noncompetitive election in which voters would decide, yes or no, whether the judge should retain his (all judges at this time were male) office. If retained in office, the judge would serve a full term and then could ask the electorate to retain him for another term on a simple yes or no ballot, what is now called a "retention election." This would continue until the judge chose not to run, reached mandatory retirement age, resigned for other reasons, or died (Carbon and Berkson 1980:2–3). The retention election was included to mollify the electorate and to create at least an appearance of accountability (Winters 1968:75). The expectation of Kales and others who advocated for a system along these lines was that the accountability was to be a matter of competence and not related to the judges' decisional propensities.

While a number of variants of Kales's plan were advanced (Carbon and Berkson 1980:7), it would be twenty years before any state actually adopted a plan with some of the innovations Kales had proposed. The first state to do so was California which in 1934 adopted a system whereby the governor nominates a candidate for a vacant or soon-to-be-vacated appellate judgeship. If the judgeship is then vacant, the nominee is presented to the Commission on Judicial Appointments (consisting of the chiefjustice, the attorney general, and a presiding judge from the Court of Appeals) for approval, and if approved the nominee assumes office; the judge or justice then stands for election the next time judicial elections are held. If the current incumbent for the position remains in office but is not going to run for another term, the nominee is placed on the ballot at the next election and, if successful, takes office upon the expiration of the incumbent's term. In either situation, the candidate runs without opposition, and the electorate is asked to vote yes or no on the question, "For [office – e.g., Associate Justice of the Supreme Court] shall XXXX be elected to the office for the term provided by law." If the judge currently holds the office, the judge's title is included with his name (e.g., "shall Associate Justice XXXX be elected...").[10] Unlike the Kales plan or methods used in states that subsequently adopted plans derived from what Kales proposed, the California system does not formally employ a nominating commission to screen potential appointees.

In 1940, Missouri adopted the second system to use retention elections (see Peltason 1945). Under Missouri's Nonpartisan Court Plan, or the "Missouri Plan" as it is often called, a nominating commission, consisting of a mix of lawyers selected by the bar, lay persons selected by the governor, and one judge screens potential nominees. The commission then forwards three names to the governor who has sixty days to make a selection from that list; if the governor fails to act, the nominating commission then makes a selection.[11] The selected person serves for one year, and then stands for retention at the next election on the question, "Shall Judge XXX be retained in office." At the end of each subsequent term, the judge stands again for retention (Watson and Downing 1969:13–14). The next state to adopt a selection system employing retention elections for members of its supreme court was Kansas in the late 1950s.

Proponents of the Missouri-type system have dubbed it "merit selection." The argument of the proponents is that the screening by a nominating commission improves the quality of those appointed to the bench. While there is an extensive academic literature comparing the judges under different selection systems dating back fifty years (Alozie 1990; Canon 1972; Dubois 1983; Esterling and Andersen 2000; Flango and Ducat 1979; Glick and Emmert 1987; Graham 1990; Jacob 1964),[12] there is no systematic evidence that judges selected using a nominating commission are better than those either appointed without the use of such a commission or directly elected by the voters (Fitzpatrick 2009).[13] Moreover, there are systems that use a nominating commission that do not use retention elections, and there are systems that use retention elections that do not use a nominating commission (e.g., California as described earlier). Given that the central focus in this book is on elections, I have chosen to use the label "retention elections" to refer to any system using such elections; where a system uses a combination of a nominating commission and retention elections, I will refer to it as a "Missouri Plan" system.

10 See Uelmen (1988) for a history of judicial selection and judicial elections in California. Only once has a gubernatorial selection for the California Supreme Court been rejected by what is now called the Commission on Judicial Appointments, and that was in 1940 when the governor nominated law professor Max Radin; after Radin's rejection, the governor nominated law professor Roger Traynor, who went on to have an illustrious career on the California Supreme Court (Smith 1951:591–94).

11 See http://www.courts.mo.gov/page.jsp?id=297 (last visited September 24, 2012).

12 There is also a substantial literature on whether the selection system used impacts the decisions that judges make; this literature is considered in Chapter 4.

13 A central problem in assessing whether one system or another produces "better" judges is defining what one means by a "better" judge in any kind of truly neutral fashion.

CHANGES IN THE USE OF JUDICIAL ELECTIONS FOR STATE SUPREME COURTS SINCE 1946

As of 1946, twenty-two states used partisan elections for their state supreme courts, fourteen states used formally nonpartisan elections in the general elections (three of the fourteen had partisan nomination systems), and two states used systems employing retention elections. The remaining ten states used appointment systems without any direct involvement by the electorate or a system of election by members of the legislature. When they entered the union, Hawaii chose to use a system of appointment without elections and Alaska adopted a Missouri Plan system involving a nominating commission, gubernatorial appointment, and retention elections. Several states employed a district-based system of election where only voters in the district from which the justice was to be selected voted; these states included Kentucky, Illinois, Louisiana, Maryland, Mississippi, Nebraska, Oklahoma (for the Court of Criminal Appeals), and South Dakota.

There has been substantial change in selection methods since 1946. Figure 2.2 graphically represents the changes that have occurred among those states using elections in some form in 1946. Only two states made changes during the 1950s: Utah from partisan to nonpartisan elections and Kansas from nonpartisan elections to a Missouri Plan system. Thus most of the change since 1946 occurred after 1959.[14] Overall, twenty-two of the thirty-six states using partisan or nonpartisan elections in 1946 for their state supreme courts have made major changes in how their justices are selected and/or retained. As the figure shows, there has been a sharp move away from partisan elections; no state has adopted partisan elections during this period. Of the twenty-two states using partisan elections in 1946, eighteen have made major changes compared to only three of the fourteen states using nonpartisan elections in 1946, all three to a system using retention elections. There is a great deal of variety in the changes made by the formerly partisan states:[15]

- Two changed initially to nonpartisan systems but within a few years shifted to a system using retention elections.
- Five changed to nonpartisan elections.
- Seven changed to a system using retention elections.

[14] This does not include changes in rules concerning elections such as occurred in the late 1940s in Minnesota, which shifted from multi-seat elections to single-seat elections and began including an indication of incumbency on the ballot.

[15] Not included here as having changed its basic method is Louisiana. In 1977, Louisiana moved to a blanket primary system ("jungle" primary) in which all candidates regardless of party stand on a single ballot with party labels; if no candidate wins a majority, the top two candidates regardless of party have a runoff. I treat this as a partisan system and hence I do not count it as a system change for purposes of my basic categorization.

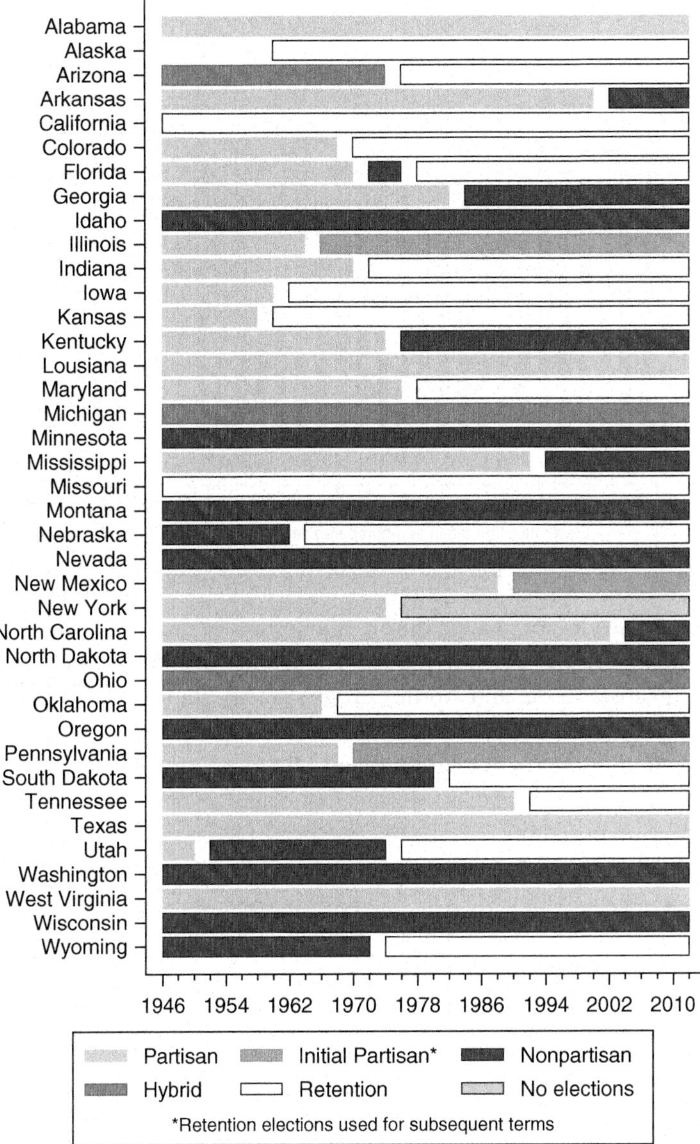

FIGURE 2.2. Changing Methods of Judicial Selection, 1946–2013.

- Three changed to a system using partisan elections for a justice's initial term, with the incumbent justice then standing for retention for subsequent terms.
- One, New York, abandoned elections entirely for its court of last resort, which in New York is called the Court of Appeals (see Philip et al. 1976).

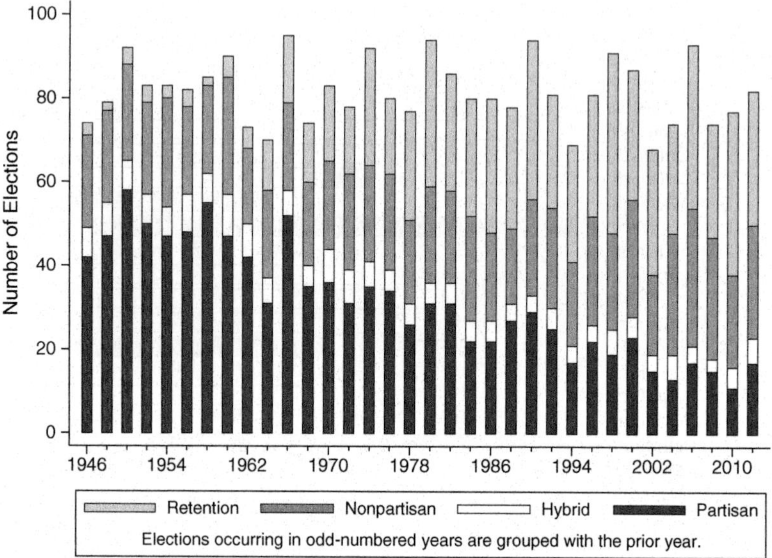

FIGURE 2.3. Number of Elections of Each Type, 1946–2013.

The peak decades for change during the postwar period were the 1960s and 1970s; as Figure 2.2 shows, much less change has occurred since 1980. Two states, Arkansas (2002) and North Carolina (2004), started using nonpartisan elections in the 2000s; the last states to start using a system employing retention elections were Tennessee (1992) and Mississippi (1996).

The result of the changes is a decline in the number of partisan elections and an increase in the number of retention elections. Figure 2.3 shows the number of elections of each type over time. In this figure, I show separately the number of elections in states (Ohio, Michigan, and Arizona prior to its switch to the Missouri Plan system) using partisan nominations but having no party labels on the general election ballots, what I label "hybrid" systems.[16] In this figure I have combined the number of elections occurring in odd-number years with the number in the prior even-numbered year (i.e., what is labeled 1960 is actually 1960 and 1961). The overall number of elections, while varying somewhat each two-year period, has changed relatively little. The number of nonpartisan and hybrid elections has been relatively stable, while the decline in the number of partisan elections has been offset by the increase in the number of retention elections.

While there has been little change over the last twenty-five years, efforts to make changes have continued. In 2010, voters in Nevada rejected adoption of the Missouri Plan, and in several states one house of the state legislature passed

16 Michigan uses party conventions to nominate candidates, Ohio uses party primaries as did Arizona prior to its adoption of the Missouri Plan (Lee 1973:53–54).

legislation for a constitutional amendment adopting the Missouri Plan, but the legislation died in the other house.[17] In other states, campaigns for change have continued without getting to the stage of presenting a formal plan to the voters (see Anderson and Anderson 2011; Goodman and Marks 2007). As noted previously, retired U.S. Supreme Court Justice Sandra Day O'Connor has played a leading role as a spokesperson for systems based on the Missouri Plan (O'Connor 2010). Even while there are efforts to adopt the Missouri Plan, criticism of that plan has begun to appear (see, for example, Fitzpatrick 2009), and in several states that have a Missouri Plan system, including Missouri itself,[18] one finds calls to move away from that system to one where elected officials or voters have more control over staffing the state's supreme court (Rosenbaum 2009; Sisk 2009).[19]

STATE SUPREME COURT ELECTION SYSTEMS TODAY

Figure 2.2 indicates that there are five systems that use popular elections in some way for selecting and/or retaining state supreme court justices:[20]

- Partisan elections for initial term and subsequent terms.
- Partisan elections for initial term with retention elections for subsequent terms.
- Nonpartisan elections for initial term and subsequent terms.
- Partisan nomination with nonpartisan elections (i.e., no party label on the ballot) for both initial term and subsequent terms.
- Appointment for initial (usually abbreviated) term followed by retention elections for subsequent full terms.

In addition, there are the states that do not use popular elections for either initial selection or retention.

Typically those writing about judicial elections distinguish between selection and retention. Those terms can be misleading given that even in states where the state constitution seems to indicate that supreme court justices are to be elected, there are provisions for appointment by the governor, or in two states the supreme court itself, to fill any vacancies that occur other than at

17 See http://www.judicialselection.us/judicial_selection/reform_efforts/failed_reform_efforts.cfm?state= (last visited October 2, 2012).

18 See http://www.newmoplan.com (last visited October 29, 2012).

19 A change along these lines was adopted by voters in Tennessee in 2014. Nomination by a formal nominating commission was discontinued and the governor's choice can be rejected by the state legislature if the legislature acts within a specified period of time; retention elections will continue to be used for terms beyond the initial appointment (see http://ballotpedia.org/Tennessee_Judicial_Selection,_Amendment_2_%282014%29, last visited December 24, 2014).

20 South Carolina and Virginia use systems involving elections by members of the legislature.

the conclusion of a justice's term. The reality is that the vast majority of state supreme court justices in states using partisan and nonpartisan elections initially obtain office by gubernatorial appointment. That is, most justices are initially selected by the governor. Consequently, for most justices in states using elections, one needs to distinguish among initial selection, election to an initial term, and election to subsequent terms.

Even this distinction only begins to describe the differences in what might best be labeled "staffing systems" for state supreme courts. As Gibson (2012:138) noted, "[V]irtually every state selection system is unique, either as to its formal or informal characteristics." In this section, I catalog the various dimensions characterizing the systems that states use in staffing their supreme courts. I limit the discussion to states that use popular elections as part of their staffing systems.[21]

Initial selection: In most states using retention elections, all supreme court justices are initially appointed by the governor. Those states generally employ some form of the Missouri Plan whereby the governor must choose from among one or more candidates identified by a nominating commission; there is substantial variation among the states using either legally required or voluntarily adopted nominating commissions on who controls the selection of members of the commission and the criteria for appointment.

In at least three states all justices, other than those holding the position on an interim basis, are initially elected. In Louisiana, if a vacancy occurs, the supreme court makes an interim appointment, but that appointee may not run in the election to fill the position; that election must occur within one year after the seat initially becomes vacant. In Arkansas, interim vacancies are filled by the governor, but those appointed to such vacancies are barred from running in the subsequent election to fill the seat by the Arkansas constitution (Amendment 29, Section 2). In Pennsylvania, while the governor fills interim vacancies by appointments, those appointees do not by tradition run for the position in the election that follows.[22]

[21] The information in this section was assembled from a wide variety of sources. The best single source is the judicial selection website maintained by the American Judicature Society (http://judicialselection.us, last visited October 9, 2012). William Blake kindly provided me with a table he compiled based on the AJS website. This website also has information on selection and retention processes used by the states that do not employ popular elections. A second good source of information on selection and retention of state court judges is the Survey of State Court Organization, which is accessible online at http://www.ncsc.org/sco# (last visited June 9, 2014). Note that the American Judicature Society closed down in the fall of 2014; its judicial selection website is supposed to be taken over by the National Center of State Courts, which also maintains the Survey of State Court Organization website.

[22] There is no legal restriction on interim appointees running, but a norm has evolved that those nominees do not seek the post in the subsequent election. Prior to Pennsylvania's adoption of retention elections for terms after the first one to which a justice is elected, interim appointees often did run for election; the last election in which an interim appointee ran was in 1979, which was before Pennsylvania adopted its current system of selection and retention.

In the other states initial selection can be either through appointment to fill a midterm vacancy or by election if a justice chooses to leave office at the end of his or her term. All but two states using appointments to fill midterm vacancies designate the governor as the appointing authority. As previously described, in Louisiana the supreme court makes interim appointments, but those selected by the court are not permitted to run in the special election that follows; in Illinois the supreme court makes interim appointments after a screening and evaluation process, and those so appointed may (and usually do) run for a full term in the partisan election that follows the vacancy. As noted, many states using gubernatorial appointments to fill midterm vacancies require the governor to use a nominating commission, while other states leave it to the governor to decide how to identify and screen candidates. Some states subject the governor's choice to some form of confirmation process either using one or both houses of the state legislature or some other body. In one state, California, if a justice chooses not to run for another term but does not step down midterm, the governor nominates a single candidate who then goes before the electorate on a "yes-no" ballot; one could call this process, which has actually occurred only twice (in 1990 and 2014), a form of gubernatorial nomination with voter confirmation.

Pre-election Term Length: States using elections vary in how they schedule the first election after a justice is appointed. In some states the justice must stand at the next election provided that the appointment is not made very close to that election. In other states the justice does not stand for election until she or he has served some minimum period of time. As discussed in Chapter 1, in Wisconsin a newly appointed justice serves until the next election at which no other justice's term is expiring.

Initial election format: The initial election format can be partisan, nonpartisan, nonpartisan after partisan nomination ("hybrid"), or retention. Since 1977 Louisiana has employed a blanket primary (sometimes referred to as a "jungle primary") at the time of the general election where all candidates with party designations are listed on a single ballot; if no candidate wins a majority, the top two candidates regardless of party stand in a runoff held in December. In Montana, if an incumbent is unopposed, the election becomes a retention election regardless of whether the incumbent has previously been elected.[23]

[23] Utah had a similar provision for several years before it switched to the Missouri Plan. Nevada includes a "none of the above" option on its ballot which makes an uncontested election a kind of retention election. In none of these states has a supreme court justice facing an election of either type been turned out of office.

Term length after initial election: In some states the initial election for a justice who had been appointed to office is for the remainder of the predecessor's term; in other states the initial election is for a full term regardless of whether the previous justice's term was ending.

Subsequent election format: Most states use the same election format for initial and subsequent elections. The exceptions are New Mexico, Illinois, and Pennsylvania, all of which use partisan elections for the initial election and retention elections for subsequent elections.

Percentage required for retention: In most states using the retention format, a simple majority of "yes" votes is required for retention. The exceptions are New Mexico (57 percent required) and Illinois (60 percent required).

Formalized evaluation process prior to retention: At least seven states (Alaska, Arizona, Colorado, Kansas, New Mexico, Tennessee, and Utah) have created by law formal evaluation processes for judges standing for retention elections.[24] However, the Kansas program, while still on the books, has been defunded. In addition, a number of state bar associations conduct evaluation surveys, and one state bar, Missouri, conducts a formal evaluation that is authorized by court rule that combines bar surveys with other evaluative mechanisms.

Length of full term: Full terms for justices in states using elections range from six to twelve years; the most common term length is six years.[25]

Individual seats: In most states justices run for individual seats. However, in Michigan, Pennsylvania, and West Virginia, when multiple seats are up for election, the seats are treated as a set, meaning that if there are X seats, the top X vote getters win those seats. In Michigan, when there are elections for both full and partial terms, they are treated separately.[26]

Number of seats at a single election: In most states the number of seats up for election at any one time is some fraction of the number of justices on the court. As previously noted, in Wisconsin terms are structured so that there is never more than one seat up for election. In South Dakota, all five members of the state supreme court stand for retention at the same time. This is also true in Tennessee, but there have been elections where only a subset of the five-member court stood for election, either because an appointment to fill a

[24] See http://www.ncsc.org/topics/judicial-officers/judicial-performance-evaluation/state-links.aspx (last visited October 8, 2012); http://iaals.du.edu/initiatives/quality-judges-initiative/implementation/judicial-performance-evaluation (last visited October 9, 2012).

[25] As discussed in Chapter 1, Minnesota has a provision that allows the governor to extend the justice's term for up to three years if during that time the justice will qualify for "full" retirement; thus, at least in theory, a justice in Minnesota could serve up to nine years without having to face the electorate.

[26] Such elections are fairly infrequent in Pennsylvania because partisan elections are only used for the initial election.

vacancy came too soon before an election or a justice had decided to serve out his or her term and not stand for retention, which produces an appointment once the seat becomes vacant. There have been other retention elections in Tennessee where a recently appointed justice stands for retention for the balance of his or her predecessor's term.[27]

Constituencies: In most states all justices run for election on a statewide basis. In Kentucky, Illinois, Louisiana, Maryland, and Mississippi, justices run in a district that comprises only part of the state with some large urban districts having multiple seats.[28] In Nebraska, associate justices run in districts while the chief justice runs statewide. In three other states (Oklahoma, South Dakota, and Tennessee) retention elections for the state supreme court are statewide but all justices are selected from a specific district.[29] In Florida there must be one justice appointed from each of five districts which means, given that the court consists of seven justices, a justice can be appointed from anywhere in the state if the departing justice is one of two from a district.[30]

Election scheduling: In most states, elections for the state's supreme court occur in even-numbered years in November along with other statewide and national elections. The exceptions are

Georgia: July (nonpartisan elections at the time of the partisan primaries with a runoff if needed in August).

Pennsylvania: November of odd-numbered years (both initial partisan and subsequent retention elections)

Tennessee: August (retention elections)

Wisconsin: April (nonpartisan elections with primaries in February)

27 One effect of the amendment to the Tennessee Constitution passed in 2014 is that retention elections will take place only after an appointee has served the term to which she or he was appointed regardless of whether this is a full or partial term. The amendment also appears to mean that all members of the Tennessee Supreme Court will stand for retention together every eight years.

28 Before shifting to the Missouri Plan, South Dakota used nonpartisan elections with districts.

29 It appears from looking at election returns in Oklahoma that during part of the period of this study, Oklahoma nominated supreme court candidates in district primaries but they then ran statewide in the general election.

30 "The present Florida Constitution requires that, at any given time, at least one Justice must have been a resident of each of the five District Courts of Appeal at the time of appointment to the Court. Thus, at-large seats are determined solely by the composition of the Court when a vacancy is filled. Under the current Court composition, an at-large seat would be vacant if one Justice from the Second or Fourth District left the Court. This is because each of these districts currently has two representatives. If a Justice representing the other three districts left the Court, the vacancy could only be filled by a qualified person living within the boundaries of that district" (http://www.floridasupremecourt.org/pub_info/documents/appointed.pdf, last visited October 27, 2012).

Louisiana holds what can amount to a primary at the November general election, with a runoff in early December if no candidate wins a majority in November; Georgia used this model in 2006, 2008, and 2010, but in 2012 reverted to the schedule noted previously, which it had started using when it switched to nonpartisan elections in 1984.[31] Mississippi holds its supreme court elections in even-numbered years along with federal elections; however, elections for governor, the legislature, and other state officials occur in odd-numbered years. Four states (Arkansas, Idaho, Oregon, and Washington) which use nonpartisan elections hold primaries even if there are only two candidates and have provisions that if a candidate wins a majority in the primary, that candidate is elected and the office is not included on the ballot at the November general election (or only the candidate winning the primary appears on the general election ballot); this effectively makes the general election a runoff.[32] The Arkansas, Idaho, and Oregon primaries are held in May and the Washington primary is held in August.[33] The majority of contested elections in these four states are determined at the primary.

Chief justice selection: Three different methods are used for selecting the chief justice: specific appointment/election to that position, selection by members of the court, and seniority (the justice with the longest service is the chief).

Incumbency indicated on ballot: Several states (Arkansas, Georgia, Idaho, Michigan, Minnesota, and Oregon) provide an indication of whether a candidate is an incumbent. For some states this involves listing the word "incumbent" with the candidate's name. Idaho uses a ballot in the form of "To Succeed Justice John Smith" and then lists the candidates, one of whom may be "John Smith" if he is running for reelection. The others show the candidate's title (i.e., list the candidate as "Justice XXX") or list the candidate's current position under his or her name (e.g., Justice of Supreme Court).[34]

Straight-ticket voting: Many states provide a way for voters to cast a "straight-party ticket" by marking a single box or some equivalent. Among

[31] During this earlier period, the supreme court justices did appear on the general election ballot, but always without opposition.

[32] Arkansas, which adopted this schedule when it switched to a nonpartisan system with the 2004 election, actually calls the November election, if it occurs, a runoff.

[33] Washington discontinued this system starting with the 2014 election; under its revised system, there is no primary if there are only two candidates, and both candidates appear on the November ballot.

[34] This is also true in California, which uses a retention-form ballot. Only two retention-type elections for the California Supreme Court have involved a candidate who was not an incumbent. In the 2014 election, the nonincumbent was listed as "Stanford University Law Professor Mariano-Florentino Cuéllar." In other states a title might also be listed for other candidates who are currently judges on other courts.

the states still using partisan elections for the state supreme court, Alabama, Texas, and West Virginia include the supreme court elections in the list of offices covered by a straight-party vote.[35] New Mexico did so until 2012, when the secretary of state decided not to include a straight-party option on the ballot.

Term limits: No state has established a limit on the number of terms a person may serve on the state supreme court. However, in Georgia a justice who chooses to continue service after being on the state supreme court for twenty-four years forfeits his or her retirement benefits.

Mandatory retirement age:[36] Fifteen of the states using elections have established a mandatory retirement age ranging from 70 to 75, most commonly 70. States vary as to how the retirement age works: retirement on the justice's birthday, retirement at the end of the month in which the birthday occurs, retirement at the end of the calendar year in which the birthday occurs, or retirement at the end of the justice's current term if less than half the term remains. An additional seven states have a maximum age (either 70 or 75) at which someone, including an incumbent, can run for a seat on the state's supreme court. One state, Arkansas, has no mandatory retirement, but a justice forfeits retirement benefits if the justice fails to retire at the end of the term during which the justice turns 70.

VARIETY IS THE SPICE OF JUDICIAL SELECTION

From the preceding discussion it should be clear that describing how state supreme courts are staffed is not a simple task. More important for the analyses presented in the following chapters is that the complexities dictate that a lot of very specific choices have to be made. For example, in states where the chief justice is elected, how should one categorize an election in which one of the candidates is the incumbent chief justice and one is an incumbent associate justice with regard to the incumbency of the two candidates? While one is an incumbent in the office, the other is also an incumbent on the court. What about an election for chief justice when the current incumbent does not run, but one of the two candidates is an incumbent associate justice; should the associate justice be treated as an incumbent? How does one code an election for chief justice where an incumbent associate justice loses but remains on the court as an associate justice?

35 Straight-party voting is not applicable in Pennsylvania given the scheduling of its elections for the state supreme court, nor in Louisiana given the blanket primary it uses.

36 The primary sources for information on mandatory retirement are Goldman (2009) and http://www.ncsconline.org/d_kis/salary_survey/retirement.asp (last visited October 8, 2012).

Not only are the staffing systems for the state supreme courts highly variable, but as discussed in this chapter they have been subject to extensive change over time. Some of the changes are large, such as New York's decision to completely abandon judicial elections for its highest court in favor of an appointive system, or South Dakota's shift from nonpartisan elections using districts to a Missouri Plan system with statewide retention elections. Some changes that may seem relatively small can have significant impacts; one such change was Minnesota's decision to list incumbency status on the ballot starting in 1950. Other changes, such as the adoption of a formal mechanism for evaluating judicial performance and communicating those evaluations to potential voters, are relatively small and probably have had little if any practical effect. Some states have had very stable systems; in Wisconsin the only major change was the adoption of the Australian ballot in the late nineteenth century, and then later formalizing that the ballot would be nonpartisan (even though no candidate had previously requested to be identified by party). Other states have made a lot of changes. Utah shifted from a partisan to a nonpartisan system in 1951, then to a nonpartisan system where an unopposed incumbent was subject to a retention election, and then to a Missouri Plan system, all in the space of less than thirty years.

In the following chapters I examine how state supreme court elections have changed over a period of sixty-seven years, 1946 through 2013. My focus is not on the changes to the formal features of the elections but rather on how key patterns in the elections have changed.

3

So What, Do Judicial Elections Matter?

An initial question to be answered about method of judicial selection generally and judicial elections more specifically is "so what?" Does the method of selection or the form of election matter in anything more than a symbolic fashion? There is an extensive body of research by political scientists starting in the 1960s (Jacob 1964) that has sought to understand what if any differences arise as a result of the way that judges are selected. Much of this research has focused on whether various selection systems produce judges with different background characteristics such as race, ethnicity, gender, religion, prior practice, type of law school attended, and local connections (Alozie 1988, 1990, 1996; Bratton and Spill 2002; Canon 1972; Dubois 1983; Dudley 1997; Emmert and Glick 1988; Esterling and Andersen 2000; Flango and Ducat 1979; Glick and Emmert 1987; Graham 1990; Hurwitz and Lanier 2003). While some of the early research considered whether the manner of selection and retention affects the decisions that judges make (Atkins and Glick 1974; Nagel 1973), starting in the early 1990s the possible impact on decisions became the central question for researchers looking at the impact of selection methods (Hall 1992, 1995; Hall and Brace 1992; Pinello 1995).

One difficulty with this body of research is that it frequently looks at the formal selection system, counting states as selecting judges through election even when most judges initially came to the bench through appointments to fill midterm vacancies. Moreover, much of the research does not consider the distinction between how judges initially obtain their positions and the mechanism through which they retain those positions. As was detailed in Chapter 2, there are many important variations, and in a large number of states there are significant differences between initial selection and retention. Drawing on ambition theory (Schlesinger 1966), one should expect that for judges who want to retain their positions – those with what Schlesinger labeled "static ambition," attention should focus on who will decide the retention question rather than on who was responsible for the judge's initial selection. While initial selection method may account for differences in judges' demographics, how judges are retained is more likely to account for what judges do when they make decisions.

A second issue regarding the impact of selection and retention is reflected in claims by critics of judicial election that "judicial elections are undermining public confidence in the fairness and impartiality of the courts" (Geyh 2003; see also Phillips 2003:144) and that election spending by special interests "threatens the integrity of our courts" (Jamieson and Hennessy 2007; see also O'Connor 2007). At least some studies of public opinion show a widespread belief that elected judges are biased toward those who contribute to their election coffers (see Gibson 2012:188n11, citing a survey done for Justice at Stake). Simple democratic theory suggests that judges who must face the electorate in order to retain their positions should be more attentive to the preferences of their constituencies than are judges who do not have to be concerned with their electoral futures (Schlesinger 1966). All of these points accord with what many people would see as common sense, but does that common sense reflect actual reality? That is the question considered in this chapter.

In thinking about the question of whether judicial elections matter, it is important to distinguish between the specific individuals who serve on a court and the processes of selection and retention. As suggested by the discussion in Chapter 1 of events related to the Wisconsin Supreme Court, it is easy to look at the outcome of a judicial election and say that if Candidate X had won rather than Candidate Y, the decision in Case A would have been different. However, the same analysis applies to judges selected through appointment processes, either in terms of who is doing the appointing or in terms of whom the appointer chooses to appoint. Imagine how the history of recent Supreme Court decisions might have been different if Richard Nixon's nomination of Clement Haynesworth had been confirmed by the Senate and Harry Blackmun had spent the rest of his career as a federal appellate judge in Minnesota, or if President George H. W. Bush had chosen someone other than David Souter, or if Thurgood Marshall had stepped down while Jimmy Carter was president and had been replaced by someone other than Clarence Thomas (Leonhart 2014). The question of concern here is not who is selected but whether elections matter in ways beyond the specific individuals who are selected or retained through an electoral process.[1]

[1] Given this focus, I do not look at studies (e.g., Echeverria 2015) that focus on the effect on court decisions of who wins an election.

This chapter examines three distinct ways that judicial elections generally and state supreme court elections more specifically can matter in real terms:

- The impact of elections and election campaigns on a court's legitimacy
- The impact of elections, direct or indirect, on the decisions judges make
- The impact of campaign contributions on the decisions judges make

The discussion that follows draws heavily on extant research, adding several new analyses concerning several specific questions.

SUPREME COURT ELECTIONS AND LEGITIMACY

There are three hypotheses that can be derived from the claim that elections undermine public confidence in the fairness and impartiality of the courts. First, if the claim is true, one would expect that, on average, citizens' views of the courts in states without elections should be more positive than in states using elections, particularly partisan or nonpartisan elections. Second, some observers have argued that the negative campaign advertisements, particularly those on television, reduces the public's respect and support for the courts (see Gibson 2008b:60).[2] Third, as suggested, the need for candidates in judicial elections to raise campaign funds may lead the public to believe that such fundraising leads to judicial bias.

Impact of Method of Selection and Retention on Legitimacy

A major challenge for research on the impact of the use of elections to select and/or retain judges on legitimacy, support, and trust in the state courts is the sparsity of survey data about state courts, particularly data that can be compared over time and/or across states. The problem is even greater if one wants to zero in on state supreme courts because most of the extant surveys asked about either "state courts" or "local courts" generally and not about state supreme courts specifically. A further complication that this presents is that, in some states, the way judges are selected varies by level of court, and in a few states even geographically with regard to trial courts. A final complication has to do with how courts are labeled or the presence of multiple courts of last resort. In New York the "supreme court" is both the trial court and the intermediate court of appeals, with the court of last resort carrying the name Court of Appeals. In Texas and Oklahoma there are two separate courts of last

[2] I leave for Chapter 5 the consideration of whether negative advertising systematically affects the outcome of state supreme court elections.

resort, with the state "supreme court" dealing with noncriminal matters and a court of criminal appeals having the final say in criminal cases. It is important to keep these complications in mind as I discuss the research that examines the linkage between selection/retention methods and legitimacy.

Wasmann et al. (1986) reanalyzed data from a national survey conducted in 1977 for the National Center for State Courts (Yankelovich, Skelly & White 1978);[3] they compared the public's view of the state and local courts across formal selection systems (appointment, Missouri Plan, partisan election, and nonpartisan election), and found little variation. Subsequently, several scholars examined the impact of the formal selection method on the public's view of "courts in your community" using a 1999 survey, again done on behalf of the National Center for State Courts (National Center for State Courts 1999). One of those analyses (Benesh 2006) reported a small impact for selection method with respondents in states relying on partisan elections having a lower level of "confidence" than those in other states.[4] However, a re-analysis of the same data using a different set of control variables (Kelleher and Wolak 2007) failed to find a relationship between partisan elections and confidence in the courts. Using a 2001 survey done for Justice at Stake,[5] Cann and Yates (2008) constructed a multi-item index of diffuse, or general, support for the state courts.[6] They found a negative relationship between diffuse support and both partisan and nonpartisan elections, but that effect was limited to those respondents who self-reported a low level of knowledge of the workings of their state court system.

Gibson (2012:49–52) briefly reported an analysis comparing citizens' views of the legitimacy of the state supreme court in states that do and do not use some form of elections to choose and/or retain members of the state supreme court. Using data from a small national survey conducted in 2007, he found that the use of popular elections of any type in choosing or retaining members of the state supreme court had no effect on the perceived legitimacy of the

3 The Yankelovich survey was the first national survey focused specifically on the public's views of the courts. There were prior studies (e.g., Curran 1977:232–34) that asked about courts in a nonspecific way; there is no way to know whether respondents in such studies were thinking of federal courts, state courts, or both.

4 One uncertainty in this analysis is how states were coded given that in some states partisan elections are used for some state courts while appointment or the Missouri Plan is used for other courts.

5 The questionnaire along with marginal frequencies for this survey can be found at http://www.justiceatstake.org/media/cms/JASNationalSurveyResults_6F537F99272D4.pdf (last visited June 5, 2013).

6 The four items in the index were "judges are trustworthy and honest," "judges are fair," "courts provide equal justice," and "court decisions are based on facts and law."

court.[7] However, drawing on studies based on survey experiments in Kentucky (Gibson 2012) and Pennsylvania (Gibson et al. 2011), Gibson (2012:107) found that "judicial elections by themselves enhance judicial legitimacy."

The most recent national study focused on the public's views of state courts is a 2009 survey conducted for the National Center for State Courts by Princeton Survey Research Associations International (2009).[8] The survey included six questions related to the public's view of the state courts:

- a question that asked respondents to indicate their level of confidence (a lot, some, not too much, no confidence) in various state institutions including "state courts";
- a question that asked respondents whether with regard to the amount of control that the governor and members of the legislature have "over state judges and the decisions they make in court," the governor and state legislators "should have more control than they do now, less control, or about . . . the same amount of control";
- four additional questions asked respondents to choose between pairs of statements regarding the state courts:
  1. Decisions are too often mixed up in politics *versus* courts put politics aside in making their decisions.
  2. State courts can be trusted to make decisions that are right for the state as a whole *versus* often don't give enough consideration to what's right for the state as a whole.
  3. The state supreme court should not be able to decide as many controversial issues as it does now *versus* it's important for the state supreme court to maintain its ability to decide such issues.
  4. It's important for judges on the state supreme court to be independent and not too influenced by what others think *versus* it's better for judges to be less independent and pay more attention to what the people think.

A simple reanalysis of the responses to these six questions individually and in the form of two scales, one combining all six items and one combining the

7 Gibson measures legitimacy using a factor score that is based heavily on three items: accepts that the decisions of the state supreme court are fair and impartial, believes that the judge can be fair and impartial, considers the state supreme court legitimate (Gibson 2009:1293). While the size of Gibson's national sample was about 350 overall, with only about 100 respondents in states without elections, the reported difference in Gibson's measure of legitimacy is zero to two decimal places.

8 David Rottman of the National Center generously made these data available to me for reanalysis.

two items that specifically referenced the state supreme court, showed no statistically significant differences among respondents based on the selection/retention system used for their state's supreme court.[9] A regression analysis that included a range of control variables also failed to produce any evidence of differences based on the type of selection system. Details of these analyses are in this chapter's Appendix A.

Impact of Election Processes on Legitimacy

Chapter 5 discusses changing patterns of campaign contributions and expenditures and the frequency of television advertising, both positive and negative. That discussion shows a clear pattern of increased spending but that negative advertising is less frequent or dominant than many critics contend. What impact do these aspects of elections have on the public's view of the courts?

Impact of Campaign Contributions and Expenditures

Critics argue that the money aspect of judicial elections puts the judges' impartiality into question ("Editorial: Money and Judges, a Bad Mix" 2014; American Bar Association 2003:viii; Caplan 2012; Kaplan 1987; Kaplan and Davidson 1998:12; Moyer 2010; Talbot et al. 1999) and that negative advertising has costs for the general legitimacy of and/or trust in the courts (National Center for State Courts 2002:7; Souders 2006:558–59). Systematic research does lend support to at least the first of these concerns. The public is cynical about judges receiving campaign contributions from those who appear before them or who have interests that are affected by court decisions (Geyh 2003:54–55; Gibson 2012:12–13; Jamieson and Hennessy 2007:901; Justice at Stake 2013; Sample et al. 2010a:56), and such contributions do appear to detract from the legitimacy of the courts (Gibson 2009).

Impact of Negative Advertising

The research regarding negative advertising provides a somewhat mixed message. Gibson (2012:12–13) found that a significant portion of the public thinks that it is acceptable for candidates for judicial office to attack their opponents.[10] Gibson

9 One caveat about the findings vis-à-vis questions asked about the "state supreme court" is that, as noted previously, in the state of New York, the "supreme court" is the higher trial court and the intermediate appellate court; the state court of last resort in New York is called the Court of Appeals.

10 Gibson also reports that 86 percent of his respondents believed the judicial candidates should be allowed to make their policy views known.

et al. (2011) found in their study of the 2007 Pennsylvania election that exposure to ads, whether positive or negative, tended to reduce support of the court, with little difference between what they labeled "traditional" ads and attack ads; they note that this finding must be understood in the context of an election that overall increased support for the court. A survey experiment study using Texas voters by McKenzie and Unger (2011) failed to find any effect of types of campaign ads on support for the Texas Supreme Court, with or without controls for and interactions with the respondents' level of sophistication.

The 2009 study for the National Center for State Courts discussed earlier provides a source of data for a simple test of whether the presence of attack ads in state supreme court election campaigns impacts the public's support for the court. Comparing states where attack ads had been aired in state supreme court elections by the time of the survey with states that had not seen such ads,[11] both states without elections and states with elections but no attack ads showed no statistically discernible differences between states with and without attack ads on any of the six items. The same was true for regression analyses that used several of the individual items and the two scales mentioned previously (one combining all items and one combining the two items that specifically mentioned the state supreme court). Details of these analyses are presented in this chapter's Appendix A. Thus, there is no evidence to date that negative advertising has significantly impacted the public's view of their state courts generally or their state's supreme court more specifically, although the research does not rule out the possibility of short-term, nonlasting effects in the wake of an election campaign that included substantial negative advertising.[12]

Summary and Conclusion

Gauging the impact of selection/retention systems is difficult because factors in specific states can impact support in many ways. The ideal approach would be to have good time series data for a state that changed from one

[11] Several states first saw attack ads in 2010; because the survey was done in early 2009, they were treated as not having seen such ads for purposes of this analysis.

[12] I located a report based on several surveys of Wisconsin residents that included questions about views of the Wisconsin Supreme Court (Jacobs et al. 2013). Regrettably, the first of these was done after the nasty 2008 election. Three surveys were conducted after the 2011 election discussed in Chapter 1. The approval of the court was actually higher in 2011 (about six months after the April election) than in spring 2012 or spring 2013. There were differences in approval between those who identified themselves as Democrats and those who identified as Republicans. Unfortunately, there is not a good comparison point from prior to the 2011 election.

selection system to another. In recent years there has been little change, with only two states, North Carolina and Arkansas, making a change between 2000 and 2013, both shifting from partisan to nonpartisan elections. As discussed in Chapter 2, since 1946 only one state, New York in the 1970s, has completely abandoned elections for its highest court,[13] although many more states have shifted to systems employing appointment combined with retention elections or from partisan elections to nonpartisan elections. Another approach could be to look at the impact on public support for lower courts in one of the three states – Arizona, Kansas, and Missouri – where some parts of the state use elections while other parts do not (Rottman and Strickland 2006:33–39); however, such an analysis would be complicated by the fact that any news coverage or advertising concerning elections would spill over into areas where judges were not elected.

To summarize, the research on the impact of method of selection on how the public views state courts provides little support for the argument that elections have systematically negative consequences for the courts' long-term legitimacy; the one broad exception is the public's concern about the implications of the money that candidates for judicial office must raise.[14] This one negative must be considered in light of the two single-state studies in Kentucky and Pennsylvania discussed earlier which found positive effects of election campaigns on legitimacy, at least as regards short-term effects. The key limitation of these two studies is that each deals with a single election cycle. One can certainly imagine a specific election that could produce at least a temporary decrease in public support for some or all of a state's courts, although a hard-fought election may produce a decrease in support among persons who preferred the loser, which could be offset by an increase by those who preferred the winner. However, the important question is not the short-term impact of any one election, but rather whether elections have enduring impacts, either positive or negative, on how the public views the courts and the public's willingness to accept the decisions made by the courts. There is no extant evidence showing long-term effects in either direction.

[13] Over the course of U.S. history, only one other state that adopted elections for its state supreme court has entirely abandoned popular elections: Virginia briefly had popular elections, but switched to a system of legislative selection during the Civil War. This is based on information posted by the American Judicature Society (http://www.judicialselection.com/, last visited June 14, 2013).

[14] Some states specifically forbid candidates for judicial office from soliciting campaign donations. In 2015, the U.S. Supreme Court will consider a challenge to such regulations in a case from Florida, *Williams – Yulee v. The Florida Bar* (No. 13-1499).

IMPACT OF ELECTIONS ON JUSTICES' AND JUDGES' DECISIONS

In Chapter 1 I argued that a key factor explaining change in judicial elections in Wisconsin was the mobilization of interest groups in response to several Wisconsin Supreme Court decisions related to tort law. As I will discuss in later chapters, decisions related to the death penalty served to mobilize opponents of sitting justices in California and Tennessee. Other hot-button issues have been abortion, property rights (i.e., restrictions on land use and development), and most recently same-sex marriage. If elections do matter for state supreme court decision-making, one would expect such effects to be most evident in these kinds of issues which are likely to be the vehicles for mobilizing voters.

There is a substantial body of research on the impact of electoral considerations on decisions related to the death penalty, some work related to sentencing more generally, and three studies of decisions regarding abortion rights. With some minor exceptions, the impact of judicial elections on decisions related to tort matters, same-sex marriage, or property rights has not been examined. In this section I will review the extant research on criminal case decisions and abortion, and I will present original analyses related to same-sex marriage and decisions regarding tort law; I am not able to shed any light on whether judicial elections impact decisions in land use matters. While most of the following discussion considers state supreme court justices, for decisions related to criminal law, I will briefly reference research on the impact of elections on decisions of trial court judges.

Method of selection and/or retention can have either direct impacts or indirect impacts on judicial decision-making. By direct impacts I mean that judges make different decisions depending on how they are selected and/or retained; for example, judges who are retained by elections of one type or another may be less likely make decisions favorable to criminal defendants than are judges who do not have to face the electorate if they want to continue in office at the end of their current terms. By indirect impacts I mean that factors influencing judges' decisions differ depending on how they are selected and/or retained; for example, judges who must face the electorate may be responsive to public opinion, while judges who do not have to face the electorate can ignore public opinion.

Criminal Cases

The Death Penalty in State Supreme Courts

Capital punishment has been a hot-button issue for courts since at least 1986, when Rose Bird and two of her colleagues lost retention elections for the California Supreme Court after a campaign that focused heavily on their decisions in death penalty cases (see Chapter 7 for a discussion of this election). It should not be surprising that the subject of capital punishment has received the most attention in studies of the impact of elections on judicial decision-making.

Relatively soon after the defeat of the three California justices, Hall (1992) looked at the possible electoral effects on death penalty decisions by state supreme court justices in four southern states (Kentucky, Louisiana, North Carolina, and Texas) during the 1980s.[15] She focused specifically on the more liberal judges in cases that upheld the death penalty. She asked in what way might the electoral situation these judges faced lead them to vote to uphold the death penalty rather than dissenting as one would predict given their broader pattern of voting in criminal cases? Her results showed that these liberal justices were more likely to vote contrary to their presumed political inclinations when they were approaching the end of their terms, if they had won their previous election by a narrow margin, if they were running in a district rather than statewide, and if they had previously run for reelection. Hall (1995) later found essentially the same pattern of relationships in an analysis of voting to uphold death penalties using all of the justices in the same four states and using all cases regardless of whether the court's decision was to uphold or strike down the death sentence. Brace and Hall (1997) extended the analysis further to include death penalty decisions by eight state supreme courts (Arizona, California, Illinois, Kentucky, Louisiana, North Carolina, Ohio, and Texas) during the period from 1983 through 1988. They found that justices were more attentive to the likely preferences of constituencies if they faced more frequent elections (shorter terms) and served in more competitive political environments.

Several analyses have been conducted using data from the State Supreme Court Data Project (SSCDP) which covers cases in all states between 1995 and 1998 (see Brace and Hall 2001). The dataset includes almost 900 cases (over 5,600 individual decisions) from 34 of the 38 states that had the death penalty at that time. Brace and Boyea (2008) examined the question of whether public support for the death penalty influenced judicial decisions and whether any such influence was conditional on the method of retention. The results of their analysis showed that decisions of justices facing reelection were correlated with public opinion in the justice's state, while the decisions of justices in states not using elections for retention did not show a similar relationship. In another analysis using these same data, Brace and Boyea (2007) found that

[15] One of the states was Texas, and for Texas she looked at decisions by the Court of Criminal Appeals which is the final court in criminal cases in Texas.

justices in the last year before retirement on courts in elective states were more likely to vote to reverse in a capital case than were non-retiring justices; there was no such effect in appointive states, where the likelihood of voting to reverse was essentially the same as for retiring justices in elective states regardless of retirement plans or requirements. They also found that in states using some form of popular election as the method of retention, justices were less likely to vote to reverse in a year when the justice was standing for election than either the year prior to or the year after the year of election. Hall (2012), also using data from the State Supreme Court Data Project, focused specifically on how mandatory retirement might condition the influence of election-related factors on decisions in death penalty cases. She found that for justices not compelled to retire prior to what would be their next election, the likelihood of voting to reverse in a capital case decreased if elections to the state supreme court had generally been competitive, if the justice had won his or her last election with less than 55 percent of the vote, and if the other two branches of state government were under unified Republican control (presumably an indicator of a conservative political environment). For justices who were barred from standing again for election, these effects were reduced or absent.

Canes-Wrone et al. (2014) report the most extensive and sophisticated analysis of the linkages between selection/retention of state supreme court justices and decisions in death penalty cases. Their analysis is based on 12,777 votes by justices in 2,078 death penalty appeals between 1980 and 2006. Their model included both the method of retention and public support for the death penalty conditional on method of retention, plus reselection proximity and indicators of whether the justice was facing mandatory retirement or was otherwise a lame duck; controls for various case and legal factors filled out the model. The authors report results for both before (Pre-Bird) and after (Post-Bird) the defeat of the three California justices. Post-Bird, they find that, after controlling for the justice's party, state public opinion, and electoral proximity, justices in both nonpartisan and retention election systems are more likely to uphold the death penalty than are justices in partisan election states. Justices in both partisan election states and states where justices are subject to reappointment are responsive to public opinion, while those in nonpartisan and retention states are not. Justices facing reselection within two years were more likely to uphold a death penalty, but judges facing retirement or otherwise in a lame-duck status did not differ in a significant way. The analysis comparing pre- and post-Bird showed that prior to the 1986 election there was no significant difference in the decision pattern comparing justices subject to partisan and nonpartisan elections, but those subject to retention elections were *less* likely to vote to uphold a death penalty; that is, the effect of retention elections reversed in the wake of the defeat of the three California justices in retention elections.

These various studies clearly show that elections have significant influences, both direct and indirect, on the decisions of state supreme court justices in death penalty cases. The studies are not entirely consistent regarding the precise nature of those influences, but it is clear that many justices, either consciously or unconsciously, consider the electoral consequences of their decisions in these cases.

The Death Penalty in State Trial Courts

While this book's focus is on elections of state supreme court justices, there is also evidence of the death penalty's electoral impact on trial judges who preside in death penalty trials. Specifically, three states (Alabama, Delaware, and Florida) authorize trial judges to impose a sentence of death when a jury has *not* recommended a death sentence for a defendant; a fourth state, Indiana, allowed such overrides until July 1, 2002. Judges in Delaware do not stand for election while judges in the other three do have to face the electorate to retain their positions. Statistics suggest that having to face the electorate inclines judges to demonstrate that they are tough on crime by imposing death sentences even when a jury has failed to recommend death.

Justice Stevens's dissent in a 1995 U.S. Supreme Court decision upholding life-to-death overrides, *Harris v. Alabama*,[16] noted that in Alabama judges had overridden life sentences forty-seven times but death sentences only five times; in Florida judges had overridden 134 recommendations of life but only 51 recommendations of death; and in Indiana judges had overridden eight recommendations of life but only four of death. Delaware did not adopt the two-way override until 1991, but between 1991 and 1994, no Delaware judge had overridden a life recommendation while seven had overridden death recommendations (Russell 1994:11n52). Several studies have updated the figures in Stevens's dissent:

- By 2011, only one Delaware defendant had been sentenced to death after a jury recommendation of life, while twelve received life sentences after the jury recommended death (Radelet 2011:798–99).[17]

[16] 513 U.S. 504, 515. In November 2013, the U.S. Supreme Court declined to revisit its earlier decision over the strong dissent of Justice Sotomayor (Liptak 2013).

[17] The Delaware defendant's initial death sentence was thrown out by the Delaware Supreme Court; after the trial judge again sentenced the defendant to death, the Delaware Supreme Court once again threw it out, and ordered the trial judge to impose a life sentence.

- In Indiana between 1977 and 2002, when the state legislature abolished the life-to-death override, eight defendants were sentenced to death (one twice) against the recommendation of the jury, while nine defendants received life sentences although the jury had recommended death (Radelet 2011:797).[18]
- In Florida, between 1972 and 2011, there were 166 instances of death sentences being imposed after a jury recommended life imprisonment; all of those overrides occurred prior to 2000 (Radelet 2011:809).[19] Through 2011 there were at least ninety-one instances in which a judge imposed life after a jury imposed death, and twenty-four of those overrides occurred after 1999 (Radelet 2011:820).[20] Exactly why judges in Florida stopped overriding jury recommendations of life is not clear (810–11).
- Through mid-2011, Alabama trial judges had overridden ninety-eight recommendations of life but only nine recommendations of death (Equal Justice Initiative 2011:7).[21] One study of death overrides in Alabama through the late 1990s found evidence that judges were more likely to override life sentences in the two years immediately before they would have to face the electorate to win a new term, and that this effect developed after the 1986 defeat of the three California Supreme Court justices (Burnside 1999:1039–41).

These statistics suggest that elections influence the action of trial judges in capital cases. While it is unclear why life-to-death overrides have ceased to occur in Florida, the overall pattern here strongly suggests that judges facing reelection are attuned to the risks of being labeled soft on crime by a potential opponent,[22] and to limit that risk they appear to choose to demonstrate their toughness in the most visible cases on their docket, those involving a possible death sentence.[23] As I will discuss, these kinds of effects are not limited to

18 None of the eight Indiana defendants who received death sentences over the jury recommendation of life was executed.

19 Four persons have been executed in Florida after being sentenced to death despite a jury recommendation of life imprisonment.

20 The uncertainty regarding the exact number of death-to-life overrides reflects the difficulty in identifying such cases, particularly if the defendant did not appeal (Radelet 2011:812). Death sentences are automatically appealed.

21 Eight of the defendants in these 98 cases had been executed by mid-2011 (Radelet 2011:802).

22 In the three electoral states that allow, or allowed, judicial overrides of a nondeath sentence, trial judges are retained through either partisan or nonpartisan elections.

23 A similar effect of electoral proximity was found in a study of capital cases tried in Cook County between 1870 and 1930. The authors of the study report that a defendant found guilty was 15 percent more likely to be sentenced to death during the year that the judge was up for election; however, except in the case of a bench trial, the death-life sentence was entirely in the hands of the jury which leaves some doubt about the mechanism leading to the reported effect (Brooks and Raphael 2002:638).

capital cases: elected trial judges dealing with criminal cases are attuned to the electoral implications of their decisions.[24]

Other Criminal Cases in State Supreme Courts

Three studies have examined the possible electoral effects on state supreme court justices across the full range of criminal case issuesand all three are limited in their focus. One study (Savchak and Barghothi 2007) looked at justices who would have to stand in a retention election. The core hypotheses of that study were (1) that justices originally appointed by Democratic governors would be more likely to vote in a fashion favorable to defendants, (2) the overall political orientation (liberal vs. conservative) of the state's residents would have an influence on justices' votes, and (3) that influence of the citizens' political orientation would increase as the end of the justices' terms approached. Using the data from the State Supreme Court Data Project, the authors found that both the party of the appointing governor and the political orientation of the state's citizens worked as hypothesized even after controlling for the justices' own political orientation. They did not find a statistically discernible additional effect of the political orientation of the state's citizens as the justices' terms approached their end, although the direction of the effect was as hypothesized.[25]

The second study (Cauthen and Peters 2003) was limited to Louisiana, and asked whether the district-based system for electing members of the Louisiana Supreme Court affected justices' decisions. Looking at 1,111 votes from 180 non-unanimous search and seizure cases decided between 1970 through 1994, the authors found that justices were more likely to render a pro-prosecution decision in cases from their home district compared to cases coming from elsewhere in the state (64 percent versus 55 percent). A logistic regression model that included a measure of district ideology and controls for the justices' own ideologies showed that justices tended to vote consistently with the ideology of their district but only in cases from their district; in fact they tended to vote in opposition to their district ideology in cases from outside their district.

[24] Lemennickier and Wenzel (2014:9–10) present some evidence they suggest indicates that executions are less likely "in states where judges are independent from voters (merit plan)." Unfortunately, they mischaracterize some states' selection system for trial-level judges and do not appear to fully understand the role of elections as a retention rather than a selection mechanism.

[25] A key variable missing from their analysis was whether the justice is barred from running for another term due to mandatory retirement provisions in the state.

The third study by Shepherd and Kang (2014) examined the impact of the volume of television advertising in supreme court elections on the decisions of state supreme court justices in criminal cases. The study was based on almost 3,100 state supreme court cases from the period 2008 to 2013 selected from thirty-two states, and used data on television advertising compiled by the Brennan Center. The analysis found that the likelihood that a justice would vote in a manner favoring criminal defendants decreased as the number of advertisements aired in elections in a justice's state increased. Importantly, the effect was related to the number of advertisements, not specifically to advertisements focused on criminal justice. The analysis controlled for a range of potentially relevant factors including case characteristics, type of retention system, and justice's political party affiliation. The authors do not report whether they also conducted an analysis that split out advertising with a criminal justice focus, which leaves the question of why justices would be responsive to advertisements unrelated to criminal justice, particularly when much of that advertising focuses on the justices' professional background, commitment, and other feel-good factors.[26]

Sentencing in Noncapital Cases

Several studies have examined the impact of elections on sentencing in noncapital cases. Two studies, one using data from Pennsylvania (Huber and Gordon 2004) and one using data from the state of Washington (Berdejó and Yuchtman 2013), considered whether sentencing behavior varied over the electoral cycle, with the hypothesis that sentences would be tougher when a judge approached his or her reelection. Both studies found the hypothesized effects.

Another pair of studies (Gordon and Huber 2007; Lim 2008) took advantage of variation in the method used to select trial judges in Kansas. The trial courts in Kansas are organized by district, with fourteen districts employing partisan elections for both initial selection and retention and seventeen employing gubernatorial appointment for initial selection and retention elections for subsequent terms. Regardless of the selection system used, trial judges serve terms of four years. Not a single trial judge has been defeated in a retention election in Kansas, while 5–10 percent of judges running for reelection in partisan elections have lost (Lim 2008:3). Using both regression techniques and case-matching techniques, Gordon and Huber found that judges in districts using partisan elections tended to impose harsher sentences both in terms

[26] The initial report of this study, which appeared as this book was in final preparation, is somewhat sketchy, and leaves a lot of questions about the study unanswered.

of the likelihood that the sentence involved a period of incarceration and the length of that incarceration (Gordon and Huber 2007:121–27). They also found that electoral proximity is influential in partisan election districts, but not in retention election districts; in fact for the latter the coefficients are negative, although not statistically different from zero (128–30). Lim looked at the sentencing tendency of judges controlling for both election type and the partisan background of the judge; she found that the sentences of the judges facing retention elections hew closer to the presumptive guidelines regardless of the judge's partisan background. In contrast, Democratic judges in partisan election districts were more likely to impose the harshest sentences while Republican judges in such districts were more likely to impose the most lenient sentences (Lim 2008: 29).

Summary: Judicial Elections and Judicial Behavior in Criminal Cases

The studies just reviewed make clear that the role and type of elections used in the retention, and possibly the initial selection, of judges are associated with broad patterns in the decisions made by both final appellate court and trial court judges in criminal cases. One might be concerned about the link between the election cycle and judicial decisions in criminal cases (Epstein 2013:220), which shows that defendants facing sentencing by a judge nearing election might have reason to fear a harsher sentence than if the defendant were facing a judge who had recently been elected or reelected; that is, an approaching election may bias at least some judges toward harsher sentencing. However, as Gibson (2013:227–28) points out, it is not obvious which is the "correct" sentence, the one given out in the absence of electoral pressures or the one given out when the judge might be under closer scrutiny by the public. In both cases the legal parameters of the sentence are specified in statutes passed by the elected representatives of the citizens. One could readily argue that judges who sentence more leniently early in their terms are failing to carry out their duty, while those toward the end of their term are faithfully executing their duty.

The death penalty override cases provide a counter to Gibson's suggestions. In those cases it is the juries who make the initial decision and presumably the juries reflect local public opinion. In fact, if anything, the "death-qualified" jurors who would have made the recommendation tend to fall on the harsher side of public opinion (see Allen et al. 1998). If such juries fail to decide that the death penalty is appropriate in a particular case, in what way would a judge's decision to override that determination and impose the death penalty reflect the "more correct" decision under the law?

Civil Cases

Abortion

A second hot-button issue for state supreme courts has been abortion. A pair of studies has examined the electoral influences on state supreme court decision-making.[27] In the first study Canes-Wrone and Clark (2009; see also, Caldarone et al. 2009) compared states using partisan elections with states using nonpartisan elections, and asked to what degree the impact of public opinion on abortion influences state supreme court decisions. They identified eighty-five abortion-related cases decided by state supreme courts in sixteen states between 1980 and 2006; those cases involved a total of 597 judge-votes. They measured public opinion by pooling national surveys across states over ten-year periods. The statistical results showed that, after controlling for key facts of the case and the partisan background of the justice, justices in nonpartisan states were responsive to public opinion with a "ten-percentage point shift in public opinion in a pro-choice direction alter[ing] the likelihood of a pro-choice decision by five percentage points" (57–58). The results revealed no statistically discernible general effect for public opinion in partisan states; in fact, the coefficient suggested that, if anything, the relationship ran opposite to the direction one would expect. Moreover, regardless of the type of election system, judges were more likely to vote in a way consistent with the tenor of public opinion on abortion in their state in the last two years of their terms.

The second study (Canes-Wrone et al. 2012) added retention election states to the mix. In the retention states there were 360 votes from fifty-nine abortion-related cases. The results showed that justices in retention states were almost as responsive to public opinion as were justices in nonpartisan states. In this analysis the authors used a more refined measure of electoral proximity that separated out effects for states where public opinion leaned toward allowing easy access to abortion from those that leaned toward greatly restricting or banning abortion; the results showed no statistically discernible effects for electoral proximity, and the authors speculated that this might be due to some other refinements in the statistical modeling approach.

While it may be surprising that public opinion had no apparent effect in partisan election states, the explanation may be that in those states, voters essentially assume that candidates for the state supreme court running as

27 An earlier article by Brace et al. (1999:1294), covering fewer cases and using a less fully specified model, found that justices facing retention through partisan or nonpartisan elections were less likely to strike down abortion restrictions than were justices who would have to stand in a retention election.

Republicans oppose abortion, while Democrats favor easy access to abortion. Essentially, it may be that abortion is so aligned with the political parties that public opinion can work indirectly through the partisan labels on the ballot rather than exerting a direct influence on voters. In contrast, views on capital punishment do not align as clearly with partisanship. One question that is left unanswered by Canes-Wrone et al.'s analyses arises from the absence in the analyses of states not using any form of popular elections for selection or retention of state supreme court justices; specifically, would an analysis including those states have shown that public opinion had no influence in nonelectoral states in line with what Brace and Boyea found in their analysis of death penalty cases?[28]

Same-Sex Marriage

Same-sex marriage is the third of the prominent social issues that has come before the courts in recent years. The concern about possible decisions by state supreme courts led thirty states to pass amendments to their state constitutions defining marriage as between a man and a woman (or allowing the state legislature to so define marriage). In some cases the amendments were written broadly to limit benefits that might flow to same-sex couples through civil unions.[29] Some of the amendments were passed in response to state court decisions, while others were intended to block courts from ruling that limitations on same-sex marriage violated that state constitution.

Mezey (2009) provides an extensive analysis of the judicial decision-making related to same-sex marriage in state and federal courts through the first part of 2009. By mid-2009, appellate courts in twenty-four states had considered cases concerned with same-sex marriage or civil unions; in one of those states the case never reached the state supreme court for a decision on the merits. In only one additional state, Montana, did a state supreme court decide a same-sex marriage case between the controversial decision by the

[28] Devins and Mansker (2010:484–88) located 27 instances where state-level public opinion polls had asked questions about issues not related to crime or criminal justice that were then the subject of a state supreme court decision; the issues included topics such as abortion, same-sex marriage, gun control, education, eminent domain, immigration, and Indian gaming. Following the work of Marshall (1988, 2005), who has examined whether U.S. Supreme Court decisions align with public opinion, they looked to see whether the state supreme court decisions were in line with state public opinion. They found that justices subject to nonpartisan elections were the most likely to vote consistently with state public opinion, with justices not having to face the electorate the least likely to vote in line with public opinion.

[29] List on Wikipedia as of July 17, 2013; http://en.wikipedia.org/wiki/List_of_U.S._state_constitutional_amendments_banning_same-sex_unions_by_type.

Iowa Supreme Court in 2009 and the *Windsor* decision;[30] the Montana court simply allowed challenges to provisions in Montana law that limited marriage to proceed in the lower courts. In a second state, Texas, a petition for review languished for more than two years before the Texas Supreme Court finally granted the petition and then heard arguments four months *after* the U.S. Supreme Court handed down its 2013 decision striking down part of the federal Defense of Marriage Act in *U.S. v. Windsor*.[31]

Is there any relationship between the outcome of state challenges to limitations on same-sex marriage, and the method of retention used for state supreme court judges? Klarman (2013:117) observes that most of the judges who declined to strike down restrictions on same-sex marriage in the years immediately after the Massachusetts Supreme Judicial Court struck down the state law limiting marriage (*Goodridge v. Department of Public Health*, 798 N.E.2d 941, 2003) were elected. More generally, Pozen (2008:237) hypothesizes that decisions "that seek to protect traditionally disadvantaged or despised groups in new ways," such as by striking down limits on same-sex marriage, "will be less likely to emerge from elected courts."

The number of state appellate decisions limits the potential for statistical analysis, but one can still discern a pattern consistent with Pozen's hypothesis and Klarman's observation. Appendix C to this chapter lists the cases from the twenty-five states through 2012, including what specific issue each case dealt with and the outcome of the case. Appellate courts in ten states made decisions or issued orders favorable to same-sex unions; courts in six of those states also made unfavorable decisions. Courts in the other fifteen states that had same-sex marriage cases made only unfavorable decisions. In some cases, both favorable and unfavorable toward same-sex marriage, courts were unanimous and in others the courts were closely divided. Of the ten states where favorable decisions were made, three use retention elections, six do not use elections, and only one, Montana, uses nonpartisan elections.[32] Of the fifteen with only unfavorable decisions, ten use contested elections (partisan, nonpartisan, or hybrid), four use retention elections, and only one does not use elections. While this shows differences related

[30] As discussed in footnote 50 in Chapter 1, a Minnesota appeals court reversed a trial court decision dismissing a challenge to the Minnesota law banning same-sex marriage; however, that case never got to trial because it became moot after the Minnesota legislature legalized same-sex marriage. Given the limited nature of the decision by the appellate court, I have not included this decision in the following discussion.

[31] The Texas case is *In the Matter of the Marriage of J.B and H.B.* which was consolidated with *State of Texas v. Angelique Naylor and Sabrina Dal* (argued November 5, 2013); as of December 31, 2014, the Texas Supreme Court had not rendered its decision.

[32] In Montana, if an incumbent is not challenged, the election reverts to a retention format.

to the retention method in use,[33] one must be cautious in drawing such a conclusion given that four of the five states with favorable decisions that used appointment are in the liberal northeast and the fifth is Hawaii, which is also politically liberal. Thus the pattern may primarily reflect the level of support for same-sex marriage rather than the method of selection; based on an analysis of state-level public opinion, Barclay and Flores (2014; see also Devins 2010:1679–83) find that state-court decisions supportive of same-sex marriage have generally come once public opinion in the state has reached the point where a majority supports eliminating restrictions;[34] this is consistent with other research that finds that adoption of policies supporting various aspects of gay rights is responsive to state-level public opinion (see Lax and Phillips 2014).

Actions in state courts largely dried up in the wake of the defeat of three justices of the Iowa Supreme Court after that court unanimously ruled that limiting marriage to opposite-sex couples violated the state's constitution. Litigation challenging restrictions on or related to same-sex marriage sharply increased after the *Windsor* decision, although many of those cases were filed in federal court.[35] As this is written, it is too soon to determine whether state supreme court judges facing electorates hostile to same-sex marriage will now strike down existing limitations or uphold such laws and thus leave the potential political fallout to judges in the federal courts.[36]

Tort Cases

Given the prominence of tort reform and tort law as motivating factors in judicial elections (Goldberg 2007:80–83; Murphy 1994),[37] one might expect to find substantial research examining whether there is a linkage between variables

33 A simple goodness-of-fit test of the resulting 2x3 table for the null hypothesis of statistical independence produces a highly significant chi square (2 df) of 13.03 ($p < .001$).

34 It may be important to take into account the public's view of the substance of an issue and whether they believe it is appropriate for the state supreme court to act on an issue. Devins and Mansker (2010:487, 508) report a 2009 poll in Iowa that found that only 30.4 percent of the respondents favored a court ruling that would allow same-sex marriage, while elsewhere Devins (2010:1680) refers to a 2009 poll that found that 60 percent of Iowans supported same-sex marriage or civil unions.

35 See http://www.marriageequality.org/lawsuits (last visited June 4, 2014).

36 By mid-2014, it might be that state courts had started to become more active; a news report of a federal district judge's decision striking down Florida's ban on same-sex marriage in August 2014 noted that in the preceding six weeks five *state* trial judges in Florida had struck down the law (Stutzman 2014).

37 A study of the amount of contributions received by candidates running in elections for state supreme court found that the proportion of the court's docket comprised of tort cases was a significant predictor of contributions (Bonneau 2007a:79).

related to judicial selection and decision-making in tort cases. However, the research on this question is surprisingly thin.

In their study of judicial politics in Texas, Cheek and Champagne (see also Carter 2006:33–34; 2004:40–43) describe how decisions moved to favor plaintiffs after justices with significant backing of the plaintiffs' bar gained a majority on the Texas Supreme Court in the early 1980s. The court swung back to favoring the defense side after justices supported by business interests recaptured control of the Court in the 1990s.[38] The continued dominance of the pro-business perspective on the Texas Supreme Court is indicated by the success of defendants in tort case appeals, winning 87 percent of those cases decided with opinions in the period 2004–05 (Anderson 2007:8).[39]

An analysis of 145 tort cases decided by the Wisconsin Supreme Court between 2002 and 2012 found a sharp decline in the likelihood that the court's decision would be unanimous (Corriher 2013:8). While the analysis implies that this is a result of the contentious judicial selection process in recent years (described in some detail in Chapter 1), there is no clear evidence of such a link. Arguably the increase in contentious elections is *more likely* caused by conflict on the court regarding tort issues than vice versa.

Brace et al. (2012) used the data from the State Supreme Court Data Project to examine whether the method of selection has a systematic impact on the decisions of state supreme courts in tort cases. Unfortunately, the structure of their analysis did not provide a test of whether method of selection or other selection-related factors influence the direction of either justices' individual votes or the courts' overall decisions. In another study using the SSCDP data, Shepherd (2009c:188) found that justices who had to stand for retention in a partisan election or a retention election and faced a Republican leaning electorate favored the defense side in several types of tort cases; the effect did not appear in nonpartisan election states, but did appear in states where a justice would potentially be reappointed by a Republican governor or Republican controlled legislature. She also finds that the effects are less or nil for justices in their final terms due to mandatory retirement (190).

Another study (Helland and Tabarrok 2002; Tabarrok and Helland 1999) looked at the possible impact of selection system on awards in tort cases, and reported that the awards were higher in states where trial judges were elected

38 The ebb and flow of the battle for control of the Texas Supreme Court is tracked in some detail over a series of articles by Walter Borges that appeared in the *Texas Lawyer* in the 1990s.

39 Some of these issues were highlighted on the *Frontline* program, "Justice for Sale," which was first broadcast by PBS in 1999; the script can be found at http://www.pbs.org/wgbh/pages/frontline/shows/justice/etc/script.html (last visited July 13, 2013). A study of campaign contributions in the election for the Texas chief justice clearly showed the role of tort lawyers, both plaintiff and defense, in funding that election (Jackson and Riddlesperger 1991).

in partisan elections; however, given that most tort awards are made by juries, it is not altogether clear what the causal mechanism might be linking judicial selection to jury awards. A third study (Yates et al. 2010) examined the impact of how state trial judges are retained on the level of tort litigation in a state; that study found that the state's political climate (level of citizen liberalism) conditioned the impact of selection system (partisan and nonpartisan elections versus reappointment or retention elections) with elections associated with a lower level of tort litigation in states with a conservative orientation and with a higher level of tort litigation in politically liberal states (805);[40] however, it is unclear what the causal process at work here would be.

To assess what if any impact electoral considerations have on state supreme court decisions in tort cases, I analyzed data from State Supreme Court Data Project used by Brace et al. and by Shepherd in their analyses of tort cases. Here I summarize the results of my analysis, with a more detailed discussion in this chapter's Appendix B. The dependent variable in my analysis was the individual justice's vote, coded as pro-plaintiff vs. pro-defendant. The key predictor variables were

- Type of retention system (no elections, partisan and hybrid elections, nonpartisan elections, and retention elections);
- Whether a justice in an election state was precluded from running for another term due to mandatory retirement age;
- Whether a justice in an election state who was not barred from another term due to mandatory retirement was in the last year of his or her term; and
- A measure of the liberalism of the state's citizens, conditional on type of retention system.[41]

The regression model included control variables for type of tort, type of legal issue, absence of an intermediate appellate court that normally handled first appeals in tort cases, whether one of the parties was a governmental unit (presumably almost always as a defendant), the number of tort reform measures in effect in the state, and justice's ideology.

[40] An earlier analysis by Hanssen (1999) looked at the rate of civil filings in state trial courts of general jurisdiction for the period 1985–94 but found no statistically discernible difference between states that use partisan and nonpartisan elections for trial judges compared to states that use a Missouri Plan system or other systems whereby judges are appointed by the governor or chosen by the legislature (229–31). Hanssen did find that filing rates for appeals in the states' high courts were significantly higher in states that did not use partisan or nonpartisan elections for the justices of the high court (227–29).

[41] I would have preferred to have a measure of state-level views of tort issues, but no such measure is available, and it's unclear exactly what questions such a measure might be based on.

Because preliminary analyses indicated that patterns were different depending on whether the appeal was brought by the plaintiff or by the defendant, the analysis was done in a way that produced separate coefficients for plaintiff appeals and for defendant appeals (see Wright 1976). The sample sizes were large, with 22,808 votes in plaintiff appeals and 13,290 in defendant appeals. While the results showed statistically significant relationships for a number of variables, the models were not particularly good predictors of the justices' decisions.

The type of retention system appears to make a difference in defendant appeals but not in plaintiff appeals. Using partisan and hybrid elections combined as the reference category, for defendant appeals plaintiffs were least successful in partisan/hybrid states and most successful in nonpartisan and retention election states, with no-election states falling between. Even though the model included a control for the political orientation of the state's citizens, I am cautious about labeling this result as demonstrating an effect of retention method given that the majority of the states using partisan or hybrid elections for retention purposes in the 1990s were located in the South; the exceptions are West Virginia, Ohio, and Michigan.

The results suggest that those justices barred from running for another term due to mandatory retirement may be less likely to side with plaintiffs in appeals brought by plaintiffs. The pattern for justices facing imminent mandatory retirement in defendant appeals was inconsistent, but probably is best interpreted as indicating no clear effect. Facing reelection within twelve months did not impact justices' votes in either plaintiff or defendant appeals.

Finally, state political liberalism had a statistically discernible effect for defendant appeals only in states using partisan or hybrid elections, with the likelihood of pro-plaintiff votes increasing with the state's political liberalism. For plaintiff appeals the effect was inconsistent, with state liberalism associated with an increased tendency to side with the plaintiff in states using nonpartisan elections, but associated with siding with the defendant in states not using elections in the retention process. Judicial ideology did generally have the effect one would expect for both plaintiff and defendant appeals, with the tendency to vote in support of the plaintiff increasing as the justice's ideology moved in a liberal direction.

Overall, while it appears that selection/retention-related issues show some relationship with the direction of state supreme court decisions in tort cases, it is hard to make an argument that there are causal relationships pointing in a consistent direction. Even though tort issues have been strong motivators for key interests in judicial elections/judicial selection, the inconsistent nature of the effects summarized here precludes drawing clear conclusions about how the retention-related factors impact state supreme court decisions in tort cases.

Other Types of Civil Cases in the State Supreme Courts

As will be discussed in later chapters, a central conflict in state supreme court elections has pitted those aligned with consumers and injury victims against business and insurance interests. The outcomes of those struggles have shaped many of the decisions made by the state supreme courts in the states where they have occurred. Ware (1999) reports how Alabama Supreme Court justices lined up on a series of cases dealing with arbitration, a process generally viewed favorably by the business community but unfavorably by consumer representatives. The thirteen cases he examined were decided between 1995 and 1999, a period during which the court had some justices who had been funded and supported by the plaintiffs' bar and others who had been backed by business interests. In those thirteen cases, business-funded justices backed a broad interpretation of arbitration agreements in 91 percent of their votes compared to only 4 percent for the justices backed by the plaintiffs' bar (667–68). In another eleven cases dealing with the issue of whether an arbitration agreement covered claims against a non-signatory defendant, the corresponding percentages were 67 percent and zero percent (p. 670). Ware found this basic pattern to hold up across a range of other types of issues related to arbitration that came before the Alabama Supreme Court.

Another study of arbitration focused on the method of selection rather than the orientation of individual judges as indicated by the judge's source of campaign contributions. LeRoy (2010) looked specifically at court review of employment arbitration decisions. He found that at the trial level, employees won only 31.2 percent of cases before judges who had (or would be) running in partisan elections, compared to 52.7 percent in states using some other form of judicial retention. The pattern slightly reversed at the appellate level, with employees winning 43.2 percent before party-affiliated judges compared to 50.0 percent before other judges (LeRoy 2010:1602). Unfortunately, the study mixes state and federal trial courts, making it difficult to have much confidence in drawing conclusions about the impact of selection systems.

Hanssen (1999) looked at the question of whether the method of selection/retention of state supreme court justices was associated with the number of appeals from decisions of the state's utility commission that the state supreme court decided in the period 1978–1982. His analysis found that courts in states using partisan and nonpartisan elections decided fewer such cases than did courts in states where judges faced either no elections or only retention elections (222–26). Unfortunately for my purposes, Hanssen did not look at whether the type of selection system was related to whether the ultimate decisions were pro-consumer or pro-utility company.

Romero et al. (2002) sought to determine if selection system had any impact on the outcome of cases dealing with racial discrimination. Using the West key number system they located 126 noncriminal cases decided over the forty-year period 1956–1996 that involved decisions on the merits (i.e., not decided on procedural questions). Their unit of analysis was the case rather than the decision of the individual justice. They found no effect at all of selection method using the four categories of partisan election, nonpartisan election, Missouri Plan, and legislative or gubernatorial selection.When might one find judges who do not have to worry about election to be attentive to some constituency? Might judges who face reappointment be more favorable to government parties than judges who face reelection? Two studies examined this question.[42]

Shepherd looked at civil cases in which the state government is a party using the data from the State Supreme Court Data Project (SSCDP). She found that justices who retain their seat through reappointment by the governor or legislature are more likely to vote for the government litigant than are judges on permanent appointments (life tenure or tenure until mandatory retirement age) or those having to stand for reelection. This effect is particularly strong for justices subject to legislative reappointment who are deciding cases involving the legislature as a litigant (Shepherd 2009a:1617). She also found that the effects strengthened as reselection approached.

Rice (2014) examined how judges decided economic cases involving the state government as a party. Using 201 cases from the SSCDP data, he found that judges who would be retained through reappointment by the governor or the state legislature were more likely to decide in favor of the state government as economic conditions worsened than were judges who would have to face the electorate.[43]

These two studies demonstrate that it is not simply the election process that leads judges interested in retaining their positions to look toward a relevant reselection constituency. This is what one would expect based on Schlesinger's analysis of static ambition.

[42] A related question is whether justices differ in their inclination to strike down as unconstitutional state laws depending on the justices' electoral situation. Leonard (2014) found no effect of formal selection system on decisions regarding constitutionality. However, she looked only at initial selection systems as formally defined, not at either how a justice actually came to be on the court or in what manner the justice would face retention.

[43] Strictly speaking, Rice contrasted those who would have to stand for election with those who would not have to stand for election, and the latter group includes justices in the states where judges serve until reaching mandatory retirement age, voluntary departure, or death without ever being subject to a retention process.

Summary: Judicial Elections and Judicial Behavior in Civil Cases

This analysis of the behavior of state supreme court justices in civil cases shows some likely effects, but overall it is best to describe the findings as mixed. For abortion cases there appears to be a relationship between state public opinion for states using nonpartisan and retention elections but not for states using partisan elections; the exclusion from that analysis of states not using elections from the studies of abortion cases leaves some question about what conclusions one might draw from the results. My analysis of same-sex marriage cases is suggestive, but the fact that nonelection states are heavily found in the liberal northeast (and the absence of any same-sex marriage cases from Virginia and South Carolina, the two southern states not using popular elections) leaves some doubt as to whether retention mechanism is a causal factor. My analysis of tort cases produces results that show linkages to election-related factors, but the nature of those linkages does not support a view that these factors generally shape justices' voting in a particular way. Importantly, to the extent that there are effects related to retention, Shepherd's and Rice's analyses of cases involving government litigants make it clear that this issue is not limited to judges facing popular elections.

Summary

The research described in this section generally supports the view that methods of judicial retention and factors related to retention can influence the decisions of judges. Not all of the effects described work in straightforward ways. The effects are clearest for criminal cases, and particularly for cases involving capital punishment. On the civil side the effects are less evident or more difficult to separate out from confounding factors. For example, while my discussion of same-sex marriage cases makes clear that courts have been most likely to be supportive of same-sex marriage in states where justices do not have to stand for election to retain their positions, that may be due to the nature of the states not using elections rather than concerns about the retention process on the part of the justices. In the tort arena, the results summarized here (and detailed in Appendix B) raise many questions about the nature of the relationships my analysis uncovered, and it is not clear why particular variables seem to work in the ways that I found.

IMPACT OF CAMPAIGN CONTRIBUTIONS ON SUPREME COURT DECISIONS

The third major question concerning the impact of elections is whether campaign contributions influence the decisions that judges make. Contributions can have direct impacts or indirect impacts, or a combination of the two. One might think of an indirect impact as the expending of funds in an election campaign to secure the election of a justice *presumed* to be favorable to the contributor's perspective, while a direct impact is buying decisions by securing the loyalty of a justice who might not otherwise be sympathetic to the contributor's interest or case (Cann 2002:263).

Indirect Effects of Campaign Contributions on State Supreme Court Decisions

In practice, campaign contributors generally direct their money to candidates the contributors believe will make decisions they prefer, what some label "friendly giving" (Roscoe and Jenkins 2005:53). Regardless of whether the candidates' spending, which is made possible by the contributions from groups interested in how the candidate will vote, actually affected the election outcome, one would expect that if a significant portion of a candidate's campaign funding came from sources with particular preferences, the candidate's decision-making tendency would accord with those preferences. Such a pattern is likely to be found even in elections where the contributions had no actual impact on the outcome.

When and how campaign spending helps a candidate secure support in an election has been a significant question in the study of elections and campaigns, particularly in the context of congressional elections (see, for example, Abramowitz 1988; Cassie and Breaux 1998; Green and Krasno 1988; Jacobson 1978, 1980, 1985, 1990; Partin 2002). The thrust of the findings of this body of research is that in elections involving an incumbent, challenger spending makes a difference by increasing the challenger's vote share; whether incumbent spending matters is less clear in part because the level of incumbent spending is often in response to challenger spending (Squire 1995:900–903).[44] There has been less attention to open-seat elections, no doubt in part because they are much fewer in number. The most comprehensive study of those elections, by Gaddie and Bullock (2000), found that spending does matter. The share of the votes received by the Republican candidate tended to increase as the Republican candidate's expenditures increased and decreased as the Democratic candidate's expenditures increased (35–43, 175–77). Another study of open-seat elections employed a dichotomous dependent variable, Republican winner, and used the expenditure ratio as a predictor, finding that as the ratio of spending went from favoring the Republican to the

[44] Examining the impact of incumbent spending presents particular methodological difficulties because of this endogeneity problem. Also, generally the literature on the impact of campaign spending predates the influx of "independent" spending.

Democrat, the likelihood of the Republican winning decreased (Duquette et al. 2008).[45]

In contrast to the sizable body of research on the impact of campaign spending in congressional elections, there has been relatively little research concerning the impact of spending in state supreme court elections.[46] In a study of 260 state supreme court elections between 1990 and 2004 in eighteen states using partisan or nonpartisan elections,[47] Hall and Bonneau (2008) found that greater spending was associated with increased voter participation. In an examination of 166 partisan and nonpartisan general elections involving incumbents for the same period, Bonneau (2007c) found that, consistent with the research on congressional elections, spending by challengers increased the challenger's percentage of the vote; he found no statistically discernible effect of increased spending by incumbents.[48] Consistent with this finding, Bonneau and Cann (2011), looking at the same elections, found that funding restrictions disproportionately harmed challengers. Regarding open-seat elections, Bonneau (2006:153–54) briefly reported an analysis of the winner's vote share which includes spending by both the winner and loser; he found that more spending by the loser decreased the winner's share but there was no discernible effect for spending by the winner.[49]

Clearly money does matter in state supreme court elections, but it is not clear how much it matters in comparison to other factors such as partisanship or the experience of the candidates. Perhaps more important, to adequately assess whether campaign spending indirectly impacts later decisions by the court, one would need to know not just whether more spending can increase a candidate's vote share, but how often campaign spending affects who actually wins the elections; there is no research examining that question in the context

45 The ratio was modeled as a set of dummy variables, and showed that the effect was nonlinear in form.

46 In a brief article, Arrington (1996) reported a fairly simple analysis of the impact of spending in 20 North Carolina statewide appellate elections (1988–1994), some of which were for the North Carolina Supreme Court. He found no evidence of a relationship with spending. His analysis did not distinguish between incumbent-running and open-seat elections.

47 This study, and the others discussed in this paragraph, also included what I have labeled hybrid elections, grouping them with nonpartisan elections because the general election ballot is technically a nonpartisan ballot.

48 The effect for incumbent spending reported by Bonneau for incumbents is in the expected direction, but does not achieve statistical significance.

49 Chris Bonneau generously provided me with an earlier draft of his article that included more detail on the results of his analysis; those results showed that the coefficient for winner expenditures, while not statistically significant, was actually *negative*, which means that, if anything, greater expenditures by the winner reduced the winner's share of the vote. Actually, what this probably indicates is that one candidate's expenditures drove the other's expenditures, and perhaps the more important expenditures came from the underdog in the election.

of state supreme court elections. One can point to specific elections, such as West Virginia in 2004 or Wisconsin in 2008, where the winner and/or outside groups supporting that winner used campaign contributions from particular interests to mount a negative campaign to defeat the incumbent whom the contributor(s) wanted to see off the bench. However, there are probably many more examples where such campaigns were unsuccessful (e.g., Michigan in 2000 – see the discussion in Chapter 6).

Direct Effects of Campaign Contributions on State Supreme Court Decisions

The tendency of campaign contributors to choose whom they fund based on the past behavior of candidates and/or by their expected future behavior greatly complicates determining whether campaign contributions have what I have labeled direct effects on elected officials' decisions. That is, past and expected behavior tends to determine contributions as much or more than contributions determine behavior. This problem of likely mutual causation makes it particularly difficult to sort out the actual causal influences. However, as with the impact of spending on election results, there is a substantial literature attempting to determine if and when contributions by interest groups directly influence the actions of members of Congress.[50]

In a review of that literature, Baumgartner and Leech (1998:131–36) described that "body of research [as] infamous for its contradictory findings" (133) and concluded that campaign contributions by PACs "sometimes strongly influence congressional voting, sometimes have marginal influence, and sometime fail to exert influence" (134). They also suggest that the inconsistencies probably also reflect variations in variable selection, modeling choices, and measurement choices. In a more recent meta-analysis of the impact of campaign contributions on legislative roll call voting, Roscoe and Jenkins (2005) found that about one-third of 357 tests drawn from the thirty-three studies they examined were statistically significant.[51] Consistent with Baumgartner and Leech's suggestion that finding a relationship was partially dependent on variables included, measurement of those variables, and modeling choices, Roscoe and Jenkins reported that statistical significance varied depending on

[50] In the legislative setting, interest groups may use political donations for things other than to directly influence a legislator's vote; they may seek "to gain or maintain access, or mobilize friendly legislators to lobby their colleagues, or alter the language of the bill, especially at the committee stage" (Roscoe and Jenkins 2005:53).

[51] The meta-analysis included studies examining roll call votes that occurred between 1973 and 1996 (p. 56). Studies of voting by members of the U.S. House of Representatives dominated the analysis.

a range of such factors. For example, 62 percent of the tests were based on models that took into account the possibility of two-way causation; 30 percent of those tests were statistically significant compared to 45 percent of the tests that did not employ a simultaneous equations model.

Whether campaign contributions influence the decisions of justices is even less clear than for decisions by legislators. A number of studies have sought to link contributions and justices' decisions (Cann 2002, 2007; Cann et al. 2012; Kang and Shepherd 2011; Liptak and Roberts 2006; McCall 2001, 2003; McCall and McCall 2007; McLeod 2008; Palmer 2010; Palmer and Levendis 2008; Shepherd 2009b; Waltenburg and Lopeman 2000; Ware 1999; Williams and Dislear 2007). Most of these studies show that the decisions of at least some justices do tend to align with the interests of the groups that provide financial support for justices' election campaigns. The central issue in looking at the correlation between decisions and campaign contributions is whether contributions follow votes or votes follow contributions. Essentially, would a justice's decision in a case have been different if not for the campaign contribution? Even if one or more votes do follow contributions for a particular justice, this does not require that a justice consciously considered how he or she should vote given the source of campaign funds; it may be that the justice is more attentive to the arguments and briefs submitted by those associated in some way with those contributions. That is, much as in the legislative setting where contributions purchase access and lead to a more attentive hearing for the group making the contribution, in the judicial setting contributions may purchase a more careful consideration on the part of the justice, which in turn leads the judge to vote differently than he or she otherwise would have.

In the context of decision-making by state supreme court justices, several of the studies cited have attempted to untangle the causal question in order to determine whether justices' voting decisions were directly affected by the sources of campaign contributions the justice received. Some of those studies focus specifically on contributions from lawyers who can be identified as representing specific interests, while others have looked at contributions more broadly. The studies tackle the methodological challenge in several different ways.

Two studies employed statistical modeling that the authors argued took into account predispositions and hence allowed them to assess the impact of contributions beyond the indirect electoral impact they might have.[52] Cann

[52] The technical description of the statistical problem is that of endogeneity. That is, anticipated (or past) votes can influence contributions and contributions can influence votes. The statistical models used to overcome this problem involve what are called instrumental variables, which require finding variables that have a causal influence on contributions but not votes and variables that have a causal influence on votes but not contributions. If one is only interested in explaining votes, one need only find an instrumental variable that causes contributions but not votes.

(2007) looked at the impact of campaign contributions on decisions of the justices of the Georgia Supreme Court in cases decided in 2003. He focused specifically on contributions by attorneys who had appeared before the court during 2003, classifying the attorneys as liberal or conservative depending on the parties they represented before the court. He found that contributions increased the likelihood that a justice would vote in favor of the party the contributor represented. Bonneau and Cann (2009) applied the same approach to look at state supreme court decisions in Texas, Michigan, and Nevada for those courts' 2005 term, and found a direct impact of contributions in Texas and Michigan but not Nevada. I am not inclined to place a lot of weight on these findings, because of the limited periods covered by the studies, the limited focus on contributions from attorneys,[53] and technical issues related to the statistical estimation strategy.[54]

A second strategy used in an attempt to demonstrate a causal linkage is to focus on justices who are deemed to have a strong predilection to decide cases a particular way and ask if they are more likely to go against their predilection if they have received campaign contributions from interests and/or lawyers who normally represent interests opposed to the justices' presumed predilections. McCall (2003) applied this approach using cases before the Texas Supreme Court between 1994 and 1997 that involved businesses as both the plaintiff and the defendant. All of the justices on the Texas Supreme Court at that time were decidedly conservative, and McCall's specific strategy was to look only at the small fraction of cases won by plaintiffs and ask whether in those cases justices voting for the plaintiff (typically a small business challenging a large business) had received more contributions from the plaintiff or the plaintiff's lawyer than from the defendant or the defendant's lawyer. Given the conservatism of all of the justices, McCall assumed that contributions were not driven by the justices' ideology or anticipated decisional inclination, an assumption that seems reasonable. She did find that justices were more likely to support the plaintiff's position when they had received more in contributions from the plaintiff's side of the case. This does suggest some possible direct influence, but this is a very limited study.

53 According to Bonneau and Cann (3), attorney contributions to state supreme court candidates in 2006 comprised only 26 percent of the contributions those candidates received.

54 The technical issue concerns the quality of the instrumental variables used in the analysis. Unless the instruments both meet the requirement of not having a causal relationship with the other dependent variable and have a sufficiently strong relationship with the dependent variable for which they are being used as an instrument, the ultimate estimate is going to be on shaky grounds (see Bartels 1991); the authors of the articles using this methodology did not provide any information on the quality of the instrumental variables, and hence it is difficult to know what to make of their results.

A third approach is to find a baseline for individual justices' decision propensity for various types of cases. This is the approach used by Palmer in his controversial study of the Louisiana Supreme Court (see Finch 2008). The first iteration of the study (Palmer and Levendis 2008) was based on flawed data, which was subsequently corrected and reanalyzed (Palmer 2010);[55] the results were generally consistent across the two versions, although the corrected version was still subject to sharp criticism by defenders of the Louisiana Supreme Court (see Tully and Gay 2010). To assess causation, Palmer compared the justices' decisions for the plaintiff or defendant in cases where the plaintiff contributed more to a justice's campaign, the defendant contributed more, and where neither the plaintiff nor defendant contributed.[56] One can think of the "no contribution" condition as a baseline, where a justice's decision would not be influenced by contributions by one or the other of the parties. The cases covered the period 1992–2006, and were limited to 177 decisions on the merits where (a) at least one justice had received a contribution from a party to the case, (b) there was at least one dissent in the case, and (c) the case was not a criminal or disciplinary matter. For most of the justices, the probability of voting for the plaintiff or defendant when neither was a contributor was virtually the same as when the plaintiff was the net contributor; however, when the defendant was the net contributor, the probability of voting for the plaintiff dropped. For one justice, the likelihood of the justice voting for the defendant appeared to *decrease* if the defendant had contributed more to the justice's election campaign than the plaintiff had contributed. For one justice, the probability of voting for the plaintiff when the plaintiff was the net contributor increased from the "no money" condition and decreased from the "no money condition" when the defendant was the net contributor. One justice had too few cases involving contributors for a meaningful assessment, and two showed no apparent shifts across the three conditions (17). While using cases where a particular justice received no contributions does provide a baseline for comparison, limiting the baseline to cases where one or more of the other justices received contributions may be problematic. A second concern is the lumping of all types of cases together; one might expect that there would be potential differences based on type of case (e.g., tort vs. consumer vs. labor/employment, etc.). In the end, this study is at best suggestive that some justices might be directly

[55] Palmer sought and received independent verification of his coding. While some coding decisions might be debatable (Tully and Gay 2010:13–16), it is unlikely that correcting any remaining errors would change the thrust of his conclusions.

[56] Palmer's analysis also included logistic regression models, but those models fail to account for the endogeneity problem, and hence tell us nothing about causation.

influenced by campaign contributions, although if one were to generalize from Palmer's study one would have to say that it is a minority, and probably a small minority.

Yet another approach involves comparing the behavior of judges who might be directly influenced by campaign contributions and those whose electoral situation would free them from such a concern. One such situation is where a justice cannot stand for reelection due to a state's mandatory retirement requirement. While a retiring justice would be freed from any worries about future campaign contributions, the justices would probably vary in whether they feel any continuing loyalty to past contributors. Still, there is enough of a difference here that retiring justices provide a potential control group.[57] Shepherd (2009b) employed this approach using data from the State Supreme Court Data Project used in several of the studies previously discussed. While she concludes that her results support a finding of difference between retiring and potentially continuing justices, at least for justices in states using partisan elections, the results are not entirely clear and the pattern is not strong (673–74).[58]

In a second analysis also relying on data from the State Supreme Court Data Project, Shepherd (2013) used another control group to try to sort out the direct influence of campaign contributions. In her second study, Shepherd focused specifically on the impact of contributions made by business interests. As one would expect, the likelihood of a pro-business vote by a justice increased as the campaign support from business increased. Shepherd looked at the level of support both in absolute terms as measured by the amount of contributions from business and relative terms as measured by the percentage of contributions from business. She also showed that the support for business was negatively related to contributions from nonbusiness sources (p. 17). The key to her causal argument was the relative influence of contributions from business for justices identifiable as Democrats as compared to those identified as Republicans once one includes controls for the state's political ideology and other factors. She reported that contributions from business sources had a greater influence on Democratic justices than on Republican justices and

57 Kang and Shepherd (2011:102–03) identified another potential comparison group that has some similarities to justices facing mandatory retirement: justices in the three states (Illinois, New Mexico, and Pennsylvania) where initial selection is by partisan election but retention is by retention elections. However, they do not seek to test for possible differential effects of campaign contributions using this comparison.

58 A major question left unanswered by what Shepherd reports is whether the differences between judges facing mandatory retirement and those not facing forced retirement differ in a statistically significant sense.

she interpreted this finding as indicating a direct causal linkage. Importantly, she did not find the reverse: Republicans did not evidence a stronger effect of nonbusiness contributions than do Democrats; if anything such contributions have a stronger influence on Democrats than Republicans. One major issue gives pause in accepting Shepherd's interpretation of the results: she reported no tests comparing whether the differences between Republicans and Democrats could be attributed to chance, and one of the key differences was very small.[59]

Summary

Based on the extant studies, the only firm conclusion that one can draw from the empirical research on the link between campaign contributions and the decisions of those benefitting from the contributions is that there does tend to be a correlation between the two variables. Convincing evidence on whether those contributions systematically influence the decisions that the justices make, either directly or indirectly, is lacking. Regarding indirect effects, while there is some evidence that contributions influence vote shares, there is no evidence of a systematic impact on election outcomes. Regarding direct effects, none of the efforts to date to test for such effects is convincing, and the extant evidence is inconsistent. Given the challenges in sorting out the causal puzzle vis-à-vis direct effects, it is unclear whether solid evidence is obtainable. Finally, future efforts to assess the impact of contributions on votes will be further complicated by the lack of good data on outside expenditures by interest groups.

SUMMARY AND CONCLUSIONS

The use of elections to select and retain judges is controversial because of the perception that the method used for selection and retention actually matters. This chapter has sought to assess whether the use of elections and factors that relate to the use of elections have measurable impacts on the behavior of judges, particularly those who sit on state courts of last resort. The analysis in this chapter suggests this broad answer to the question of whether the use of

[59] At first glance one might ask why she includes no control for the justices' ideology given that justices may vary even if they share a partisan identification. The likely reason is that the usual method of measuring the ideology of a state supreme court justice, what is known as the PAJID scores (see Brace et al. 2000), is so closely related to the justice's partisan background that it would not provide enough additional information to be worth including in a statistical model.

elections for choosing and retaining state supreme court matters: *Elections do not matter as much as one might think:*

- To those who are concerned that elections – and the campaigns and money that go with elections – are harmful to the legitimacy of the court: there is little or no evidence that elections do, in fact, have the feared effect, and there is even some evidence that the use of elections with all of their warts actually increases the public's support for the courts.
- To those who are concerned that campaign contributions are a corrupting influence on state supreme courts, directly or indirectly buying the outcomes desired by the contributors: we have little or no evidence that campaign contributions *systematically* influence either who wins elections or lead to justices making decisions that would have been different in the absence of contributions.
- To those who are concerned that the need to run for reelection inappropriately influences the decisions that judges and justices make in specific cases or affects the willingness of judges and justices to make unpopular decisions: yes, there are such effects, but they are more limited than one might expect. Such effects are most evident in cases involving the death penalty; they are harder to detect in other kinds of cases.

These findings do not mean that some form of more sophisticated, more developed analysis could not show that some of the undesirable effects that critics of judicial elections espouse actually do exist. They do not mean that elections will never have some of the allegedly negative effects. They do not mean that further changes in how judicial elections are conducted could not have negative consequences for the public's view of the court. But, at least for now, most of the claimed negative consequences remain as hypotheses rather than as confirmed actualities.

This absence of evidence for most of the negative effects of elections that concern critics does not mean that there are no problems with those elections. Participation tends to be low in the absence of a highly visible top-of-the-ticket election, and even with some other election to bring voters to the polls, large numbers of voters do not participate; that lack of participation reflects the combination of low visibility for most of what courts do and the absence of the kinds of cues that voters rely on in elections. Judges do have to take time, in some situations a lot of time, to attend to election needs, both fundraising and campaigning. Given that even in electoral systems, most judges initially come to their positions by appointment, this is primarily an issue for sitting judges who might better devote time to their duties as judges. Many highly qualified persons who would make excellent judges choose not to seek judicial positions because they do not want to undertake the burdens involved in the electoral process, or do not have the personality or style to be effective political candidates.

The fact that elections do not have some of the problems often attributed to them does not mean that elections are the most desirable way to staff American courts. Nor does the general absence of the problems discussed in this chapter mean that a better system that includes elections could not be devised. In the final chapter, I will turn to the issues involved in designing systems of judicial selection, and consider what systems might be better than state systems currently in use, and the realpolitik that limits possibilities for significant change.

APPENDIX A: REGRESSION MODELS OF LEGITIMACY

As discussed in this chapter, the most recent national survey that focuses on the public's view of state courts was conducted in 2009 for the National Center for State Courts. This appendix reports the details of the statistical analyses summarized in the chapter regarding whether there are significant differences in legitimacy related to whether the respondent's state employs elections to select and/or retain state supreme court justices and whether there are any such differences related to past airing of attack advertising in connection with a state's supreme court elections.

Dependent Variables

Four different measures of public support were employed as dependent variables, with all coded so that higher values indicated more support. Two of these were single items: The first was a question asking respondents to rate their level of confidence in state courts using the alternatives of "a lot," "some," "not too much," or "no confidence" with the responses coded 0 to 3; the mean response was 1.93 with a standard deviation of .81. The second was a question asking whether the control the governor and members of the legislature had "over state judges and the decisions they make in court" should be increased, left as is, or decreased ("should have more control than they do now, less control, or about … the same amount of control"), with responses coded 0 to 2; the mean was .99 and the standard deviation .68. Logistic regressions were also done with the confidence question collapsed into "a lot of confidence" versus other responses.

Two scales were constructed. The first was the simple sum of the two dichotomous choice questions that specifically referenced the state supreme court:

- The state supreme court should not be able to decide as many controversial issues as it does now *versus* it's important for the state supreme court to maintain its ability to decide such issues.
- It's important for judges on the state supreme court to be independent and not too influenced by what others think *versus* it's better for judges to be less independent and pay more attention to what the people think.

For these questions interviewers also recorded a voluntarily provided response of "neither" or "both equally," and these were coded as falling between the two forced choice responses. The second scale was a single factor score based on the first principal component extracted from all six items. It is important to note that neither of these scales was particularly coherent. Cronbach's alpha for the two-item scale was an extremely low .19; a scale employing all four forced choice items (which was not used) had an alpha of .43. For the six items, the principal components results actually yielded two components with an eigenvalue greater than 1; the first two eigenvalues were 1.70 and 1.02, and the first component only accounted for 28 percent of the variation. A simple summated version of the six items produced an alpha of .53.

Independent Variables

Key Variables

The key variables of interest here are either the nature of advertising in the elections or the method of selection/retention. For the former, the predictor was a dichotomy coded 1 if any of the supreme court elections in the state prior to 2009 involved attack advertising, 0 otherwise. This variable was based primarily on the advertising identified by CMAG (see Chapter 5 for a discussion of the CMAG data), but could be coded as 1 if it was known that elections prior to 1999 (when the CMAG data start) involved attack advertising. For method of selection/retention two different versions were used; the first was a set of dummy variables using the categories, partisan elections, hybrid system (Ohio and Michigan), nonpartisan elections, retention elections, no elections (meaning no *popular* elections); the second collapsed partisan, hybrid, and nonpartisan elections with retention and no elections as the remaining categories. For both versions "no elections" was used as the reference category; also for both, states that combined retention elections with partisan elections (Illinois, New Mexico, and Pennsylvania) were coded as having partisan elections.

Control Variables

Nine control variables were also included in the regressions:

1. An index of knowledge that equaled the number of branches of government the respondent could identify, plus 1 if the respondent knew that the state supreme court could declare an act of the state legislature unconstitutional plus another 1 if the respondent correctly knew whether "the state supreme court" was elected. Note that for this latter item, respondents from New York were treated as having given a correct answer if they responded "Yes" because the trial division of what is called the supreme court in New York is elected even though the highest court in New York, the Court of Appeals, is not elected. This index ranged from 0 to 5 with a mean of 2.24 and a standard deviation of 1.49.
2. An index of the level of attention paid to the news based on three items asking about how closely the respondent followed national news, news about their state in general, and news about the town or neighborhood where the respondent lived. The response choices for each item were "very closely," "somewhat closely," "not too closely," and "not at all." The three-items scale with an alpha of .64. The scale ranges from 0 to 9, with a mean of 6.69 and a standard deviation 1.82.
3. An index of confidence in government other than the courts which was comprised of responses to the same question used to measure confidence in the state courts, but with the object of the questions being "the office of the governor," "the state legislature," and "local government where you live." The three-items scale with an alpha of .64.[60] The scale ranges from 0 to 9, with a mean of 5.44 and a standard deviation of 2.02.
4. A dichotomous item indicating whether the respondent had "direct experience, contact, or involvement with a court case which brought [the respondent] into a courthouse, including being called in for jury duty"; "yes" was coded 1, and 56 percent had responded "yes."
5. The respondent's sex, coded 1 male and 0 female; 53 percent of respondents were male.
6. Respondent's total household income in the previous year (2008) coded into four categories: under $25,000 (25 percent), $25,000 to under $50,000 (26 percent), $50,000 to under $75,000 (17 percent), $75,000 or

[60] Including the item asking about confidence in the state courts would produce a scale with an alpha of .72.

more (31 percent). This variable was used as a four-point scale ranging from 1 to 4; it had a mean of 2.54 and a standard deviation of 1.17.

7. Respondent's level of education coded into seven categories, and treated as a scale ranging from 1 to 7; the mean was 4.61 with a standard deviation of 1.66.[61]
8. An indicator of the respondent's race or ethnicity coded as non-Hispanic white (77 percent), non-Hispanic black (8 percent), Hispanic (9 percent), and other non-Hispanic (4 percent). This was treated both as a four-category set of dummy variables and as a two-category dummy variable where the latter three categories were collapsed; for both versions, non-Hispanic white served as the reference category.
9. An indicator of the respondent's political party identification, coded simply as Republican (24 percent), Democrat (40 percent), or Independent (33 percent); respondents who volunteered that they had "no preference" were grouped for purposes of analysis with Independents. In the analysis, party identification was treated as a set of dummy variables with Independent as the reference category.

Selected Results

Regression analyses were run using the five different measures of support previously described:

- single item, four-point measure of confidence;
- single item, dichotomous measure of confidence (logistic regression);
- single item, three-point measure of control that should be asserted by legislators and governor over court decisions;
- the two-item index combining the two forced choice questions about the supreme court;
- the six-item index combining the two single items with four forced choice items.

Additional variations in the analysis involved whether method of selection was treated as a three-category (no election, retention election, other type of election) or a five-category (separating out partisan, hybrid, and nonpartisan elections) variable. These various combinations produced a large number of regression models – too many to present. Tables 3.A1 and 3.A2 show selected models that are representative of the results.

[61] Category 4 was "technical, trade, or vocational school after high school"; category 5 was some college or university work, including an associate degree but not a four-year degree.

TABLE 3.A1. Regression Models Testing Impact of Selection Method on Support for State Courts

	Confidence		Very Confident		Support Index		Control	
	b	std. err.	b	std. err.	b	std. err.	b	std. err.
Type of Election	F=1.05, p=.384		χ^2=1.07, p=.898		F=2.34, p=.054		F=1.49, p=.203	
Partisan	–.072	.075	–.195	.302	.006	.105	–.095	.073
Hybrid	–.012	.094	.131	.365	**.340**	.132	.071	.091
Nonpartisan	.070	.078	–.054	.299	.117	.109	.040	.075
Retention	.018	.068	–.126	.269	.135	.096	–.045	.066
No Elections	.000		.000		.000		.000	
Knowledge Level	***.065***	.017	***.250***	.068	***.124***	.024	**.051**	.017
Attention to News	**.032**	.012	.000	.053	.002	.017	–.010	.012
Confidence Scale	.216	.011	***.656***	.061	***.164***	.015	***–.041***	.011
Experience in Court	***–.185***	.047	–.315	.189	**–.228**	.066	–.028	.045
Party Identification	F=0.60, p=.548		χ^2=1.90, p=.386		F=2.82, p=.060		F=0.39, p=.679	
Republican	–.035	.059	–.275	.229	*–.179*	.083	–.030	.058
Democrat	.031	.054	.007	.220	–.007	.076	–.045	.052
Independent	.000		.000		.000		.000	
Gender (1=male)	.041	.045	**.533**	.187	*.160*	.064	.075	.044
Income Scale	.043	.022	–.058	.091	***.151***	.032	*.078*	.022
Education Scale	–.008	.016	.000	.068	.031	.023	**.041**	.016
Race/Ethnicity	F=3.81, p=.038		χ^2=2.40, p=.430		F=5.50, p<.001		F=3.80, p=.010	
Non-Hispanic Black	**–.198**	.080	–.494	.375	**–.282**	.108	–.122	.076
Hispanic	–.120	.075	.117	.319	**–.352**	.103	**–.228**	.072
Other	–.136	.098	–.322	.482	–.210	.140	–.025	.097
Non-Hispanic White	.000		.000		.000		.000	
Intercept	.463	.136	–5.601	.662	–1.543	.191	.845	.131
R^2 or Pseudo-R^2	.336		.197		.241		.138	
n	950		950		808		904	

Italics indicates p< .05; **bold indicates p< .01;** and ***bold italics indicates p< .001.***

TABLE 3.A2. Regression Models Testing Impact of Attack Ads on Support for State Courts

	Confidence		Very Confident		Support Index		Control	
	b	std. err.	b	std. err.	b	std. err.	b	std. err.
Attack Ads Run	.020	.051	–.154	.201	.021	.072	–.001	.049
Knowledge Level	***.070***	.020	*.213*	.076	***.139***	.028	**.052**	.019
Attention to News	**.043**	.014	.055	.058	.006	.019	.003	.013
Confidence Scale	***.221***	.012	***.642***	.067	***.162***	.017	***–.041***	.012
Experience in Court	***–.197***	.052	–.315	.209	**–.292**	.072	–.063	.050
Party Identification	F=1.51, p=.222		χ^2=4.84, p=.089		F=4.27, p<.05		F=0.16, p=.855	
Republican	–.097	.065	–.536	.254	–.252	.092	–.020	.063
Democrat	.003	.060	–.111	.240	–.039	.085	–.032	.058
Independent	.000		.000		.000		.000	
Gender (1=male)	.015	.050	*.503*	.204	.091	.070	.035	.048
Income Scale	.048	.025	.017	.101	***.160***	.036	***.084***	.024
Education Scale	–.014	.018	–.009	.074	.023	.025	*.035*	.017
Race/Ethnicity	F=2.70, p<.05		χ^2=1.32, p=.724		F=4.94, p<.01		F=4.42, p<.01	
Non-Hispanic Black	*–.201*	.086	–.258	.385	*–.261*	.117	–.128	.081
Hispanic	*–.163*	.080	.256	.331	**–.385**	.109	**–.267**	.076
Other	–.083	.119	–.146	.598	–.095	.169	–.092	.116
Non-Hispanic White	.000		.000		.000		.000	
Intercept	.407	.138	–5.847	.697	–1.374	.197	.777	.131
R^2 or Pseudo-R^2	.340		.194		.235		.122	
n	793		793		672		756	

Italics indicates p< .05; **bold indicates p< .01;** and ***bold italics indicates p< .001.***

Impact of Selection/Retention System

Table 3.A1 shows selected results for the analysis of the impact of selection/retention method: the type of election, if any, used for selection and/or retention of judges. None of the tests of the set of selection/retention variables achieve statistical significance, and only one individual coefficient achieves statistical significance. That significant coefficient is in the model for six-item support index, and it shows that support is significantly greater in the two states using the hybrid system compared to the reference category of no election; while the coefficients comparing the other three types of election states to the reference category do not achieve statistical significance, they are all positive, suggesting that support may be *increased* by the use of elections. However, the fact that this pattern appears only for this one measure suggests caution in drawing any conclusions.

Several other variables show patterns worth noting. Experience in court appears associated with a decrease in support. Knowledge level and confidence in other political institutions are associated with an increase in support; income may be associated with an increase in support but the pattern is not consistent. All of the coefficients for the race/ethnicity variables are negative, meaning that non-Hispanic whites tend to have a higher level of support than the other four groups; however, only a fraction of these coefficients differ significantly from zero, which again suggests caution in interpreting this pattern.

Impact of Negative (Attack) Advertising

Table 3.A2 shows the regression results for the same set of dependent variables but replacing type of selection system with whether attack ads had been aired in the state prior to 2009 (the year of the survey) in connection with supreme court elections. For the models included in the table, the showing of attack ads has no discernible impact on any of the measures of support. The results shown in the table include California and Texas among the states where attack ads had been run, even though it had been ten years or more since any such ads had been used; the analysis was also run including Texas and California with states that had not seen attack ads, but the results changed little if at all. Also, the results in Table 3.A2 are based on regressions that excluded states not using elections. Making the attack ads variable into two dummy variables, attack ads shown and no elections with elections without attack ads serving as the reference category, does not change the results.

APPENDIX B: ELECTORAL IMPACTS ON STATE SUPREME COURT DECISIONS IN TORT CASES

Data, Variables, and Method

My analysis of the relationship between election-related factors and state supreme court justices' decision-making in tort cases relied on the data produced by the State Supreme Court Data Project. As noted previously, this dataset covers state supreme court decisions from 1995–1998 by state courts of last resort; if a court decided more than 200 cases in a given year, a sample of 200 cases was drawn, otherwise all of the cases were included (Brace and Hall 2000:263). For purposes of my analysis I created a version of the dataset that used the justice's vote as the unit of analysis, omitting the votes of judges sitting temporarily on the court. I obtained information on most of the individual level characteristics from a version of the SSCDP dataset that had previously been organized by justice-vote and that was posted on the Dataverse website; I then filled in as much of the missing information as I was able to locate, as well as correcting a number of coding errors I came across.[62] I selected from the dataset cases involving tort issues; because of the way that cases were coded this included a category that combined both workplace torts and appeals related to workers' compensation.[63] Overall, tort issues were involved in 21.7 percent of justices' votes with the states varying widely in this percentage, from a high of 36.6 percent in Alabama, to a low of 9.0 percent in Indiana. Overall, 37,116 of the 171,319 votes of identifiable justices involved tort issues, and 36,098 had information for all variables included in the analysis.[64]

The dependent variable in the analysis is the justice-vote coded 1 as voting in favor of the plaintiff and 0 as voting in favor of the defendant; hence, positive coefficients indicate support for the plaintiff's position and negative coefficients support for the defendant's position. As predictors I included the following variables:

- method of retention (partisan elections, nonpartisan elections, retention elections, no elections) as a set of dummy variables using partisan elections as the reference category, and grouping the hybrid states of Michigan and Ohio with the partisan states (Nelson et al. 2013);
- whether the justice was barred from running for reelection due to mandatory retirement;
- whether the justice was in the final twelve months of his or her current term;

62 I created my own version of the judge-vote dataset because I discovered a number of problems in the version on Dataverse that I was able to correct by creating my own version.

63 Given that the interests involved in workplace torts and workers' compensation are essentially the same, grouping them together for this analysis does make sense. Omitting this category of cases did not appreciably change the results.

64 One issue in the dataset is that two categories of cases that do not appear to be torts got lumped into the two general tort issue indicators (there was one indicator for private cases and one for cases involving government); these were discrimination cases and a category described in the data documentation as "other labor disputes." I omitted these cases from my analysis.

- a measure of the state's liberalism (Wright et al. 1985), scaled as a z-score with a mean of 0 and a standard deviation of 1 using the mean and standard deviation for the original variable at the state-year level;[65]
- a measure of the justice's ideology (Brace et al. 2000);
- whether the appellant was the original plaintiff;
- type of tort issue (automobile accident, premises liability, medical malpractice, products liability, toxic tort, work injury, other) as a set of dummy variables using toxic tort as the reference category for the analysis of all torts and automobile accidents as the reference category when the analysis was restricted to personal injury cases);
- whether one party to the case was a governmental entity;[66]
- whether the state lacked an intermediate appellate court that hears most civil appeals;[67]
- an index of the number of tort reforms in effect in the state in the year of the decision – see Kritzer and Beckstrom (2007:993–94) for a list of the twenty-two reforms included in the index;
- types of legal issues presented in the appeal, including separate, nonexclusive indicators of each of the following types of legal issues: abuse of discretion/ clearly erroneous decision, evidentiary issue, failure to state a claim, summary judgment, standing, mootness/ripeness (includes failure to exhaust the administrative process), governmental immunity, and jury instruction issues.

Preliminary analyses indicated strong interactions based on whether the appeal was brought by the plaintiff or by the defendant; consequently, I used a conditional model (Wright 1976) which produced separate estimates for plaintiff appeals and for defendant appeals. Preliminary analyses also indicated that the influence of state ideology interacted with type of retention system; consequently, state ideology was included as separate terms for partisan/hybrid election states, nonpartisan election states, retention election states, and nonelection states. Table 3B.1 shows summary statistics for the predictor variables separately for appeals brought by plaintiffs and appeals brought by defendants.

65 The analysis was also run using the measure of citizen liberalism developed by Berry et al. (2010; 1998); the results differed little from the analysis using the Wright et al. measure. For both of these measures, I merged in the indicators from the original sources.

66 Unfortunately, there was no way to determine if the governmental party was the plaintiff or defendant; however, I believe it is safe to assume that in the vast majority of tort cases the governmental party would have been the defendant.

67 While North Dakota has a procedure that allows for an ad hoc court of appeals to hear an appeal, the procedure is seldom used. It is unclear whether the Court of Appeals in Utah hears a significant number of civil appeals other than in the family law area or in the form of appeals from administrative agency decisions; I ran the analysis both including Utah as not having an IAC that hears tort cases and as having an IAC that hears tort cases; the results did not differ appreciably.

TABLE 3.B1. Summary Statistics

	Plaintiff Appeals		Defendant Appeals	
Variable	Mean or Percentage	Std. Dev.	Mean or Percentage	Std. Dev.
Plaintiff won (dependent variable)	48.7%		43.2%	
Retention System				
Partisan & hybrid elections	21.6%		29.0%	
Nonpartisan elections	23.0%		21.2%	
Retention elections	34.6%		32.4%	
No elections	20.7%		17.4%	
Barred by mandatory retirement age	5.1%		6.0%	
Last year of current term	8.7%		10.5%	
State Political Liberalism				
Partisan & hybrid election state	–0.53	0.48	–0.60	0.42
Nonpartisan election state	–0.62	0.76	–0.30	0.74
Retention election state	–0.32	0.76	–0.23	0.75
No election state	0.60	0.81	0.61	0.81
Judicial Ideology	39.22	22.72	38.94	22.07
Tort Reform Index	6.05	2.67	6.49	2.59
No IAC for tort cases	24.7%		14.7%	
Government Party	24.4%		21.7%	
Type of Case				
Toxic tort	1.3%		1.6%	
Auto (traffic) accident	12.1%		10.8%	
Products liability	6.0%		7.5%	
Premises liability	11.8%		11.5%	
Medical malpractice	9.1%		8.5%	
Libel	2.9%		3.6%	
Work injury	16.4%		16.2%	
Other tort	63.4%		64.6%	

(*continued*)

TABLE 3.B1. *(continued)*

Variable	Plaintiff Appeals: Mean or Percentage	Plaintiff Appeals: Std. Dev.	Defendant Appeals: Mean or Percentage	Defendant Appeals: Std. Dev.
Legal Issues in Case				
Abuse of discretion	30.4%		29.6%	
Evidentiary issue	29.5%		31.7%	
Failure to state a claim	5.3%		3.4%	
Summary judgment	22.4%		15.9%	
Standing	6.2%		5.2%	
Mootness/ripeness	3.3%		2.6%	
Governmental immunity	4.4%		5.2%	
Jury instruction	6.3%		9.0%	
N	22,808%		13,290%	

The analysis of votes/decisions of members of collegial courts presents methodological issues for which there is no definitive solution. Specifically, the observations are not statistically independent, and the dependence lies on multiple dimensions. The same judge/justice votes on many cases and any given case involves votes by multiple judges/justices. For state supreme courts, there may also be interdependence on the dimension of states as well. In fact, the variables listed previously are all measured at one of three levels: state (type of selection system, presence of an intermediate appellate court, and state liberalism), justice (ideology, age-barred, and last year of current term), and case (government party, type of tort, legal issues in the appeal). For purposes of this analysis I used generalized estimating equations (GEE), an estimating technique that allows one to specify how observations should be grouped (Zorn 2001).[68] Because there is no definitive answer to which method of grouping

[68] In very preliminary analyses, I also used logistic regression with robust standard errors to adjust for clustering. The results of those preliminary analyses did not differ from the GEE estimates I obtained in those preliminary stages, and I chose to rely on GEE as the estimating method for the final analyses. One apparent peculiarity of GEE estimation is that the results vary depending on how a model is specified in contrast to logistic regression where several different

is correct or best, I ran the analysis twice, once grouping by justice and once by case. As the accompanying tables show, the choice of grouping does make a difference in the actual estimates as well as in the standard errors of those estimates. This suggests caution in interpreting the results.[69]

Results

The results of the GEE estimates grouping by judge are shown in Table 3.B2 and by case in Table 3.B3. The first pair of columns of each table shows the results for plaintiff appeals and the second pair shows the results for defendant appeals. Coefficients that are statistically significant at the .05 level or better are shown in bold and those significant at the .10 level are shown in italics; the predictor label is shown in bold or italic to indicate that there is a statistically significant difference between the coefficients for plaintiff and defendant appeals. The overall test for significant differences between the two models is shown in the last line of each table (labeled "Interaction: Wald chi square").

Drawing clear-cut conclusions about the impact of judicial elections from the results shown in the two tables is difficult. The reasons for this difficulty are the large differences between the results for plaintiff and defendant appeals and the differences between results for estimates using grouping-by-case and results for estimates using grouping-by-justice.

For example, depending on which side appealed, the impact of type of retention system on support for the plaintiff runs in opposite directions for some methods of retention, although the effects achieve statistical significance only for defendant appeals. Using partisan and hybrid elections combined as the reference category, for defendant appeals plaintiffs were least successful in partisan/hybrid states and most successful in nonpartisan and retention election states, with no-election states falling between. While for plaintiff appeals none of the coefficients for retention system differed significantly from zero, the least success for plaintiffs came in retention election states when grouping was by case. Regardless of which grouping method was used, the difference in the effect between defendant and plaintiff appeals for retention elections was statistically significant.

specifications, such as a model with multiplicative interaction terms and the equivalent model with conditional effects, produced mathematically identical results. Importantly, the variations I observed with GEE estimation were inconsequential vis-à-vis the conclusions to be drawn from the analysis.

69 I also attempted to run a multi-level model but the software failed to produce a solution.

TABLE 3.B2. Impact of Elections on Tort Decisions (Grouping by Judge)

	Plaintiff Appeals		Defendant Appeals	
	b	se{b}	b	se{b}
Retention System				
Partisan & hybrid elections (reference)	0.0000	–	0.0000	–
Nonpartisan elections	0.1072	0.1179	**0.3863**	**0.1048**
Retention elections	–0.0413	0.1011	**0.3218**	**0.0991**
No elections	–0.0588	0.1107	0.1679	0.1162
Barred by mandatory retirement age	–0.1876	0.1150	0.1006	0.1474
Last year of current term	–0.0195	0.0563	–0.0281	0.0826
State Political Liberalism				
Partisan & hybrid election state	0.1304	0.0905	**0.2619**	**0.1213**
Nonpartisan election state	**0.3413**	**0.0756**	–0.0009	0.0632
Retention election state	*0.0731*	*0.0428*	0.0470	0.0660
No election state	**–0.1855**	**0.0605**	–0.0119	0.0687
Judicial Ideology	0.0004	0.0012	**0.0045**	**0.0014**
Tort Reform Index	0.0055	0.0122	**–0.0436**	**0.0133**
No Intermediate Appellate Court for tort cases	**–0.1971**	**0.0808**	**0.2115**	**0.0888**
Government Party	**–0.1403**	**0.0475**	**0.1368**	**0.0541**
Type of Case				
Toxic tort (reference category)	0.0000	–	0.0000	–
Auto (traffic) accident	**0.2160**	**0.0915**	**0.3307**	**0.1361**
Products liability	–0.0852	0.0976	*0.1967*	*0.1163*
Premises liability	0.0972	0.0945	**0.3660**	**0.1341**
Medical malpractice	*0.1682*	*0.0979*	**0.2219**	**0.1394**
Libel	**0.2301**	**0.1058**	0.1403	0.1473
Work injury	*0.0884*	*0.0466*	**0.3834**	**0.0539**
Other tort	0.0602	0.0960	0.1487	0.1273
Legal Issues in Case				
Abuse of discretion/arbitrary, capricious, or clearly erroneous standard	–0.0165	0.0310	**0.1113**	**0.0463**
Evidentiary issue	**–0.0939**	**0.0333**	**0.2417**	**0.0399**
Failure to state a claim (Rule 12(b)(6)	**–0.2360**	**0.0589**	–0.0853	0.1082
Summary judgment	–0.0069	0.0383	**–0.1895**	**0.0567**
Standing	*–0.1042*	*0.0610*	0.0493	0.0997
Mootness/Ripeness	0.0205	0.0732	**0.5731**	**0.1096**
Governmental immunity	*0.1455*	*0.0775*	**–0.3049**	**0.1042**

	Plaintiff Appeals		Defendant Appeals	
	b	se{b}	b	se{b}
Jury instruction	0.0668	0.0462	–0.0502	0.0621
Constant	0.0333		–0.7356	
n	22,808		13,290	
Wald chi square (26 df)	**181.33**		**282.73**	
Interaction: Wald chi square (25 df)	**274.95**			

Bold indicates statistical significance at the .05 level or better; *italics indicates statistical significance at the .10 level*. Variable names in bold or italic indicate statisitically significant differences between the coefficients for plaintiff and defendant appeals. The dependent variable is coded 1 for a vote in favor of the original plaintiff and 0 for a vote in favor of the original defendant; hence positive coefficients indicate voting that favor's the plaintiff.

What about the impact of state political liberalism conditional on retention method? Using the grouping-by-judge results, state political liberalism has positive effects on the justices' voting in favor of plaintiffs who appealed in states using nonpartisan elections but negative effects in states not using elections for judicial retention; neither of those effects are apparent when it is the defendant who appealed (the coefficients are not only nonsignificant but are zero to two decimal places). In defendant appeals, political liberalism increased the likelihood of justices' favoring the plaintiff in states with partisan and hybrid elections; while the corresponding coefficient was positive for plaintiff appeals, it was nonsignificant. Using the grouping-by-case analysis, the only significant coefficient for political liberalism is the positive effect of political liberalism for plaintiff appeals in nonpartisan states, although the coefficients for partisan and hybrid election states is positive and would be statistically significant at the .10 level; the coefficient for no-election states is negative and would also be statistically significant at the .10 level. None of the political liberalism coefficients for defendant appeals achieve statistical significance when grouping is by case, although the actual value for partisan and hybrid election states is slightly larger than for the grouping-by-judge results. The only clear conclusion that can be drawn from these results is that the state's political liberalism does not appear to have any kind of *consistent* effect on justices' voting when considered in relation to the method of retention.

The two other election-related variables are whether a justice in a state using elections is barred from running for another term due to mandatory retirement and whether a justice in an election state who is not so barred but is in the last twelve months of his or her current term. Last year of term shows

TABLE 3.B3. Impact of Elections on Tort Decisions (Grouping by Case)

	Plaintiff Appeals		Defendant Appeals	
	b	se{b}	b	se{b}
Retention System				
Partisan & hybrid elections (reference)	0.0000	–	0.0000	–
Nonpartisan elections	0.0756	0.1187	**0.3156**	**0.1551**
Retention elections	–0.1615	0.1035	**0.2766**	**0.1413**
No elections	–0.1215	0.1233	0.1990	0.1710
Barred by mandatory retirement age	**–0.1542**	**0.0364**	**–0.1861**	**0.0514**
Last year of current term	–0.0036	0.0258	0.0517	0.0390
State Political Liberalism				
Partisan & hybrid election state	*0.2175*	*0.1308*	0.2753	0.1755
Nonpartisan election state	**0.3008**	**0.0816**	–0.1647	0.1132
Retention election state	0.0370	0.0673	–0.0045	0.0966
No election state	*–0.1346*	*0.0805*	–0.0428	0.1105
Judicial Ideology	**0.0023**	**0.0003**	**0.0035**	**0.0005**
Tort Reform Index	0.0142	0.0117	–0.0238	0.0169
No Intermediate Appellate Court for tort cases	**–0.2044**	**0.0713**	0.1494	0.1145
Government Party	*–0.1488*	*0.0864*	0.1030	0.1169
Type of Case				
Toxic tort (reference category)	0.0000	–	0.0000	–
Auto (traffic) accident	0.2170	0.2153	0.3158	0.3012
Products liability	–0.0344	0.2153	0.1723	0.3019
Premises liability	0.1252	0.2186	0.3352	0.3006
Medical malpractice	0.2437	0.2230	0.2113	0.3190
Libel	0.1785	0.2695	0.0929	0.3573
Work injury	0.0566	0.0931	**0.3805**	**0.1211**
Other tort	0.0887	0.2125	0.1358	0.2991
Legal Issues in Case				
Abuse of discretion/arbitrary, capricious, or clearly erroneous standard	–0.0199	0.0681	0.1232	0.0895
Evidentiary issue	–0.0788	0.0661	**0.2860**	**0.0868**
Failure to state a claim (Rule 12(b)(6)	*–0.2368*	*0.1335*	–0.0826	0.2271
Summary judgment	0.0056	0.0752	–0.1805	0.1190
Standing	–0.0924	0.1227	0.0190	0.1774
Mootness/Ripeness	0.0247	0.1753	**0.5818**	**0.2411**
Governmental immunity	0.1523	0.1489	–0.2612	0.1888
Jury instruction	0.0874	0.1291	–0.0260	0.1371

	Plaintiff Appeals		Defendant Appeals	
	b	se{b}	b	se{b}
Constant	−0.0966		−0.7782	
n	22,808		13,290	
Wald chi square (27 df)	**106.54**		**145.92**	
Interaction: Wald chi square (25 df)	**102.32**			

Bold indicates statistical significance at the .05 level or better; *italics indicates statistical significance at the .10 level*. Variable names in bold or italic indicate statisitically significant differences between the coefficients for plaintiff and defendant appeals. The dependent variable is coded 1 for a vote in favor of the original plaintiff and 0 for a vote in favor of the original defendant; hence positive coefficients indicate voting that favor's the plaintiff.

no effect on the justices' votes regardless of which side appealed or method of grouping. Being barred by mandatory retirement reduces the likelihood of voting in support of the plaintiff regardless of which side appealed when grouping is by case. Grouping by justice, this variable does not achieve statistical significance either for plaintiff or defendant appeals; the sign of the coefficients is negative for plaintiff appeals and the magnitude is about the same as when grouping is by case, but the sign is positive for defendant appeals which is the reverse of the results when grouping is by case. This inconsistency again makes it difficult to draw firm conclusions.

Several of the control variables merit comment. The direction of judicial ideology is as one would expect, with support for plaintiffs increasing as the justice's ideology moves in the liberal direction, although the coefficient does not achieve statistical significance for plaintiff appeals when grouping is by justice. The absence of an intermediate appellate court that routinely handles tort cases runs in opposite directions depending on who appealed (although the coefficient is not statistically different from zero for defendant appeals when grouping by case), essentially indicating that the lack of such a court is associated generally with support for the respondent. A similar pattern applies when a governmental unit is a party to a case, although the coefficients are not statistically different from zero when grouping by case; the magnitude of the coefficients is about the same as when grouping by justice. While I could not discern whether the governmental party was the plaintiff or defendant, it would seem safe to assume that in the vast majority of tort cases involving a governmental unit, the government is the defendant. The level of tort reform that has occurred in a state does not produce a consistent pattern, although when grouping is by justice, the likelihood of voting to support the plaintiff increases in defendant appeals as the number of reforms that had been adopted increased.

Some of the indicators of case-type are statistically significant, although the pattern varies depending on the method of grouping and whether the plaintiff or defendant appealed. While all of the coefficients for case-type are positive with the single exception of products liability in plaintiff appeals, it is important to take note that the reference category is toxic torts, and thus the positive coefficients indicate a lower likelihood of favoring the plaintiff in a toxic tort case compared to other types of cases. It is interesting to note the coefficients for defendant appeals are generally higher than the coefficients for plaintiff appeals, but this probably simply reflects a broad pattern of the outcome of appeals more likely to favor the respondent.

Finally, some legal issue indicators are statistically significant, although the pattern varies depending on the method of grouping and whether the plaintiff or defendant appealed. Note that the legal issue variables do not constitute a set of exclusion categories; a case can raise one or more of the issues. Here is what the estimates suggest expressed in terms of the likelihood of a vote favoring the plaintiff:

- plaintiff appeals: possibly increases when there is an issue of governmental immunity;
- plaintiff appeals: decreases when there is an evidentiary issue or a failure to state a claim issue, and possibly decreases when the appeal involves a standing issue;
- defendant appeals: increases when there is an issue of abuse of discretion, an evidence issue, of a mootness/ripeness issue.
- defendant appeals: decreases when there is a summary judgment issue or a governmental immunity issue.

Note that there is some variation here depending on whether grouping is by case or by judge. The more consistent patterns are found in plaintiff appeals involving failure to state a claim, and defendant appeals involving either evidentiary issues or mootness/ripeness.

Conclusion

My general conclusion from this analysis is that there is at best some weak evidence that method of retention and other variables related to elections or conditioned on elections influence the decisions of state supreme court justices in tort cases. More specifically, the influences that the analysis does show do not run consistently to favor plaintiffs or to favor defendants; some of those influences run one way when the plaintiff appeals and the opposite way when the defendant appeals. Moreover, while the analysis does show both some statistically significant individual effects and that the overall set of coefficients differs from zero, one must keep in mind the large number of observations. Simply stated, the fit of the models is not particularly strong; GEE does not typically provide a measure of overall fit, but if I fit a model using logistic regression the pseudo-R^2 is less than .02.

Thus, while it appears that selection/retention-related issues show some relationship with the direction of state supreme court decisions in tort cases, it is hard to make an argument that there are causal relationships pointing in a consistent direction. Even though tort issues have been strong motivators for key interests in judicial elections/judicial selection, the inconsistent nature of the effects precludes drawing clear conclusions about how the retention-related factors impact state supreme court decisions in tort cases.

APPENDIX C: STATE APPELLATE DECISIONS RELATED TO SAME-SEX MARRIAGE, 1973–2012

State	Year	Case	Decision
AK	1998	*In Brause v. Bureau of Vital Statistics* 1998 WL 88743 (1998)	State must recognize same-sex marriages performed in other states; mooted by constitutional amendment (state had previously passed amendment limiting marriage to opposite-sex couples)
AK	2001	*Brause v. Department of Health & Social Services* 21 P.3d 357 (2001)	Whether statute precluding same-sex marriage was valid was not ripe for adjudication
AZ	2007	*Arizona Together v. Brewer* 149 P.3d 742 (2007)	Rejected attack on state constitutional amendment on grounds that it was not single issue
AZ–app	2003	*Standhardt v. Superior Court* 77 P.3d 451 (2005)	Intermediate appellate court upheld state DOMA; SSC denied petition for review w/o comment (*Standhardt v. MCSC*)
CA	2004	*Lockyer v. City and County of San Francisco* 95 P.3d 459 (2004)	City officials lacked authority to solemnize same-sex marriages, which had no legal effect

(*continued*)

APPENDIX C *(continued)*

State	Year	Case	Decision
CA	2005	*Knight v. Superior Court* 26 Cal.Rptr.3d 687 (2005)	Domestic partners statute did not violate constitutional requirement of voter approval for amendment of marriage initiative; enactment of domestic-partnership statute was not legislative creation of "same-sex marriage" under the guise of another name
CA	2009	*Strauss v. Horton* 207 P.3d 48 (2009)	Upheld validity of state constitutional amendment banning same-sex marriage that was passed by voters in November 2008
CT	2002	*Rosengarten v. Downes* 802 A.2d 170 (2002)	Court did not have jurisdiction over complaint seeking dissolution of foreign same-sex civil union
CT	2008	*Kerrigan v. Commissioner of Public Health* 957 A.2d 407 (2008)	Struck down state ban on same-sex marriage
FL	2004	*Kantaras v. Kantaras* 884 So.2d 155 (2004)	Wife's marriage to postoperative female-to-male transsexual was void *ab initio*
GA	2006	*Perdue v. O'Kelley* 280 Ga. 732 (2006)	Rejected attack on state constitutional amendment on grounds that it was not single issue
HI	1993	*Baehr v. Lewin* 74 Haw. 645 (1993)	Reversed lower court dismissal of complaint from couple seeking marriage license
HI	1997	*Baehr v. Miike* 950 P.2d 1234 (1997) Table	Affirmed lower court ruling against state, but not effective because superseded by state constitutional amendment
HI	1999	*Baehr v. Miike* 994 P.2d 566 (Table)	Reversed lower court judgment; case now moot due to constitutional amendment
IA	2009	*Varnum v. Brien* 763 N.W.2d 862 (2009)	Struck down state ban on same-sex marriage
IN-app	2005	*Morrison v. Sadler* 821 N.E.2d 15 (2005)	Intermediate appellate court upheld state DOMA; not appealed to the Indiana Supreme Court

State	Year	Case	Decision
KY	1973	*Jones v. Hallahan* 501 S.W.2d 588	Female persons were not entitled to have issued to them a license to marry each other
LA	2005	*Forum for Equality PAC v. McKeithen* 893 So.2d 715 (2005)	Rejected attack on state constitutional amendment on grounds that it was not single issue
MA	2003	*Goodridge v. Department of Public Health* 798 N.E.2d 941(2003)	State must allow same-sex civil marriage
MA	2004	*In re Opinions of the Justices to the Senate* 802 N.E.2d 565 (2004)	Banning marriage, but permitting civil unions, for same-sex couples violates equal protection
MA	2006	*Cote-Whitacre v. Department of Public Health* 446 Mass. 350 (2006)	Upheld prohibition on same-sex marriage performed for nonresidents whose home states did not allow same-sex marriage
MA	2012	*Elia-Warnken v. Elia* 463 Mass. 29 (2012)	In-state, same-sex marriage was void *ab initio* when one partner had undissolved civil union from other state
MD	2007	*Conaway v. Deane* 932 A.2d 571 (2007)	Upheld state's limitation of marriage to opposite-sex couples
MD	2012	*Port v. Cowan* 44 A.3d 970 (2012)	Valid, out-of-state same-sex marriage was cognizable in the state for purposes of application of state's divorce law
MI	2007	*National Pride At Work, Inc. v. Governor of Michigan* 732 N.W.2d 139 (2007)	Public employers' recognition of domestic-partnership agreements for employment benefits violated marriage amendment
MN	1971	*Baker v. Nelson* 191 N.W.2d 185 (1971)	Minneosota law "does not authorize marriage between persons of the same sex and that such marriages are accordingly prohibited." Also finds that the statutory prohibition "does not offend the First, Eighth, Ninth, or Fourteenth Amendments to the United States Constitution."

(*continued*)

APPENDIX C *(continued)*

State	Year	Case	Decision
MT	2012	*Donaldson v. State* 292 P.3d 364 (2012)	Appeal challenging every state statute excluding committed same-sex couples from protections granted to opposite-sex, married couples, denied; Court ruled that cases challenging specific statutes could move forward
NJ	2006	*Lewis v. Harris* 908 A.2d 196 (2006)	Found that same-sex couples were entitled to civil unions that granted all benefits of marriage; did not find that this meant state must allow same-sex "marriages" but left that as an option.
NJ	2012	*Garden State Equality v. Dow* 2012 WL 540608	Plaintiffs stated claim against defendants on the basis that Civil Union Act violated the Equal Protection Clause of the Fourteenth Amendment granted reconsideration
NM	2004	*Victoria Dunlap v. Patricia Madrid and Hon. Louis P. McDonald* Sup Ct, NM, July 8, 2004, index No. 28730	Affirmed and extended restraining order preventing the issuance of marriage licenses to same-sex couples but never ruled on the legality of licenses
NY-app	1997	*Storrs v. Holcomb* 666 N.Y.S.2d 835 (1997)	Challenge to same-sex marriage ban failed when necessary party was not joined (transfer by Appellate Division as direct appeal to NYCA previously denied; 88 N.Y.2d 1063 (1996))
NY	2006	*Samuels v. New York State Dept. Of Health* 811 N.Y.S.2d 136 (2006)	There was rational basis for limiting marriage to one man and one woman
NY	2006	*Hernandez v. Robles* 7 N.Y.3d 338 (2006)	Upheld state's limitation of marriage to opposite-sex couples
NY	2010	*Dickerson v. Thompson* 897 N.Y.S.2d (2010)	Trial court had subject matter jurisdiction over action for dissolution of same-sex civil union
NY-app	2008	*Martinez v. County of Monroe* 50 A.D.3d 189 (2008)	Appellate court upheld state official's decision that state would recognize same-sex marriages that were performed in states where they were legal; NYCA dismissed motion for leave to appeal

State	Year	Case	Decision
NY-app	2009	*Lewis v. New York State Dept. of Civil Service* 60 A.D.3d 216 (2009)	Recognition of valid foreign same-sex marriages for purposes of state employee health benefits was permissible
OH	2003	*In re Marriage License for Nash* 2003 WL 23097095	Public policy in Ohio prohibited postoperative female-to-male transsexual from marrying female
OR	2005	*Li v. Oregon* 110 P.3d 91(2005)	Ruled that Oregon law limited marriage to opposite-sex couples and any same-sex licenses that had been issued were invalid
RI	2007	*Chambers v. Ormiston* 935 A.2d 956 (2007)	Family Court was without jurisdiction to entertain divorce petition involving same-sex couple who were married in Massachusetts
TX-app	2006	*Ross v. Goldstein* 203 S.W.3d 508 (2006)	Appellate court would not adopt "marriage-like relationship" as equitable remedy upon death of one same-sex partner
TX-app	2010	*In the Matter of the Marriage of J.B. and H.B.* 326 S.W.3d 654 (Tx. 5th Cir. Ct of Appeal 2010)	Same-sex couple married in Massachusetts now living in Texas filed for divorce in Texas. State appealed after trial judge ruled that same-sex marriage ban violated Fourteenth Amendment; three-judge appellate court unanimously reversed trial court. Decision by Texas Supreme Court pending as of March 1, 2015.
VT	1999	*Baker v. State* 744 A.2d 864 (1999)	State must allow same-sex civil unions
WA	1974	*Singer v. Hara* 247 522 P.2d (1974)	Statutory prohibition against same-sex marriages did not violate constitutional provision that "equality of rights and responsibility under the law shall not be denied or abridged on account of sex"
WA	2006	*Andersen v. King County* 158 Wash.2d 1 (2006)	Upheld state's limitation of marriage to opposite-sex couples

4

Contestation and Competitiveness in State Supreme Court Elections, 1946–2013

In this chapter, I examine one aspect of change in state supreme court elections: contestation and competitiveness.[1] Specifically, has the likelihood increased that elections for seats on the various courts will be contested and, for those that are contested, are the elections more likely to be competitive? Democratic theory would lead one to see competitive elections as a good thing because it would be indicative of active public debate, and this is just as true for judicial elections as for elections to other types of public office (see Bonneau and Hall 2009). Moreover, elections can serve to increase the legitimacy of the courts even if citizens have some qualms about the electoral process in the judicial context (Gibson 2012). Ironically, many observers view increased competition in judicial elections as a negative because it leads candidates to do things deemed to be incompatible with the judicial role such as raising money, stating positions on issues, and attacking opponents (Geyh 2003, 2007). Thus, for proponents of reform, such as retired U.S. Supreme Court justice Sandra Day O'Connor who chairs the O'Connor Judicial Selection Initiative (see Schwartz 2009), increasing levels of competition in elections for judges would be a primary reason to move to alternative systems of judicial selection.[2]

[1] An earlier version of most of this chapter appeared in the *Journal of Empirical Legal Studies* (Kritzer 2011). This chapter differs in three ways from the earlier article. First, it extends the analysis through elections held in 2013 (the earlier article ended with elections in 2009). Second, it defines competitive elections as those in which the winning candidate received less than 55 percent, while the earlier article defined competitive elections as those where the winning candidate received less than 60 percent; this change reflects that the 55 percent threshold has been more commonly used as an indicator of a competitive election. Third, it includes data from two states (Maryland and South Dakota) omitted from the earlier analysis.

[2] It is worth noting that while the debate is expressed in terms of "judicial elections" generally, the concern has been primarily with state supreme court elections. The vast majority of research on judicial elections focuses on state supreme courts; we know much less about elections to lower courts (but see Arbour and McKenzie 2010; Frederick and Streb 2008, 2011; Nelson 2011; Streb and Frederick 2009; Streb et al. 2007; Streb et al. 2009).

The extant evidence regarding increased competition in recent years is limited. Melinda Gann Hall examined the question of whether state supreme court incumbents were challenged in elections (both partisan and nonpartisan) over the period 1980–2000, and found that the percentage challenged grew from about 50 percent at the beginning of the period she examined to 75 percent or more at the end of the period (Hall 2007, 171). However, her analysis did not reveal any clear trends in the competitiveness of elections where challengers entered the race or in patterns of competition in open-seat elections (175–82).[3]

Hall's analysis covered a relatively short twenty-year period. It is possible that the starting point for her research, 1980, represents not the end of a period of stability vis-à-vis challenges to incumbents but either just one point on a longer trend of secular change or even a low point in what could be a cyclical pattern. One needs to examine a longer period in order to put relatively recent changes in the competitiveness of elections into a more meaningful perspective.[4] Moreover, as will be discussed in Chapter 5, the period since 2000, the endpoint of Hall's analysis, has been marked by a sharp increase in expenditures on state supreme court elections. The availability of increased funds may have encouraged more challengers to come forward in state supreme court elections involving incumbents, and the greater amount of advertising those funds have made possible may have increased the competitiveness of elections, both those involving incumbents and those for open seats.

In this chapter I analyze the patterns of contestation and competitiveness in judicial elections for positions on state supreme courts and also the pattern of outcomes in retention elections. The first sections examine partisan, hybrid, and retention elections over a period covering sixty-eight years, 1946 through 2013. The unit of analysis for these elections is the seat up for election. I examine whether the elections for those seats were contested and how close the elections were. Thus, this chapter will answer the closely related questions of whether the likelihood that elections are contested has increased since the mid-1940s and whether elections that are contested are more likely to be competitive. The analysis shows that *while there has been change, that change is largely limited to partisan elections in southern states.*

By definition, retention elections do not involve competition but one can ask whether justices standing for retention face an increased threat of not being

3 In an earlier article, which examined elections between 1980 and 1994, Hall showed that competitiveness in state supreme court elections was actually fairly similar to the competitiveness in elections for the U.S. House of Representatives (Hall 2001, 319).

4 Dubois (1980, 50) provides some data on competitiveness of state supreme court elections for the period 1948–1974. However, his analysis excludes southern states and primary elections. Moreover, it does not control for the presence of an incumbent in the election.

retained, measured either by actually losing the retention election or by being retained by a reduced margin. The last section of this chapter considers retention elections, covering *all* retention-type elections for state supreme court since the first such election in California in 1936.[5] I find that there is evidence that the percentage voting in favor of retention has declined over time, but that change largely reflects a drop from very high positive votes (often exceeding 80 percent) in the early years of retention elections;[6] from the late 1970s through 2013 the average percentage voting in favor of retention fluctuated between 70 percent and 75 percent.[7] Arguably, there has been an increase in the percentage of retention elections in which the positive vote was less than 60 percent, although this peaked at just more than 20 percent of retention elections in the early 1990s and through 2013 did not exceed 10 percent of elections.[8]

As will be clear from the analyses in the following pages, the conclusion to be drawn from those analyses is that there has been much less change in contestation and closeness of state supreme court elections than might be inferred from much of contemporary rhetoric about the need for changes in judicial selection and retention.

DATA

For this analysis I sought to assemble data on every state supreme court election conducted on a partisan or nonpartisan basis between 1946 and 2013, including primary elections, primary runoffs, and general elections;[9] these elections filled a total of 2,058 seats on state supreme courts.[10] The sources for these data varied from state to state. For recent elections, virtually all of the needed information was available online from state election office websites. For earlier elections, some states routinely published detailed election reports which I was able to obtain from one of several libraries. For other states the necessary information was provided to me by state election offices. For still other states, the information had been shipped off to state archives, and to obtain the information I sought, it was necessary to arrange to have someone go to the archive and

5 I include in the analysis one California election which technically did not deal with the retention of a sitting justice but rather constituted a confirmation of the appointment of a person to fill a seat that was being vacated at the end of a justice's term.

6 The statistics regarding retention elections are based on four-year periods.

7 In 2014 the average percentage voting in favor of retention was 68.5 percent.

8 In the 2014 election, in 21 percent of the 33 retention elections, the positive vote was less than 60 percent.

9 As previously noted, Texas and Oklahoma have separate courts of last resort for criminal and noncriminal cases; for those states, I have included elections for both courts.

10 If three seats are up for election, for purposes of this book I count that as three elections.

retrieve the information on my behalf. For a few primary elections, I relied upon newspaper reports of overall election results.[11]

For those elections involving contested primaries but an uncontested general election, I employed information from the primary election computing relevant percentages based only on the candidates that continued to the general election or the top two candidates if the primary determined the winner of the seat. If there were both primary and general elections for a seat,[12] I used as my indicator of closeness the election with the closest vote involving the incumbent (or the victor in the case of an open-seat election).[13] States with multi-seat elections in which candidates did not run for specific seats (i.e., if two seats were contested, the top two vote getters win), what I label "unassigned multi-seat elections," raise some specific issues. First, how should one handle the situation where the number of candidates is less than twice the number of seats (i.e., three candidates running for two seats)? In those elections, if there was one fewer candidate than twice the seats, I treated the top vote getter as unopposed; so, for example, if there were three seats and five candidates, one seat was deemed unopposed and two as opposed (with the top vote getter assigned to the unopposed seat). The second issue is how to determine how close the elections are in unassigned, multi-seat elections? I adopted the convention of pairing first the highest and lowest vote getters, then the second highest and second lowest, on down. For unassigned multi-seat partisan elections, I paired the highest Democrat with the lowest Republican, the highest Republican with the lowest Democrat, and then the middle pair or pairs.[14]

One final issue needs to be noted. Some competition is best described as symbolic rather than real. For example, while through the 1940s, '50s, and into the '60s, elections in most of the South were one-party affairs, there were a small number of southern state supreme court elections during those years in which Republicans did appear on the ballot. To say that such candidates did not stand a chance of winning is an understatement: usually they received less

[11] The newspaper reports were usually unofficial and often provided less than complete results. However, given the way I have categorized election results, it is unlikely that complete returns would shift an election from one category to another.

[12] If there was a primary runoff and that election was closer than the primary, or closer than both the primary and general election where both occurred, I used the primary runoff result in the analysis.

[13] In a handful of elections, the incumbent was defeated in the primary election, and the winner of the primary went on to face opposition in the general election. In those cases, I employed the results of the primary election in my analysis. In partisan election states where the nonincumbent loser in the general election had run in a contested primary election, I ignored the primary result involving the general election loser even if it was closer than the general election.

[14] Undoubtedly there are other ways that this could be handled. However, given that relatively few states have unassigned, multi-seat elections, it is unlikely that adopting a different approach would have a significant impact on the results that I report in this chapter.

than 15 percent of the vote. More recently, some of the southern states have become essentially one-party Republican in state supreme court elections, but in a number of elections not contested by Democrats, Libertarians entered the general election to challenge the Republican candidate; typically the Libertarians get at most 25 percent of the vote. Because of this phenomenon,[15] I have chosen not to focus simply on contested versus uncontested elections, but rather to classify elections into five categories: uncontested, symbolically contested (winner got 75 percent or more of the vote, but faced an opponent listed on the ballot), noncompetitive (winner got 55–75 percent), competitive (50–55 percent for the winner),[16] and incumbent defeats;[17] the latter category applies only when there was an incumbent, either recently appointed or previously elected, running to retain his or her seat. No rounding was done in creating the categories, and no election had a result falling at a precise category; hence "50–55%" means from just more than 50 percent to less than 55 percent, and "55–75%" means from just more than 55 percent to less than 75 percent.

In addition to the partisan and nonpartisan elections, I assembled data on every supreme court election conducted on a retention basis since the first election in 1936 in California. Prior to 1960, the only state in addition to California using this format was Missouri, which held its first retention election in 1942. Kansas had its first retention election in 1960, followed by Alaska in 1962, and Iowa, Illinois, and Nebraska in 1964. Through 2013 there had been 736 retention-type elections for state supreme courts, 699 of those having occurred between 1960 and 2013.[18] Two states with nonpartisan elections use, or did use, a retention-type ballot in elections where an incumbent is unopposed; these twenty-one elections are included both in the analysis of nonpartisan elections (where they are counted as "uncontested") and in the analysis of retention elections discussed in this chapter.

15 In a number of the elections involving what I label "symbolically contested" general elections there was a much closer primary election, and that primary election is used for the statistical analysis.

16 I include in this category elections where the ultimate winner was not the top vote getter in a first round (usually a primary) but did win the runoff.

17 In computing the percentage, I focus on the top two vote getters; for example, if there were three candidates in a primary, getting 45 percent, 40 percent, and 15 percent respectively, I took the top two and recomputed the percentage focused on those top candidates. In this case, that percentage would be 100×(45/85) = 52.9 percent. My rationale for this approach is that it is the closeness between the top two candidates that matters to the winner. This also applied to general elections with more than two candidates, some of whom were third-party candidates; in no election with both candidates from the major parties and candidates from one or more third parties did a third-party candidate obtain a higher percentage of the vote than did either of the two major-party candidates.

18 I refer to "retention-type" elections because, as discussed in Chapter 2, California technically uses the yes-no type ballot for candidates nominated by the governor to assume a seat on the California Supreme Court for justices who choose to serve out their terms and not run for retention.

ANALYSIS OF PARTISAN AND NONPARTISAN ELECTIONS

The analysis that follows is presented mostly in the form of stacked bar graphs, all of which divide the vertical bar proportionately among the four to six categories being considered. One can think of each of these stacked bar graphs as representing a series of pie charts. The advantage of these graphs is that they allow one to quickly see how the distribution among the categories has shifted over time. The disadvantage is that it takes a bit of effort to estimate a specific percentage other than for the category shown at the bottom of the graph. In all of the stacked bar graphs for partisan and nonpartisan elections, the top-most section of each bar represents the proportion of elections that were uncontested.[19] The section just below the top section represents the proportion of elections that were symbolically contested (the winner received at least 75 percent of the vote). The middle section represents the proportion of noncompetitive elections in which the winner received at least 55 percent but less than 75 percent. For elections involving incumbents, the section of each bar at the bottom of the graph represents the proportion of elections in which the incumbent lost and the section just above represents the proportion of elections that the incumbent won with less than 55 percent of the vote. For open-seat elections, the bottom section represents the proportion of elections won with less than 55 percent of the vote.[20]

Most state supreme court elections take place in even-numbered years. In a small number of states, some or all such elections are held in odd-numbered years. For purposes of analysis and presentation, I have grouped elections occurring in odd-numbered years with the prior year. For open-seat elections, I have grouped the elections into four-year sets, labeled with the year of the presidential election; hence, the data point for open-seat elections labeled 1948 captures the judicial elections that occurred from 1946 through 1949.

Elections Involving Incumbents

All Elections with Incumbents

Figure 4.1 shows the overall pattern of contestation and competitiveness in 1,611 state supreme court elections involving incumbents between 1946 and 2013.[21] To avoid clutter, Figure 4.1 and subsequent figures do not show the numbers of elections upon which the percentages reflected in the figures are based; I include this

19 I ignore the presence of write-in candidates.

20 As noted previously, in computing all of these percentages, I look only at the top two vote getters.

21 Omitted from this analysis are the two elections from Tennessee in which incumbents were not renominated by party conventions; the candidates that were nominated ran unopposed in the general election.

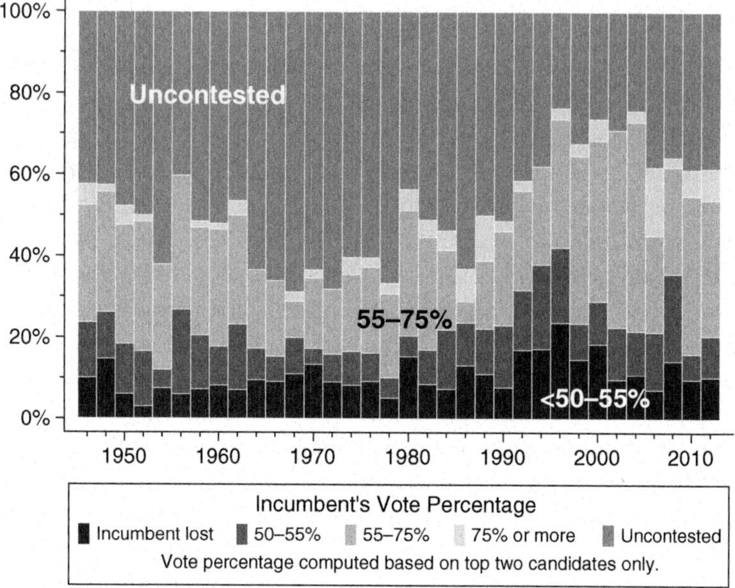

FIGURE 4.1. Contestation and Competitiveness, All Elections Involving Incumbents, 1946–2013.

information as a chapter appendix in Table 4.A1. For some of the figures the number of elections reflected in a data point is quite small, and those figures need to be treated with caution. One can read Figure 4.1 by looking at a particular year and estimating the percentage for that year. For example, for 1990–91 there were thirty-nine elections with incumbents running, and the figure shows that in

- 8 percent of the elections (three elections) incumbents lost
- 15 percent of the election (six elections) incumbents won with less than 55 percent of the vote
- 23 percent of the elections (nine elections) incumbents won with at least 55 percent but less than 75 percent of the
- 3 percent of the elections (one election) incumbents won with 75 percent or more of the vote
- 51 percent of the elections (twenty elections) incumbents were unopposed

As the figure shows, there is a lot of year-to-year variation; my interest is in patterns of change over the entire period.

A first point to note is that while Figure 4.1 shows some shifts, they are generally relatively subtle as opposed to striking. There is no clear pattern in the likelihood of incumbents being defeated (the bottom-most section of each bar), although arguably there is a slight increase starting around 1990. If one combines elections where incumbents lost in which the incumbent got less than 55 percent (i.e., combine the bottom two sections), there does appear to be some pattern of increase starting around 1980. And while the graph shows a decrease in the proportion of incumbents who were unchallenged (the top-most section of each bar), one also sees that there was a period when the likelihood of being unchallenged actually increased; thus, while percentage unchallenged in the current period is lower than earlier periods, how much lower depends on what one chooses to use as a baseline.

One obvious question is whether the pattern of change is random or reflects systematic differences. To address this question, I compared the twelve years 1946–1957 (the "early period," n = 384) with the twelve years 2002–2013 (the "late period," n = 222), and I collapsed the first two categories (elections in which the incumbent lost and elections in which the incumbent received less than 55 percent of the vote) and the last two categories (in which the incumbent was unopposed or won with 75 percent or more of the vote. A simple goodness-of-fit (GOF) chi square test for all elections involving incumbents shows that the difference between the early and late periods is not statistically significant ($\chi^2 = 4.88$, df = 2, p = .088). What about the dip in the middle of the period? To assess whether this introduces a statistically significant difference, I created a twelve-year "middle" period covering 1966 through 1977 (n = 297); the GOF chi square test using three periods is statistically significant ($\chi^2 = 39.19$, df = 4, $p < .001$), confirming that the dip in competition during the period 1966–1977 reflects a statistically significant difference from the early and late periods.[22]

22 There is one technical issue raised by the use of the simple goodness-of-fit chi square test. That test assumes that all observations are statistically independent, something that is clearly untrue given that there are multiple elections from a given state, often in the same year. The impact of this kind of nonindependence tends to inflate the statistical significance of the tests because the practical effect of such dependence is that one has less information than the test assumes. Hence, when the chi square fails to achieve statistical significance, one can be confident that an adjustment for the clustering of observations within states would not change the conclusion from nonsignificant to statistically significant. However, when the simple goodness-of-fit chi square does achieve statistical significance, it is possible that an adjusted test would not be statistically significant. One can adjust for this nonindependence problem. To obtain a test adjusting for clustering, I used the statistical software package Stata to fit simple bivariate or multinomial logistic regression models with one or two dummy variables as appropriate for the time period. For these models I obtained robust standard errors clustered on state, and then instructed the software to conduct a joint general linear hypothesis test of the estimates for the dummy variables. This test employs the robust standard errors and produces a statistic called a Wald chi square. This test does not work with some of the figures because the number of observations in some cases is too small, and the estimation procedure breaks down. For almost all tests run for this analysis the results obtained adjusting for clustering by state were consistent with those using simple tabular analysis, and consequently I do not report the results of the individual tests that I performed unless there is an inconsistency; when results are reported they will appear in a footnote.

While the middle period does show a reduced level of competition, exactly what accounts for that reduction is unclear. One problem with interpreting this overall pattern is that, as discussed in Chapter 2, over the period shown in Figure 4.1 there have been major changes in the distribution of types of elections. While in the 1940s the majority of elections were (at least nominally) partisan, by the 2000s a majority were nonpartisan, and while the number of nonpartisan and hybrid-system elections have remained roughly constant, the number of partisan elections has sharply declined. Because of this shifting distribution of election types it is necessary to look separately at partisan and nonpartisan elections to begin to understand the nature of changes in contestation and in competitiveness that may have occurred.

Elections with Incumbents Controlling for Election Type

Figure 4.2 replicates Figure 4.1 but for nonpartisan elections only, not including the hybrid elections that group more appropriately with partisan elections given the active and explicit role of parties in the process of getting candidates on the ballot and supporting those candidates (see Nelson et al. 2013). Figure 4.2 shows some decline in the percentage of nonpartisan elections involving an unchallenged incumbent (the top section of each bar shown in the graph). However, the decline in unchallenged incumbents is not accompanied by an increase in competitive elections (or defeated incumbents); the increase comes in the noncompetitive elections. The difference between the early and late periods comes close to achieving statistical significance (GOF $\chi^2 = 5.84$, $p = .054$), although the pattern is not particularly strong. Including the middle period produces a test that is significant (GOF $\chi^2 = 10.35$, $p = .035$), but this primarily reflects the fact that two-thirds of the elections were uncontested or symbolically contested in the middle period compared to 59 percent and 50 percent in the early and late periods respectively.

Figure 4.3 provides the same information for partisan and hybrid elections. Here one sees initially an increase in unchallenged incumbents (the top section of each bar in the figure) into the 1970s followed by a sharp decline with a concomitant increase in competitive elections and defeated incumbents (the bottom two sections), although competitiveness seems to have declined in the most recent years. Simple GOF chi square tests, either comparing just early and late periods, or including the middle period, 1966–1977,[23] achieve

[23] If one were designating a middle period based purely on Figure 4.3, one would probably extend it back to start in 1964, and possibly extend it forward to 1979; doing so does not change the results of the statistical test.

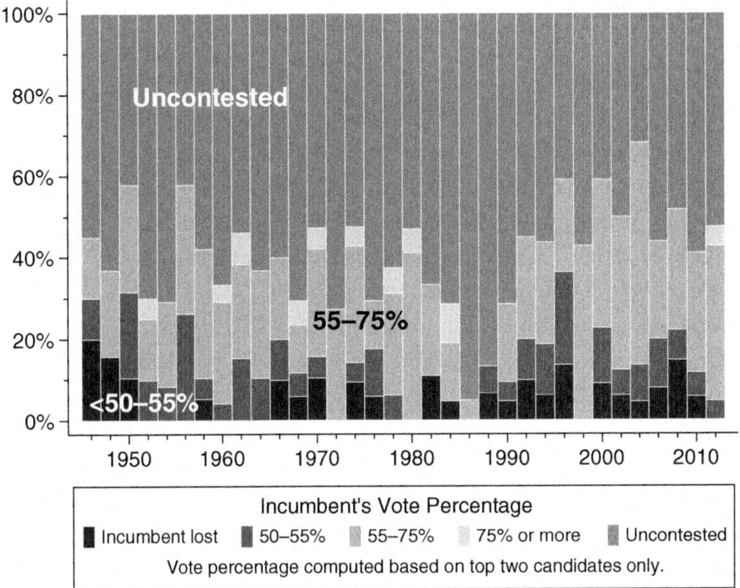

FIGURE 4.2. Contestation and Competitiveness, Nonpartisan Elections Involving Incumbents.

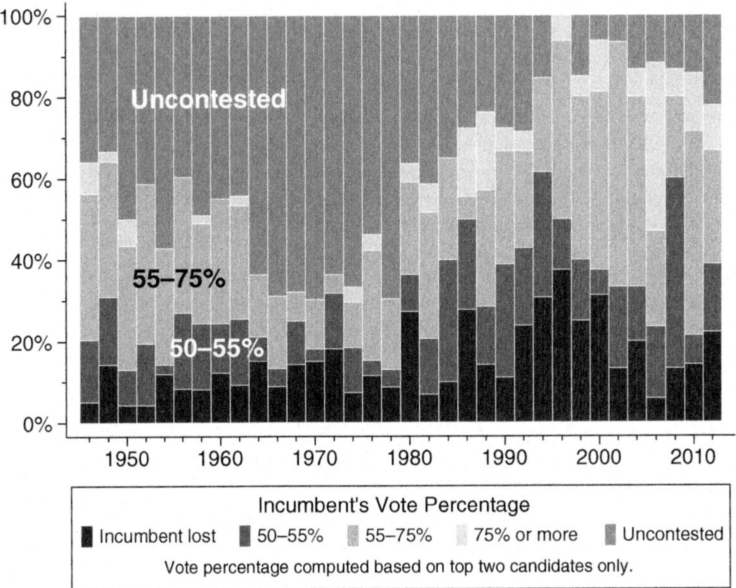

FIGURE 4.3. Contestation and Competitiveness, Partisan and Hybrid Elections Involving Incumbents.

statistical significance ($\chi^2 = 11.41$, $p = .003$, comparing early and late; $\chi^2 = 47.35$, $p < .001$, comparing three periods). Initially, this pattern may seem surprising given that one might expect parties to make an effort to find and support candidates. However, one must keep in mind that a substantial number of the partisan elections are from states in the formerly one-party South and there have been huge political changes in that region over the period under consideration. The change in the South suggests looking separately at southern and nonsouthern states that use partisan (and hybrid) elections.

Figure 4.4 shows the pattern separately by region with the South defined as Alabama, Arkansas, Florida, Georgia, Louisiana, Mississippi, North Carolina, Tennessee, and Texas.[24] For the South (Figure 4.4a) there are very substantial changes, both in the decline of unchallenged incumbents (the top section) and in the increase in competitive elections and incumbent losses (the bottom two sections). The rise in uncontested elections starting in the mid-1960s largely reflects the disappearance of contested Democratic primaries. In the most recent years, there is an increase in symbolic challengers. Both the two- and three-period tests are statistically significant.[25] In contrast, in the nonSouth, there was a decrease in unchallenged incumbent elections (the top-most section) but it occurred prior to 1980; the pattern of competitive elections and incumbent losses shows no pattern of change during the period under consideration. The two-period test is not statistically significant ($\chi^2 = 1.08$, $p = .584$); however, the three-period test does achieve statistical significance ($\chi^2 = 16.84$, $p = .002$).

24 The other two states traditional considered part of the South, Virginia and South Carolina, do not use popular elections for either judicial selection or judicial retention. For purposes of these figures, I have grouped the border states of Kentucky and Oklahoma with the nonSouth states; grouping Kentucky (which switched to nonpartisan elections in 1976) and Oklahoma (which switched to the "merit" system starting in 1968) with the southern states makes little or no difference.

25 Two questions that might be raised about the pattern in Figure 4.4a are (1) whether it is driven by changes in which states in the South employed partisan elections, and (2) whether it was driven by one or two states. As for the first question, all of the states were present for the first two periods, and hence the drop during the middle period does not reflect a change in the states represented in Figure 4.4a. Arkansas, Florida, Georgia, Mississippi, and Tennessee abandoned partisan elections before the start of the late period; however, restricting the analysis to the remaining states (Alabama, Louisiana, North Carolina, and Texas) produces the same pattern, and the pattern shows statistically significant shifts over time (GOF χ^2=39.25, p<.001). As for the second question, in the late period, Texas provides 38 of the 60 elections, so an obvious question is whether Texas is driving the results. Separate tabulations for Texas and for the other states as a group (Alabama, Louisiana, and North Carolina) show that the pattern holds for both Texas and the other states, and that the pattern of change is statistically significant both for Texas (GOF χ^2=21.25, p<.001) and for the other three states (GOF χ^2=21.06, p=.001 for the other three states). Note that the sample sizes here were too small to apply the multinomial logit analysis.

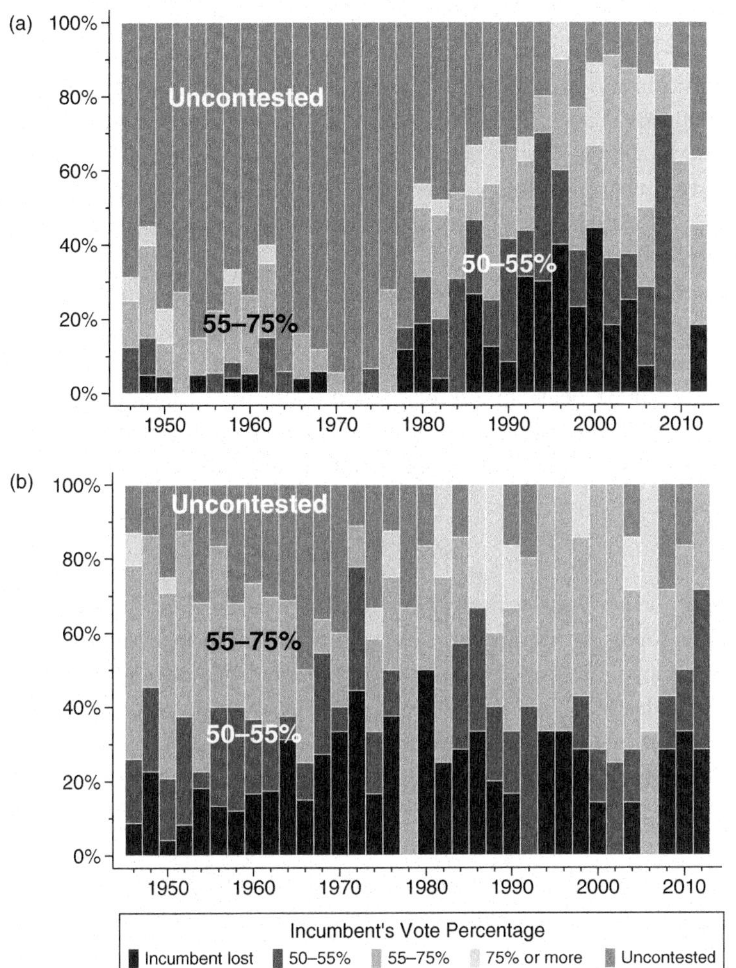

FIGURE 4.4. Contestation and Competitiveness, Partisan Elections Involving Incumbents by Region; (a) South, (b) Nonsouth.

How might one account for the pattern in the South? The initial decline in competition may have been in response to the perceived threat to the "southern way of life" created by legal challenges to segregation that started in the 1950s and peaked in the 1960s. Then, with the increase in competition coming as the South transitioned to a two-party system (see Black 2004:1002–07), elections to the state supreme courts started to become competitive. The marginal decline in the most recent years is probably due to the overwhelming dominance of the Republican Party in many southern states (Cohn 2014). This is of course speculative, but it is consistent with the timing of both the drop in competition around the 1964 election between Lyndon Johnson and Barry Goldwater (which came soon after the passage of the landmark 1964 Civil Rights Act) in which southern states felt particularly challenged vis-à-vis maintaining segregation, and the growth in competition starting around 1980 as the Republican Party began to gain substantial strength in state-level contests in the southern states with the election of Ronald Reagan.

To summarize the pattern of change for elections involving incumbents, the major change is concentrated in southern states with partisan elections. In nonpartisan elections and in partisan (and hybrid) elections outside the South there have been at most relatively modest shifts, largely a decline in the number of uncontested elections. However, that decline has not translated into substantial increases in competitive elections.

Open-Seat Elections

There are fewer open-seat elections for state supreme courts than there are elections involving incumbents. In part this is the normal pattern of incumbents seeking reelection, but it also reflects the fact discussed in Chapter 2 that in most states that ostensibly elect the members of the state supreme court, midterm vacancies are filled through an appointment process with appointees subsequently running as incumbents. Cutting the other way are three states (Illinois, New Mexico, and Pennsylvania) that rely on retention elections to retain incumbents but which require a partisan election when a vacancy occurs. While during the 1946–2013 period there were 1,611 elections involving incumbents, during that same time there were only 445 open-seat elections; one of those 445 elections was conducted entirely on a write-in basis and is omitted from the analysis that follows. As noted previously, I have grouped open-seat elections into four-year intervals; thus the years shown in the figures for those elections include the two years prior plus the one year after (e.g., 1948 covers elections from 1946 through 1949).

Figure 4.5 shows the pattern for all open-seat elections. There appears to be an increase in the likelihood of the winner receiving less than 55 percent of the vote (the bottom-most section shown in the figure) during the 1980s and 1990s, but the most recent years look more like the pattern in the early 1950s. Comparing the early and late periods does not reveal any statistically significant change, nor are there any significant differences if I include the middle period. As before, we need to look separately at nonpartisan and partisan plus hybrid elections.

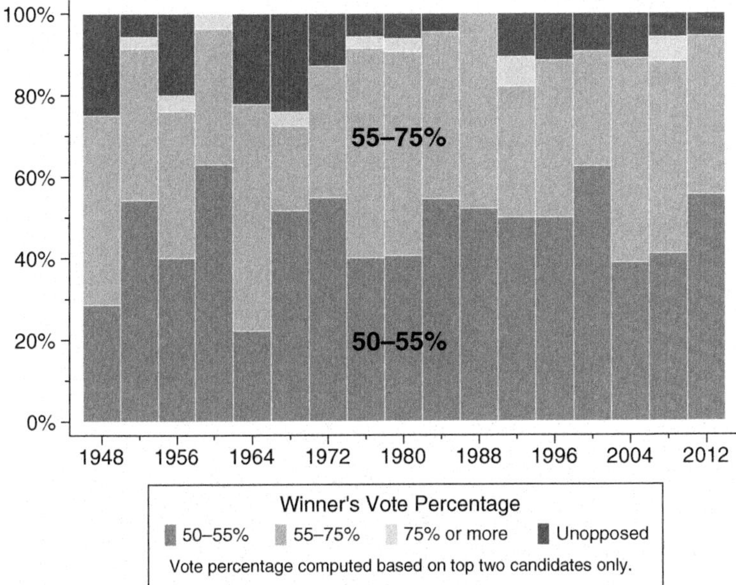

FIGURE 4.5. Contestation and Competitiveness, All Open-Seat Elections, 1946–2013.

Figure 4.6 shows separate patterns for the two broad types of elections. While the patterns appear to differ, we need to treat those differences with caution because GOF chi square tests for examining change over time for each of these two subsets all fail to achieve statistical significance. For nonpartisan elections, while the percentage of elections that are competitive is greater than it was during the earliest years shown, the period of highest competitiveness appears to be in the middle of the period (about 1970 to the mid- or perhaps early 1980s). In contrast, in partisan and hybrid states, the later t years show the highest levels of competition and there is a period of lesser competition in the middle years (about 1960 to around 1980). Exactly why the patterns for the two broad types of elections may differ is not obvious, although some of what is going on here could again reflect differences due to partisan elections in the South.

Figure 4.7 shows partisan and hybrid open-seat elections separately for southern and nonsouthern states. In both regions one sees an increase in competitiveness over time, although given the small number of observations, none of the two-period or three-period comparisons achieve statistical significance, although the two-period test for the South comes close. For the nonsouthern states, this increase occurred in the 1980s. In the South, similar to what occurred in elections with incumbents, there was a decline in

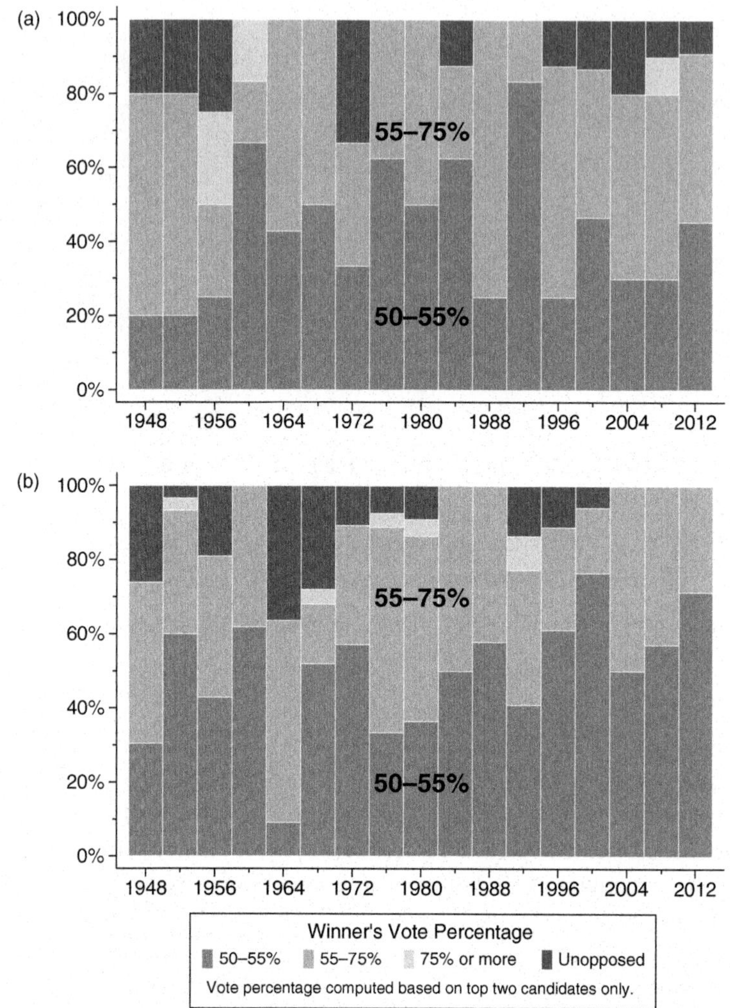

FIGURE 4.6. Contestation and Competitiveness, Open-Seat Elections Controlling for Election Type; (a) Nonpartisan Elections, (b) Partisan and Hybrid Elections.

competitive elections in the 1960s and 1970s compared to the level in the years examined before 1960, with an increase starting in the late 1970s or early '80s. For the nonSouth, there appears to be an increase in the likelihood that an election will be competitive; again, however, neither the two-period nor the three-period test reaches statistical significance. One noteworthy difference between the South and the nonSouth is that no open-seat partisan elections have gone uncontested outside the South.

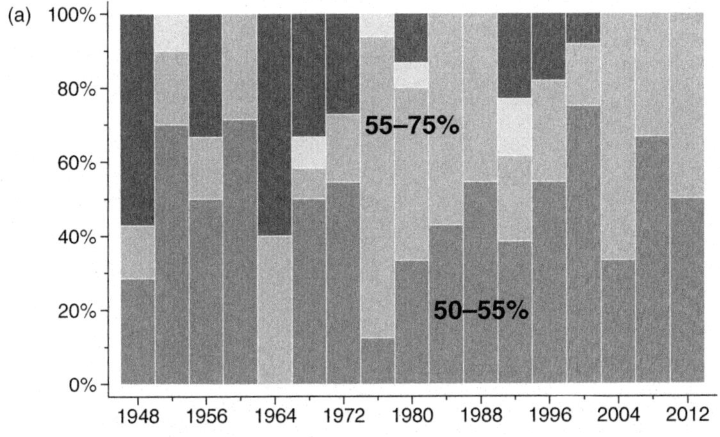

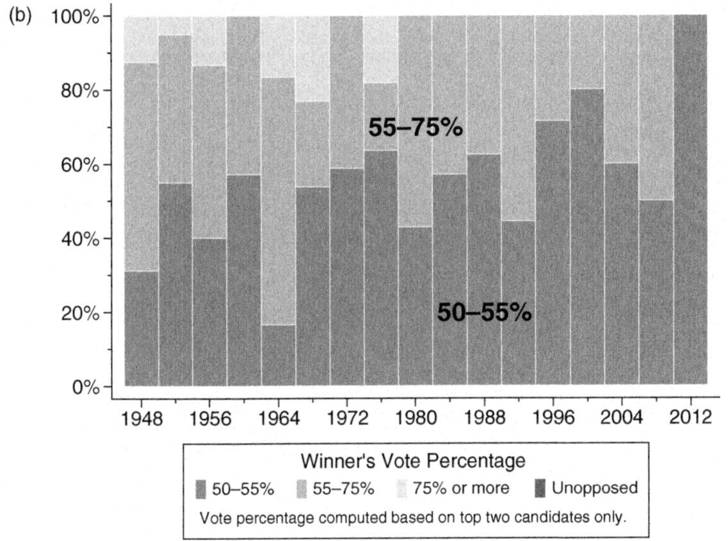

FIGURE 4.7. Contestation and Competitiveness, Partisan and Hybrid Open-Seat Elections Controlling for Region; (a) South, (b) Nonsouth.

Change in the South: Further Analysis

As I noted previously, I believe that the best explanation for what has transpired in the South, and hence the bulk of the change that has occurred in the competitiveness of state supreme court elections, reflects the shift of the southern states from essentially noncompetitive one-party political systems to two-party systems. There is no clear way to "prove" that this is the explanation, but the timing of the shift of the South's patterns seems more consistent

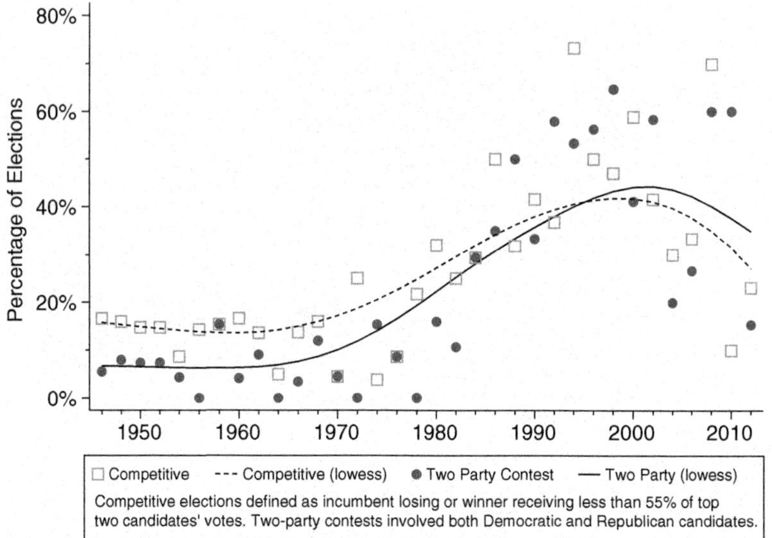

FIGURE 4.8. Competitiveness and Contested Partisan General Elections in Southern States.

with this explanation than the alternatives, and it explains why the bulk of the change has occurred in southern states. Figure 4.8 provides a bit more evidence in support of this explanation. The figure shows two trend lines for partisan elections in the southern states. The hollow squares connected by the broken line show the percentage of elections in which the incumbent lost or the winner obtained less than 55 percent. The solid circles connected by the solid line show the percentage of elections with candidates from the two major parties. The similarity of the two lines is quite strong, and the two series correlate .74. I interpret this strong relationship as indicative that competitiveness in this set of elections was strongly related to two-party competition.

Undoubtedly there was some increase in expenditures and campaign activity with the emergence of the Republican Party in the South. However, it is likely that those increases were in response to the increased competition rather than being a cause of increased competition. One aspect of the recent debate regarding state supreme court elections has been over whether the sharp increases in expenditures and advertising seen during the last decade have changed the nature of competition in state supreme court elections. What I am suggesting is that the changes in the South started around 1980 and were internal to the party system rather than reflecting the role of external players such as interest groups that provide campaign funds and run advertisements. As the Republican Party became more successful in the South, various external actors increased their activities. Importantly, while such actors also increased their involvement in both partisan and nonpartisan elections outside the South, one does not see any evidence of significant increases in the amount of competition coinciding with increases in advertising or involvement of external actors.

Summary, Partisan and Nonpartisan Elections

The foregoing analysis shows that it is accurate to say that overall state supreme court elections have become more competitive, both in terms of more challenges to incumbents and in terms of a higher proportion of elections falling in what I have defined as the competitive range (including incumbents being defeated). However, that broad pattern hides important variations, and the analysis shows that there are differences if one looks separately at nonpartisan states, partisan and hybrid states outside the South, and partisan states in the South.

The one strong pattern revealed by this analysis is that much, perhaps most, of the change that has occurred has been concentrated in southern states that hold partisan elections for their state supreme courts. Whatever change there has been in contestation and competitiveness in nonpartisan states and in nonsouthern partisan states is fairly modest. For open-seat elections there may be a slight pattern of increased competition in partisan and hybrid elections in both the South and the nonSouth, although the specific pattern differs slightly; for nonpartisan states, there has actually been, if anything, a decline in the competitiveness of open-seat elections during the last twenty years or so covered by the analysis.

RETENTION ELECTIONS

Between 1936 when the first retention election was held in California and 2013, only eleven incumbents have failed to be retained out of 736 who sought retention.[26] Six of those eleven nonretentions occurred in just two elections, 1986 in California (Wold and Culver 1987) and 2010 in Iowa (Schotland 2011), when three incumbents in each state lost their bids to be retained. The other five nonretentions are scattered across five states, with the first occurring in Alaska in 1964.[27] For purposes of analysis, I have combined the retention elections into four-year periods; because until 1960 only two states, California and Missouri,

[26] None of the 33 supreme court justices standing for retention in 2014 were defeated. Justice Lloyd Karmeier had the closest call, receiving a positive vote of 60.8 percent in Illinois, which requires a 60 percent positive vote for retention.

[27] The other four nonretentions occurred in Wyoming (1992), Nebraska (1996), Tennessee (1996), and Pennsylvania (2005).

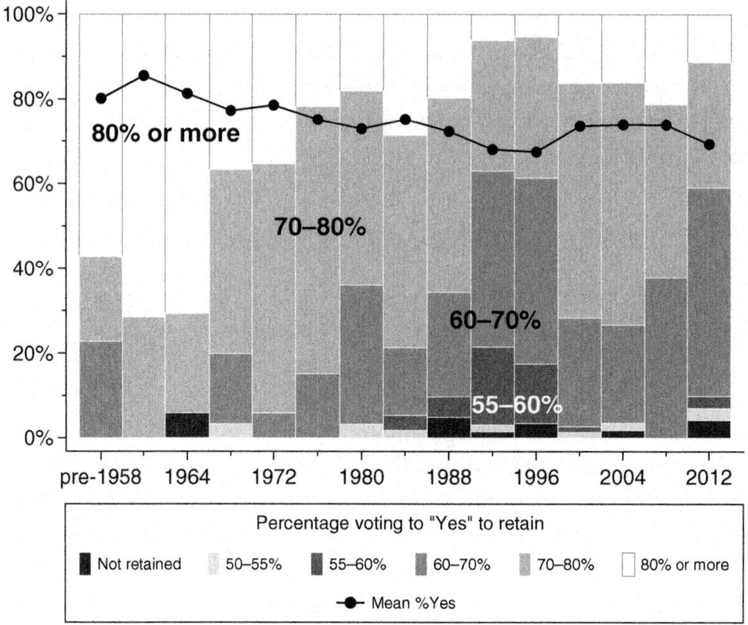

FIGURE 4.9. Voting "Yes" to Retain.

employed such elections,[28] I collapsed all elections through 1956 into a single data point for Figure 4.9. The results shown in the figure are grouped into six categories: the incumbent was not retained, the incumbent was retained with a yes-vote of less than 55 percent, the incumbent was retained with a yes-vote of 55–60 percent,[29] the incumbent was retained with a yes-vote of 60–70 percent, the incumbent was retained with a yes-vote of 70–80 percent, and the incumbent was retained with a yes-vote of 80 percent or more of the vote.[30]

Figure 4.9 makes it clear that the likelihood of an incumbent being retained with 70 percent or more of the vote has declined over the last fifty years, and that the likelihood of being overwhelmingly retained with 80 percent or more

[28] In the years prior to 1960, there were a total of 37 supreme court retention elections in these two states (22 in California and 15 in Missouri).

[29] I used a different division for the retention results for two reasons. First, two states require more than a 50 percent positive vote: 57 percent in New Mexico and 60 percent in Illinois. Second, an examination of the overall distribution showed that very few elections fell below 60 percent (and even fewer below 55 percent) and there were a substantial number in the earlier years with yes-votes exceeding 80 percent.

[30] As with the analysis of partisan and nonpartisan elections, no rounding was done prior to creating the categories, and hence there is no actual overlap in contiguous categories despite their sharing a boundary.

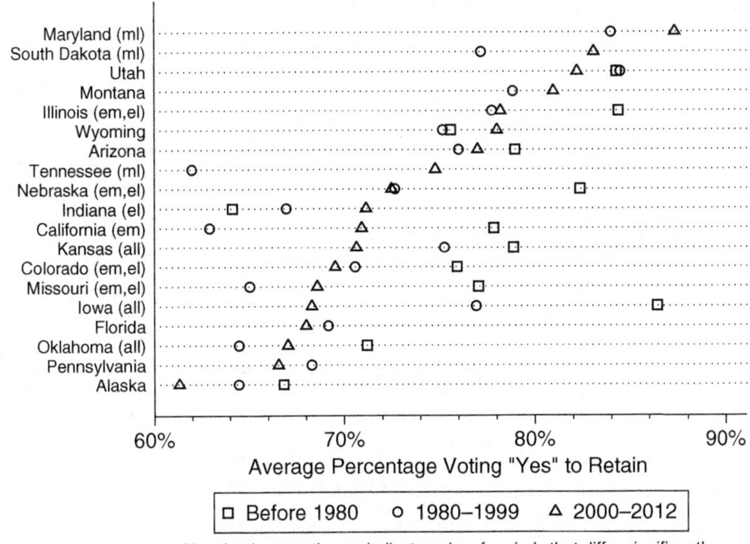

FIGURE 4.10. Percentage Voting "Yes" to Retain for Three Time Periods.

has all but disappeared. The line in Figure 4.9 represents the average percentage voting yes for each four-year time period; that line shows that there was a steady decline over the period 1960–1996, but since 1996, the average has been relatively stable. It is difficult to see any definitive pattern of change in the percentage of elections resulting in nonretention or even very close votes on retention. The change that has occurred is largely a shift from winning with a yes-vote of 70 percent or more to winning with a yes-vote of 60–70 percent.

For further analysis I split the data into three periods: prior to 1980, 1980–1999, and 2000–2013. A one-way analysis of variance shows that there are statistically significant differences between the earliest period and the later two periods, but the change from the middle period to the later period is not significant.[31] However, these overall results mask important differences among the states.

Figure 4.10 is a dot plot showing the average for each period for each state having four or more retention elections in at least two periods.[32] The states are

[31] F ratio = 35.32, $p<.001$ (df=2, 733); both pairwise t-tests and Scheffé comparisons show no difference between the middle and late periods. One technical issue in this analysis is that the data clearly violate the assumption of independent observations; however, even if one treated the statistical results as involving many fewer observations, the results will still achieve statistical significance.

[32] New Mexico is omitted entirely from Figure 4.10 because it started using retention elections in the 1990s, but only three such elections had occurred prior to 2000.

ordered using the mean for the latest period. The squares represent the mean for the early period, the circles for the middle period, and the triangles for the latest period. The notation in parentheses indicate for which pairs of periods the average vote to retain differed using the criteria of statistical significance.[33] The figure shows a great deal of variation among the states in the pattern of change, or lack thereof. The yes-vote percentage did decrease substantially in five states (Colorado, Illinois, Iowa, Kansas, and Nebraska) but it actually increased in four states (Indiana, Maryland, South Dakota, and Tennessee).[34] Three states showing increases did not start using retention elections until some time in the middle period;[35] only Indiana showed increases over all three pairs of periods. Three states (California, Missouri, and Oklahoma) show a mixed pattern decreasing from the earliest period to the middle period, and then increasing from the middle period to the late period.[36] The variation among the three periods in five of the states (Alaska, Arizona, Montana, Pennsylvania, and Wyoming) is not sufficient to be statistically significant, and the nature of that limited variation differs with increases in the yes-vote in two states, decreases in two, and a decrease followed by an increase in one. While some of these variations may be readily explainable, such as the pattern in California which reflects a series of elections in the 1980s (which are discussed in detail in Chapter 7), the dynamics behind most are not at all clear.

33 The statistical significance was determined using pairwise t-tests; the highest p-value was .028, although most of the significant p-values were <.001. One test, Indiana comparing middle and late, produced a p-value of .059. It is important to keep in mind that the statistical test results are driven by a combination of the size of the change and the number of observations. The amount of change in Alaska looks quite similar to that in Oklahoma, but all of the comparisons in Oklahoma are statistically significant while none of those in Alaska are; the difference reflects that the numbers of elections in each period in Oklahoma were 26, 49, and 36, compared to 9, 9, and 7 in Alaska.

34 I should note that in the 2014 retention elections in Tennessee, the three incumbents were targeted for removal by conservatives, including the leadership of the state Republican Party (Blinder 2014a), and while all three were retained in the August retention election, the margins of retention were well under 60 percent (Blinder 2014b). Hence, if 2014 were to be included in the analysis of Tennessee retention elections, the statistically significant increase in Tennessee would disappear.

35 Maryland actually did start using retention elections in 1978, and the two elections that occurred that year were the only retention elections in Maryland prior to the start of the middle period; hence those two elections were excluded from the results depicted in Figure 4.10. The mean percentage voting yes for those two elections was 83.8, compared to 84.0 for the middle period.

36 One might ask whether this pattern for California and Missouri reflects their adoption of retention elections in the 1930s and 1940s, and hence cover a much longer period. The pattern holds with little change if one restricts the analysis to elections after 1958; the means for the early period drop only slightly, from 77.8 percent yes to 74.6 percent in California and from 77.1 percent yes to 75.5 percent in Missouri.

CONCLUSION

The surprising conclusion that flows from the analysis in this chapter is that, controlling for type of election that is used, there has been relatively little net change since the 1940s in terms of whether incumbents in state supreme court elections face competition or defeat, or whether open elections involve highly competitive races. There are certainly changes that flow from the electoral structure, and as discussed in Chapter 2 there has been a great deal of change moving away from partisan elections and toward nonpartisan or retention election systems.

The one very clear exception to this summary is partisan elections in the southern states. Changes in those elections almost certainly reflect broader political changes in the South. As the South emerged from the period of resistance to desegregation and began to move first from one-party Democratic systems to two-party competitive systems, and then in many southern states to overwhelming dominance by the Republican Party, one sees first a drop in contestation and competition, then an increase, and possibly most recently a decrease. Thus, the overall analysis presented here does not support the proposition that patterns in *aggregate* election results have changed markedly due to any changes over the last 15–20 years in the way state supreme court campaigns are conducted. Leaving aside the broad changes that have occurred in the southern states, the picture that emerges from this analysis is, perhaps surprisingly, one of relative stability.

The other clear change has been the *overall* decline in the percentage voting "yes" in retention elections. However, that overall change primarily represents a shift from the early years of retention elections rather than a recent shift. Moreover, as the state-level analysis shows, there is a lot of variation in what has happened in this regard.

APPENDIX

TABLE 4.A1. Numbers of Elections Represented in Figures

	Incumbent Running					Open Seat					Retention
	All	Non-partisan	Partisan or Hybrid	Partisan or Mixed		All	Non-partisan	Partisan or Hybrid	South	Nonsouth	All
				South	Nonsouth						
	Figure 4.1	Figure 4.2	Figure 4.3	Figure 4.4a	Figure 4.4b	Figure 4.5	Figure 4.6a	Figure 4.6b	Figure 4.7a	Figure 4.7b	Figure 4.9
1946	59	20	39	16	23						
1948	61	19	42	20	22	28	5	23	7	16	
1950	65	19	46	22	24						
1952	66	20	46	22	24	36	6	30	10	20	
1954	66	24	42	20	22						
1956	67	19	48	18	30	25	4	21	6	15	35
1958	68	19	49	24	25						
1960	73	24	49	19	30	27	6	21	7	14	7
1962	56	13	43	20	23						
1964	52	19	33	17	16	18	7	11	5	6	17
1966	65	20	45	25	20						
1968	45	17	28	17	11	29	4	25	12	13	30
1970	52	19	33	18	15						
1972	44	22	22	13	9	31	3	28	11	17	34
1974	48	21	27	15	12						
1976	43	17	26	18	8	35	8	27	16	11	46
1978	39	16	23	17	6						

1980	39	17	22	16	6	32	10	22	15	7	61
1982	47	18	29	25	4						
1984	41	21	20	13	7	22	8	14	7	7	56
1986	38	20	18	15	3						
1988	36	15	21	16	5	23	4	19	11	8	61
1990	39	21	18	12	6						
1992	41	20	21	16	5	30	6	24	15	9	65
1994	29	16	13	10	3						
1996	38	22	16	10	6	26	8	18	11	7	57
1998	34	14	20	13	7						
2000	38	22	16	9	7	32	15	17	12	5	74
2002	31	16	15	11	4						
2004	37	22	15	8	7	18	10	8	3	5	56
2006	42	25	17	14	3						
2008	42	27	15	8	7	17	10	7	3	4	66
2010	31	17	14	8	6						
2012	39	21	18	11	7	18	11	7	4	3	71
Total	1,611	662	949	536	413	447	125	322	155	167	736

5

Changes in Supreme Court Election Campaigns, Money, and Advertising

Over the last quarter century, American election campaigns have changed in many ways (Medvic 2011). The role of the political parties has changed, while the role played by groups other than the parties or the candidates themselves has greatly increased. Campaign consultants have emerged as key players. The Internet has become both a medium of campaign communication and a major vehicle for campaign fundraising. The amounts of money being spent on campaigns have steadily increased. And, the quantity and quality of television advertising has changed. While these changes are most visible and most talked about in the context of presidential elections, they extend to both congressional and state level elections, including elections for state supreme courts. Three of these changes have been the subject of particular discussion in the context of state supreme court elections: the amount spent on campaigns, the amount and nature of television advertising, and the role played by outside groups in funding campaigns and sponsoring advertising. By the early years of the twenty-first century, judicial campaigns had become, in the words of the title of one brief commentary, noisier and nastier (Herrnson and Abbe 2002).[1]

While it has become common to decry the role of corporate interest groups in supreme court elections (e.g., Corriher 2012), it has long been common for those with strong interests in the decisions of those courts – trial lawyers, labor

[1] "Noisier and nastier" actually comes from an earlier article by Roy Schotland published seventeen years earlier in which Schotland asserts that "elections which used to be uncontested, and which even if contested were personal, quiet and inexpensive, have now become *noisier, nastier and costlier*" (1985:76). Schotland was not referring specifically to state supreme court elections, but to judicial elections more generally. He was writing before the 1986 election which saw the nonretention of Rose Bird and two other members of the California Supreme Court, discussed later in this chapter. Schotland does note (p. 67) that in 1978 Justice Bird had been retained with only 51.7 percent of the vote.

organizations – to contribute to campaigns (Champagne 2001; Mahtesian 1998), and to be otherwise active in judicial selection at the state level (Watson and Downing 1969). One might actually ask why it took until the 1980s or later for groups such as state and national chambers of commerce and business-supported tort "reform" advocacy organizations to become significant players in judicial elections. In the late 1980s, Texas business groups together with the Texas Medical Association mobilized after trial lawyers had succeeded in capturing control of the Texas Supreme Court from conservative Democrats who had long been friendly to business; by 1990, pro-business conservative justices, then mostly Republicans, were back in control of the Texas court (Champagne and Cheek 2002:911–16; Cheek and Champagne 2004:37–54). Business groups got involved in at least some states in response to decisions by elected state supreme courts striking down limitations on tort litigation that the business interests had pushed through state legislatures (Champagne 2001; Echeverria 2000:289–90; Mahtesian 1998; Ware 1999:657–61). These efforts by the conservative business-oriented groups are part of the broader agenda of conservative legal interests to reshape both federal and state courts (Southworth 2008; Teles 2008).

The year 2000 seems to constitute something of a turning point, at least for national business-oriented groups. In 2000, the U.S. Chamber of Commerce and affiliated organizations devoted about $10 million in soft money to state supreme court elections in Michigan, Mississippi, and Ohio, although the results of the Chamber's efforts were mixed (Heller 2000; Heller and Ballard 2000). While support from the Chamber of Commerce was not entirely new in 2000 (Flesher 1998), the Chamber's spending in that election combined with advertising by groups opposed to tort reform represented an early volley of the televised "issue ads" that have come to be a factor in hard-fought state supreme court elections.

Starting with the 2000 election cycles, the Brennan Center for Justice has released a series of reports with the title "The New Politics of Judicial Elections" (Goldberg et al. 2000; Goldberg et al. 2004; Goldberg and Sanchez 2004; Sample et al. 2007; Sample et al. 2010b), with the 2010 edition carrying the subtitle, "Decade of Change." The argument of these reports (summarized by Sample et al. 2010a) is that the nature of state supreme court elections has changed, and that change is due to a huge influx of money, a "money explosion," into those election campaigns, much of which is used for television advertising (see also Champagne 2002). Moreover, business-oriented interests seeking to elect judges who will "serve their narrow interest, not the public interest"[2] are the dominant sources of the money flowing into judicial

[2] From http://www.justiceatstake.org/about/index.cfm (last visited April 13, 2013).

elections. The examples discussed in Chapter 1 of the campaigns in Wisconsin in 2008 resulting in the defeat of Louis Butler, and in 2011 resulting in the reelection of David Prosser, are consistent with this argument,[3] as are a number of other specific examples cited in the Brennan Center reports. The issue examined in this chapter is the nature of any broader pattern of change that has occurred regarding funding of state supreme court election campaigns and the use of television advertising in those campaigns.

Unfortunately, data on both questions are limited in important ways. First, both kinds of data are only available for a much shorter time period than for the other aspects of the analyses in this book. Systematic data on television advertising only began with the 1999 election year, and are limited to channels that broadcast over-the-air; that is, we do not have national data on advertising aired on cable-only channels or purchased directly through a cable company. With a small number of exceptions, data on campaign contributions to supreme court candidates are available going back only to 1990, and are generally limited to data on contributions to the candidates' campaigns. There is almost no good, longitudinal data on campaign-related expenditures by so-called independent groups. In a very small number of states public interest organizations or government agencies have sought to compile such data;[4] in addition, some inferences about independent expenditures can be made drawing on information regarding spending on television advertising because it is possible to determine who or what group probably paid for a specific advertisement. In this chapter I examine the available evidence concerning the increasing amounts of money involved in state supreme court elections and the increase in and changing nature of television advertising in these elections. I also consider the evidence regarding what, if any, effects campaign spending and television advertising have on the elections themselves.

MONEY IN STATE SUPREME COURT ELECTION CAMPAIGNS

While one major aspect of the contemporary debate over judicial elections generally and state supreme court elections more generally has focused on the role of money, and particularly the source of that money, in judicial election

3 The 2013 Wisconsin Supreme Court election was not as controversial as either the 2008 or 2011 elections, but conservative groups again dominated in terms of outside spending in support of the reelection of Patricia Roggensack (http://www.wisdc.org/pr072513.php, last visited July 28, 2014).

4 The state of Washington began requiring reports of independent expenditures in state supreme court elections in 2006. Groups were required to report expenditures prior to 2006, and to list the candidates whom they were supporting or opposing, but apparently were not required to allocate their expenditures among the candidates they were supporting or opposing.

campaigns, this issue is by no means new. In a long article published in 1985, Roy Schotland raised concerns about the amounts that had been spent on state supreme court elections during the preceding decade as well as the source of the funds (1985:59–64). In Schotland's view, judicial elections had changed, reflecting "the decline of strong political parties, the sharp rise in the amount of campaign spending, the increase in the numbers of contested elections, the use of professional management, and the appearance of more 'single-issue' groups and contests" (76). Fifteen years earlier, Texas Supreme Court Justice Joe Greenhill gave a speech at Baylor Law School in which he decried the cost of judicial elections, calling them "staggering" particularly for statewide races (Greenhill and Odam 1971:219).

As discussed in this chapter, there is no question that the amounts being spent in some recent state supreme court elections dwarf the amounts that were spent at some earlier time. However, it is important to recognize that spending in many of those elections has remained relatively modest. Moreover, the fact that spending has increased substantially for some elections is not necessarily a reason for concern. One must put the expenditures in judicial elections into some broader perspective: how do the increasing amounts spent on judicial campaigns compare to spending increases in election campaigns more generally? To some observers the source of campaign expenditures, both expenditures by groups operating formally independently of candidates' campaigns and contributions to campaigns by those with business before the courts, is of equal or greater concern. This section examines both the changing magnitude of contributions and expenditures in supreme court elections, and, to a lesser extent, changes in who is doing the spending.

Campaign Expenditures: Compared to What?

Drawing on data collected by the National Institute on Money in State Politics, Sample et al. report that the aggregate spending by state supreme court campaigns in the 2000s (2000–2008) totaled $206.9 million, compared to $83.3 million in the 1990s (Sample et al. 2010b:5), a 148 percent increase. This is certainly a large increase.[5] While the aggregate increase in campaign expenditures in state supreme court elections is large, it is important to put that increase into a broader perspective if we are going to understand the nature of that change.

The 1986 campaign in California that led to the ouster of Rose Bird and two of her colleagues on the California Supreme Court involved expenditures

5 If one adjusts for inflation, the degree of increase goes down, but remains substantial. In 2010 dollars the sum of expenditures for 2000–2008 is $229.3 million compared to $121.5 million in the 1990s, an 89 percent increase in real terms.

estimated to be $11.4 million (Hansen 1998:70).[6] In 2010 dollars, this would be almost $23 million. The 2012 election in Michigan involving three seats may be the most expensive through 2013 in nominal dollars, costing in excess of $15 million.[7] Expenditures for the 1988 Texas Supreme Court election, involving six seats, totaled $11.5 million (Champagne and Cheek 2002:914), or about $21 million in 2010 dollars. If the Michigan election is in fact the most expensive in nominal dollars, it is substantially surpassed in real terms by California in 1986 and Texas in 1988.

More important, the costs of elections in the United States have been rapidly increasing for at least thirty years, and most likely since the 1950s when television advertising began to be part of major election campaigns. In 1980, presidential candidates spent a total of $92.3 million; eight years later it was $210.7 million; in 2000 the total was $343.1 million; and in 2008 it was $1,324.7 million – that is, over $1.3 *billion*,[8] a figure that dropped by about $75 million in 2012.[9] Expenditures by campaigns for the U.S. House of Representatives increased from $115 million in 1980, to $225 million in 1988, $515 million in 2000, $929 million in 2010, and $924 million in 2012.[10] The parallel figures for the U.S. Senate are $74 million, $184 million, $384 million, $568 million, and $588 million.[11] That is, the spending on congressional elections increased from under $200 million in 1980 to $1.5 *billion*, thirty-two years later in 2012. The increase in spending is by no means limited to races for federal offices; the increased proportion of state governments under single-party control may be in part due to sharp increases in spending on state legislative races (Stassen-Berger and Howatt 2013:A9). What this suggests is that it is important to put the change in the amounts of money involved in state supreme court elections into the broader perspective of the increasing expenditures on elections in the United States more generally.

Campaign contributions and campaign expenditures are closely related, and because the former are more readily available, I have relied on data on

6 There were actually six seats up for retention in California in 1986, but the other three were noncontroversial, and probably attracted minimal expenditures. While the public campaign against Bird and two of her colleagues focused primarily on criminal justice issues, particularly the justices' votes in death penalty cases, business interests concerned about business-related issues that came before the court contributed heavily to that campaign (Galante 1986:10; Grodin 1989:174, 178; Hearn 1986; Thompson 1988:2038); the campaign in support of Bird and her colleagues received substantial financial support from a combination of the plaintiffs' bar and labor interests.

7 See http://www.mcfn.org/press.php?prId=171 (last visited May 16, 2012).

8 See http://www.opensecrets.org/pres08/totals.php?cycle=2008 (last visited April 13, 2013).

9 See http://www.opensecrets.org/pres12/expenditures.php (last visited May 19, 2012).

10 See http://www.cfinst.org/data/pdf/VitalStats_t2.pdf (last visited August 30, 2013).

11 See http://www.cfinst.org/data/pdf/VitalStats_t5.pdf (last visited August 30, 2013).

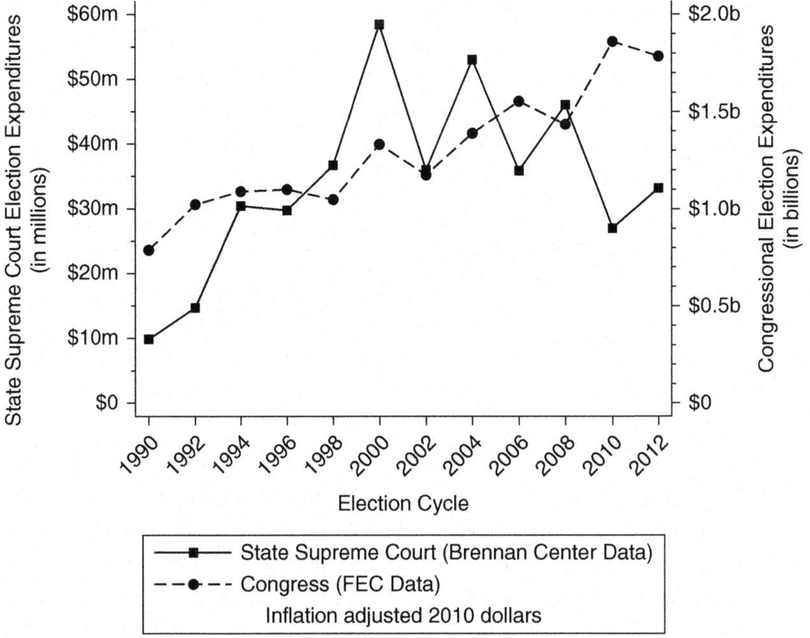

FIGURE 5.1. Total Campaign Contributions, 1990–2012.

contributions for much of the analysis that follows. Because of the lack of systematic data across the states on either contributions or expenditures in state supreme court elections prior to 1990, I concentrate my analysis on the period starting with 1990. Figure 5.1 draws on data from the Federal Elections Commission on campaign contributions to congressional candidates for both the U.S. House of Representatives and the Senate, plus figures on contributions to state supreme court candidates compiled by the Brennan Center. [12] The data have been collapsed into two-year election cycles.[13] All values have been adjusted for inflation to 2010 dollars.[14]

12 The figures for 1990–2008 for state supreme court elections are found in Sample et al. (2010b:5); the figures for 2009–2010 come from Skaggs et al. (2011:5), and the figures for 2012 from Bannon et al. (2013:5). Note that in this analysis I do not include the Texas Court of Criminal Appeals because neither Brennan nor NIMSP treats those as supreme court elections. The figures for congressional elections are from the Federal Elections Commission (FEC) website.

13 Unlike in other chapters, where odd-numbered years were collapsed with the preceding even year, here I have collapsed odd-numbered years with the following even years because that reflects the funding cycle for most elections. What this means is that the data actually start with 1989 rather than 1990, although I will refer to the starting point as 1990.

14 The inflation adjustment is based on the annual figure reported by the CPI by the Bureau of Labor Statistics, using the BLS table found at ftp://ftp.bls.gov/pub/special.requests/cpi/cpiai.txt (last visited, April 14, 2013).

Figure 5.1 plots the change in total contributions to candidates for the state supreme court (solid line) and the change in total contributions to candidates for Congress (broken line). From 1990 through 2000 there was a clear and sharp increase in the level of contributions to supreme court candidates, from about $10 million (in 2010 dollars) to more than $58 million, almost a 500 percent increase. If one combines 1990 and 1992 and compares that pair to the combination of 1998 and 2000, the increase is "only" about 300 percent. Over the same 10-year period, contributions to congressional candidates grew at a slower rate, increasing by only about 69 percent (in constant, 2010 dollars). However, since 2000, contributions to the campaigns of state supreme court justices have actually fallen (in real dollars) while contributions to congressional candidates have continued to increase, growing by another 33 percent in constant dollars.

The jaggedness of the line in Figure 5.1 for state supreme court elections almost certainly reflects variation in the number of contested supreme court elections from cycle to cycle. That number ranges from 24 to 42; eliminating those elections labeled in Chapter 4 as symbolically contested (the winner received at least 75 percent of the vote), the number ranges from 24 to 40.[15] Figure 5.2 shows the total contributions for all elections in each cycle (solid line), the mean of the contributions computed by dividing the total by the number of contested elections (long-dashed line), and the modified average contribution computed by dividing the total by the number of contested elections omitting from the count those where the winner received 75 percent or more of the vote (short-dashed line). What is evident from this figure is that the basic pattern shown in Figure 5.1 holds up. There was a substantial increase during the 1990s; contribution levels held generally stable through most of the first decade of the twenty-first century, but have actually dropped over the last two election cycles. Regardless of which figure one looks at, the contribution level for the 2011–12 election cycle, adjusting for inflation, approximates the pattern in the mid-1990s.

The patterns in Figures 5.1 and 5.2 may not accurately reflect recent developments in the funding of state supreme court elections because the data are limited to contributions made to the candidates' campaigns. In its report on the 2009–10 state supreme court elections, the Brennan Center reported that a total

[15] A total of 15 elections between 1990 and 2012 fall into this category. Six of those elections are from Texas and all of those involve a Republican incumbent facing competition only from a Libertarian candidate; one additional election, from Alabama, involved a Republican incumbent facing a Libertarian challenger. Six of the 15 elections (four in Texas) occurred in 2006, the one year where there is a noticeable difference between the average and what I label the modified average in Figure 5.2; one of the other election cycles has two such elections in this category, and the remaining cycles have only one. Note again that the Texas Court of Criminal Appeals is not included in this analysis.

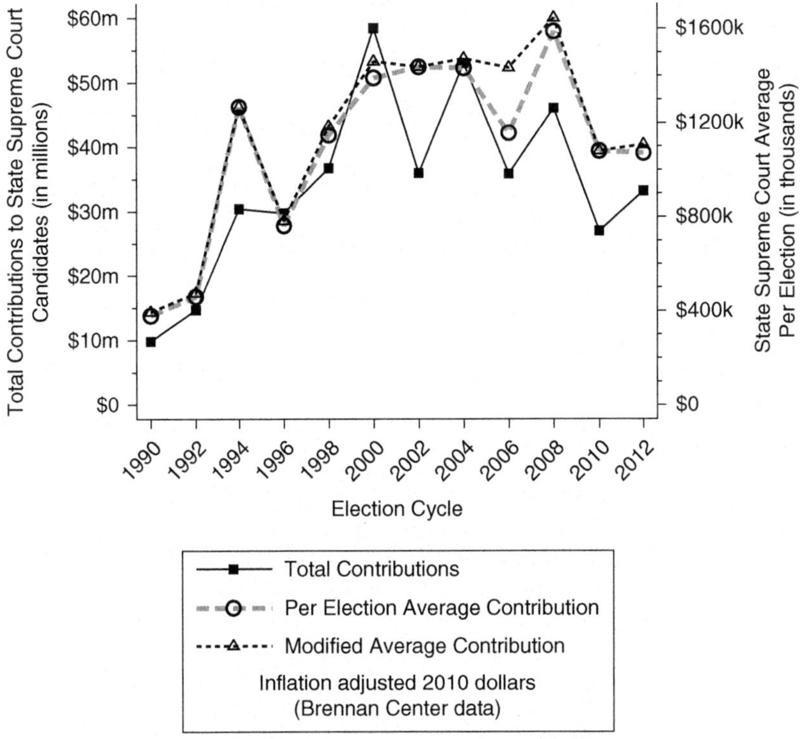

FIGURE 5.2. Averages of Campaign Contributions, 1990–2012.

of more than $38 million had been spent on those elections; however, the total contributions to candidates in those two years was only $27 million (Skaggs et al. 2011:1). That is, about 30 percent of the campaign expenditures in the 2009–10 election cycle was not funneled through the candidates' campaigns, and hence does not show up on the candidates' contribution or expenditure reports. The authors also note that this constituted a substantial increase over 2005–06. In the 2011–12 election cycle, total spending exceeded $56 million, but only $32 million of that total was spent by the candidates' campaigns. Total spending in 2005–06 was similar to that in 2011–12, but spending had shifted sharply from the candidates' campaigns to outside groups: 22 percent in 2005–06 compared to 43 percent in 2011–12. However, 85 percent of the outside spending in 2011–12 reported by the Brennan Center came from elections in just four states: Michigan, Wisconsin, Florida, and North Carolina (Bannon et al. 2013:5–6).

As documented in the various Brennan Center reports, noncandidate groups sponsor a significant portion of the advertising in state supreme court elections. Figure 5.3 plots the campaign contributions received by candidates

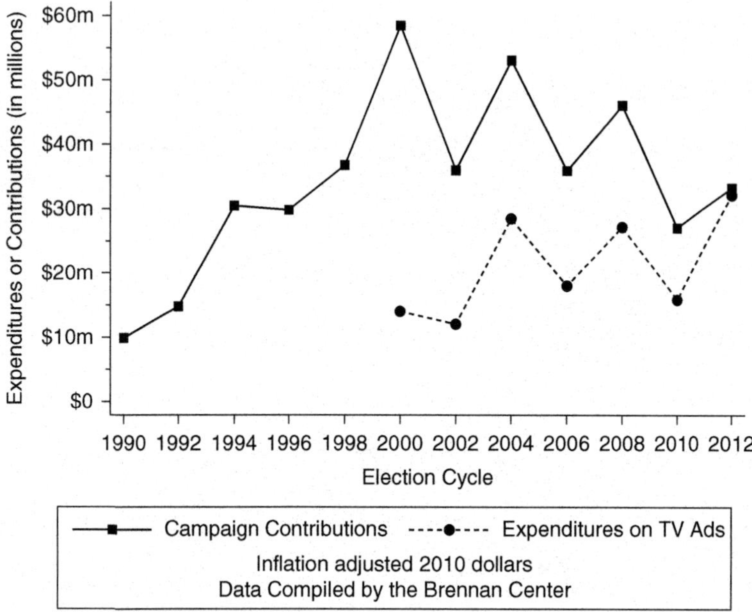

FIGURE 5.3. Campaign Contributions and Television Advertising Expenditures.

and the amount of money spent on television advertisements both by the candidates themselves and by noncandidate groups. The growth in television advertising expenditures during the early part of the decade starting in 2000 is evident. After that initial growth the expenditures move in parallel with contributions to the candidates running about 50 percent of those contributions, until the last two-year period, 2011–12, when more was spent on television advertising than the candidates' campaigns received in contributions. In this last period, outside groups, which include political parties, sponsored 60 percent of the television advertising cost, compared to 42 percent in the prior cycle;[16] more specifically, nonparty outside groups sponsored 36 percent of the television advertising costs in 2011–12 compared to only 15 percent in 2009–10. However, as I will discuss in detail later in this chapter, in 2009–10 the percentage of television advertising costs attributable to outside groups was actually the lowest of the period examined, and the percentage funded by such groups in the 2007–08 cycle was almost the same as in the 2011–12 cycle.

[16] Based on information posted by the Brennan Center, outside groups paid 61 percent of the cost of television advertising in the 2013–14 election cycle; nonparty groups paid 33 percent of those costs. See http://www.brennancenter.org/analysis/buying-time-2014 and http://www.brennancenter.org/analysis/buying-time-wisconsin-judicial-election-2013 (last accessed December 28, 2014).

Variation in Campaign Contribution Trends

In the previous chapter I showed that one had to control for region and type of election system to understand the changes that have occurred in competition and competitiveness in state supreme court elections. Is the same true with regard to trends in campaign contributions? In particular, does the time trend vary by type of election and/or region? In order to look at the question of variation in the time trend, one must turn to other sources of data because the data on campaign contributions reported by the Brennan Center are limited to aggregate figures by election cycle. The National Institute on Money in State Politics (NIMSP) through its website FollowTheMoney.org provides data on contributions to candidates running for state office.[17] Unfortunately, NIMSP has only partial data for 1990–98 on state supreme court elections.[18] However, Chris Bonneau collected similar data for the period 1990–2000 and has made those data available as part of a replication dataset in connection with an article on contributions to state supreme court candidates (Bonneau 2007a).[19]

Figure 5.4 shows the candidate-level average contribution for each election cycle along with the averages based on Bonneau's data tracked by the long-dashed line and averages based on the NIMSP data tracked by the short-dashed line;[20] the solid line plots the average computed by election rather than candidate, which is the same as the long-dashed line in Figure 5.2. The fact that the averages for the one cycle shared by the two candidate-level data sources are virtually identical provides a measure of confidence that the combined data produce valid inferences in assessing variation in the trends in campaign contributions over time. This is reinforced by the similarity in the patterns shown for the candidate-level and election-level averages (the latter appears as the solid line). However, there are differences in what the two data sources cover, which means that some caution needs to be exercised in moving from the 1990s to the 2000s. Specifically, Bonneau's data do not include primary losers but do include the Texas Court of Criminal Appeals, while the

17 The NIMSP maintains data at the level of the contribution, and one can extract the information from the website at that level. Denise Roth Barber, the managing director at NIMSP, generously produced a candidate-level aggregation for me.

18 As noted previously, the NIMSP does not include the Texas Court of Criminal Appeals as a state supreme court.

19 Bonneau's analysis focused on factors influencing contributions received by individual candidates for the period 1990–2000. The factors that he found to have a significant influence included incumbency, nonincumbents' experience as a judge, the percentage of the state supreme court's docket comprised of tort cases, partisan election system (negative relationship), number of seats up for election (negative relationship), odd-year elections, and professionalism of the state supreme court.

20 Note that in computing the averages, candidates reporting no contributions were omitted.

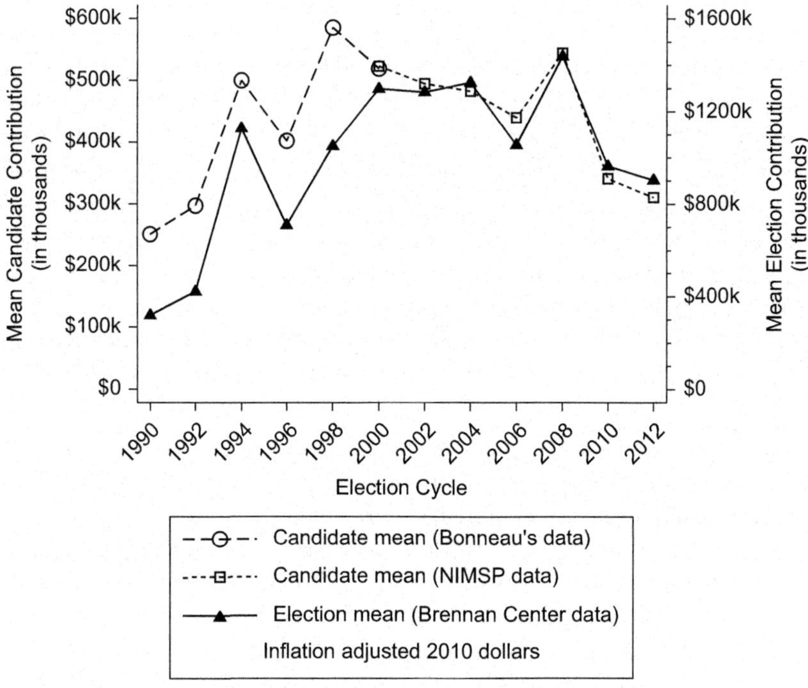

FIGURE 5.4. Candidate Average Campaign Contributions, 1990–2012.

NIMSP data include primary losers but exclude the Texas Court of Criminal Appeals.

Figure 5.5 shows the trend in the candidate average contribution totals separately for nonpartisan (solid line), partisan (long-dashed line), and hybrid (short-dashed line) elections. The striking finding in the figure is the much lower, and essentially constant, average for candidates running in nonpartisan elections. This seems inconsistent with the hard-fought nonpartisan elections that have occurred in recent years in Wisconsin and Washington. However, it almost certainly reflects that the heavy spending in elections in those states came not from the candidates themselves but from interest groups aligned with the candidates.

For the hybrid election system currently used only in Michigan and Ohio, there is substantial variation from election to election; however, if one were to omit the 2000 election and possibly the 2002 election, one could argue that this fluctuation was around a fairly constant overall average. The pattern for the hybrid elections also makes clear how important the period examined is. If one looks at the decade of 1990–2000, it appears that there is a strong pattern of increase in the amount of contributions candidates are receiving in states using the hybrid system; however, if one looks at the period 2000–12, one would

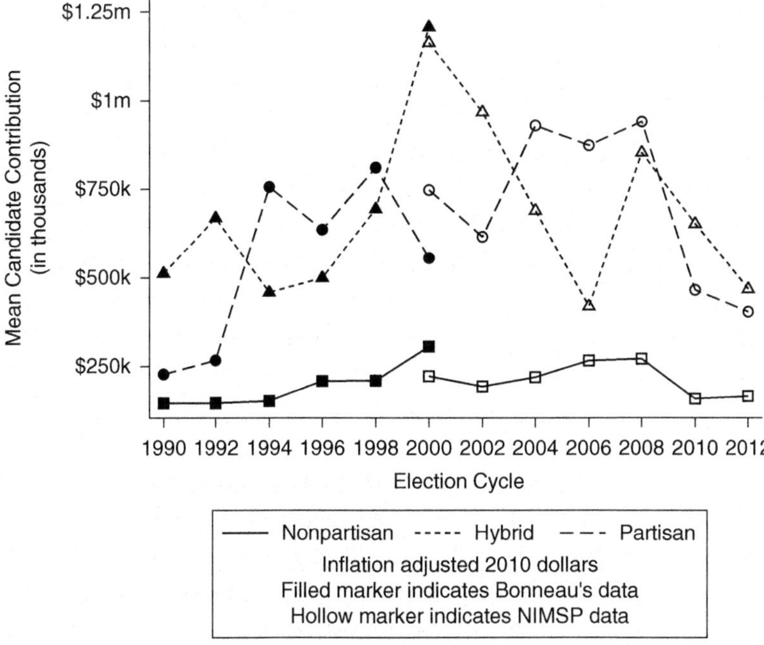

FIGURE 5.5. Average Contributions by Election Type, 1990–2012.

conclude that the average contribution, controlling for inflation, is declining. Over the entire twenty-two-year period for which I have data, the best conclusion is that there has been no systematic change in contribution averages in the two states using hybrid elections. This does not mean that the amount being *expended* in these states has not changed, given that the amounts examined include only contributions made to the candidates' campaigns; neither expenditures by the political parties nor by interest groups are included.

What about partisan states? There is a clear pattern of increase from 1990 through 2004. However, the average amount of contributions candidates received leveled off starting in 2004, and then plummeted down in 2009–10 and 2011–12 to levels not seen since the mid-1990s. Whether this drop was an anomaly, or possibly reflected a decline in competitive elections in some of the partisan states (especially Texas and possibly Alabama), is not clear, and cannot be discerned from these data given that the decline involves only two election cycles as this is being written.

Figure 5.6 separates the partisan and nonpartisan elections by region, with nonsouthern states shown by heavy lines and southern states by lighter lines; hybrid states are omitted because both are nonsouthern. The patterns shown are essentially the same for southern and nonsouthern states, although for

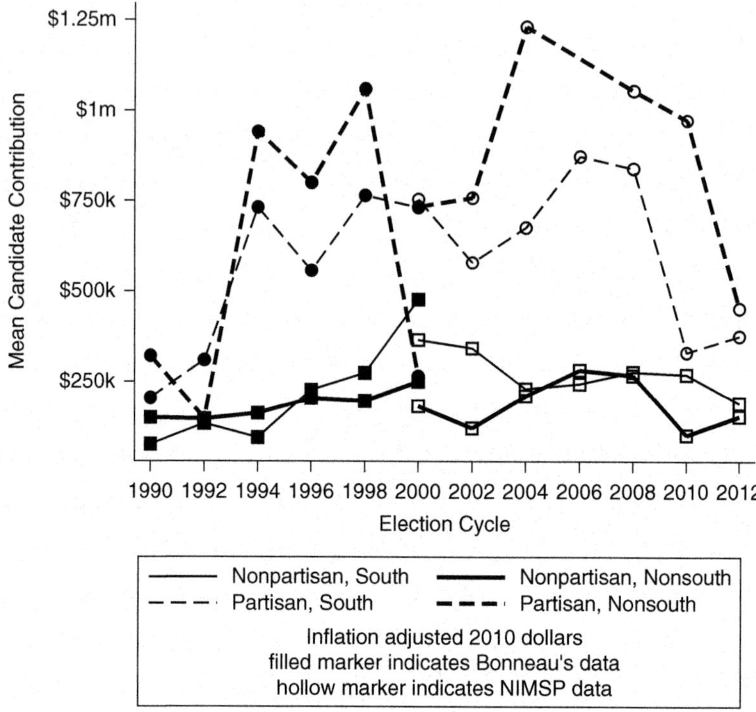

FIGURE 5.6. Average Contributions by Election Type and Region, 1990–2012.

partisan elections the averages for nonsouthern states tend to be higher than in the southern states. The cycle-to-cycle variations are greater controlling for region but this undoubtedly reflects the smaller number of observations upon which each of the averages is based.

Moving Beyond Campaign Contributions

As noted at the beginning of this chapter, a major limitation in the study of the financing of state supreme court elections is that systematic data are available nationally only for contributions to candidates.[21] This leaves the important

[21] Chris Bonneau has compiled data on expenditures by candidates from the state agencies to which candidates are required to report (Bonneau 2004, 2005, 2007b, 2007c; Bonneau and Cann 2011); the correlation between contributions to campaigns and expenditures by those campaigns is extremely high, and the pattern in the volume of spending will by and large mimic the pattern in the volume of contributions. The degree to which there will be expenditures outside the candidates' campaigns will depend in part on state law regarding limits on campaign contributions and state law regarding reporting requirements. For example, I was told that generally there has been relatively little outside spending in Texas Supreme Court elections because the campaign contribution rules are so loose that there is no reason not to simply give the funds to a candidate's campaign and let the campaign decide how to spend it.

question of the volume of campaign financing that does not pass through the candidates' campaign organizations. However, starting in 2006 the state of Washington has had a very broad reporting requirement with a facility for easily extracting and aggregating information that has been reported,[22] and in two additional states, Wisconsin and Michigan, there are state-based organizations that have undertaken to assemble more complete information, although that information does have some gaps. In this section I briefly examine what can be discerned from these three states; I also examine the role of outside groups in funding over-the-air television advertising.

Washington

As I will discuss in the next chapter, Washington is a state that elects its state supreme court justices through a nonpartisan ballot but which, like Wisconsin, has witnessed a sharp shift in the nature of those elections. Between 1978 and 1988, there were twenty supreme court elections in Washington, only six of which were contested. There were eighteen elections between 1990 and 1998, fourteen of which were contested, but most were noncontroversial. Things changed starting in 2000; between 2000 and 2012 there were twenty-two elections, eighteen of which were contested. While saving the detail for the next chapter, there were heated contests in many of the elections reflecting conflict between major interests in the state, particularly between those interested in property development and environmentalists. Issues such as abortion and same-sex marriage were also factors in some of these elections.

Public disclosure requirements in the state of Washington may be the most comprehensive in the country. Since 1978 the Public Disclosure Commission has published a "Fact Book" giving details about campaign contributions and showing the amounts expended by candidates. As noted previously, starting in 2006, spending by independent groups has had to be reported, including the name of the candidate being supported or opposed.[23] Importantly, the

[22] According to the National Institution on Money in State Politics, several other states have fairly comprehensive reporting requirements that cover independent expenditures and "electioneering communications"; however, the reports are filed on paper forms which, while individual forms can be accessed, do not allow for ready aggregation; see http://www.followthemoney.org/press/ReportView.phtml?r=495&utm_campaign=ealert-indep-spending-scorecard-2013&utm_medium=email&utm_source=nimsp-contacts (last visited May 19, 2013).

[23] The change, which became effective in January 2006, was specifically targeted at advertising. Expenditures on advertising had to be reported if the ad (1) clearly identifies a candidate, (2) appears within 60 days of an election in the candidate's jurisdiction, (3) is produced through radio, TV, mail, billboard, newspaper, or periodical, and (4) either alone, or in combination with other communications by the sponsor identifying the candidate, has a fair market value of at least $5,000. In 2012, the threshold dropped to $1,000.

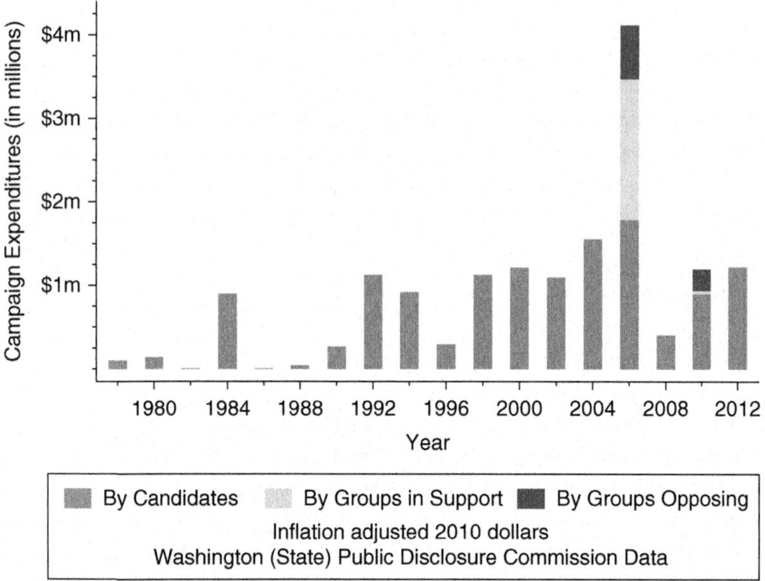

FIGURE 5.7. Campaign Expenditures in Washington, 1978–2012.

reporting is electronic and goes into a database that allows searching and easy aggregation for years starting in 2000. Using a combination of the database and earlier Fact Books, I compiled data on expenditures in Washington Supreme Court elections between 1978 and 2012.[24]

Figure 5.7 is a stacked bar chart showing the results of this compilation of spending in Washington's Supreme Court elections starting with 1978. Given the small number of contested elections prior to 1990, the minimal spending in most of the period 1978–1988 is what one would expect. Perhaps a bit more surprising is that there is not a greater difference in spending by candidates starting in 2000 compared to the 1990s. While one might be tempted to attribute this to the absence of information on outside group spending for 2000–2004, it is only in 2006 that such spending was a major element of the overall spending on supreme court campaigns. In that year outside spending totaled $2.2 million, constituting 57 percent of the total spent on supreme court campaigns. Noteworthy is the fact that 52 percent of the outside spending was either in support of or opposition to a single candidate, John Groen, an attorney who had worked on behalf of property rights interests; another

[24] The Fact Books are accessible at http://www.pdc.wa.gov/home/factbook.aspx (last visited May 19, 2013).

26 percent of the outside spending was focused on Stephen Johnson, who was also allied with property rights interests and had been a proponent of Washington's Defense of Marriage Act eight years earlier. While outside interests were big spenders in 2006, that role was not repeated in 2008, 2010, or 2012, even though there were a number of contentious elections in those years.[25]

Michigan

The Michigan Campaign Finance Network (MCFN) has sought to compile and make public information on the financing of Michigan Supreme Court elections starting with the 1984 election. MCFN seeks to capture independent expenditures both by the political parties that nominate candidates for the court and by interest groups. Information on expenditures on television advertising includes both over-the-air and cable-only outlets and comes from the outlets' actual invoices.[26] Based on the MCFN reports, one can separate out expenditures by the candidates, by the parties, and by interest groups. One complication in looking at these data is that the number of seats in play ranges from one to three, and this variation needs to be taken into account, although it is not uncommon for advertisements sponsored by political parties or other outside groups to endorse or attack all the candidates of a particular party.

Figure 5.8 shows the trend in expenditures over the full term of the MCFN data, both total expenditures and expenditures per seat. Prior to 1994, all of the expenditures found by MCFN were by the candidates. MCFN reported the first expenditures by the parties in 1994 (about 4 percent of total expenditures) with both parties and interest groups making expenditures in 1996 (26 percent by parties and 7 percent by interest groups). In 1998, almost all of the expenditures were again by the candidates, with none made by interest groups and only 2 percent by the parties; however, in that election there were signs of increasing concern by both the parties and the interest groups ("Advocates Do Battle as Court Candidates Keep Low Profile" 1998). The big change came in 2000, both in terms of volume of expenditures and major involvement of both parties and interest groups. That year stands as the high water mark of total expenditures when measured in constant dollars,[27] although it falls below 2008 if one takes into account the number of seats at play in the election – there

[25] These later elections are discussed in Chapter 6.

[26] MCFN's expenditure compilations are available at http://www.mcfn.org/MSC1984_2012.php (last visited May 2, 2013).

[27] Measured in nominal dollars, the high point in total expenditures was the 2012 election.

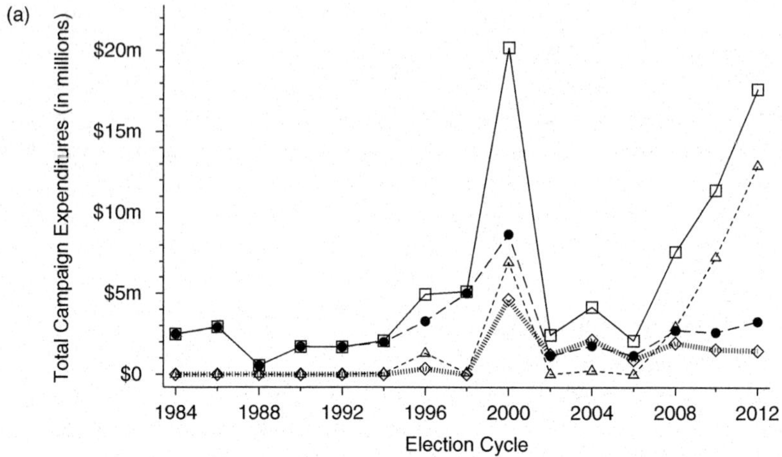

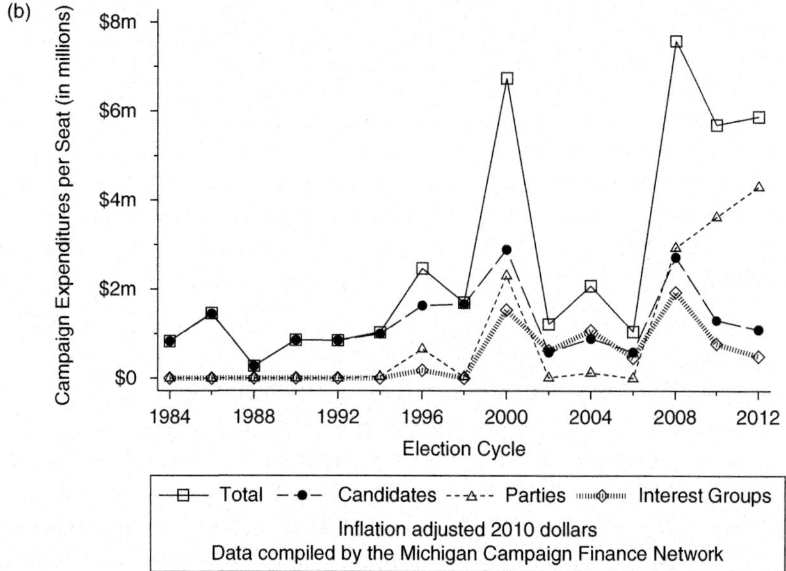

FIGURE 5.8. Campaign Expenditures in Michigan, 1984–2012; (a) Expenditures across All Seats, (b) Expenditures per Seat.

were three seats in 2000 but only one in 2008, the only election cycle among the fifteen with only one.

As previously stated, a substantial share of total expenditures were made by all three sets of players in 2000: candidates (43 percent), parties (34 percent), and interest groups (23 percent). Since that time there have been major shifts among the candidates, parties, and interest groups in the share of expenditures by each. This is visually illustrated in Figure 5.9 which tracks the share of

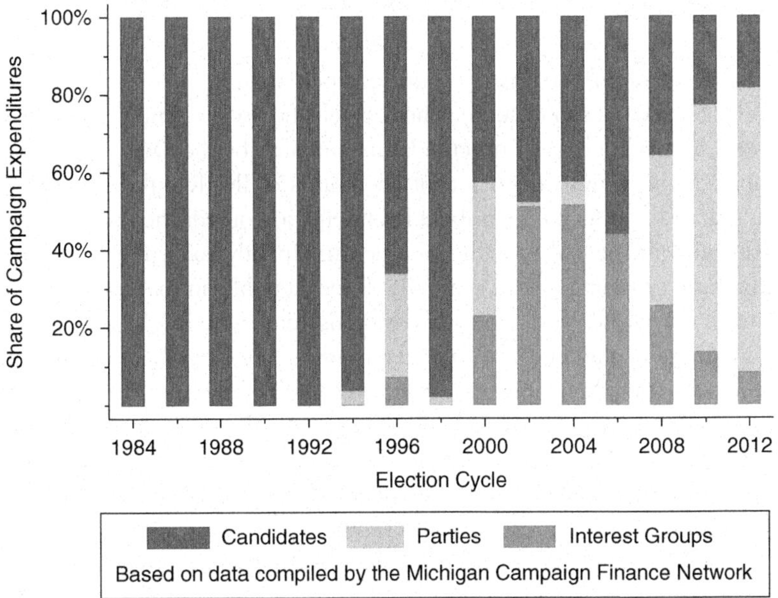

FIGURE 5.9. Relative Role of Candidates, Parties, and Interest Groups in Financing Michigan Supreme Court Elections.

expenditures over the entire period as a stacked bar graph similar in form to the graphs used in Chapter 4. In 2002, 2004, and 2006, interest groups played a major role with parties largely on the sidelines; starting in 2008, parties took over from the interest groups, and in the last election reported, party expenditures amounted to almost three-quarters of the total expenditures found by MCFN. In fact, there is less of a shift from interest groups to parties than might first appear because the interest groups have simply funneled their contributions through party organizations. Regardless, while prior to 2000 most spending in Michigan's Supreme Court elections was by the candidates' committees, in the later years covered by this analysis the bulk of the spending was by interest groups or by party organizations functioning as surrogates for interest groups.

One might ask what specifically set off the change in Michigan? As previously discussed, Michigan has a hybrid system of judicial elections for its supreme court, in which the parties nominate candidates, but the candidates then appear on the general election ballot without party designations. A longtime political issue in Michigan is the tension between business and labor. While generally the Republican Party nationally is thought of as aligned with business interests and the Democratic Party with labor interests, the alignment is particularly strong in Michigan. This division has long extended to the Michigan Supreme Court, as evidenced in appointment of justices to the court (Schubert 1959a), and decision-making patterns on the court (Feeley 1971; Ulmer 1962, 1966). The 2000 election was essentially a battle for control of the Michigan Supreme Court initiated by the Democratic Party, which sought to unseat two recent appointees of the Republican governor plus a third Republican incumbent in anticipation of redistricting battles that might arise in the wake of the 2000 census. In July 2000, the Democratic Party started running ads attacking the three Republican incumbents which prompted responses in the form of ads sponsored by the Michigan Chamber of Commerce. After the Democratic convention, the Chamber of Commerce ran ads attacking the Democratic nominees, as did the Michigan Republican Party (LaBrant 2004). Why then did the pattern of substantial expenditures not continue in the elections immediately after 2000? One likely explanation was that none of those elections was going to produce an outcome that would immediately change the control of the court.

In some states the impetus for interest groups' engagement in state supreme court elections has been decisions striking down tort reform measures. While Michigan has seen a number of rounds of tort reform, the Michigan Supreme Court has not struck down any of the statutes passed by the legislature (Fosmire et al. 2013:8). However, the prospect of challenges to tort reform in response to tort reform proposals being considered, and subsequently passed, by the Michigan legislature probably accounted for the uptick in expenditures and the start of interest group and party involvement in the mid-1990s (LaBrant 2004:44).

Wisconsin

The Wisconsin Democracy Campaign (WDC) has undertaken an effort similar to that of the Michigan Campaign Finance Network, although WDC's information does not start until the 1997 Wisconsin Supreme Court election. As does MCFN, WDC seeks to obtain access to actual invoices for television advertising; however, WDC does not attempt to collect information from cable systems. In Wisconsin, PACs making expenditures in support of candidates must register with what is now called the Wisconsin Accountability Board and file reports of their expenditures. However, this requirement does not extend to expenditures on activities and advertisements that do not specifically call on citizens to vote either for or against a particular candidate; WDC seeks to identify expenditures in this category but this is very difficult for activities other than television advertising.

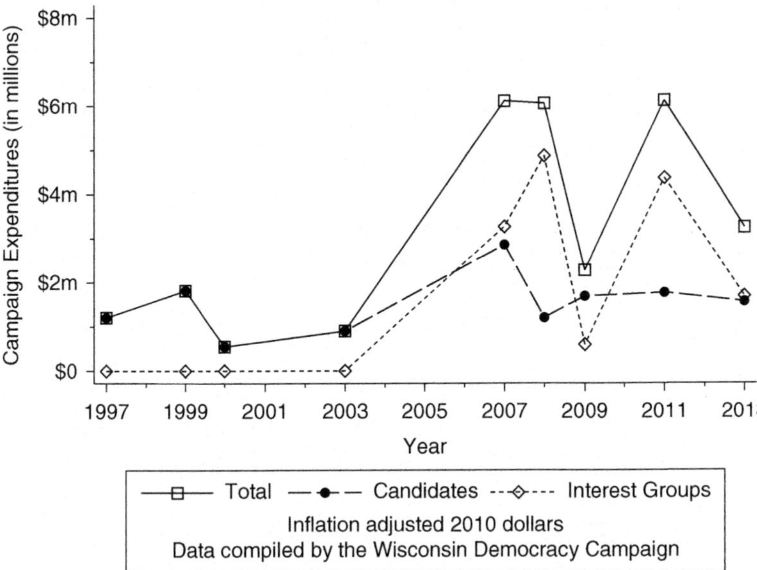

FIGURE 5.10. Campaign Expenditures in Wisconsin, 1997–2013.

Figure 5.10 shows the pattern in expenditures by candidates and interest groups in Wisconsin Supreme Court elections starting in 1997 as compiled by WDC. There is no need to control for the number of seats being contested because in Wisconsin there is never more than one seat up for election in a given year. The figure shows that interest groups first entered the picture with independent expenditures in Wisconsin in the 2007 election. Prior to that time there was variation from year to year in candidate expenditures, with a peak of about $2 million (in 2010 dollars, about $1.4 million in nominal dollars) in the 1999 election; that election pitted Chief Justice Shirley Abrahamson against challenger Sharren Rose, with Abrahamson's campaign accounting for about 54 percent of the total.

What happened between 2003 and 2007 that accounts for the sharp increase in total spending, including the entry of interest groups making independent expenditures? As discussed in Chapter 1, in July 2005 the Wisconsin Supreme Court in a 4-3 vote struck down a $350,000 cap on noneconomic damages that the legislature had passed in 1995.[28] The decision was something of a surprise because most observers viewed the court as having a conservative majority; however, one member of that perceived conservative majority, Patrick Crooks (Ross 2005), joined with the court's three liberals to strike down the

[28] *Ferdon v. Wisconsin Patients Compensation Fund*, 701 N.W.2d 440 (Wis. 2005).

cap.[29] Crooks again joined with the liberal faction in the case that made it easier for victims claiming they had been harmed by lead paint to bring suit if they could not identify the specific manufacturer(s) of the paint to which they had been exposed.[30] Business interests chose not to mount a challenge to Crooks when he ran for reelection the following year,[31] perhaps because it would have been difficult to challenge his overall record given that he had a solid record as a law and order trial judge and his votes in criminal cases in his ten years on the Supreme Court generally aligned with the conservative wing of the court.[32]

The big jump came in 2007 when a seat became open as a result of the decision by a member of the court's conservative wing not to run for reelection. The April election pitted Madison immigration attorney Linda Clifford against conservative circuit (trial) judge Annette Ziegler from Washington County. Clifford was backed by liberal interests, particularly labor, while Ziegler's backing came from business interests. As suggested by Figure 5.10, those interests poured significant money into the campaign and Ziegler won the election.[33]

The next year interest groups played an even greater role in a challenge to incumbent Louis Butler. Butler had been appointed to the court in 2004 to replace Diane Sykes when she was appointed to the Seventh Circuit Federal Appeals Court. Butler, who is the only African American to ever serve on the court, had been defeated by Sykes in 2000 when he opposed her in her first election after she had been appointed to fill a court vacancy in 1999. Conservative interests opposed Butler because his defeat would shift the court firmly to a conservative majority given that Crooks was increasingly aligning himself with the three liberals on the court. Butler's opponent was Michael Gableman, a trial court judge from Burnett County in the northwest part of the state. The election was nasty; more than 12,000 television spots aired, about 7,000 of which were attack ads. Gableman won, but as mentioned in

29 Crooks had been elected to an open seat in 1996. Prior to becoming a trial court judge, Crooks had been a Republican activist in the Green Bay area, and had once run unsuccessfully in a Republican primary for the state senate (Segall 1996:9A).

30 *Thomas ex rel. Gramling v. Mallet*, 701 N.W.2d 523 (Wis. 2005).

31 Between 2003 and 2007 one other incumbent, Ann Walsh Bradley was unopposed for reelection in 2005; Bradley had been elected to the court in 1995 to fill an open seat.

32 An alternate explanation suggested by a longtime observer of the Wisconsin Supreme Court was that a number of liberal judges were considering opposing Crooks (Ross 2005), and conservative interests may have feared that if they also mounted a challenge that would ultimately lead to Crooks being weakened in a way that would lead to the election of someone much more liberal than Crooks.

33 Subsequent to her election, Ziegler faced disciplinary proceedings for conflicts of interest while sitting as a trial judge; Ziegler had presided over cases involving a bank on whose board her husband served. The Supreme Court ultimately issued a reprimand.

Chapter 1, he then faced charges that one of the ads he ran made false statements about Butler regarding a criminal case from the time he was a public defender; the Supreme Court ultimately divided 3-3 over the ethics charge and hence took no action against Gableman.[34]

The dip in interest group activity in 2009 between the high points of 2008 and 2011 (the Prosser election discussed in detail in Chapter 1) may appear to be an anomaly but is easily explained. In 2009, Chief Justice Abrahamson stood for reelection for a fourth ten-year term facing a conservative challenger, Jefferson County Circuit Judge Randy Koschnick. However, conservative interest groups chose not to mount a challenge to Abrahamson, probably for two reasons. First, with four conservative members in place, defeating Abrahamson would not shift the majority, and second, Abrahamson was a proven vote getter who had cultivated a wide range of supporters during her more than thirty years on the court.

I suggested in Chapter 1 that a significant part of the explanation for elections for the Wisconsin Supreme Court having become strongly polarized with substantial involvement of interest groups was the court's decisions on issues that would activate conservative business interests. This analysis of spending in recent Wisconsin elections clearly accords with this explanation of the broader changes that have occurred in the state.

Television Advertising Expenditures

Estimates of the amounts spent on television advertising come from the Campaign Media Analysis Group (CMAG). Importantly, CMAG's estimates do not capture advertising placed through local cable providers and its estimates are based on the standard rates charged by various outlets rather than representing the actual amounts campaigns pay for the ads.[35] Given that television outlets are able to charge premium rates close to election day when there is a high demand for advertising slots, CMAG's figures, even for the ads they do capture, are likely to be underestimates. However, the consistency of CMAG's approach over time provides a basis for examining trends. Much of the information from CMAG appeared in reports prepared by the Brennan

34 As noted in Chapter 1, it was during the court's consideration of the charges against Gableman that Justices Prosser and Bradley came to blows. Gableman subsequently faced other ethics issues including sitting on cases involving a law firm that had represented him without charge during the first ethics case.

35 CMAG does track advertising on some national cable services, but those services would not themselves be running ads for state and local elections; any such ads would be inserted by the local cable distribution system.

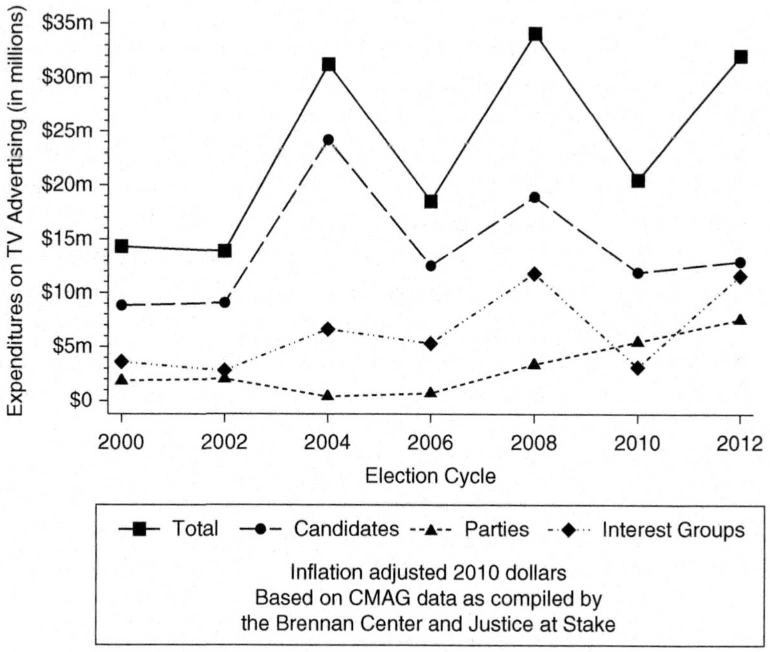

FIGURE 5.11. Television Advertising Expenditures, 1999–2012.

Center; additional information was provided to me either by the Brennan Center or by Justice at Stake. Some information is missing for ads broadcast in 2000. Finally, CMAG's market coverage has increased over the years. In 2000, it covered only the seventy largest television media markets, encompassing more than 80 percent of the national audience (Goldstein and Freedman 2002:727n5); from 2002 through 2007, it covered the one hundred largest markets constituting 86 percent of television households nationally (Ridout et al. undated:9); starting in 2008, CMAG has covered all 210 media markets in the country.

The CMAG data provide information on the sponsor of the ad, the number of airings, and the estimated costs of the air time. Figure 5.11 shows the CMAG figures on expenditures, in constant 2010 dollars, for each election cycle starting with 1999–2000, both the total expenditures and expenditures separately for candidates, parties, and interest groups. The pattern goes up and down between presidential election years (except 2000, probably reflecting in part the smaller number of markets covered that cycle) and mid-term election years. While one might be tempted to attribute the ups and downs to differences in the number of contested seats at each election, this is not entirely true.

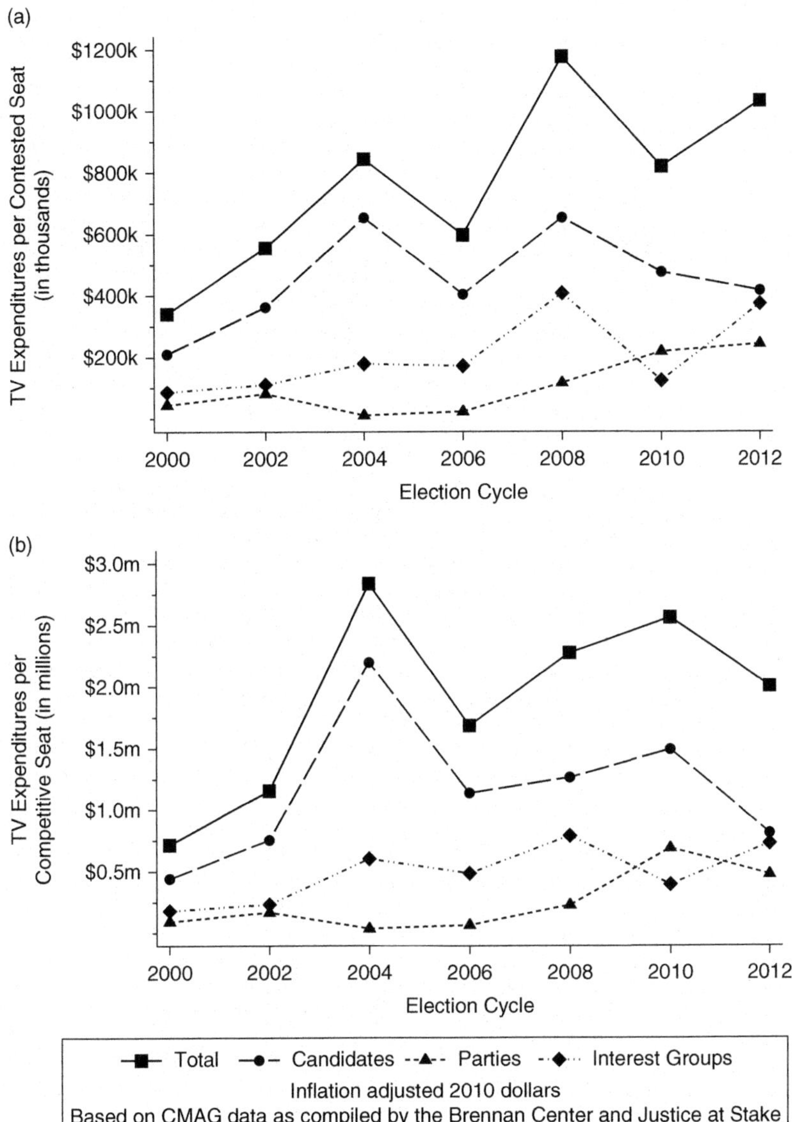

FIGURE 5.12. Average Television Advertising Expenditures, 1999–2012; (a) Per Contested Seat, (b) Per Competitive Seat.

Figure 5.12 shows the pattern controlling for the number of contested seats (5.12a) and controlling for the number of competitive seats (5.12b).[36]

[36] Competitive here is determined post hoc, and is defined as a seat where either the incumbent lost or the winner (compared to his or her closest competitor) got less than 55 percent either in the general election or in a primary election.

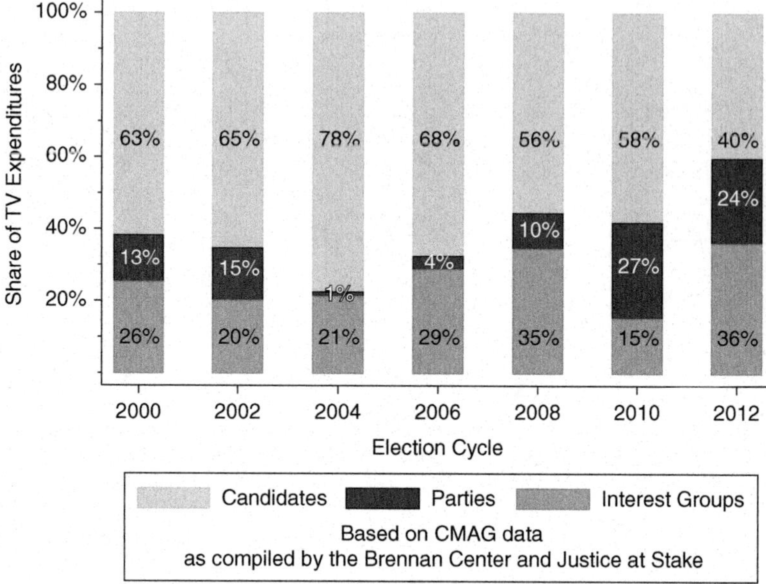

FIGURE 5.13. Sponsorship of Television Advertising, 1999–2012.

Looking at the average per contested seat, one sees that the up-down pattern continues, although it is slightly muted compared to the pattern for the total expenditures. If one looks at the average expenditure per competitive seat, the alternating up-down pattern disappears, although some ups and downs remain.[37] The one clear conclusion from Figures 5.11 and 5.12 is that over the period under consideration there has been some increase; it is less clear whether one should label the increase as fairly steady (with some ups and downs) or more of a jump between the 2001–02 election cycle and the 2003–04 election cycle.

Another point that is clear in Figures 5.11 and 5.12 is that there have been some shifts in the pattern of sponsorship of the television advertising in state supreme court elections. This is most clearly seen in Figure 5.13, which uses stacked bars representing the percentage of advertising expenditures by candidates, parties, and interest groups. Until the 2011–2012 election cycle, candidate expenditures as measured by CMAG constituted the majority of expenditures on TV advertising, ranging from 55.5 percent in the 2007–08 election cycle to 77.5 percent in the 2003–04 election cycle. Only in the last

[37] The average per competitive seat is computed using the total expenditures (regardless of whether the expenditure was in connection with a competitive seat) divided by the number of seats that turned out to be competitive as previously defined.

election cycle, 2011–2012, did noncandidate spending exceed candidate spending, which fell to 40.3 percent of expenditures.[38] Also notable is the growth in spending by parties over the last two cycles shown in Figure 5.13, but as discussed earlier that significantly reflects the channeling of some interest group money through party organizations.

Summary: Patterns of Change in Campaign Spending

This analysis makes it clear that spending has increased in state supreme court elections between 1999 and 2012. In some ways the year 2000 seems to demarcate a point of change, particularly as regards spending on television advertising and spending by noncandidate groups. On the other hand, election spending, both generally and in state supreme court elections, has been increasing steadily as far back as one can find good, comparable data, and the impact of broadcast advertising on those expenditures is by no means a new question (see Abrams and Settle 1976). The analysis presented here does indicate that there were significant increases in spending on state supreme court elections through the 1990s; the analysis is less clear as to whether there was significant change after 2000. The change through the 1990s may represent a "catching up" of spending in state supreme court contests compared to other contested elections. A challenge in assessing the change after 2000 has been the increased role of parties and interest groups. Some of this increased role has been a shift from candidate to noncandidate spending. However, it is important to keep in mind that spending in state supreme court elections has tended to concentrate on a small number of elections in each cycle rather than being spread across a substantial proportion of the seats actually contested in an election cycle.

NATURE OF ADVERTISING: IS IT NASTIER OR JUST NOISIER?

Advertising in American Politics and Elections

The increased polarization in American politics over the last quarter century is evident in a variety of ways – the nature of election campaigns, campaigns to persuade members of Congress to support or oppose specific legislation, and the inability of Congress and the president, or the two

[38] In the 2013–2014 election cycle, candidates' campaigns paid for 39.1 percent of television ads, according to data reported by the Brennan Center.

parties in Congress (Hare and Pool 2014), to find common ground on many policy issues. One manifestation of this polarization has been the growth of attack ads in election campaigns, both those placed by candidates and parties and ads placed by interest and ideological groups (Hollihan 2009; Mark 2009). Neither advertising generally nor attack ads specifically are new in American politics (West 2014:1–2). Advertising in one form or another has been around as long as there have been elections, but the nature of the advertising has changed as the media available for advertising has changed (Hollihan 2009:136–66), and advertising has long included attacks on candidates.

Negative television advertisements appeared in the first presidential election that included any television ads, the 1952 election between Dwight Eisenhower and Adlai Stevenson (West 2014:2), although the birth of the television attack ad is sometimes traced to the "Daisy Spot," an advertisement run by Lyndon Johnson's presidential campaign in 1964 (Mark 2009:39–53).[39] Over the fifty years following the Daisy Spot, negative advertising became a central aspect of television advertising in presidential elections. Geer examined negative advertising from 1960 through 2008 by coding the appeals in ads run by the candidates and parties but not outside interest groups (Geer 2006:35); for the period 1960 through 2000, this amounted to 9,950 separate appeals in 795 ads.[40] In 1960, about 10 percent of appeals in the ads were negative; this jumped to 30 percent in 1964 and then fluctuated between about 20 percent and 25 percent through 1988. In 1992, more than 40 percent of the appeals were negative, jumping to 50 percent in 2004, and then about 65 percent in 2008 (Geer 2012:422).

The Wisconsin Advertising Project (WAP) and its successor, the Wesleyan Media Project (WMP), compiled television advertising information for all presidential and congressional elections between 2000 and 2012, except for 2006, using the resources of CMAG. The projects obtained from CMAG

39 The one-minute ad actually ran only once. It was an attack on the Republican presidential candidate, Senator Barry Goldwater of Arizona, whom Johnson wanted to portray as someone who would have an itchy finger on the nuclear trigger. The ad shows a young girl standing in a field picking petals off a daisy, and counting the petals as she does so. After a few seconds, her voice is replaced by a booming man's voice counting down for a missile launch, "Ten, nine, eight . . . " The ad closes with the visual switching to a nuclear explosion accompanied by the sound of a blast, followed by a final visual, "Vote for President Johnson on November 3," and the announcer saying, "The stakes are too high for you to stay home" (Hollihan 2009:155) .The ad is on YouTube, http://www.youtube.com/watch?v=63h_v6ufoAo (last visited, May 7, 2013).

40 Geer did not code ads by third-party candidates (e.g., Perot in 1992 and 1996). Geer's report (2012) extending the analysis through 2008 does not provide information on the number of appeals or ads coded.

information on number (and timing) of airings and estimated costs, and coded each ad both for content themes and for tone: whether the ad was promoting one candidate (promote), attacking a candidate (attack), or contrasting two or more candidates (contrast).[41] The percentage of airings comprised by attack ads increased from about 30 percent in 2000 to about 64 percent in 2012 in presidential general elections and from 32 percent to 52 percent in congressional elections (Fowler and Ridout 2013:58–59). If one combines attack ads with contrast ads which typically include negative content about the opposing candidate along with positive content about the favored candidate, the jumps are 60 percent to 86 percent in presidential general elections and 40 percent to 74 percent in congressional elections.[42] To state this another way, the proportion of positive, promote ad airings in presidential general elections dropped from 40 percent in 2000 to 14 percent in 2012; positive, promote ads in congressional went from 40 percent of airings to 26 percent of airings.

What about state-level elections? WAP and WMP have compiled and coded television advertisements that were run in gubernatorial elections for the same years for which they compiled data on congressional elections. In the 2000 election, 28 percent of airings in gubernatorial elections were attack ads, 22 percent were contrast ads, and 50 percent were promote ads. In 2010 and 2012, attack ads constituted 27 and 28 percent of airings;[43] between 2000 and 2012, promote ads have fluctuated between 46 and 60 percent, and contrast ads between 15 and 25 percent.[44] As I present the analysis of television advertising in state supreme court elections, it is important to put it into the

41 See Franz et al. (2008:36-5, 145–178) for details on the coding.

42 An analysis of congressional elections in 2000 and 2004 showed that the tone in competitive elections (accounting for about three-quarters of airings) was much less positive than in non-competitive elections (Franz et al. 2008:56).

43 Data for most years have now been released for analysis by other scholars, and I compiled most of the figures on advertising in gubernatorial from the raw data; the 2012 data have not yet been released, but the figures on ads in gubernatorial elections appeared in a conference paper (Salamone et al. 2014:15).

44 The full pattern (percentages may not add to 100 due to rounding) for gubernatorial elections is

	Promote	Attack	Contrast
2000	50%	28%	22%
2002	57%	27%	15%
2004	60%	24%	16%
2008	46%	29%	25%
2010	52%	27%	20%
2012	53%	28%	19%

perspective of political advertising more broadly, both in the longer term as described by Geer and in the period I will cover in some detail for which data are available from CMAG.

A related development has been the appearance of "issue ads" intended to put pressure on legislators considering proposed legislation or the confirmation of appointees by mobilizing or shifting public opinion. A prominent example in the judicial arena involved the nomination of Robert Bork to the U.S. Supreme Court, which produced a torrent of television advertising, heavily weighted in opposition to Bork's confirmation (Bronner 1989:147–49). Arguably one of the most successful issue ad campaigns appeared in 1993–94 in opposition to President Clinton's proposed healthcare reforms, particularly the ads featuring "Harry and Louise," a couple discussing how they would be hurt by the proposed reforms, which were sponsored by the Health Insurance Association of America (Brodie 2001; Kolbert 1995; West 1996).[45]

To the development of issue advertising one must add elements of the Supreme Court's 1976 decision in *Buckley v. Valeo* which limited the application of the Federal Election Campaign Act of 1971 to communications that employed one or more of what became known as the "eight magic words" in connection with the name of a candidate.[46] One result was to emphasize advertisements that omitted the eight magic words while criticizing or praising candidates for their positions or votes on issues. Some states extended the coverage of campaign regulation and reporting to include what has become known as "electioneering communications" which includes advertisements that clearly identify a candidate for elective office regardless of whether they use any of the eight magic words. In those states, expenditures on such communication may be subject to regulation and reporting if the advertisement is run within some specified period before the election, typically within thirty days before a primary or sixty days before a general election. While electioneering ads can attack candidates, promote candidates, or compare candidates, they are a particularly common vehicle used to attack a candidate.

Advertising in State Supreme Court Elections before 2000

As I will discuss, there appears to have been a change in television advertising in state supreme court elections around 2000, both in quantity and possibly

[45] At least some of the Harry and Louise ads are posted on YouTube.

[46] 424 U.S. 1 (1976). The "eight magic words" are actually eight words or phrases, or variations on those words or phrases: "vote for," "elect," "support," "cast your ballot for," "Smith for Congress," "vote against," "defeat," and "reject."

in tone. Unfortunately, systematic data regarding either the quantity or nature of advertising generally, or television advertising more specifically, in state supreme court elections do not exist for elections prior to 1999. Anecdotally we know that television advertising in state supreme court elections has been around since at least the 1970s (Philip et al. 1976:83), and negative television advertising since at least the 1980s (Brandenburg and Schotland 2008:1236). Attack ads were used in at least three states in the 1980s: Ohio, California, and Texas. In Ohio there was negative advertising in both 1984 and 1986 generally aimed at Chief Justice Frank Celebrezze, regarding his leadership and his decisions.[47]

As I will discuss in more detail in Chapter 7, Rose Bird was a controversial appointment as Chief Justice of California and attracted opposition from the start of her tenure. Under California law she had to stand for what in California is technically "confirmation" by the voters at the first nonpresidential general election which came in 1978. Bird's opponents had prepared television ads that opposed her confirmation (Rood 1978), and planned to spend $200,000 in the month before the election airing those ads around the state.[48] However, in the end they were able to air the ads only in some smaller markets (Endicott 1978c:7) because of the reluctance of stations to run the ads due to efforts by Bird's supporters, who complained that the ads were "inflammatory and inaccurate" and asked that they be given equal time if the ads were run.

Negative advertising figured prominently in the expensive and successful campaign eight years later in 1986 to unseat Bird and two of her colleagues on the California Supreme Court (Yoachum 1986). Crime Victims for Court Reform, one of the groups prominent in opposing Bird, "aired emotional, but effective, television advertisements against the justices" (Culver and Wold 1993:155; see also Thompson 1988:2039). One of those ads depicted "a mother complaining that the [California] Supreme Court had set aside the death penalty judgment against the murderer of her child and implying that the murderer was on the loose as a result" (Grodin 1989:178).[49] Another ad "told voters that if they wanted to keep the death penalty in California they should vote no on Bird, Reynoso, and Grodin" (179).

After some hesitation Bird and her colleagues did try to respond to these attacks, but the television ads that they ran were relatively low-key (Grodin 1989:179; Wold and Culver 1987:350; Yoachum 1986). In one of Bird's ads there

47 My thanks to Lawrence Baum, a longtime observer of supreme court elections in Ohio, for this information.

48 One of those ads was shown on the CBS Evening News, October 6, 1978.

49 The ad did not reveal that a second trial had occurred and the defendant had again been convicted and again sentenced to death.

is a very mild attack on those running ads against her, labeling them politicians. Grodin described three ads he ran, one picturing a superior court judge endorsing him, one promoting the fact that he had been endorsed by two police organizations, and a third picturing Grodin "saying something banal about the law" (Grodin 1989:179). Reynoso ran some ads similar to Grodin's (Hager 1986). Late in the campaign, one of the consultants Bird had dismissed was hired by a citizens' group that had been formed to defend the justices. That firm created an ad that depicted an assassin "assembling a machine gun out of paper money supplied by special interests funding the campaign to defeat the justices"; in the ad, "[a]s the assassin took aim at the justices, the narrator asked voters not to let the special interests use this weapon against the court" (Zimmerman 1986). Bird condemned the ad, which ran only a small number of times due to the limited funds available to purchase television time.

In Texas, negative advertising had started by 1986 when one candidate filed a grievance with the Judicial Conduct Commission against his three primary opponents, and then ran an ad proclaiming that his opponents were under investigation. The negative advertising in Texas increased in the 1990s. In a race in 1992, a candidate ran an ad along the lines of "I've studied [my opponent], and in my opinion he's going to jail."[50] Another Texas ad, run during the Democratic primary for the Texas Supreme Court that pitted a conservative Democratic incumbent against a challenger backed by the state's trial lawyers (Champagne and Cheek 2002:915–16), attacked the incumbent for having never handed out a death sentence since becoming a member of the court, ignoring the fact that appellate courts do not hand out sentences and that the Texas Supreme Court does not handle appeals in criminal cases.

The 1990s saw some particularly nasty advertising in contests for the Alabama Supreme Court. In the 1994 election, Ernest "Sonny" Hornsby ran an ad accusing his opponent, Perry Hooper, Sr., of "releasing a burglar who later murdered a woman," which prompted ads in response labeling Hornsby as "a typical trial attorney, exploiting victims in order to further [his] shallow political objectives" (Becker and Reddick 2003:15; Russakoff 1996). Two years later, things got even nastier in an election in which Democratic incumbent Justice Kenneth Ingram was challenged by Republican Harold See. A group calling itself the Committee for Family Valuesthat actually was financed by several trial lawyers, ran advertisements accusing See of having a "secret past" and of having "abandoned his wife and two children, [having] had a love affair... and [having] fled

50 While this may seem like an absurd claim to make about an opponent, recall the discussion on Don Yarbrough in Chapter 2; while he did win the 1976 election for the Texas Supreme Court, he eventually ended up in jail (see Holder 1980:190–93).

Illinois for Alabama" (Russakoff 1996). Ingram ran what became known as the "skunk ad" which featured a picture of a skunk fading into a picture of See with the words "Slick Chicago Lawyer" plastered over See's face.

Television advertising in Wisconsin Supreme Court elections goes back to at least the 1980s, and there was at least one negative ad run in the 1990 election between incumbent Justice Donald Steinmetz and challenger, Appeals Court judge Richard Brown; Steinmetz ran an ad that linked his challenger to trial lawyers who in fact were supporting Brown. In the 1997 election incumbent Jon Wilcox, who had been appointed by Republican governor Tommy Thompson in 1992, was opposed by Walt Kelly, a civil rights and labor lawyer from Milwaukee (Segall 1997). Wilcox's campaign ran television ads "assailing the fact that the American Civil Liberties Union had honored Kelly ... [and] also denounced Kelly's role in the early 1970s as the executive secretary" of an agency "that funded and staffed a citizens committee that recommended closing prisons and considering legalizing marijuana" (Pommer 1997). Earlier campaigns in Wisconsin had seen television advertising as well, although it is unclear whether any of that advertising had a negative tone (Jones 1995; and "Editorial: Voters Can Judge for Themselves" 1996).

While the elections and states described stand out by the presence of negative TV ads, we also know that advertising occurred in other state supreme court elections as well. In Michigan, a consortium of business groups known as M-Law spent more than $300,000 on television advertising in 1996 and around $50,000 in 1998 (Echeverria 2000:278, 285).

Advertising in State Supreme Court Elections in the Twenty-first Century

As noted previously, the Brennan Center has assembled much of the CMAG data on advertising in state supreme court elections. For many of the years, staff at the Center coded each spot as to whether it "promotes" a candidate, "contrasts" two or more candidates, or "attacks" a candidate. For the other years, I coded the spots into one of the three categories.[51]

[51] Brennan staff did not code elections in odd years, nor had they coded the 2012 election ads by the time of my analysis. Brennan staff had coded the ads from the 2000 election, and Goldberg et al. (2000:15–17) report some summary tallies; unfortunately, the original codings appear to have been lost, which meant that the ads from 2000 had to be recoded. For the 2012 ads I had access to all of the storyboards, and they were the basis of my coding. For the other years I had access to most of the storyboards. Where no storyboard was available I coded based on the ad title if that title seemed pretty clear; where the title was unclear, I sought out additional information either by contacting people who I thought might recall the ad or by doing searches based on the ad title. In the end, I was able to code almost all of the ads for which no coding information was available from the Brennan Center. The data and coding for several years were provided to me by Melinda Gann Hall.

Between 1999 and 2013, there were 226 retention elections plus 242 contested seats in states using partisan, nonpartisan, or hybrid elections; only 153 of these 468 elections involved any television advertising. At the extreme, opponents or supporters ran television advertisements in only sixteen of the retention elections. Four of these were a set of elections in Oklahoma which featured a single ad promoting a "Yes" vote to retain all four justices. Another four were in Iowa (2010 and 2012), three were in Florida (2012), three were in Pennsylvania (2005 and 2007), and there was one each in Alaska (2010) and Illinois (2010).[52] Advertising was much more common in the contested supreme court seats in states using partisan, nonpartisan, or hybrid elections. Among those 242 elections, 137 (56 percent) involved at least one television advertisement, but only 49 (20 percent) involved one or more attack ads. Television advertising was slightly more likely in open-seat elections (62 percent vs. 54 percent), but attack ads were slightly more likely in elections with an incumbent (21 percent vs. 17 percent); however, neither of these differences was even close to achieving statistical significance.[53] Looking at the form of election, the two states with hybrid elections (Michigan and Ohio) stand out with 97 percent of the elections between 2000 and 2012 involving at least some television advertising; only one of the thirty-one contested elections in those two states during this period did not involve advertising.[54] Regarding partisan and nonpartisan states, there was at best a small difference, with televised ads appearing in 47 percent of partisan elections and 54 percent of nonpartisan elections. Regarding the use of attack ads, 42 percent of the contested elections in hybrid election states involved attack ads, compared to 17 percent and 16 percent in the partisan and nonpartisan states.[55]

The larger question here is how has advertising changed, if at all, over the period 1999 to 2012?[56] It is possible that there has been a major change in the volume and/or tone of advertising in state supreme court elections other than in retention elections where advertising has remained quite rare. Figure 5.14

[52] Four of the thirty-three retention elections in 2014 involved television advertising, and it was heavily in the form of attack ads. In fact, 69 percent of the expenditure on attack ads in 2014 occurred in these four elections, one of which was in Illinois. with the remaining three in Tennessee.

[53] The respective chi squares were 1.36 and 0.39; 69 of the 241 elections were open-seat elections, leaving 172 that involved incumbents.

[54] All five of the 2014 election campaigns in Michigan and Ohio involved television advertising.

[55] Chi square tests involving the three categories of election types were statistically significant (chi squares of 24.49 and 10.87, df=2).

[56] Because for purposes of the advertising analysis I have grouped odd-year elections with the following even year, the 2013 Wisconsin election, which involved contrast ads but no attack ads, is not included here.

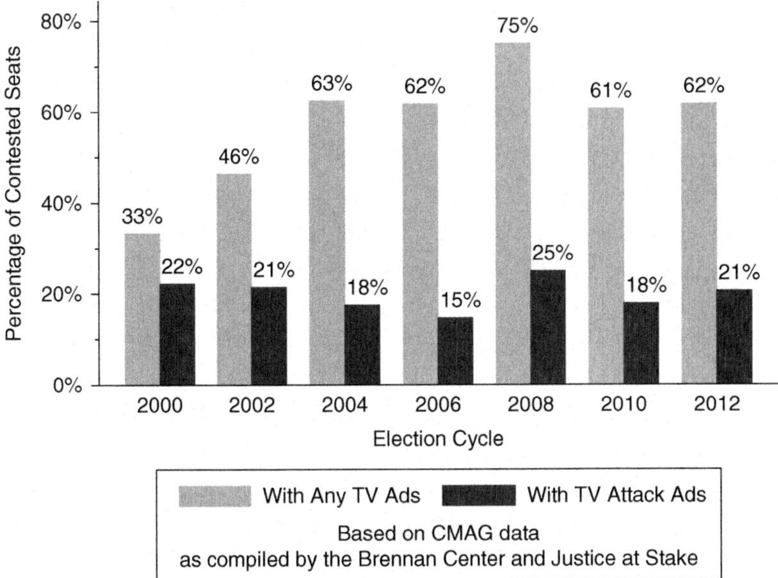

FIGURE 5.14. Appearance of Television Advertising, 1999–2012.

shows the percentage of contested seats in partisan, hybrid, and nonpartisan elections that involved any type of television advertising and the percentage that involved one or more attack ads. Assuming that the 2000 election cycle did not represent a drop in television advertising from prior years, television advertising has become more common, rising from about a third of contested state supreme court elections in the 2000 election cycle to a bit under two-thirds of elections by the 2012 election cycle. Importantly, the proportion of contested elections that involve attack ads has essentially remained constant, fluctuating around 20 percent. Both the percentage of contested elections with any advertising and the percentage with attack ads appear to have peaked in the 2008 election cycle.

Has the intensity of the advertising increased over the period? Figure 5.15 shows the number of airings for each type of advertisement along with the total number of airings. Consistent with the increased spending on advertising, the total number of airings has increased over time (even taking into account that fewer markets were covered in earlier election cycles). However, the bulk of the increase has been in the form of ads promoting a candidate. There clearly was a blip in attack ads in the 2007–08 election cycle when the number of attack ad airings jumped to 21,780 from 7,008 in the 2005–06 election cycle, an increase of 14,772. Almost all of that increase can be explained by Wisconsin where, combining the two elections that occurred in 2007 and

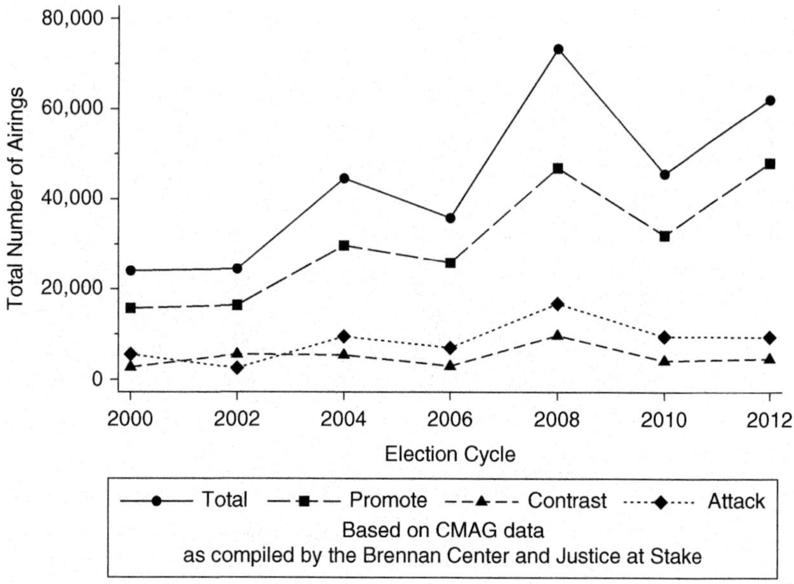

FIGURE 5.15. Number of Television Ad Airings by Ad Tone, 1999–2012.

2008, there were 13,380 airings of attack ads; another 4,796 attack ad airings occurred in Michigan in 2008. After that election cycle, the number of attack ads fell back to a level close to what occurred in 2003–2006, while the number of promote and contrast ads fell only very slightly. Clearly there has been at least some increase in the number of attack ads, but leaving aside 2007–08, that increase is best understood as part of the overall growth in the number of ad airings in state supreme court elections.

Figure 5.16 shows the distribution among promote, contrast, and attack. This figure makes it clear that with the exceptions of 2000 and 2008, attack ads have consistently constituted 20 percent or less of ad airings identified by CMAG. There is no evidence that over the seven election cycles between 2000 and 2012 television advertising in state supreme court elections got nastier in relation to the overall volume of television ads aired in those elections, and that is true even after controlling for whether an election is partisan, nonpartisan, or hybrid. Arguably, state supreme court elections became somewhat nastier after 2000 in the sense that there was much less television advertising prior to that year, and hence voters were not likely to see many attack ads. However, as discussed earlier in this chapter, there has been negative television advertising in state supreme court elections at least as far back as the 1980s, but we have no way of knowing whether the proportion of ad airings comprised of attack ads has in fact increased or stayed the same compared to that earlier period

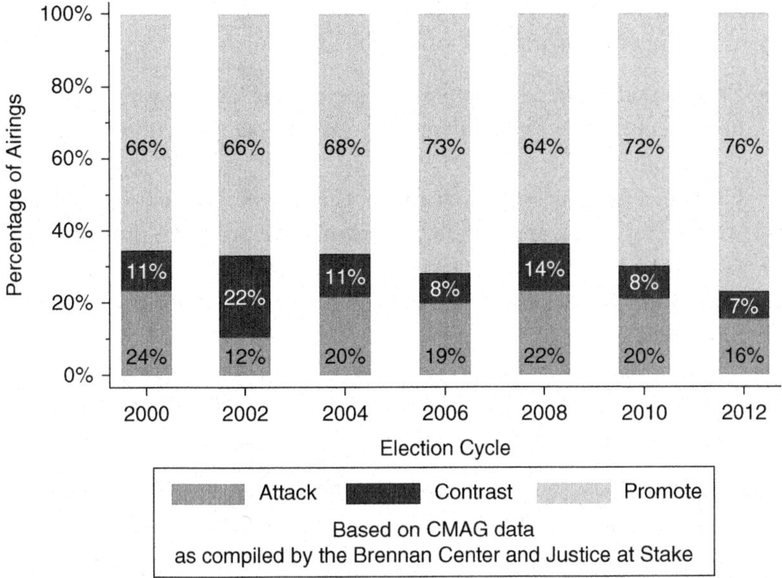

FIGURE 5.16. Distribution Ad Airings by Tone and Election Cycle, 1999–2012.

because no systematic data are available on the nature or volume of television advertising in state supreme court elections prior to 1999.[57]

One interesting implication of these findings is that, contrary to some predictions (see Caufield 2007), there does not appear to have been a significant impact on the *relative* tone in state supreme court elections as a result of the 2002 U.S. Supreme Court decision in *Republican Party of Minnesota v. White*,[58] which lifted many of the restrictions on what candidates running in judicial elections can say. The election that took place only months after the *White* decision actually had the lowest level of attack ads over the period examined, and later years resembled the pattern in the period just before the decision. The absolute number of television airings of attack ads has increased somewhat since 2002, but that is more a part of the overall increase in the number of ad airings.

Finally, the relative tone of television advertising in state supreme court elections continues to be very different from what one sees in the other

57 To my knowledge, the only organization to systematically collect data on televised campaign advertising is CMAG. While CMAG first began operation in April 1996 (Goldstein and Freedman 2002:727n7), the first available ads for state supreme court elections are from 1999.

58 536 U.S. 765 (2002).

elections that attract substantial television advertising. Just to use the 2012 election as a point of comparison, consider the following:

- Presidential (general) election: 64 percent of airings were attack ads, 86 percent were either attack or contrast, 14 percent were positive ("promote") ads.
- Congressional elections: 52 percent of airings were attack ads; 74 percent were either attack or contrast; 26 percent were positive ("promote") ads.
- Gubernatorial elections (2011–12): 28 percent of airings were attack ads; 47 percent were either attack or contrast; 53 percent were positive ("promote") ads.
- State supreme court elections (2011–12): 16 percent of airings were attack ads; 24 percent were either attack or contrast; 76 *percent were* ***positive*** *("promote") ads*!

Compared to television advertising in other relatively visible elections, state supreme court election advertising overall continues to be very positive.

Impacts of Advertising in State Supreme Court Elections

What impact, if any, has television advertising, particularly negative advertising, had on state supreme court elections? There are at least two types of impacts negative advertising might have on elections: on voter participation and on voter choice.

Political scientists have debated the question of whether negative advertising serves to turn off voters and hence reduce participation in elections, or alternatively serves to mobilize voters and increase participation (Ansolabehere and Iyengar 1995; Lau 2007; Lau et al. 1999; Wattenberg and Brians 1999).[59] In the context of state supreme court elections, Hall and Bonneau (2013) examined elections in 2002, 2004, and 2006, and found no decrease in turnout in state supreme court elections with attack ads. If anything, the turnout in those elections was higher, but whether there is a causal effect is debatable. A later analysis extended the years covered to include 2008, with no change in the results or conclusions (Hall 2014a:147–57).

A second question concerning the impact of negative advertising on elections is whether attack ads help or hurt a candidate's performance in the election. Hall (2014b) looked at three election years (2002, 2004, and 2006), focusing on elections in which an incumbent was challenged. She found that challengers in nonpartisan elections increased their vote share by airing more

[59] See Hall (2014a:129–31) for a brief review of the literature on the impact of negative advertising.

negative advertising than did the incumbent; she found no effect in partisan elections. Again, extending the analysis to include 2008 does not change the overall results or conclusions, although there is some evidence that advertising that attacks incumbents in partisan elections is, if anything, associated with an *increase* in the incumbent's vote share (Hall 2014a:113).

SUMMARY AND CONCLUSION

The core questions addressed in this chapter were whether change had occurred either in the cost of state supreme court campaigns or in the nature and/or volume of television advertising in those campaigns. The information available limits the span of time available for systematic analysis to a shorter period than is the case for the discussions in other chapters. The basic answer to both the question of whether there has been change regarding campaign expenditures and the question of whether change has occurred in television advertising is "yes," but that answer must be conditioned on what baseline one chooses to use.

If the baseline for comparison is 1980 or earlier, we can say that state supreme court elections have changed along the dimensions discussed in this chapter. However, one must take note that these same changes took place for elections more generally, and reflected the changing technology available for election campaigns as well as broad shifts in the dynamics of politics in the United States. What the analysis in this chapter indicates is that the period of change was 1980–2004, and that between 2004 and 2012 there was relatively little additional change, with one possible exception. That exception is the growth in the role of groups not associated with the candidates' campaign committees. However, even that may depend in significant part on state law with regard to campaign contributions and expenditures. In some states it does appear that outside groups have changed the nature of the campaigns (e.g., Wisconsin), while in others the change may be more of a shift of the center of gravity without a lot of change in the content or tone of campaigns (e.g., Michigan).

An important caveat regarding any change that has occurred is that it is far from universal. As shown in Chapter 4, a large proportion of state supreme court elections continue to be uncontested, which means there is little or no campaign expenditure in those elections. Only a relatively small proportion of state supreme court elections feature any televised attack ads, although television advertising more generally does appear now to be a common part of supreme court elections involving two or more candidates, while remaining rare in retention elections. Regardless of whether change continued after 2004 or simply reflects the broader changes in electioneering more generally, critics of judicial elections look aghast at how at least some state supreme court elections are now conducted (Brandenburg and Schotland 2008; Geyh 2003; O'Connor 2010).

So what has been the impact of the shift to noisier, nastier, and more costly election campaigns to obtain and retain seats on state supreme courts? Undoubtedly in some elections it has affected the outcome of the election. Examples would almost certainly include the 2008 election in Wisconsin discussed in Chapter 1, the recapture of control of the Texas Supreme Court by conservative business interests in Texas in the late 1980s and early 1990s, the 2004 election in West Virginia that ultimately led to the U.S. Supreme Court's 2009 decision in *Caperton v. A.T. Massey Coal Co.* (Leamer 2013), the defeat of Rose Bird and two of her colleagues on the California Supreme Court in 1986, and probably the defeat of the Iowa justices in 2010. Elections do produce outcomes, and those outcomes have winners and losers. It is very clear that the American electorate likes elections, and that extends to selecting judges. There are many issues created by use of elections for lesser offices, only some of which are unique to judgeships.[60] However, elections do require voters to obtain information, and voters tend to be passive recipients rather than seekers of information to inform their votes. Election campaigns, and campaign advertising more particularly, provide information. Negative advertising, while it can be deceptive and dishonest, often provides information that is more useful than the more common judicial ad which either pictures a judicial candidate talking about his or her background and experience or features someone endorsing the candidate.

Critics of elections see fundraising and advertising as two evils that undermine the public's confidence and trust in the courts. Regarding the former, as discussed in Chapter 3, the public is concerned about the contributions that judicial candidates must have to mount an informative campaign, but that appears to be offset by the positive effects of the elections themselves. As for negative advertising, there is no evidence to date that such advertising has negative consequences for the public's view of the courts, perhaps in part because voters have become somewhat inured to such ads by the overwhelming dominance of negative ads in other elections that involve a lot of television advertising.

[60] Chapter 2 discusses some of these issues, particularly the problem of name confusion.

6

Patterns of Partisanship in Contested Elections

In Chapter 1 I introduced the "partisan correlation": the correlation between the county-level vote pattern in the gubernatorial election and the county-level vote pattern in the state supreme court election. In that chapter I showed how the partisan correlation in Wisconsin had increased starting in 1997, while in Minnesota it was essentially stable over the period starting in 1950. Examining changes in the patterns of partisan correlations provides a vehicle for assessing the changing politics of state supreme court elections, and in this chapter I extend my analysis of partisan correlations to include all states using partisan, nonpartisan, or hybrid statewide elections between 1946 and 2013. Importantly, the absence of a strong partisan correlation does not indicate the absence of politics in an election because elections by definition involve politics, but the partisan correlation is a useful indicator of a certain type of politics.

Historically, the avoidance of the politics of party partisanship was a major goal of reform advocates who supported the switch to nonpartisan elections and those reformers who later worked for the adoption of the Missouri Plan. While nonpartisan elections and the Missouri Plan change the nature of the politics involved in judicial selection and retention, they by no means remove politics. Moreover, for purposes of understanding the nature of much of the politics involved in contemporary judicial selection and retention, the partisan correlation is useful because divisions on the kinds of issues that often generate controversy in state supreme court elections – the death penalty, abortion, same-sex marriage, property rights, and tort reform – tend to align with the perceived positions of the Democratic and Republican parties.

In the following sections of this chapter I will first discuss prior research that has considered partisanship in judicial elections, including several studies that have relied on the partisan correlation measure followed by a discussion of various data and methodological issues. The analysis section of the chapter considers separately the patterns of stability and change for partisan, nonpartisan, and hybrid supreme court elections. The analysis shows that, not surprisingly, there has been a consistent pattern of strong partisan correlations in partisan elections, but that there are important changes in many, *but not all,* states that use nonpartisan or hybrid elections. Through discussions of specific elections producing strong partisan patterns in states using nonpartisan elections, I argue that it is past or anticipated court decisions on issues with strong partisan overtones that account for much of the strong partisanship in those elections. Thus, analysis supports one of the main contentions introduced in Chapter 1 in my comparison of Wisconsin and Minnesota: voters will respond in partisan ways when asked to vote on judicial candidates tied to positions on issues that divide the electorate along partisan lines, and partisan voting patterns will not develop when courts have not had to decide highly partisan issues. Moreover, repeating an observation by G. Alan Tarr quoted in Chapter 1, there has been an "increasing involvement of courts, particularly in recent decades, in addressing issues with far-reaching policy consequences" (Tarr 2003:6).

PRIOR RESEARCH ON PARTISAN PATTERNS IN STATE SUPREME COURT ELECTIONS

Studies Relying on Aggregate Data

The earliest empirical research on judicial elections was by Edward Martin (1936a; see also Martin 1936b), who examined judicial elections for trial courts in Chicago. Martin's primary focus was on the role of the bar, not on the role of partisanship. However, Martin did devote a chapter to discussing how partisan politics affected the influence of the bar (249–310). According to Martin, the political parties played a central role in the selection of candidates through a system of sponsorship that served the parties' goal of doling out patronage (252–57). To counter the role of partisan politics, the local bar association attempted to put forth an "independent" slate of candidates for the bench, but those slates were overwhelmed by the party-backed candidates (271). Unfortunately, Martin presented no data on voting patterns in these elections that would have provided information on how the voters responded to the partisan slates.[1]

[1] Given that the elections were conducted on a partisan basis, and voters had the option of voting straight-party tickets as indicated in a sample ballot for the Municipal Court judgeships included in Martin's book (228), strong patterns of partisan voting were highly likely. More recently, Champagne (2006; see also Jefferson and Kourlis 2010; Tolson 2012) has discussed the impact of straight-ticket voting in some Texas trial court elections in the last decade.

In states that elect judges on a partisan basis, it would not be surprising that the votes cast for judicial candidates for a particular party closely track votes for other partisan offices elected at the same level. An early study from West Virginia showed this rather dramatically. Davis (1959: 27) compared the percentage of the vote going to the Democratic candidate for the West Virginia Supreme Court of Appeals on a quadrennial basis from 1928 through 1956 to the average percentage voting Democratic for the other state-level officers comprising the Board of Public Works (omitting the governor), and found that the difference was never more than three-quarters of a percentage point.[2] He also looked at voting for the Circuit Court (judges) in 1952, and found a similar, but less stark, pattern (28). Again, the presence of partisan patterns of voting in partisan elections should not be surprising.

Kathleen Barber (1971) may have been the first scholar to examine empirically the role of partisanship in state supreme court elections that are nominally nonpartisan. Barber focused her attention on Ohio, one of the two states that continue to employ the hybrid system whereby parties are central to the nominating process either through primaries or conventions but the general election ballot is nonpartisan with no party designation for candidates for the state supreme court. This system raises interesting questions, including to what degree voters respond in partisan patterns in the absence of partisan signals on the ballot when candidates are designated through a partisan system. To look at this, Barber employed what I have labeled partisan correlations. She showed that across adjacent partisan elections for offices such as governor, the correlations approached or exceeded .90 (778). The correlation between the partisan elections and elections for the Ohio Supreme Court tended to be lower, varying around .50 (779); she highlighted the anomalous election mentioned in Chapter 2 in which there was a partisan correlation of −.42 arising from candidates whose names mistakenly led some voters to think that the Republican was a Democrat and that the Democrat was a Republican.[3]

Adamany and Dubois (1976: 756–60) extended the use of partisan correlations to two states employing partisan elections (New York and Pennsylvania),

[2] Davis explains that he omitted vote for governor "on the assumption that a less partisan vote was cast for that office"; he goes on to note that "[h]ad the vote for governor been included, ... the percentage would not have changed substantially" (28).

[3] The candidate nominated by the Democratic Party was named Allen Brown and the candidate nominated by the Republicans was named J.J.P. Corrigan, names that at the time in Ohio had been long associated with the Republican and Democratic parties respectively. The "Brown" phenomenon in Ohio Supreme Court elections is interesting. Between 1960 and 1980, 12 of 60 candidates in contested supreme court elections were named Brown, and two were Brown v. Brown (Barber 1982: 30). Between 1982 and 2012, only three Browns ran for the Ohio Supreme Court, and all three were Democrats.

two states employing the hybrid system (Ohio and Michigan), and one nonpartisan state (Wisconsin), examining elections for the period 1958 through 1969. They limited their analysis of Wisconsin elections to three contested elections in which the candidates were clearly identified with the two parties (omitting five contested elections during the period in which the candidates were not so identified). Not surprisingly, the average partisan correlations for the two partisan states were very high, .86 and .92 for New York and Pennsylvania respectively. For the hybrid states, the average partisan correlations were .41 and .51 for Michigan and Ohio respectively. For the three Wisconsin elections examined, the average partisan correlation was only .21, even though many knowledgeable voters would probably have been aware of the partisan backgrounds of the candidates in those elections.

In subsequent work, Dubois (1978, 1979, 1980) extended the analysis to all nonsouthern states employing partisan or nonpartisan statewide general elections sometime during the period 1948 through 1974. Even for the states covered, there are two limitations to Dubois's study. First, he excluded elections in nonpartisan states in which he could not link at least one of the candidates with a political party (Dubois 1980: 73). The second limitation was that he considered only general elections which eliminated many contests in those nonpartisan states where no general election was held if a candidate won a majority in the primary; as discussed in Chapter 2, in those states a primary is held even if there are only two candidates. This means that all two-candidate elections, plus some three-candidate elections, in Washington, Oregon, and Idaho were determined in the primary. Because between 1948 and 1974 only one election in Oregon had been contested at the general election, Dubois omitted that state entirely from his analysis (Dubois 1980: 75).

Dubois correlated the county-by-county pattern for a supreme court election with either the contemporaneous gubernatorial election or the immediately preceding gubernatorial election if there was no contemporaneous gubernatorial election. Dubois reported an average partisan correlation of .84 for partisan states, .44 for hybrid states,[4] and .22 for nonpartisan states (Dubois 1980: 74–76). For partisan states, the state-level means ranged from .67 to .92, with all but one .78 or higher; for the hybrid states the state-level means ranged from .40 to .47; for nonpartisan states the range was .03 to .37 (Dubois 1980: 75).[5]

4 Dubois included Arizona among the hybrid states; Arizona changed to a "merit" system in 1974.

5 Dubois also reports the ranges for the states and the standard deviations. For the partisan states the standard deviations are, with one exception, less than .10; for the other states the standard deviations are, with one exception, greater than .10 and range up to .33. For the hybrid and nonpartisan states, a number of elections produce negative correlations, with the highest being −.49 in an election in Wyoming. Dubois describes the Wyoming election, which occurred in 1956, as having "defied explanation" (Dubois 1978: 172).

The use of aggregate data in this fashion raises the question of the often discussed problem of ecological correlations (Robinson 1950). Specifically, there can be problems inferring individual behavior from correlations based on aggregate data. One issue is that the strength of the relationship measured at the aggregate level will normally be much stronger than what one would find at the individual level. For the analysis here, that means that if one were to look at individual level voting data and compute the correlation between an individual's votes for governor and for state supreme court, the relationship one would observe would be much weaker than those I report for the aggregate data. Nonetheless, the correlations I present based on the aggregate data are generally good indicators of the *relative* strength of the underlying individual voting patterns, and it is the relative strength, both across different types of election systems and across time, that is the focus of my interest.

However, the problem with ecological correlations is not necessarily limited to the aggregate correlations exceeding what one would find at the individual level. It is possible that the direction of the relationship observed at the aggregate level would be the opposite of what one would obtain if the analysis were based on individual level data (King 1997:15). This would be a potential problem if one is computing a small number of aggregate correlations. However, the analysis that follows is based on almost 900 correlations, and the likelihood that more than a small handful of these correlations reflect a mischaracterization of the direction of the relationship is virtually nil. Finally, my interest here is not in attempting to estimate the correlation for the individuals; my interest is in the aggregate patterns themselves because they are a good indicator of how the structure of the election affects broad electoral patterns.

Studies Relying on Individual Level Data

The research examining the role of partisanship in voting for state supreme court justices using individual level data is much more limited. Lawrence Baum, working with two different collaborators, has conducted a series of analyses of voting in Ohio Supreme Court elections using survey data (Baum 1987; Baum and Klein 2007; Klein and Baum 2001; Rock and Baum 2010). These surveys included nonpresidential year elections occurring over a twenty-year period, 1986 to 2006, plus 1984. The thrust of these findings is that, even in the absence of party labels on the general election ballot, the voters' party identification does predict which of the party-nominated candidates the voters back. Moreover, the size of the effect of party identification is greater in elections with substantial media attention and substantial campaign expenditures.

The only national study that looks closely at voting in state supreme court elections with a primary focus on partisanship is by Bonneau and Cann (2015). Their research employed national surveys from 2010 and 2012, and included ten states in each of the two election years, covering a total of thirty-one contested single-seat elections (40).[6] They report strong partisanship effects, both in a simple tabular analysis and using a multivariate model, for *both* partisan and nonpartisan elections (41–49).[7] At least for 2012, for which they had a large sample, the partisanship effect is stronger in partisan elections, as one would expect. These patterns hold up even after controlling for the voter's ideology and the amount of spending by the candidates' campaigns which the authors intend as a proxy for election intensity (49–55).

The work by Baum and colleagues and by Bonneau and Cann support the significance of partisanship as a factor in state supreme court elections regardless of ballot form. However, each has limits. Baum et al. focused on only one state, Ohio, and that state's hybrid system using party primaries to select candidates to run in nonpartisan general election is unique. Bonneau and Cann's work covers only two recent elections which cannot tell us what, if anything, has changed over time. Additionally, while their analysis includes a range of control variables, those variables do not fully capture state differences; that is, the pattern for nonpartisan elections may depend significantly on developments in the states involved, and particularly the kinds of issues that the state supreme court has been called on to decide. The advantage of the aggregate analyses presented in this chapter is that they allow for an examination of patterns in individual states and for identification of where change has and has not occurred over the sixty-eight years covered by my analysis.

DATA AND METHOD

The analysis presented here replicates and extends Dubois's analysis. I assembled data on the county-level votes for all contested partisan and nonpartisan statewide elections for state supreme court for the period 1946 through 2012. I included the southern and border states that Dubois excluded, although for the period Dubois considered there were a very small number of contested *general* elections. Two states, Texas and Oklahoma,[8] have separate courts of last resort for criminal cases, and I included elections for those courts if they

6 Their analysis excluded multi-seat elections in Michigan and West Virginia.

7 In the analyses Bonneau and Cann report, they treat Ohio as a nonpartisan state; however, they also report (5) that they repeated the analysis treating Ohio as partisan, and this had "no substantively meaningful effect on the results."

8 Oklahoma switched to a "merit" system in 1967.

otherwise fit my criteria for inclusion. For nonpartisan states in which winning a majority in the primary obviates the need for a general election, I included data on those primaries in which the leading candidate obtained an absolute majority. Unlike Dubois, I did not limit the nonpartisan elections to those where one or both candidates could somehow be identified with a political party. The analysis presented includes 393 partisan contests, 172 contests from hybrid states, and 328 from nonpartisan states.

As discussed in Chapter 2, there have been many changes in how states select and retain justices for their highest courts since 1946, and consequently the states included in the analysis constituted a changing cast of characters, as detailed in Figure 2.2. As indicated in that figure, Illinois,[9] New Mexico, and Pennsylvania now use partisan elections for the election following the occurrence of a vacancy on the court with the winner of that election standing in a retention election if the incumbent desires to remain in office for additional terms.[10] By 2012, there were thirteen fewer states using partisan or nonpartisan elections for retention and sometimes for initial selection compared to 1946, plus three states that use partisan elections only for selection for an initial full term.

As discussed in Chapter 4, data for recent elections were generally available online.[11] For earlier elections I relied on the variety of sources previously described. Where the county-level data were not in machine-readable form, I OCR'ed or keyed the data by hand. Part of the data entry process involved cross-checking the totals from the data entry with the election totals. In a small number of cases I was not able to match my total to the reported total, and I have no way of knowing whether the reported total was incorrect or whether one or more counties were incorrectly recorded. In some cases the problem may lie in the readability of copies obtained from archives. For a few

9 Illinois, along with Kentucky, Louisiana, Mississippi, Maryland, South Dakota (through 1978 after which the state changed to a "merit" system with retention elections on a statewide basis), and Nebraska (except for the chief justice) elect or retain members of the supreme court by district; except for elections for Nebraska's chief justice, these states are omitted from the analysis in this chapter. Several other states associate members of their courts of last resort with districts (presumably requiring residence in the district), but all voters in the state can vote on all members.

10 In New Mexico and Pennsylvania, the governor can appoint someone to fill the vacancy when it occurs, and the appointee can then run in the subsequent partisan election, although by tradition interim appointees do not run in Pennsylvania. In Illinois the remaining members of the supreme court select someone to fill the vacancy and that person can run in the subsequent partisan election.

11 The county-level gubernatorial data came primarily from either the Interuniversity Consortium for Political and Social Research for years through 1990 (in ICPSR Studies 1 and 13), or from machine readable information available through CQ Press's Voting and Elections Collection for most later years. The most recent years came from state election websites.

elections, I was able to identify what appeared to be a clear error for a county and could make a correction that allowed me to match the overall total. In a small number of elections no information was available for a small number of counties, and those counties were omitted from the calculation of the correlation coefficient for that election.

For judicial elections that were not concurrent with a gubernatorial election, Dubois used the county-level results for the previous gubernatorial election (which was usually two years before).[12] I adopted a slightly different approach. Specifically, when there was no concurrent gubernatorial election, I averaged the county-level percentages from preceding and succeeding gubernatorial elections. In those situations in which the supreme court election was one year from one gubernatorial election and three years from the other, I used a weighted average of the county-level percentages for the two elections.[13]

Another issue is how to handle multi-seat elections in which the candidates do not run for specific seats. In those elections, if there are X seats up for election voters can cast X votes, and the top X candidates win the seats. I followed Dubois's handling of this issue for partisan elections (Dubois 1980: 274n42): I paired the top vote-getting Republican with the bottom Democrat, the top Democrat with the bottom Republican, and the middle Democrat with the middle Republican if there were three seats open. In nonpartisan elections, I matched the candidate with the most votes with the candidate with the least votes, the candidate with the second most with the candidate with the second least, etc. If there were more than twice the number of candidates running as there were seats, I dropped the lowest candidates and then matched the remaining candidates as described. If there were fewer than twice the number of candidates as seats (there was never more than one fewer), I treated the candidate getting the most votes as unopposed and did not include that candidate in the analysis I present here.

[12] Dubois (1980:273n42) does not explain his choice in this regard. The approach that I used sought to make the best use of information on contemporaneous voting patterns in gubernatorial elections; using the average of preceding and succeeding elections provides a more robust estimate of what the gubernatorial voting pattern would have been if the supreme court and gubernatorial elections had been contemporaneous. Moreover, unlike Dubois, I had access to that information in electronic form using ICPSR studies that were not released until 1984, several years after Dubois's book was published; to use my approach, Dubois would have had to key a lot of additional sets of election returns.

[13] For nonpartisan states in which winning an absolute majority in the primary was determinative, I treated the primary as occurring at the time of the general election for purposes of matching to gubernatorial election returns. In the case of Wisconsin, which holds judicial elections in April, I treated the April election as if it occurred the previous November (or the following November if there was a gubernatorial election in the same calendar year).

While most elections involved only two candidates on the ballot, there were occasional situations with more than two candidates. This could arise when a third-party candidate ran, or in one of the nonpartisan states where there would not be a general election if a candidate won more than 50 percent in the primary. In either of these situations, I computed the vote percentage based only on the top two candidates in the statewide results.

Lastly, as noted previously, I included all contested nonpartisan elections. Unlike Dubois, I did not limit my analysis to those nonpartisan elections in which one or both candidates had some link to one of the political parties, and I made no effort to identify those candidates who could be linked to a party. Consequently, for nonpartisan elections I present results based on the absolute value of the correlation. I treat hybrid systems separately for purposes of this analysis; this includes all elections in Michigan and Ohio, and elections in Arizona prior to its switch to the Missouri Plan.

ANALYSIS

General Patterns

For the entire period studied, the average partisan correlations are .87 for partisan elections, .48 for hybrid elections, and .34 for nonpartisan elections.[14] Controlling for election system, the average partisan correlation differs little depending on whether or not an incumbent is running: .88 with an incumbent and .85 without an incumbent for partisan election states, .47 and .51 for hybrid election states, .33 and .37 for nonpartisan election states.[15] Consequently, in the analysis that follows, I do not differentiate between elections involving incumbents and open-seat elections.

14 For the period examined by Dubois (1948–74), the corresponding averages are .86, .43, and .27. The averages reported by Dubois (1980: 74–76) are .84, .44, and .22. Dubois's averages are actually the average of the state averages rather than the average correlation across all elections of a given type. Computing across the elections, the means for Dubois's data are .85, .44, and .24 (computed from data listed in table 10 in Dubois, 1980: 75; there appears to be a minor typo in the table: the mean for Washington should be shown as .24 not .18). As noted previously, I used absolute correlations for the nonpartisan states; the average of the absolute values of the correlations Dubois reports for the nonpartisan states is .29.The correlations for individual elections are reported in Dubois's dissertation (1978:143–45, 150–53).

15 T-tests for each of these comparisons show that the differences for hybrid and nonpartisan states are not statistically significant, while the smaller difference for partisan states, which is actually a *decline*, is significant at the .05 level. The statistical significance reflects the combination of larger n's and lower standard deviations; the standard deviations for hybrid and nonpartisan states are around .24 while for the partisan states the standard deviations are less than half that.

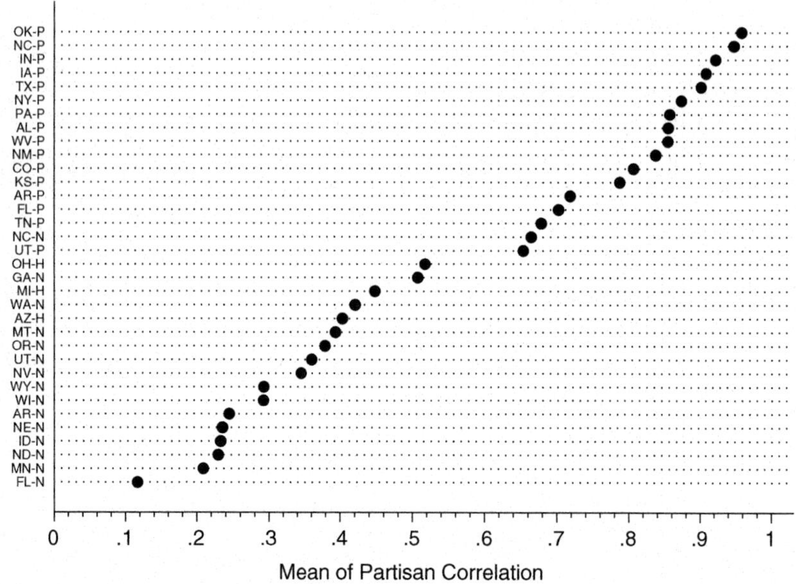

Note: The letter following the state abbreviation indicates the type of election: **P** for partisan, **N** for nonpartisan, **H** for hybrid.

FIGURE 6.1. Mean Partisan Correlations by State.

Figure 6.1 shows the mean correlation by state over the entire time period. The letter appended to the state abbreviation indicates the type of electoral system (**P**artisan, **H**ybrid, or **N**onpartisan). For states that shifted from partisan to nonpartisan elections, the state is shown twice except for Georgia, where there had been no contested partisan elections between 1946 and 1982, after which it switched to nonpartisan election. While the patterns shown in the figure are as one would expect, there are some interesting anomalies. Prior to switching to nonpartisan elections as of 2004, North Carolina was one of the most partisan of the partisan states in its state supreme court elections; that partisanship dropped with the introduction of nonpartisan elections, but remained relatively high, above the partisanship in the hybrid states. Georgia also remained fairly partisan in its elections after adopting nonpartisan elections in 1983, falling between the two states currently using hybrid elections.

Figure 6.2 shows the mean partisan correlation by decade for each of the three types of elections. An interesting feature of all three lines is a dip ending around 1970. For partisan elections, the pattern over the period has been fairly stable except for this slight dip; the average partisan correlation in the most recent decade is virtually the same as in the original decade. It is worth reiterating that a number of states that used partisan elections at the beginning

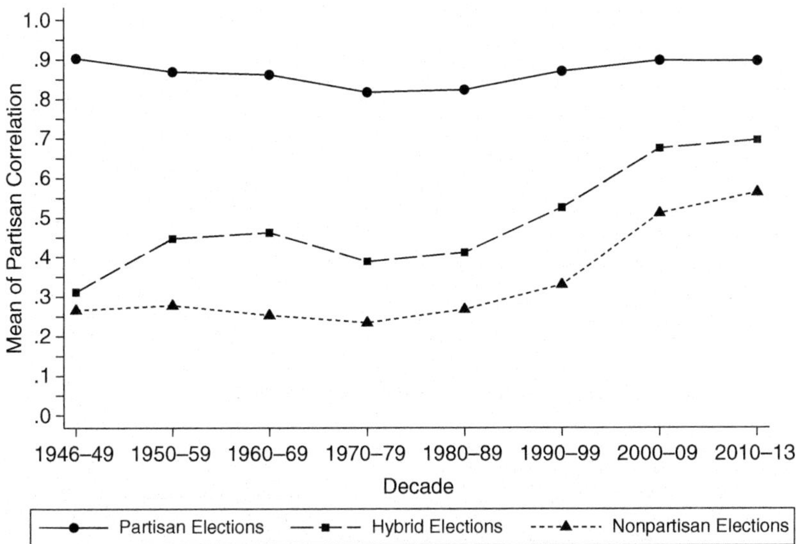

FIGURE 6.2. Mean Partisan Correlation by Decade and Election Type.

of the period have since switched to other selection methods, and several of the states conducting large numbers of partisan general elections are southern states that in the early period had few general election contests due to the overwhelming dominance of the Democratic Party. The two states still using hybrid elections, Ohio and Michigan, show a marked increase in the mean partisan correlations over the last two decades; there was also an earlier increase in the 1950s and 1960s over the 1940s followed by a dip in the 1970s and 1980s. Nonpartisan states were fairly stable through the 1980s, showing a slight dip in the 1970s; as with the hybrid states, the nonpartisan states show a marked increase in the mean partisan correlation in the last two decades.

One question that might be asked about the nonpartisan states is how much of the recent increase reflects the adoption of nonpartisan elections by Georgia and North Carolina which, as noted previously, have a relatively high mean partisan correlation for their nonpartisan elections. Figure 6.3 shows mean partisan correlations for partisan and nonpartisan elections controlling for region (it omits hybrid elections because none of those elections were outside the South); lines with solid markers represent the nonsouth and those with hollow markers, the South. As the figure shows, even omitting Georgia and North Carolina (plus a small number of elections in Florida and Arkansas), there is an upward shift in the mean partisan correlation for nonpartisan states outside the South. Also of note in Figure 6.3 is the drop in the mean partisan correlation for partisan elections in the South during the 1970s. However, this

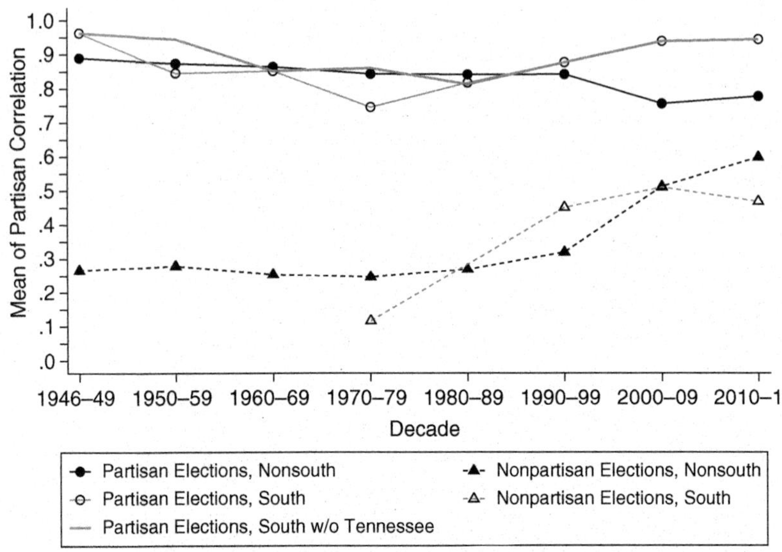

FIGURE 6.3. Mean Partisan Correlation by Decade and Region.

is due to the pattern in Tennessee as shown by the heavier line without markers which omits Tennessee; without Tennessee the dip in the 1970s disappears. Finally, the pattern for partisan elections outside the South shows a very slight downward trend, with a sharper drop in the last decade.

State Level Patterns of Change

Looking at patterns nationally, or even regionally, obscures important differences among states. Figure 6.4 replicates Figure 6.1 but shows separate means for the two periods: 1946 to 1979 and 1980 to 2013. Statistically significant changes (based on t-tests comparing the means of the correlations for the two periods) are indicated by asterisks next to the state identifiers. Among partisan states, there have been statistically significant changes for Pennsylvania, Tennessee,[16] Texas,[17] and West Virginia, all showing a significant *decrease* in the partisan correlations. The remaining states with partisan elections in both time periods (Alabama,[18] New Mexico, and North Carolina) do not evidence statistically significant changes. In both of the hybrid states, Ohio and Michigan, the mean partisan correlation

16 Tennessee switched to a "merit" system early in the second period, and the second period mean for Tennessee includes only four elections.

17 As noted previously I have included both the Texas Supreme Court and the Texas Court of Criminal Appeals, which is the court of last resort in Texas for criminal cases.

18 Graphically the change in Alabama looks large; however, only one contested general election occurred in the pre-1980 period.

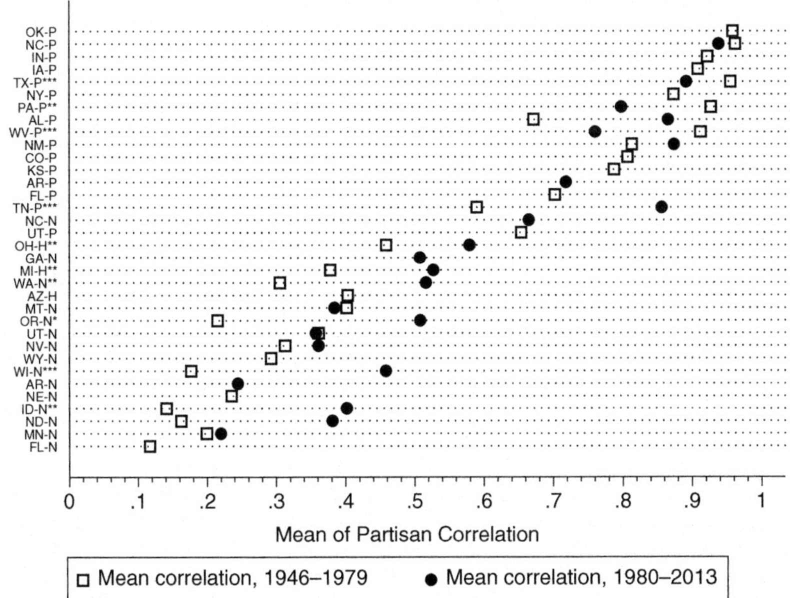

Note: *p<.05, **p<.01, ***p<.001 (for t-test of change). The letter after the state abbreviation indicates the type of election: **P** for partisan, **N** for nonpartisan, **H** for hybrid.

FIGURE 6.4. Mean Correlations by State for Two Time Periods.

increased significantly over the two periods, by 0.11 in Ohio and 0.15 in Michigan. The nonpartisan states show a variable pattern, with no appreciable change in the mean partisan correlation in Minnesota, Montana, and Nevada.[19] Four nonpartisan states, Idaho, Oregon, Washington, and Wisconsin, show a statistically significant increase in the mean partisan correlation; North Dakota would be statistically significant at the .10 level (two-tailed) but, as I will explain, the apparent difference reflects a single, outlier election.

Figures 6.5, 6.6, and 6.7 are scatterplots of individual correlations by year for those states that continued to use elections through all or most of the period.[20] I have grouped the scatterplots by election type; for the two states that switched

[19] Utah shows no change as well, but it switched to a "merit" system early in the second period, and there is only one nonpartisan election included in the computation of the mean for the later period for Utah. The mean shown for the early period for Utah when it employed partisan elections is based on only three elections.

[20] Because some states have multiple elections in a given year, I have employed Stata's "jitter" capability to make individual points visible; one side effect of employing the jitter capability is that some elections may appear to have occurred earlier or later than they did, and for states that changed selection methods some of the elections occurring after the change may appear on the graph before some of the elections before the change.

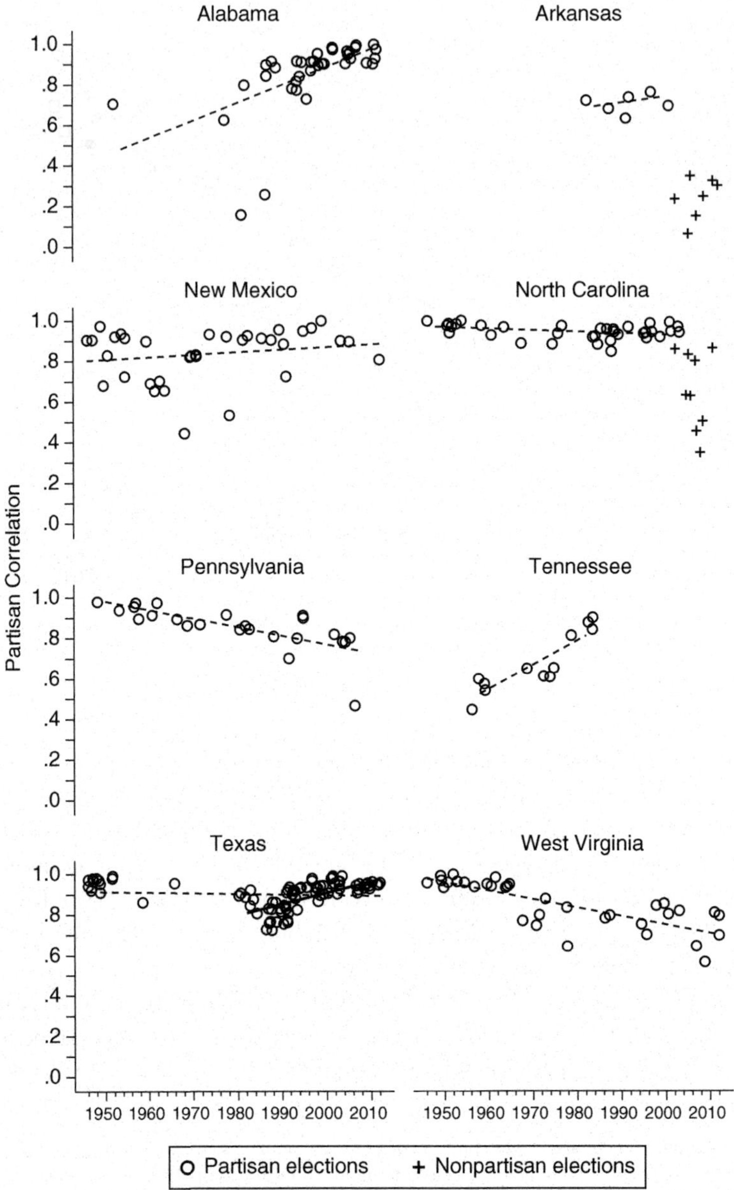

Note: Each data point represents the partisan correlation for one election.

FIGURE 6.5. Partisan Correlations in States with Partisan Elections.

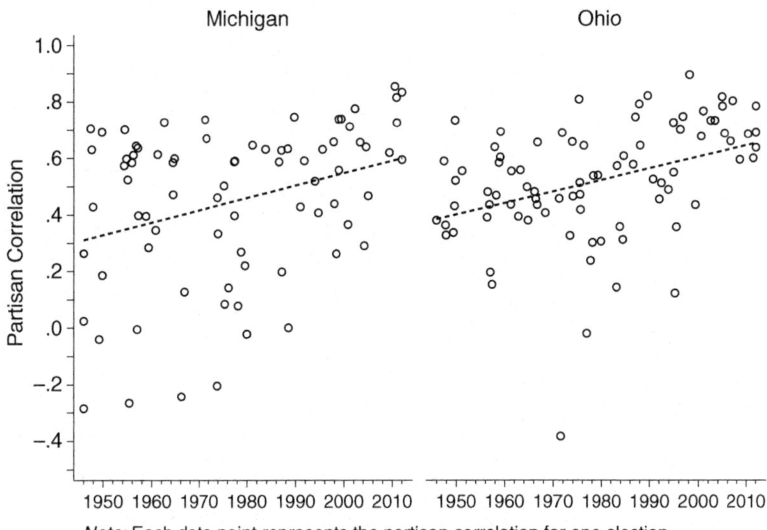

Note: Each data point represents the partisan correlation for one election.

FIGURE 6.6. Partisan Correlations in States with Hybrid Elections.

to nonpartisan elections after 2000, North Carolina and Arkansas, I have plotted all the elections on a single graph grouped with the partisan states, showing the nonpartisan elections with a different symbol from the partisan elections that existed through most of the period I am considering.

Partisan States

Figure 6.5 shows the eight states that employed partisan elections through most of the time period.[21] As a test for whether there is a time trend, I computed simple regressions predicting the correlation from year; the broken lines shown in the figure represent the fitted lines. Table 6.1 shows the numerical results of these regressions; with some noteworthy exceptions, the results of the regressions conform to the pattern shown in Figure 6.4. For Texas, the inconsistency reflects the impact of a small number of contested general elections during the period when Texas was essentially a one-party Democratic state. Limiting the regression for Texas to after 1958, the slope is positive and statistically significant ($b = .0036$, $p < .001$, $r^2 = .274$), and if I limit the period to after 1980 (shown in Figure 6.5 by the solid line), I get an even stronger slope ($b = .0055$,

[21] Since 1968 in Pennsylvania and 1988 in New Mexico, partisan elections have been used only for the initial election to the court; previously elected incumbents seeking additional terms now stand in retention elections in those two states.

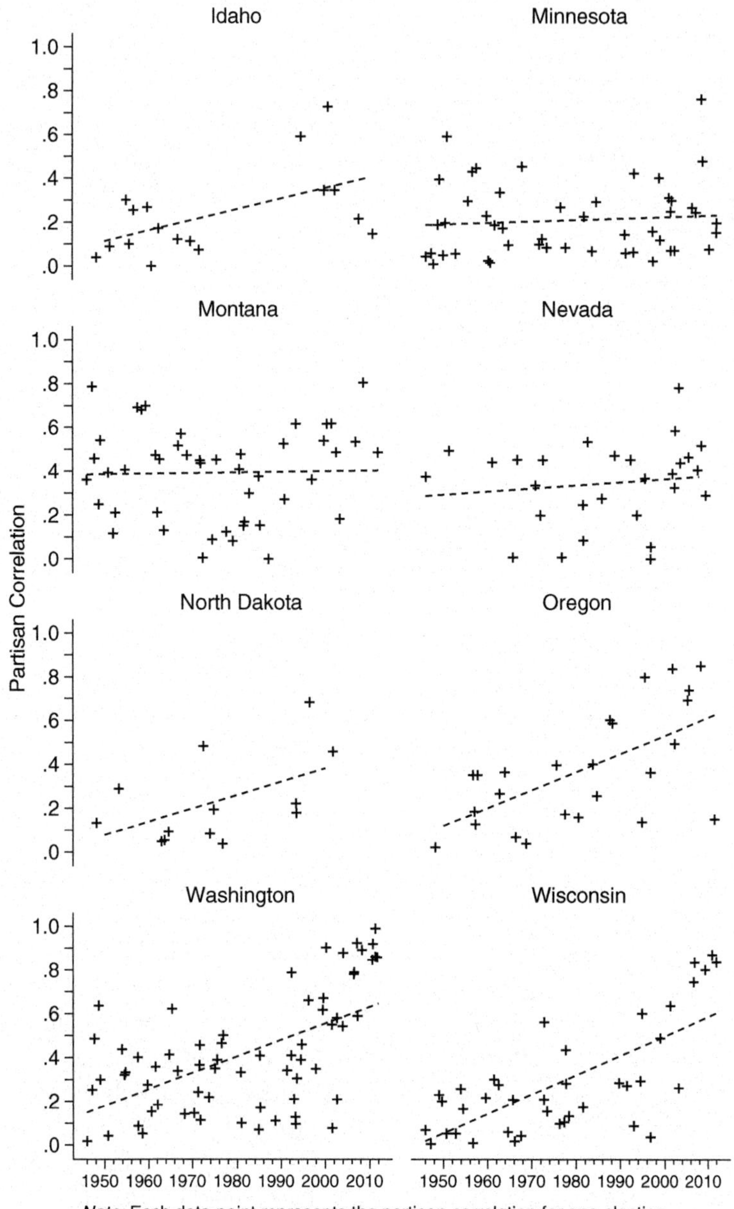

FIGURE 6.7. Partisan Correlations in States with Nonpartisan Elections.

TABLE 6.1. Over-Time Regressions for Partisan and Hybrid States

State	Slope (b)	r^2	p	N
Partisan States				
Alabama	0.0088	0.324	<.001	37
Arkansas	0.0031	0.486	0.486	6
New Mexico	0.0012	0.034	0.287	35
North Carolina	−0.0007	0.139	0.139	35
Pennsylvania	−0.0042	0.548	<.001	24
Tennessee	0.0112	0.724	<.001	12
Texas	−0.0003	0.007	0.442	84
(post-1980)	0.0055	0.4821	<.001	69
West Virginia	−0.0042	0.622	<.001	34
Hybrid States				
Michigan	0.0044	0.106	0.004	77
Ohio	0.0034	0.414	<.001	84

$p < .001$, $r^2 = .482$). Alabama shows two elections with very low correlations; these occurred in 1980 and 1988. One of these elections involved a candidate running for reelection who had switched parties in anticipation of the election; it may be that this switch produced voter confusion, leading many people to vote for the incumbent thinking he was still a Democrat despite contrary information on the ballot. Omitting these two elections from the regression diminishes the slope (from .0088 to .0056) but actually increases the r^2 (from .324 to .576).[22] Finally, Pennsylvania has one anomalous election which occurred in 2009;[23] while it produced a partisan correlation of only .548, even omitting that election Pennsylvania shows a declining pattern of partisanship.[24] I have been unable to come up with a good explanation for the anomaly in 2009, although one possibility is that Republican candidate Joan Orie Melvin was endorsed by major newspapers in the Democratic strongholds of Philadelphia and Pittsburgh, and this election did not coincide with other statewide partisan elections which probably means that the party organizations did not undertake

[22] I explored the question of whether the pattern in Alabama might be nonlinear with a decreasing increase in the correlation over time. There is some evidence of this if the 1980 and 1988 elections are included, but not if they are excluded.

[23] As previously discussed, in 1968 Pennsylvania modified its existing partisan election system so that partisan elections are held only for a justice's initial 10-year term; to retain their seats at the end of the initial term, justices run in a retention election. Also, by custom the partisan elections since 1968 in Pennsylvania have all been open seat contests.

[24] I did t-tests with and without the 2009 election; both are statistically significant ($p<.001$).

major get-out-the-vote drives. Also, Melvin had lost a close election for the Pennsylvania Supreme Court in 2003, and having run in that earlier statewide election likely enhanced her name recognition.[25]

Arkansas had very few contested general elections between 1946 and its switch from a partisan system to nonpartisan elections starting in 2002, and it shows no change over time in the partisan correlation for the small number of partisan elections that did occur. The switch to nonpartisan elections produced a sharp drop in the partisan correlations, with a mean for partisan elections of .718 versus .241 for nonpartisan elections;[26] there are six elections of each type, and the difference is statistically significant ($t = 9.24$, $p < .001$). North Carolina, which appears to show no significant change in partisan correlation between 1946–1979 and 1980–2002, does show a slight but statistically significant *decline* in partisan correlation over the entire time period 1946–2002. Of greater interest is how the partisan correlation changed with the transition to nonpartisan elections in 2004. Unlike Arkansas, which showed an immediate sharp drop, in North Carolina there was a pattern of decline over time; in the last four partisan elections (two in 2000 and two in 2002), the mean partisan correlation was .962, dropping to .852 in 2004 (two nonpartisan elections), .644 in 2006 (four nonpartisan elections), and .408 for 2008–10 (one partisan election in each even-numbered year). In 2012 there was a strongly partisan result in North Carolina with a partisan correlation of .878; in that election the Republican Party strongly backed the incumbent Paul Newby, who defeated challenger and appellate judge Sam Ervin, IV, who was backed by the Democratic Party, and who was the grandson and namesake of a longtime Democratic senator from North Carolina.[27]

Why did North Carolina and Arkansas differ so greatly after they switched to nonpartisan elections? The two states have not differed substantially in the mix of incumbent running and open-seat elections, either immediately before or after they each changed their election systems for their state supreme courts. One possible explanation for the difference is that Arkansas adopted a system in which if a candidate wins a majority in the primary, which is always the case if only two candidates are running, the primary decides the election and no

[25] In May 2012, Melvin was charged with nine counts of improperly using government resources in her election campaigns; in February 2013 she was convicted and in May 2013 was sentenced to 3 years of house arrest followed by 2 years of probation. She resigned from the Pennsylvania Supreme Court effective May 1, 2013.

[26] The one contested election in Arkansas in 2014 produced a partisan correlation of .34.

[27] The 2014 election for four seats on the North Carolina Supreme Court produced partisan correlations that returned to the level found in the partisan elections prior to 2004: .72, .78, .91, and .92. One of the candidates was Sam Ervin IV; the partisan correlation for that seat was .78.

general election takes place; thus, there is an election for state supreme court in November only if there are three or more candidates and no candidate wins a majority at the time of the primary.[28] Since Arkansas changed to nonpartisan elections starting in 2004, only one Arkansas Supreme Court election has required a runoff in November. A second possible factor is that persons appointed to fill a vacant seat on the Arkansas Supreme Court are prohibited from running for that seat in the subsequent election; this reduces the potential of a partisan signal that might be created by the party of the governor who would have appointed the incumbent to a vacant seat.

Hybrid States

Figure 6.6 shows the partisan correlations for the two hybrid states; this figure shows both positive and negative correlations because, as noted previously, in a small number of elections voters were confused by candidates whose surnames were associated with one party but who had been nominated by the other party. Table 6.1 shows (at the bottom) the results for the over-time regression for these two states; both regressions are statistically significant, but the fits are not as tight as for the partisan states because of the amount of scatter in the states' patterns. For Michigan, the relationship is produced in part by the small number of negative correlations; if those correlations are omitted, the slope coefficient is halved, although it is still statistically different from zero ($p = .030$). Moreover, a t-test comparing the mean correlations for the two time periods in Michigan is statistically significant with the negative correlations included (means .38 and .53, $t = 2.46$, $p = .016$) but misses achieving significance at the .05 level (two-tailed) with the eight negative correlations excluded (means .47 and .56, $t = 1.90$, $p = .062$). In contrast, for Ohio the pattern of increase changes little when the two negative partisan correlations are excluded; the slope with the negative correlations is .0040 compared to .0038 with the negative correlations excluded. Clearly, the partisanship in Ohio's hybrid system has increased over time; for Michigan any increase, once voter confusion is discounted, is at best modest.[29] This may reflect the fact that the

[28] Arkansas labels the nonpartisan judicial elections at the time of the party primaries as the "non-partisan judicial general election," and labels any vote in November as "non-partisan judicial run-off election."

[29] What if we treat mistaken partisanship the same as partisanship, and look at the absolute value of the partisan correlations? For Ohio, this makes little difference in the results, either for the two-period t-test or for the regression. For Michigan, the results are somewhat ambiguous. The two-period t-test is not statistically significant (means .43 and .50, $t= 1.561$, $p=.123$, .062 for one-tailed) but the slope marginally just misses one-tailed statistical significance ($p=.052$).

TABLE 6.2. Over-Time Regressions for Nonpartisan States

State	Slope (b)	r^2	p	N
Idaho	0.0049	0.3	0.023	17
Minnesota	0.0007	0.008	0.537	48
Montana	0.0003	<.001	0.856	46
Nevada	0.0014	0.018	0.496	28
North Dakota	0.0061	0.244	0.086	13
Oregon	0.0082	0.373	0.001	25
Washington	0.0073	0.324	<.001	64
Wisconsin	0.0083	0.457	<.001	38

Ohio court and its justices have been involved in several major controversies over the last twenty-five years (Cook and West 1983; "Dispute Injects Politics into Judicial Races in Ohio" 1984; Glaberson 1999, 2000b; Liptak and Roberts 2006; "Ohio Justices Say School System Is Legal but Must End Disparities" 2001; Sharkey and Ricks 1984).

Nonpartisan States

Figure 6.7 shows the pattern of partisan correlations for eight states that have had nonpartisan elections throughout the period 1946–2013.[30] Table 6.2 shows the results of the over-time regressions for each state; four states (Idaho, Oregon, Washington, and Wisconsin) show significant increases in partisan correlations; three states (Minnesota, Montana, and Nevada) show no apparent increase; and one state (North Dakota) shows what appears to be a marginal increase. One interesting aspect of the patterns in Idaho and North Dakota is that both states experienced a hiatus in contested elections. In Idaho, there were no contested elections for a twenty-year period from 1972 through 1992. North Dakota had a somewhat shorter hiatus during that same period.

The graph for Idaho suggests that the increase there might reflect the impact of two elections which produced partisan correlations of .76 and .59; however, even omitting those two elections there is a modest upward trend (just barely

[30] Another state that could have been included here is Georgia which has had nonpartisan elections since 1983 (and where there were no contested general elections between 1946 and 1982). There have been nine contested nonpartisan elections in Georgia, the first one actually occurring in 1990, and the most recent in 2010. An over-time regression for these elections produced a nonsignificant slope of .0102 ($p=.149$; $r^2=.273$).

achieving .05 one-tailed significance). It is noteworthy that both of these elections, one of which occurred in 1994 and the other in 2000, involved Cathy Silak who "had been appointed by a Democratic governor, had married into a well-known Democratic family, and had been involved in liberal causes" (Champagne 2001:1402). In 1994 Silak, who had been appointed to the court the previous year by Democratic governor Cecil Andres, defeated Wayne Kidwell; Kidwell was a prominent Republican who had been the Republican majority leader in the Idaho State Senate in the early 1970s, had run unsuccessfully in the Republican primary for Congress in 1972, won election as the state attorney general 1974 by defeating the Democratic incumbent, and served in the Reagan administration as an associate deputy attorney general. Silak subsequently lost the 2000 election, and is the only incumbent supreme court justice in Idaho to have been defeated between 1946 and 2012.[31] The opposition to Silak in 2000 arose from her role in a decision that upheld a federal water rights claim in several wilderness areas (Echeverria 2000:39–54). Her opponent had backing from leaders of the Republican Party and a range of conservative groups (Champagne 2001:1402).

The marginal pattern of increase in North Dakota is the result of a single election in 1996 which produced a partisan correlation of .685. The 1996 election pitted Mary Maring, who had been appointed to the court by Republican governor Ed Schafer earlier in 1996, against Sarah Vogel, who was completing her second term as the elected agriculture commissioner (Selzer 2006:226–27). In addition to having run for statewide office as a candidate of the Democratic-NPL Party,[32] Vogel had a long record of activism with that party (Fedor 1996). The recent appointment of Maring by the Republican governor combined with Vogel's long-standing identification with the Democratic-NPL Party probably accounts for the high partisan correlation. If the 1996 election is omitted, the resulting regression does not come close to achieving statistical significance ($b = .0033$, $p = .280$, $r^2 = .116$).

Among the nonpartisan states, Oregon, Washington, and Wisconsin exhibit strong and clear patterns of increased partisanship as indicated by the partisan correlations. Washington produced the strongest correlations between 2002 and 2012 with six exceeding .90 and only one falling below .50.[33] However,

[31] The previous defeat of a sitting justice in Idaho was in 1944, and there were losses by incumbent justices during the 1930s.

[32] The Democratic Party in North Dakota is known as the Democratic-Nonpartisan League, or Democratic-NPL, Party.

[33] In 2014, two of four elections in Washington were contested; the two contested elections, neither of which was close and neither of which involved challengers closely identified with partisan-tinged issues, produced partisan correlations of .24 and .25.

the pattern of increase in Oregon over the entire period is marginally stronger both in slope and r^2 compared to Washington, although the highest correlation in Oregon is lower at .851. As I will discuss later, the increased partisanship in both of these states reflects the involvement of those states' supreme courts in controversial cases dealing with issues such as same-sex marriage, property rights, land use, and economic development – issues that align strongly with partisan interests. As discussed in Chapter 1, the increase in partisan voting in Wisconsin, the strongest increase as measured by the change in slope, arises from other types of issues, most strongly several controversial decisions dealing with tort law and in the 2011 election of an incumbent who was seen as closely aligned with the new governor and his controversial policies related to union rights and other partisan issues.

The role of issues with partisan import can be seen fairly clearly in elections in Washington in the period after 2000. James Johnson ran twice for the Washington Supreme Court,[34] unsuccessfully in 2002 against Mary Fairhurst, and successfully in 2004 against Mary Becker. Both of these elections were for open seats, and in both of them the correlation between the nonpartisan judicial election pattern and the partisan gubernatorial election was on the order of 0.90 (0.90 in 2002 and 0.91 in 2004). Johnson, a prominent lawyer who had previously served as an assistant state attorney general for twenty years, was known for having represented a number of conservative political and business interests, particularly in cases involving property rights (O'Hagan 2004). Johnson received endorsements from both the state Republican Party and the state Libertarian Party (Modie 2002). In the 2002 election, Johnson's opponent was the senior assistant attorney general and a former president of the state bar association, who was backed by the state Democratic Party as well as by organized labor, environmental groups, and Indian tribes (Galloway 2002). The election was a squeaker, and was not resolved until all absentee ballots were counted; in the end, Fairhurst won with 50.1 percent of the vote (Herrington 2002).

In 2004 James Johnson tried again, facing appeals court judge and former Democratic state legislator, Mary Kay Becker.[35] Again conservative interests lined up behind Johnson; liberal groups backed Becker. Johnson collected a record-setting campaign war chest of more than half a million dollars, surpassing the record he set two years before. Johnson won this time with 52 percent

34 For a discussion of judicial elections up until about 1995 in Washington, see Sheldon and Maule (1997:53–68).

35 Becker had served on the appeals court for ten years (O'Hagan 2004).

of the vote (Thomas 2006b).[36] When Johnson ran successfully for reelection in 2010, one newspaper headline in advance of the election read "Sharp ideological contrasts in state Supreme Court race" (Martin 2010); the article went on to describe Johnson as "the court's most consistent and avowed conservative" who "champions the rights of crime victims and private property owners … usually sides with businesses, [and] vigorously defends marriage as being between a man and woman." Johnson described himself as "without a doubt conservative, libertarian conservative," and drew support from a wide range of conservative groups. Johnson's opponent, Stan Umbaugh, drew support from progressive groups; his law practice focused on workers' compensation and representing plaintiffs, and he served on the board of Planned Parenthood.

In 2006, there was something of a replay of the 2004 election, with an incumbent justice, Gerry Alexander, challenged by another conservative attorney John Groen, who was associated with groups concerned about property rights. Alexander narrowly won the two-candidate primary which produced a partisan correlation of .78 (Thomas 2006a). A second race involved an incumbent, Susan Olson, who had faced four challengers in the primary. In the general election she faced a Republican state senator, Steve Johnson, who was also allied with property rights interests and had been a leading proponent of the state's Defense of Marriage Act in 1998. Olson won easily with almost 60 percent of the vote (carrying all but four of Washington's thirty-nine counties); given Johnson's prominence as a conservative Republican activist (Kelleher 2006), it is not surprising that the partisan pattern was strong, with a correlation of .90.

While the 2010 (James) Johnson-Rumbaugh election produced a strong partisan correlation (.83), that correlation was not as strong as in Johnson's 2004 election (.91) or the election for another seat on the Washington Supreme Court in 2010.[37] The most partisan election in 2010 pitted incumbent Richard Sanders against two challengers; while Sanders won a 47 percent plurality in the primary, he had to face attorney Charlie Wiggins, who won 40 percent of the primary vote, in the November general election. Sanders lost the general election by about 13,000 votes (out of almost 2 million votes cast), and that election had a partisan correlation of .90. Sanders has been described as "a libertarian who defies easy labels" (Miletich 2010); while much of his

[36] In the wake of the 2004 Washington state supreme court election, the Washington legislature extended limits on campaign contributions, which had not applied to judicial elections, to cover those elections. Presumably, this would preclude large contributions from groups (or individuals) such as Cruise Specialists, who contributed $112,000 to Johnson's campaign because it was upset with an appellate decision upholding a multimillion-dollar judgment against it that had been authored by Mary Becker, Johnson's opponent.

[37] It is unlikely that these correlations differ statistically.

support came from groups typically aligned on the conservative side of the spectrum (property rights advocates, anti-abortion supporters, and gun ownership proponents), he also drew support from groups more associated with the left (criminal defense attorneys and personal injury attorneys). Sanders had gotten himself in some hot water over charges of conflict of interest resulting in his being admonished in a disciplinary proceeding. While the disciplinary proceeding may have increased his electoral vulnerability, it was probably his siding with the majority in a 2006 decision in a case that upheld the state's ban on same-sex marriage that led to the strongly partisan voting pattern combined with his endorsement by the Republican and Libertarian parties and Wiggins's endorsement by the Democratic Party (Johnson 2010). Importantly, while many of the highly partisan nonpartisan elections reflect mobilization by conservatives in opposition to liberal decisions, this election may represent an example of liberal mobilization in response to a conservative decision.

In 2012, Richard Sanders sought to regain a seat on the Washington Supreme Court. He was one of four candidates seeking an open seat, and he finished second in the primary. In the general election he faced Sheryl McCloud, who was a lawyer with an appellate practice representing criminal defendants. McCloud won the election with 55 percent of the vote. The partisan correlation for the election was .96, the strongest I found for any ostensibly nonpartisan election. The other two 2012 elections were easily won by incumbents at the primary, even though one of the incumbents faced two challengers. The partisan correlations for those two elections were both .85, although there does not appear to have been any significant campaigning by the challengers in either election. One of the incumbents was a recent appointee with a Hispanic name, Steve Gonzalez. His single challenger, Bruce Danielson, was a little-known lawyer from Seattle who raised no money, did not meet with newspaper editorial boards, and participated in no candidate forums; Danielson reportedly did have a website that provided information on what was described as his conservative legal ideology, but it is unlikely that many voters had seen it. The other incumbent was Susan Owens, who had first been elected in 2000; her two previous elections produced partisan correlations of .62 and .91. She won the primary with 63 percent of the vote.

The increasingly partisan pattern in Washington almost certainly arises from the fact that the Washington Supreme Court has made major decisions on issues that are highly salient to voters and interest groups. For example, in July 2006, the Washington Supreme Court handed down its decision in *Andersen v. King County* upholding the state's ban on same-sex marriage (see Liptak and Timothy Egan 2006).[38] The controlling majority on the court,

[38] 138 P.3d 963 (Wash. 2006).

which included Richard Sanders, found that the same-sex marriage ban met rational basis scrutiny. Justice Alexander concurred, joined by Justice (James) Johnson, arguing that the same-sex marriage ban would survive strict scrutiny because there is "a compelling governmental interest in preserving the institution of marriage." Justice Mary Fairhurst, who had defeated Johnson in 2002, was the author of the dissenting opinion.

What about Oregon, which is the third state using nonpartisan elections that has seen an apparent increase in partisan voting patterns? First, it is important to note that while in Washington eighteen of the twenty-two elections between 2000 and 2012 were contested, in Oregon only six of seventeen elections during that period were contested, and four of those were for open seats.[39] None of the contested elections in Oregon have had a partisan correlation as strong as several Washington elections. The strongest correlation was .85 in 2010 followed very closely by .84 in 2000; both of these elections were for open seats. The 2010 election involved a five-candidate primary from which emerged Court of Appeals Judge Paul DeMuniz and lawyer Greg Byrne. DeMuniz did not come into the election with any particular political alignment, but Byrne did; he had been associated with Bill Sizemore, a well-known Oregon conservative who had been the Republican candidate for governor in 1998, and had led the effort to pass a 1996 initiative rolling back property taxes after having founded Oregon Taxpayers United in 1993. Moreover, during both the primary and general election campaigns, Byrne made clear his conservative credentials and viewpoints (Farrell 2000a, 2000b, 2000c).

The 2010 election did not appear to involve strong partisan overtones of the kind that occurred in 2000. The 2010 election pitted another Court of Appeals Judge, Jack Landau, against Allan Arlow, an administrative law judge serving with the Oregon Public Utilities Commission. One article described the election as "a lot quieter than some appellate-court campaigns of the past decade" ("Two Face Off for Oregon Supreme Court Seat" 2010). No reports I found suggested that there had been significant interest group involvement or high campaign expenditures in the election. The only hint of something that might account for the strong partisan pattern was that Landau was associated with court decisions favoring "equal rights for gays and lesbians," particularly a 1998 opinion ruling that employers could not discriminate against gay and lesbian couples in providing health insurance benefits ("Elect Judge Jack Landau to Oregon Surpeme Court" 2010).

[39] The two Oregon elections in 2014 both involved incumbents, neither of whom faced a challenger.

The third open seat election occurred in 2006, and produced a partisan correlation of .69. The election, pitting Court of Appeals judge Virginia Linder against former state labor commissioner Jack Roberts, was hard fought and expensive ($1.5 million),[40] breaking Oregon's record of expenditures on judicial campaigns. Roberts drew support from business groups, including those supporting limits on lawsuits. Linder's supporters included plaintiffs' attorneys, gay rights groups, and unions (Green 2006). However, the strong partisan pattern was most likely due to the fact that Roberts had run five times in the prior twelve years in statewide races, including as the Republican candidate for governor in 2002 ("Supreme Court Runoff is a Low-Key Race" 2006), and hence had both name and partisan recognition among many voters ("Voting in the Dark" 2006). While Roberts led in the three-candidate primary with 41.8 percent versus 38.6 percent for Linder, Linder won the general election with 51.8 percent.

The fourth open-seat election occurred in 2012. Three candidates entered the primary; one was a judge of the state appellate court, one was a trial court judge, and the final candidate was a trial lawyer. Early comment viewed the appellate judge, Timothy Sercombe, as the front-runner because the previous four open seats had been won by appellate judges, and since 1969 when the Oregon Court of Appeals was created, only one appellate judge who had run for the Oregon Supreme Court had been defeated. However, Judge Sercombe came in third in the primary. Attorney Nena Cook led the primary field, followed by Judge Richard Baldwin. Baldwin won the November election with 51 percent of the vote. The partisan correlation was only .14, the lowest since 1994. There do not appear to have been any strong issues in the campaign, nor did there seem to be significant news coverage of the election; both candidates ran television ads, but those were positive ads promoting the candidate. Prior to becoming a judge, Baldwin was a legal aid lawyer and Cook's practice included plaintiffs' personal injury work and criminal defense.

The remaining contested elections in Oregon since 2000 were both in 2004, and both involved incumbents. The election pitting incumbent Rives Kistler against solo practitioner James Leuenberger produced a partisan correlation of .73, and the election involving incumbent William Riggs and circuit (trial) court judge Rudolph Murgo resulted in a somewhat more modest .50. While not raised explicitly by his challenger, the fact the Justice Kistler was openly gay may have contributed to the partisan pattern in that contest, particularly given that Leuenberger had represented the leader of a group that had

[40] Most of this $1.5 million was spent during the primary election that included a third candidate in the primary ("Supreme Court Runoff is a Low-Key Race" 2006).

sponsored anti-gay-rights ballot measures in four preceding elections ("Judge, Lawyer Battle for Seat on High Court; the Challenger and Incumbent Avoid Discussing Sexual Orientation" 2004).[41]

What about the nonpartisan states where there has been no change – Minnesota, Montana, and Nevada? As discussed in Chapter 1, the Minnesota Supreme Court has not been put into a position where it has had to decide highly charged issues likely to activate interest groups, and while it has had some politically important cases, it has often managed to decide those cases without dissent. Montana's pattern is interesting; it appears to be parabolic, with a strong decrease in the middle period and then rising again in the later period. In fact, if I add a quadratic term to the regression to account for this apparent shape, the regression achieves statistical significance ($p = .013$, $R^2 = .188$) and both coefficients in the regression model are statistically significant.[42] Thus Montana represents a particularly strong example of the dampening of partisanship in the middle of the period I am examining. Both Minnesota and Nevada show a recent election with a partisan correlation exceeding .70, but these are outliers.

Interestingly, in the Nevada election with the high correlation, both candidates for the open seat were identified in the press as Republicans, although a group calling itself the Republican Judicial Caucus sent out "sample ballots" that only identified one of the candidates, former Republican Party state chairman John Mason, as a Republican – the correlation was in Mason's direction (Neff 2004). This election came as part of a flurry of controversy regarding the Nevada Supreme Court in the wake of *Guinn v. Legislature of the State*,[43] a 2003 6-1 decision temporarily setting aside a state constitutional provision requiring a two-thirds majority in both houses of the state legislature in order to increase taxes; the ruling came amidst a budget impasse in the Legislature.

The second highest correlation in Nevada also occurred in 2004, and involved Michael Douglas, an incumbent who had been appointed to the court in January 2004, and hence was not on the court at the time of the 2003 decision; Douglas, as the first African American on the Nevada Supreme Court, attracted endorsements from prominent figures from both parties. The first incumbent who had been on the court at the time of the 2003 decision to stand for reelection was Nancy Becker, whose term was up in 2006; she was

[41] Some of the groups supporting Leuenberger may have highlighted the issue of sexual orientation.

[42] For this, and the other regressions, I did not enter the raw year, but rather what I labeled "baseyear" which was the year 1946; thus "baseyear" runs from 0 to 66. In the nonlinear model I included both baseyear and the square of baseyear as predictors; the resulting coefficients were $-.0165$ ($t = -2.97$) and $.00028$ ($t = 3.12$).

[43] 71 P.3d 1269 (Nev. 2003).

opposed by Nancy Saitta, a trial court judge. In the campaign, Becker was attacked for her vote in the controversial decision, and despite endorsements from leading newspapers, lost the election, garnering only 45 percent of the vote. Her defeat may have been partly due to her participation in a unanimous Nevada Supreme Court decision two months before the election that removed from the ballot an initiative to limit the powers of both the legislature and the governor on spending and taxes (Bills 2008:47–55). While one might expect a strong correlation in an election that dealt with these kinds of issues and which resulted in the defeat of an incumbent, the partisan correlation in the Becker-Saitta election was a moderate .46.

There were two elections in 2008, both contested. One was for an open seat and produced a partisan correlation of .50. The other involved Mark Gibbons who had voted with the majority in the controversial *Guinn* decision in 2003; Gibbons won with 68 percent of the vote and the election produced a partisan correlation of .28. All of the elections in 2010 and 2012 involved incumbents, and none have faced opposition.[44] Overall, it appears that aside from the controversy surrounding the *Guinn* decision the Nevada Supreme Court, like the Minnesota Supreme Court, has escaped the kinds of controversial issues that have led to partisan voting patterns in a number of the states employing nonpartisan elections.

* * *

A question one might ask about the changing patterns of partisan correlations is whether there is any difference in the pattern depending on whether one looks at elections in which the incumbent loses, the incumbent wins, or there is no incumbent, either for partisan or nonpartisan elections? Figure 6.8 plots the partisan correlations over time showing the two types of elections (partisan and nonpartisan) using different symbols for the three types of electoral situations; in addition, for each subset of elections, the figure shows a "lowess" line, which uses a method of line fitting that allows for nonlinearity (Cleveland 1979). There is little variation and minimal change for partisan elections. However, for nonpartisan elections one sees the overall increase discussed previously; moreover, while there is an increase for all three situations shown, the increase in partisan correlations is greatest for elections in which the incumbent lost.[45]

[44] The two incumbents running in 2014 also faced no opposition.

[45] It is unclear whether this difference is anything other than random variation (i.e., achieves statistical significance). If I split the data into two periods, pre-1990 and 1990 and later, the means of the partisan correlations for the three nonpartisan election situations in the earlier period are essentially the same, ranging from .24 to .27; in contrast for the later period the mean for elections where the incumbent lost is .600 compared to .42 and .47 for incumbent-won and open-seat situations. However, there are only six elections in which an incumbent lost in the later period, and if I do a one-way analysis of variance, the result is not statistically significant (or even close to statistical significance).

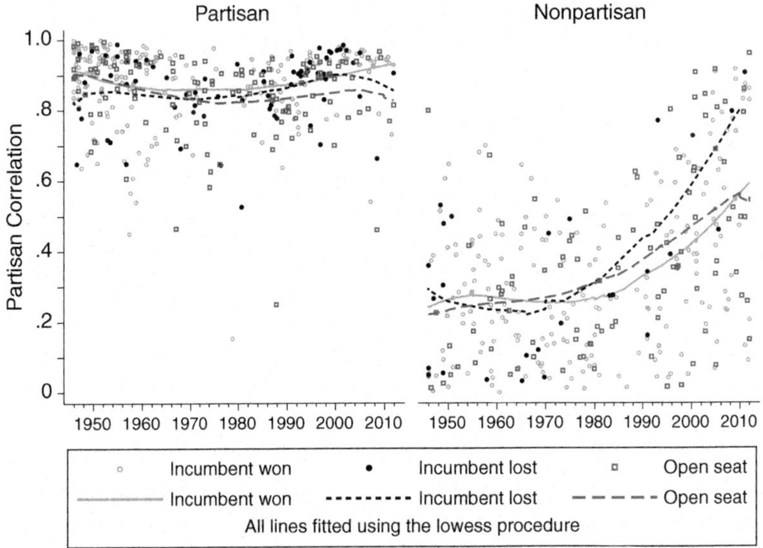

FIGURE 6.8. Partisan Correlations Controlling for Election Situation and Outcome.

Another question with regard to nonpartisan elections is what impact has there been as a result of the explosion of television advertising? As discussed in the previous chapter, the Brennan Center and Justice at Stake have compiled data on television advertising in judicial elections starting in 1999; given the absence of data prior to that time, it is necessary to restrict any consideration of the impact of advertising to this latter period. Between 1999 and 2013, there were eighty-eight contested nonpartisan statewide elections for state supreme court; television advertisements were run in forty of those elections. As discussed in Chapter 5, the Brennan Center codes the tone of the advertisements into three categories: promote, contrast, and attack; thirty-eight elections saw ads in the promote category, twenty-three of which had only promote ads, ten saw contrast ads, and eleven saw attack ads; seventeen had either contrasts or attacks, or had both, but only two of those seventeen did not also have promote ads. There are a variety of ways to slice up these eighty-eight elections; I chose to use three groups: no television advertisements, only promote ads, and either or both contrast or attack ads. Table 6.3 shows means, medians, quartiles, and the maximum for the three groups. A first point the table makes clear is that advertising is not a necessary condition for very high partisan correlation; the nonpartisan election with the highest such correlation did not involve any television advertising, and all three categories had one or more elections with a partisan correlation exceeding .9. Second, it appears that the typical partisan correlation may be higher

TABLE 6.3. Possible Impact of Television Advertising on Partisan Correlations

Type of Advertisments	Mean	Median	1st Quartile	3rd Quartile	Maximum	N
No TV ads	0.52	0.53	0.30	0.76	0.96	48
Promote only	0.48	0.45	0.27	0.78	0.91	23
Contrast or attack	0.59	0.63	0.43	0.79	0.90	17
Total	0.52	0.50	0.30	0.78	0.96	88

for elections with attack and/or contrast ads compared to either elections with no television advertising or with only promote ads. However, neither a one-way analysis of variance test of the means ($F = 0.98$, $p = .389$) nor a one-tailed t-test comparing the mean partisan correlation in elections with attack and/or contrast ads to the other two groups combined ($t = 1.20$, $p = .116$) achieves statistical significance indicating that the apparent differences are likely to reflect random variations. Finally, regression models (not shown) predicting the partisan correlation that included dummy variables for the nature of advertising, dummy variables for whether the election was an open seat or resulted in a defeat of an incumbent, and the winner's percentage of the vote produced neither a significant overall fit nor significant individual effects.[46]

CONCLUSION

Elections for state supreme courts have changed. The focus in this chapter has been on whether there has been an increase in partisanship in the voting patterns in state supreme court elections. The analysis shows that in states where elections for the court(s) of last resort are conducted on a partisan basis, the elections usually result in highly partisan voting patterns, and there has been little change in those patterns over the 1946–2013 period; where there has been change, it varies in direction with some states experiencing an increase in partisanship and others a decrease. In the two states continuing to use the hybrid system, where the voting patterns have long had a partisan tinge, there has been some increase in the degree of partisanship, although that change is clearer in Ohio than in Michigan. In states with a nonpartisan election

[46] Joint tests of each of the two sets of dummy variables also failed to achieve statistical significance. I also ran regressions using the natural logarithm of the number of airings of ads (adding one so that 0 converted to 0 when the log was taken); this again did not produce anything of statistical significance. Replacing the correlation with the Fisher's little-z transformation did not change the results.

system, the pattern varies, with some states showing sharp increases in partisan patterns and some maintaining the relatively low level of partisanship that has historically characterized nonpartisan supreme court elections in those states.

What accounts for the presence or absence of partisan patterns in nonpartisan elections? Occasionally a partisan pattern may simply reflect the fact that at least one of the candidates is closely identified with a political party, either because of prior political activity or perhaps because of political activity of a family member bearing the same last (or occasionally, first *and* last) name, or because the candidate has a last name closely identified with a political party. As noted in Chapter 1, one such example occurred in 1950 in Minnesota when one candidate was the son of a former Republican governor of the state and shared his father's first as well as last name.[47] Patterns of change reflect something more than the name-party nexus. Some of the most recent change probably reflects a growing pattern of the political parties endorsing and/or working on behalf of candidates running in nonpartisan elections. This may account for patterns in one of the 2010 Minnesota elections, and more generally for part of the shift in Washington. However, the most important factor is the involvement of a state supreme court in controversial issues, either past or anticipated, that align with party positions. In Washington in particular, the state supreme court has decided some controversial cases dealing with property rights and same-sex marriage. In Wisconsin, the court has decided some controversial issues dealing with torts and tort reform (DeFour 2011), and in 2011, issues related to the sharp curtailment of public sector unions that occurred that year after Republicans won control of the governor's office and both chambers of the legislature in the 2010 election.

This analysis shows that if courts decide high-visibility cases with strong partisan political import and voters have the opportunity to respond in the voting booth to courts' decisions on those issues, voters will often act in a partisan fashion. This will be helped along by interest groups with a stake in the issues in question, and the magnitude of that assistance has undoubtedly been affected by the U.S. Supreme Court's decisions in *Citizens United v. Federal Election Commission*,[48] and will be further affected by *American Tradition Partnership, Inc. v. Bullock*,[49] which made clear that the principles enunciated in *Citizens United* apply to state elections as well as federal elections.

47 One element I do not examine is the potential for name confusion producing *negative* correlations. This has sometimes happened when a candidate has a last name associated with a political party but in fact is personally associated with the other party, such as the 1970 election in Ohio discussed earlier.

48 558 U.S. 50 (2010).

49 567 U.S. ___ (2012).

This should not be surprising. The purpose of elections is to hold public officials accountable to the electorate not just to ensure their honesty and competence but also for the substance of their policies. Voters voting against judges or judicial candidates who are identified with policies the voters disagree with is the nature of the electoral process. Moreover, if courts decide issues that are important to powerful actors, the fact that those actors will attempt to influence the membership of the courts should also not be surprising or unexpected, particularly when there is little or no constraint on what those actors, whether individual persons, organized groups, or corporations, can do to advance their interests.

Does this analysis support the campaign long waged by supporters of the so-called merit system of judicial selection, the Missouri Plan, with periodic retention elections where voters are asked to decide whether a judge or justice should retain his or her office on a simple yes or no ballot? As shown in Chapter 4, justices have seldom been turned out of office in retention elections, although there have been some spectacular exceptions, including three justices of the Iowa Supreme Court defeated in 2010 after the court ruled in favor of same-sex marriage and three justices of the California Supreme Court in 1986 who were attacked for being soft on crime. In the next chapter I apply the method of partisan correlations to look at voting patterns in state supreme court retention elections as a means of examining whether the kinds of changes found for some nonpartisan states also appear for states that have adopted retention elections.

7

Patterns of Partisanship in Retention Elections

Historically, judicial retention elections have been low-key affairs. News coverage is minimal or nonexistent, voter participation is relatively low, and the incumbent is retained with a positive vote of 60 percent or more. As discussed in Chapter 4, out of the 736 retention elections for state supreme courts from the first such election in 1936 through 2013, voters have turned only eleven (1.5 percent) justices out of office.[1] While the probability that a supreme court justice will be turned out of office in a retention election is low, it is higher than for lower level courts.[2]

The 2010 election cycle included the dramatic defeat of all three Iowa Supreme Court justices who were standing for retention that year. Their defeat came after a campaign launched by those opposed to the court's unanimous 2009 decision in *Varnum v. Brien* which struck down the Iowa law that limited marriage to heterosexual couples (Schotland 2011).[3] This was almost twenty-five years after the similar defeat of Rose Bird and two of her colleagues on the California Supreme Court in 1986 (Culver and Wold 1986). In both the 2010 Iowa election and the 1986 California election there were strong partisan correlations. Specifically, the correlations between the county-level percentage voting to oust the justice and the county-level vote for the Republican candidate for governor ranged from .84 to .93. This is not particularly surprising given that the issues that led to the campaigns against the incumbents

1 This figure, and the analysis that follows, includes the Oklahoma Court of Criminal Appeals as well as the Oklahoma Supreme Court.

2 Larry Aspin, who has been tracking judicial retention elections at all levels in 12 states (Alaska, Arizona, Colorado, Illinois, Indiana, Iowa, Kansas, Missouri, Nebraska, New Mexico, Utah, and Wyoming), reports that from 1964 through 2010 only 0.9 percent of the 7,689 elections resulted in a judge being turned out of office (computed from Aspin 2011:225).

3 763 N.W.2d 862 (Iowa 2010).

closely aligned with party positions on the central issues of the death penalty in California and same-sex marriage in Iowa.

However, as I will show, partisan patterns in voting in state supreme court retention elections are not limited to elections in which incumbents are defeated, nor are they limited to elections in which there are partisan-oriented campaigns challenging the incumbent. Moreover, there has been substantial change in the partisan patterns in some states over time. In at least one state, California, there has been a shift from a positive correlation between the county-level vote to retain and the county-level vote for the Republican gubernatorial candidate to a positive correlation between the vote to retain and the county-level vote for the Democratic gubernatorial candidate. An important question that I will address in the analysis presented in this chapter is whether there are any systematic factors that can account for the broader patterns in partisanship that I describe. In the next section I present a discussion of partisan patterns in state supreme court retention elections where the incumbent garnered less than a 60 percent yes-vote. The next section of this chapter presents a descriptive analysis of the full set of statewide supreme court retention elections including how, if at all, patterns have changed over time. The last section examines possible explanations for variation in the partisan correlations in retention elections.

CLOSE STATE SUPREME COURT RETENTION ELECTIONS

Table 7.1 provides some summary information on the 736 state supreme court retention elections that have taken place through 2013.[4] The table shows that, in addition to the eleven justices turned out of office, there were thirty-seven incumbents who received yes-votes of less than 60 percent, with nine less than 55 percent. As noted, six of the defeats occurred in California (1986) and Iowa (2010); the remaining five occurred in Alaska (1964), Nebraska (1996), Pennsylvania (2005), Tennessee (1996), and Wyoming (1992). A total of twelve of the twenty states using retention elections experienced "close" elections using less than 60 percent as the cutoff; if one uses less than 55 percent as the cutoff criterion, the number of states drops to eight, and the number of "close" elections drops to twenty. In the discussion that follows, I use the 60 percent criterion for inclusion while

[4] Included among the retention elections used in the analysis in this chapter are those from Utah and Montana which defaulted to the retention format because the incumbent did not face a challenger.

TABLE 7.1. State Supreme Court Retention Elections between 1936 and 2013

State	First Year	Number	Defeats	50–54.9%	55–59.9%
Alaska	1962	25	1	2	2
Arizona	1976	30	0	0	0
California	1936	73	3	2	5
Colorado	1970	33	0	0	1
Florida	1980	42	0	0	2
Illinois	1964	21	0	0	0
Indiana	1972	23	0	0	1
Iowa	1964	64	3	1	0
Kansas	1960	60	0	0	0
Maryland	1978	31	0	0	0
Missouri	1942	50	0	0	4
Montana	1974	15	0	0	0
Nebraska	1964	50	1	0	1
New Mexico	1994	12	0	0	0
Oklahoma[a]	1968	111	0	1	12
Pennsylvania	1981	17	1	2	0
South Dakota	1984	17	0	0	0
Tennessee	1994	13	1	1	0
Utah	1970	20	0	0	0
Wyoming	1974	29	1	0	0
Total		736	11	9	28

[a] Includes elections for both the Oklahoma Supreme Court and the Oklahoma Court of Criminal Appeals.

distinguishing between positive retention votes between 50 percentand 55 percent from those between 55 percent and 60 percent.[5] For purposes of the analysis of retention elections, partisan correlations were computed by correlating the county-level yes-vote percentage with the county-level vote for the Democratic candidate for governor. Thus, a negative correlation indicates that the yes-vote percentage tended to be higher in counties leaning more Republican in their gubernatorial voting.

[5] I used the criterion of 60 percent to define "close" elections for this analysis for two reasons. First, two states require a judge seeking retention to obtain a positive vote greater than 55 percent: 60 percent in Illinois and 57 percent in New Mexico. Second, increasing the cutoff to 60 percent provides more "close" cases for consideration. There were two elections in Illinois that produced results within 10 percentage points of removing the incumbent, but given the 60 percent criterion in Illinois, these are not treated as "close" for purposes of my analysis.

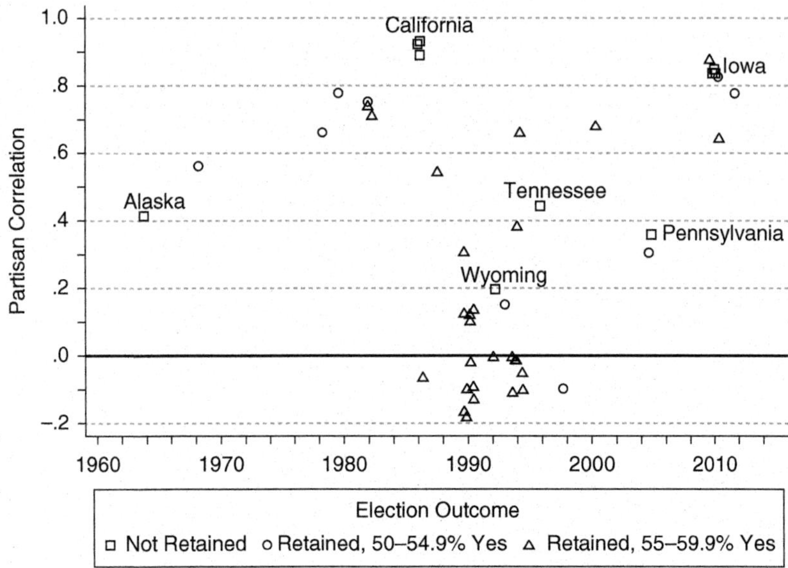

FIGURE 7.1. Partisan Correlations in "Close" Statewide Retention Elections.

Combining the defeats and the close elections, there are forty-six elections that were conducted on a statewide basis and hence for which it is possible to compute the partisan correlations; the other two elections that were close or resulted in defeats occurred in Nebraska on a district basis and hence are not included in the analysis of partisan correlations.[6] Figure 7.1 plots the partisan correlations for the forty-six elections by year, showing the elections in which the justice was not retained with square markers, those retained with 50–55 percent as circles, and those retained with 55–60 percent with triangles; positive correlations are those above the heavy horizontal line and negative correlations are those below the heavy line. What is evident in the figure is that strongly partisan retention elections are not limited to elections in which the incumbent was defeated.

While some of the strongest partisan correlations in 2010 were in Iowa, hovering around .84, several other 2010 elections in which the justices involved were retained produced strong partisan correlations. A retention election in Colorado actually produced the highest correlation in 2010, .88, but the justice, Alex Martinez, was retained with a 59.5 percent yes-vote. Two other Colorado justices, Michael Bender and Nancy Rice, were also up for retention, but did slightly better than Justice Martinez, with 60.4 percent and 61.9 percent of the

[6] One of these elections involved the defeat of Justice David Lanphier (1996) and the other, involving Justice C. Thomas White (1986), fell just under 60 percent (59.3 percent).

voters favoring retention; while the partisan correlations for Justices Bender (0.82) and Rice (0.85) differed little from Justice Martinez, they are not included in Figure 7.1. The challenge to these Colorado justices was spearheaded by conservative groups associated with a range of issues including property rights (eminent domain), taxes, and congressional districting (Cardona 2010a).[7]

In Alaska, Justice Dana Fabe was retained with a 54.7 percent yes-vote; that election produced a partisan correlation of .83. Ten years earlier, Justice Fabe was retained with a 55.7 percent yes-vote that produced a partisan correlation of .68. In that earlier election Justice Fabe was attacked by conservatives for an opinion that said that "a hospital that accepted government money could not ban legal abortions" (Toomey 2000); in 2010 her critics raised issues related to her "rulings on abortion, gay marriage, benefits for same-sex partners of state workers, and prisoner rights" (Demer 2010).

One retention election in Florida in 2010 produced a fairly high partisan correlation of .63, although the justice involved, Jorge Labarga, was retained with a 59.0 percent yes-vote. Three other Florida justices were on the ballot for retention, James Perry, Ricky Polston, and Charles Canady; their yes-votes were 61.7 percent, 66.1 percent, and 67.5 percent respectively, and the corresponding partisan correlations were .64, .48, and .45. Justices Labarga and Perry were attacked by Tea Party groups at least in part due to the justices' joining the Florida Supreme Court 5-2 majority that struck from the November ballot a measure that asked Floridians to vote on whether Florida should exempt itself from the provisions of the Patient Protection and Affordable Care Act – AKA Obamacare (Haughney 2010); interestingly, Justices Canady and Polston constituted the two dissenters in the case (their yes-vote percentages were in line with patterns over the prior 20 years).[8]

Figure 7.1 shows only one 2012 retention election.[9] That election occurred in Iowa and involved Justice David Wiggins, the one member of the Iowa

7 One might speculate that the Colorado justices were helped in their retention campaigns by very strong positive evaluations conducted by the state's Commission on Judicial Performance (Cardona 2010b). This may also be true for Dana Fabe; the Alaska Judicial Council also conducts evaluations in advance of retention elections.

8 As noted by Aspin (2011:228), the four justices up for retention for the Kansas Supreme Court also had opposition campaigns spearheaded by an anti-abortion group (Kansans for Life); however, all four were retained by yes-votes from 61.5 percent to 62.8 percent; the partisan correlations ranged from .241 to .409.

9 Seven of the thirty-three retention elections in 2014 produced yes-votes under 60 percent; in addition, the election in Illinois, where 60 percent is required for retention, produced a yes-vote of 60.8 percent. Five of the seven elections, those in Kansas and Tennessee where campaigns to defeat the incumbents were mounted, produced partisan correlations in the range of .61 to .73. The other two elections were both in Oklahoma but just barely met the under 60 percent criterion; the partisan correlations in those two elections were −.13 and −.19.

Supreme Court standing for retention in 2012 who had participated in the unanimous decision striking down Iowa's law precluding same-sex marriage. The same groups that campaigned successfully to reject the three sitting justices running for retention in 2010 sought to oust Justice Wiggins (Pettys 2013:56–63). The anti-Wiggins campaign included television advertising which, as discussed in Chapter 4, is rare in retention elections.[10] Unlike 2010, there was a counter campaign supporting Wiggins's retention (pp. 63–72), and he was retained with a 54.5 percent yes-vote; however, the partisan correlation at .79 was only moderately lower than for the Iowa justices defeated two years earlier. The three justices appointed to replace those defeated in 2010 were also on the 2012 ballot in Iowa; they were all easily retained with positive votes of almost 75 percent and partisan correlations on the order of .20.

Figure 7.1 shows with state labels all of the statewide retention elections that resulted in defeats. The strongest partisan correlations occurred in the 1986 California retention elections: .89, .93, and .93.[11] While the 1986 election is well known due to its result, which is usually attributed to the justices' routine reversal of death penalty cases (see Culver and Wold 1986), in terms of partisanship the 1986 election was something of a culmination of a pattern that had built over the years following Rose Bird's appointment as chief justice by Governor Jerry Brown in 1977. When Justice Bird first stood for retention in 1978, she barely survived with a 51.7 percent yes-vote, in an election with a partisan correlation of .66.[12] Three other justices were up for retention in 1978 and they obtained

[10] In 2012, retention elections were held in 11 states, involving 23 justices running for retention; in only two other states, Florida and Oklahoma, were any television advertisements aired in connection with the retention election, and the one ad that ran in Oklahoma was supportive of retention. The only other year for which the Brennan Center shows television advertisements in retention elections is 2010, when ads were run in Iowa, Colorado, and Alaska. Note as discussed in Chapter 5 that the Brennan data start in 1999, so I have no systematic information on the use of advertising in the earlier high-visibility retention elections such as those in Tennessee in 1996 (discussed later) and California in 1986, although as discussed in Chapter 5 there was some significant television advertising in 1986 in California, and even in earlier elections involving Rose Bird.

[11] In 1986 there were actually six justices up for retention. The three who were not challenged were Malcolm Lucas, Edward Panelli, and Stanley Mosk, all of whom received yes-votes well above 70 percent (79.5 percent, 78,7 percent, and 73.6 percent); the partisan correlations for the three unchallenged justices were .54, .49, and .74, suggesting that the campaigns against Rose Bird, Cruz Reynoso, and Joseph Grodin had at least some carryover effect in terms of the patterning of the vote.

[12] News stories around the time of the election reported that two separate campaigns had been "mounted to unseat her but neither one really jelled" (Endicott 1978a, 1978b). The morning of the election there was a story in the *Los Angeles Times* that reported the court had voted 4-3, with Justice Bird in the majority, to strike down a law mandating prison time for offenders convicted of using a gun during a violent crime (Endicott and Fairbanks 1978).

yes-votes of from 61.2 percent to 72.6 percent.[13] While not included in Figure 7.1, it is noteworthy that the partisan correlations for the other three elections in California in 1978 were similar to the correlation in the vote regarding Justice Bird: .65, .59, and .57; this suggests that there might have been some carryover effect from the negative attention directed at Justice Bird.[14]

The challenge to Justice Bird in 1978 was not the first California election in which one or more of the justices up for retention came under attack. In 1966, in the wake of the California Supreme Court's decision overturning an anti-fair housing measure that voters had approved in a referendum in 1964, four of the five justices standing for retention came under attack by "right wing" groups (Endicott 1978b). The campaign was not particularly successful, and the four targeted justices – Roger Traynor, Paul Peek, Stanley Mosk, and Louis Burke – were all retained with yes-votes in the range of 62–65 percent; the campaign did reduce the yes-vote for the targeted justices as indicated by the fact that the one justice up for retention not targeted, Marshall McComb, obtained a yes-vote of 79.2 percent. In that election the partisan correlations ranged from .34 to .47; the partisan correlation for the unchallenged Justice McComb was actually one of the higher ones at .44.

There was one set of retention elections between 1978 when Justice Bird had her close call and 1986 when she and two colleagues were ousted; the 1982 election forebode what was to occur in 1986. Four justices stood for retention, three of whom were recent appointees of Governor Jerry Brown and one of whom had been appointed by Governor Ronald Reagan. An organization called Californians for Judicial Reform (CJR) sought the ouster of the three Brown appointeess – Cruz Reynoso, Allen Broussard, and Otto Kaus – whom CJR deemed to be too liberal. CJR was more or less a front for leaders of the Republican Party including the Republican gubernatorial candidate, California attorney General George Deukmejian, who hoped to win the election and then to be able to replace the three justices with people more to his own liking ("The Encouragement of Ugliness" 1982; Hager 1982a, 1982b).[15]

13 One intriguing aspect of the vote in this election was that Justice Bird actually got more yes-votes than one of the other candidates, and not much fewer (about 20,000) than a second; however there were over 100,000 more no-votes for her than for these other two justices.

14 The next set of retention elections for the California Supreme Court came in 1990. One candidate in that election, Armand Arabian, got less than a 60 percent yes-vote (55.8 percent), but the partisan correlation for Arabian was only .31. The remaining three justices standing for retention got yes-votes in the range of 66–69 percent, and the partisan correlations were –.03, –.08, and .30 (the negative values for the first two indicate that the yes-vote percentages were in the direction of the Republican vote).

15 California holds retention elections every four years, coinciding with the gubernatorial election.

The three challenged justices survived, but all had yes-votes less than 60 percent (52.4 percent, 56.2 percent, and 57.0 percent); the one justice not challenged, Reagan appointee Frank Richardson, received a 76.2 percent yes-vote. The partisan correlations for the three challenged justices were .76, .71, and .75; the partisan correlation for the unchallenged Richardson was .43.[16]

The best known of the other defeats of state supreme court justices in retention elections is the 1996 Tennessee election that resulted in the ouster of Penny White. The campaign against Justice White focused on her vote in a unanimous decision that overturned a death sentence in a particularly brutal murder case; the court upheld the conviction but ordered a new sentencing proceeding. The effort to remove Justice White was spearheaded by the Tennessee Conservative Union, and brought together victims' rights groups, religious conservatives, and law enforcement organizations (see Reid 1999).[17] Given the strength of the partisan correlation in other elections raising highly visible and partisan issues, it may be surprising that the partisan correlation in Tennessee in 1996 was a relatively modest .45. The relatively low correlation may be because in Tennessee the death penalty issue did not, at least at the time, align in a strongly partisan way.

The 1992 ouster of Wyoming justice Walter Urbigkit demonstrates that an effort to defeat a justice standing for retention need not produce a partisan voting pattern. The successful campaign to oust Justice Urbigkit focused on the justice's record in criminal cases, with his critics claiming he was soft on crime ("Foes Want Voters to Fire Judge; Battle Rages in Wyoming, Spurred by Claim that Supreme Court Justice Is Too Easy on Criminals" 1992). However, that campaign did not lead to a partisan pattern; the partisan correlation was only .19.

[16] Squire and Smith (1988) report the results of a survey of registered California voters carried out several months before the 1982 election in which respondents were asked whether they would support the retention of each of the four justices who would be on the November ballot. Half the respondents were told who had appointed each justice and half were not given this information. Those given the information about the appointer were less likely to say they had no opinion on retention and increased the likelihood of saying they would not support retention regardless of who the appointing governor was. Importantly, there was a greater willingness to support retention of the Reagan appointee regardless of whether the information on who was the appointer was provided. The authors found no evidence that party identification predicted support (with or without information on the appointer), although support for Governor Brown was a predictor when information was provided. It is difficult to draw conclusions about what this says about actual voting which occurred more than two months after the survey, a period during which the campaign to reject the three Brown appointees would have been under way.

[17] Somewhat similar issues were the basis of the campaign that led to the ouster of Nebraska justice David Lanphier that same year (Reid 1999); because that was a district-based election, I could not compute a partisan correlation.

Exactly why this election did not produce a stronger partisan pattern is unclear. One possible explanation is that calls to be tough on crime simply did not, and still might not, register in a partisan way in Wyoming.

The 2005 retention elections in Pennsylvania may be somewhat unique (Goodman and Marks 2006). The effort to defeat the two justices standing for retention, Justices Sandra Newman and Russell Nigro, flowed not from high salience, partisan issues, but from a broad frustration with state government more generally arising from the legislature's decision to increase salaries for itself and other state officials. Justices Nigro and Newman had the misfortune of being the only state officials on the statewide ballot in 2005, the first statewide election after the legislature's action (Dao 2005). As things worked out only Justice Nigro was ousted; Justice Newman was retained with a 54.1 percent yes-vote. There was no specific link to issues with a partisan overtone, and it is not surprising that the partisan correlation for Justice Nigro was a modest .36; for Justice Newman the partisan correlation was slightly lower at .31.

Alaska justice Harry Arend has the distinction of being the first state supreme court justice ousted through a retention election. His election in 1964 was only the third retention election for a justice of the Alaska Supreme Court; two other justices had been retained in 1962 in Alaska's first retention election for its supreme court. Arend's defeat resulted not from any broad political controversy or from any issues of competence but as a by-product of a fight between the state bar association and the Alaska Supreme Court over the system of attorney discipline then in use in Alaska. Frustrated by the system that had been adopted by the court, members of the bar campaigned against Justice Arend when he stood for retention. Justice Arend did not campaign in his own defense and was not retained (Olsen 2005). The partisan correlation was .41.

In every case where a justice was not retained on a statewide vote, the partisan correlation was positive. That is, counties with higher Democratic votes for governor tended to provide higher percentages of yes-votes, while it was the more Republican counties that tended to provide higher percentages of no-votes. Among the forty-six statewide elections producing yes-votes of less than 60 percent, only fourteen produced negative correlations (shown below the heavy horizontal line in Figure 7.1), and only five of those were stronger than −.10; the strongest negative correlation was .19. Of the thirty-two positive correlations, seven fell below +.20 and nineteen exceeded +.50. The question this raises is why is there such a strong pattern that links Republican-leaning counties to having stronger votes against the retention of justices in the relatively close retention elections? Where there have been strong Democratic links with the pattern of yes-votes in close elections the positions of the targeted justices have been such that those justices align with Democratic policy preferences. Justices facing retention whose positions align with Republican policy preferences have not activated campaigns against retention that resulted in close elections. As I will show in the next section, there are elections in which yes-votes exceeded 60 percent where the Republican-leaning counties were more likely to favor retention.

ALL STATEWIDE SUPREME COURT RETENTION ELECTIONS

General Patterns

In this section, I extend the descriptive analysis to all 639 statewide supreme court retention elections.[18] Figure 7.2a shows the distribution of partisan correlations for all of the statewide retention elections. The figure shows that while there is some difference in the overall range of correlations on the Republican (left of zero) and Democratic sides (right of zero), it is not as dramatic as for the close elections. The largest absolute value on the Republican side is .73 compared to .93 on the Democratic side.[19] Importantly, there is little difference in the number falling on the two sides: 296 (46 percent) on the Republican side compared to 343 (54 percent) on the Democratic side.[20] Figure 7.2b, which shows the distribution of the partisan absolute correlations, which is how I will refer to the absolute values of the partisan correlations, makes it clear that the majority of correlations fall in the middle range (between −.5 and +.5). However, as can be seen in Figure 7.2a, there is a larger proportion of values outside this range on the Democratic side (25 percent) than on the Republican side (9 percent).[21]

[18] The number is 639 rather than 640. It was not possible to compute the correlation for the 1972 retention election in Alaska. Alaska does not have counties but does have election districts, the number of which has ranged from 19 in 1962 to 40 since 1992. I used the election districts in lieu of counties. The number of election districts in 1972 differed from the numbers in both 1970 and 1974 when gubernatorial elections were held. This made it impossible to compute the partisan correlation for the 1972 election. This also is why Table 7.1 shows 25 elections for Alaska, while Table 7.2 shows 24.

[19] The California election in 2014 involving nominee Mariano-Florentino Cuéllar produced a partisan correlation of .94. Two sitting justices of the court were on the ballot, Kathryn Werdegar (appointed by Republican Pete Wilson) and Goodwin Liu (appointed by Jerry Brown); the partisan correlations for those two elections were .87 and .91 respectively. I could find no indication that campaigns were staged in connection with any of these three elections; the only newspaper article about the election that I could locate was headlined "justices face easy election road" (Mintz 2014).

[20] I'm not suggesting that this is a random distribution; a single sample difference of proportions test against 0.5 produces a statistically significant Z-value of 1.70 (one-sided $p = .0440$).

[21] This is far from a random difference; a difference of proportion test yields a Z of 5.31 ($p < .0001$).

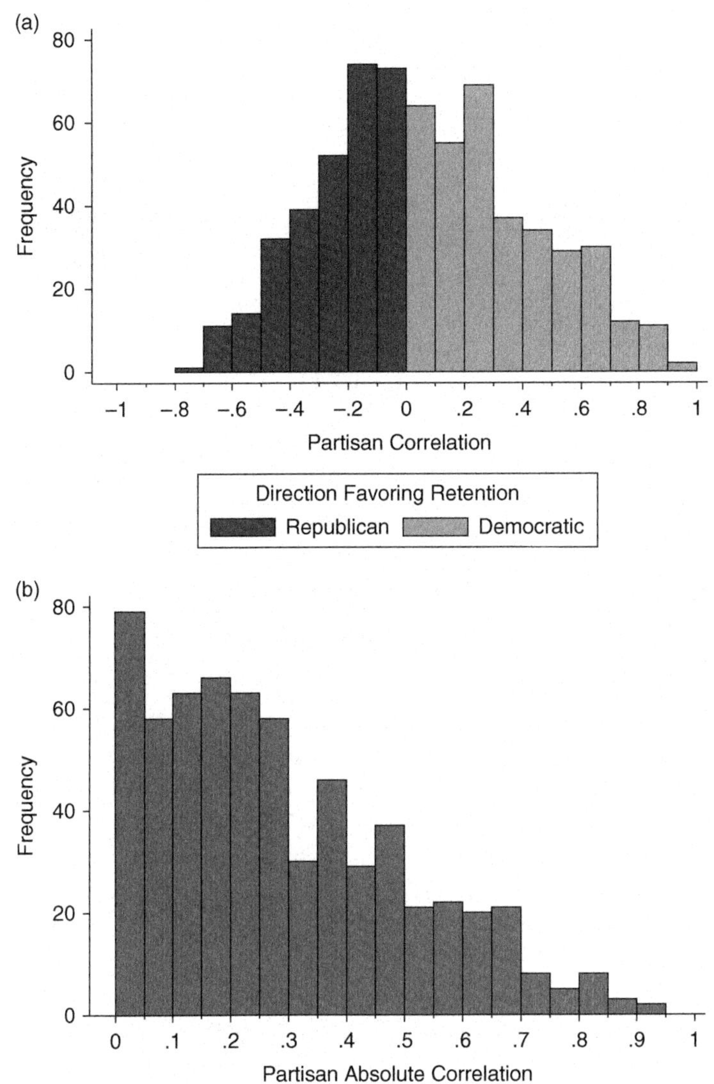

FIGURE 7.2. Distribution of Partisan Correlations for All Statewide Retention Elections, 1936–2013; (a) Showing Directionality, (b) Absolute Correlations.

While the tendency for partisan correlations in retention elections is to lean more in the Democratic direction, my central question in this book is whether judicial elections have changed over time, and here that question becomes whether partisan correlations have changed over time, either in magnitude or direction. Figure 7.3 plots all of the partisan correlations for state supreme

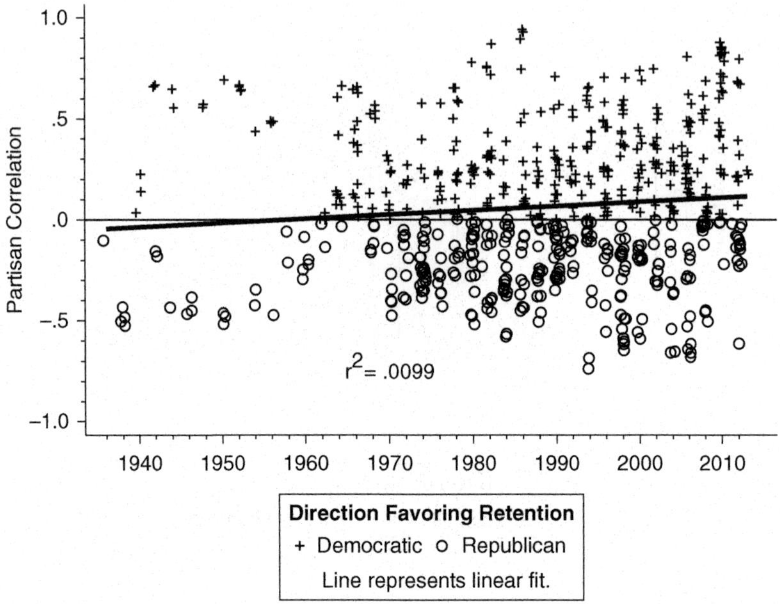

FIGURE 7.3. Partisan Correlations, All Statewide Retention Elections.

court retention elections from 1936 through 2013; plus signs indicate partisan correlations in the direction of Democratic counties being more supportive of retention, and circles indicate partisan correlations in the direction of Republican counties being more supportive. The figure also shows the regression line predicting the partisan correlation from the year, and the associated r^2. There is a very modest, albeit statistically significant, relationship indicating an increase in the correlation over time of .0021 per year, or an overall increase of about .14 in the average partisan correlation over the period 1936–2013. If I limit the period covered to 1960 (when many states began adopting retention elections) to 2013, the r^2 increases from .0099 to .0147 and the slope increases to .0030, which translates to an increase in the average correlation of .158 between 1960 and 2013). Thus, when looking across all of the states using retention elections for their supreme courts, there has been only a modest change over time.

The analysis based on Figure 7.3 does not really answer the question of whether partisanship has increased because I have included directionality. It may simply be that partisanship has shifted from Republicans to Democrats being more supportive of retention. In fact, as shown in Figure 7.4 which plots the partisan absolute correlations over time, that does appear to be the case. The fitted line is nearly flat, and the regression coefficient (.0002) is not statistically significant,

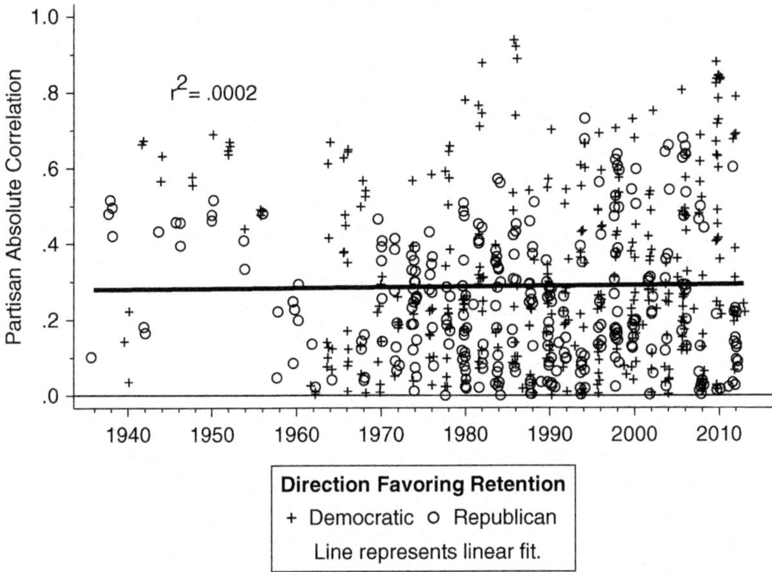

FIGURE 7.4. Partisan Absolute Correlations, All Statewide Retention Elections.

or even close to being statistically significance (t = 0.40).[22] Hence overall, there does not appear to have been any major change in the degree of partisanship in state supreme court retention elections, although there appears to be a small shift in the nature of that partisanship with Democratic-leaning counties becoming more supportive of retention and Republican-leaning counties less supportive.

State-Specific Patterns

The overall pattern is interesting and important, but it masks significant state-level variations. Figure 7.5 replicates Figure 7.3 individually for each state that conducts statewide retention elections for its supreme court;[23] because of the longer experience of retention elections in California and Missouri, those states are shown at the end of Figure 7.5 rather than alphabetically with the other states. The variation among the states in the trends over time is striking. Some states go from leaning Republican, by which I mean Republican

[22] If the analysis is limited to elections starting in 1960, there is a statistically significant slope of 0.0028 (r^2 = .0303), which indicates that over the 50 years between 1960 and 2010 the partisan absolute correlation increased by about .14, at best a very modest change.

[23] For completeness I have included Nebraska, which has statewide retention elections only for the chief justice; there were only six statewide retention elections for Nebraska's chief justice through 2012.

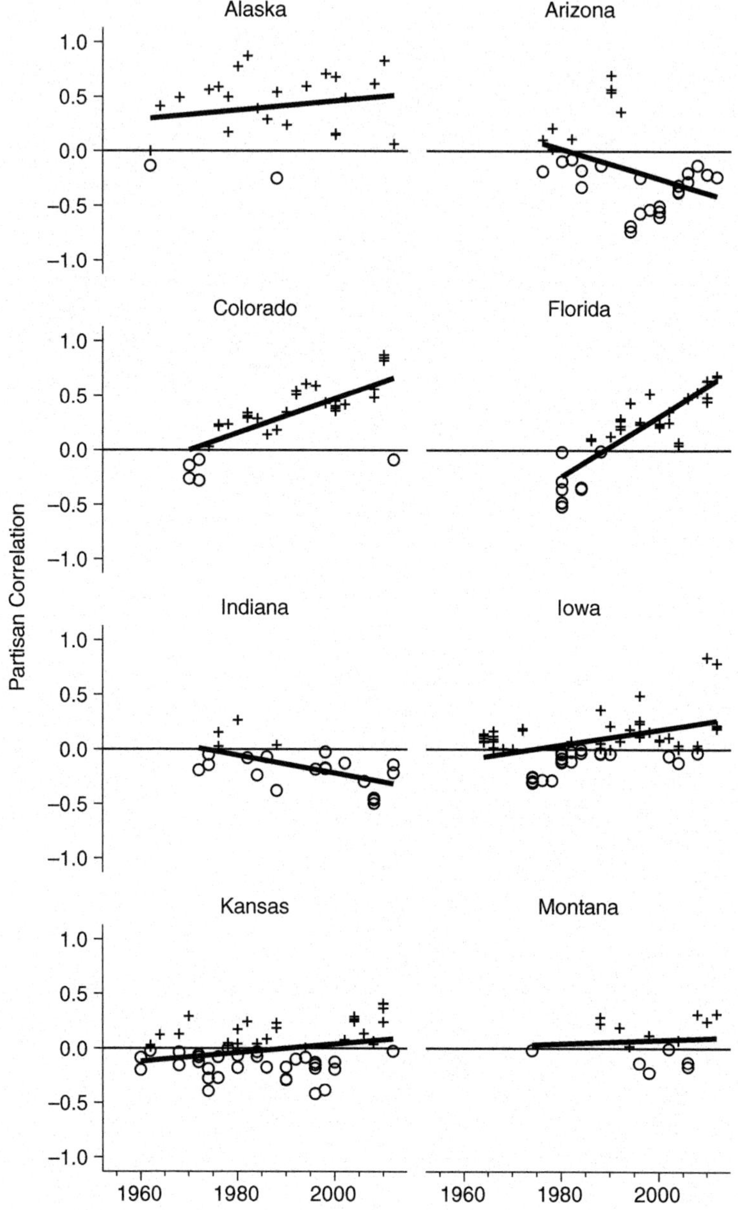

FIGURE 7.5. Partisan Correlations by State.

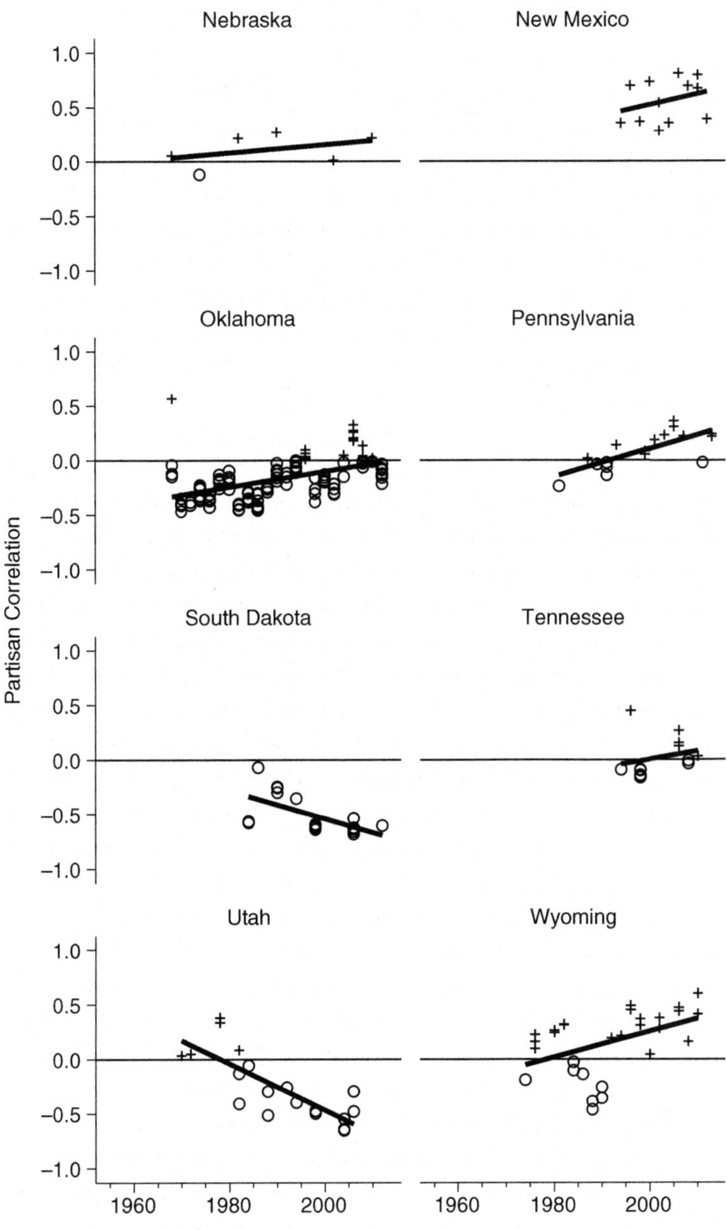

FIGURE 7.5. (*continued*)

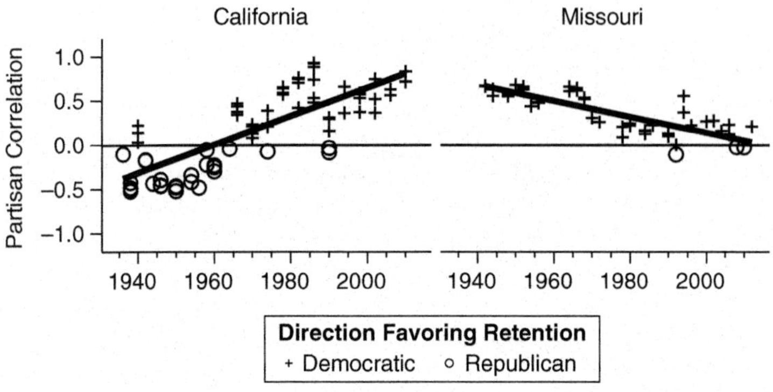

FIGURE 7.5. (*continued*)

counties tend to be more supportive of retention which is indicated by a negative correlation shown as a circle to leaning Democratic shown as a plus sign (California and perhaps Colorado and Florida). Some go from no clear lean to either a Democratic lean or a Republican lean (Utah, Indiana, Arizona). Some go from a lean in one direction or the other to no lean (Missouri, Oklahoma). Some show essentially no shift (Kansas, Montana). Other states evidence a shift more strongly on the same side of the partisan divide (South Dakota, New Mexico, Alaska). I have not mentioned Iowa here, and because I have combined Oklahoma's two courts, it may be that there is a difference between those courts; I will return to both of these states. There is a clear tendency for the shifts to be such that Democratic-leaning counties have become more favorable toward retention; thirteen of the eighteen states show a positive slope with only five showing a negative slope, the latter being indicative of a shift toward Republican-leaning counties more favorable toward retention.

Figure 7.6 shows the partisan absolute correlations separately for each state; California and Missouri are again at the end of the figure. The figure makes clear that regardless of whether states have shifted toward a higher percentage of yes-votes as a county votes more Democratic in gubernatorial elections, the magnitude of the relationship between voting in state supreme court retention elections and partisanship in the gubernatorial election has tended to increase. Of the eighteen states shown in Figure 7.6, fifteen states show a positive slope indicating that the absolute values of the correlations have tended to increase over time. The only states showing a decline in partisanship are Missouri, Oklahoma, and Tennessee.[24]

[24] The 2014 election in Tennessee might change that state's pattern (see Blinder 2014a, 2014b); the partisan correlations in that election ranged from .67 to .73.

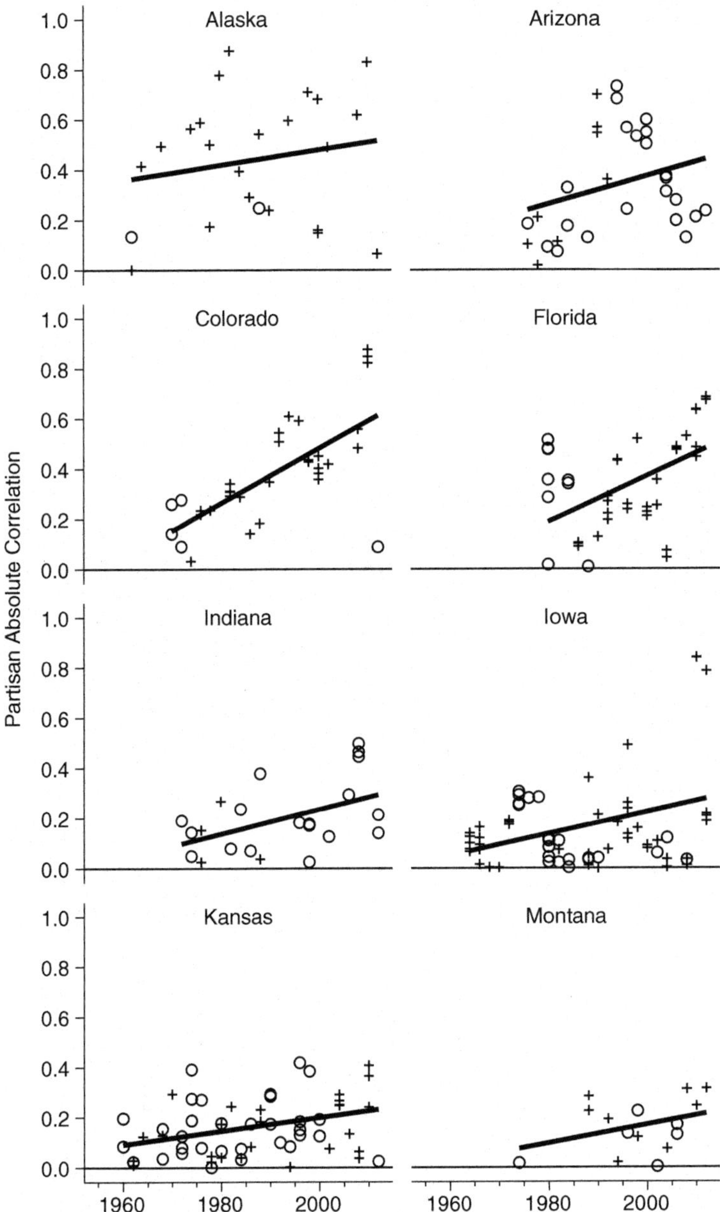

FIGURE 7.6. Partisan Absolute Correlations by State.

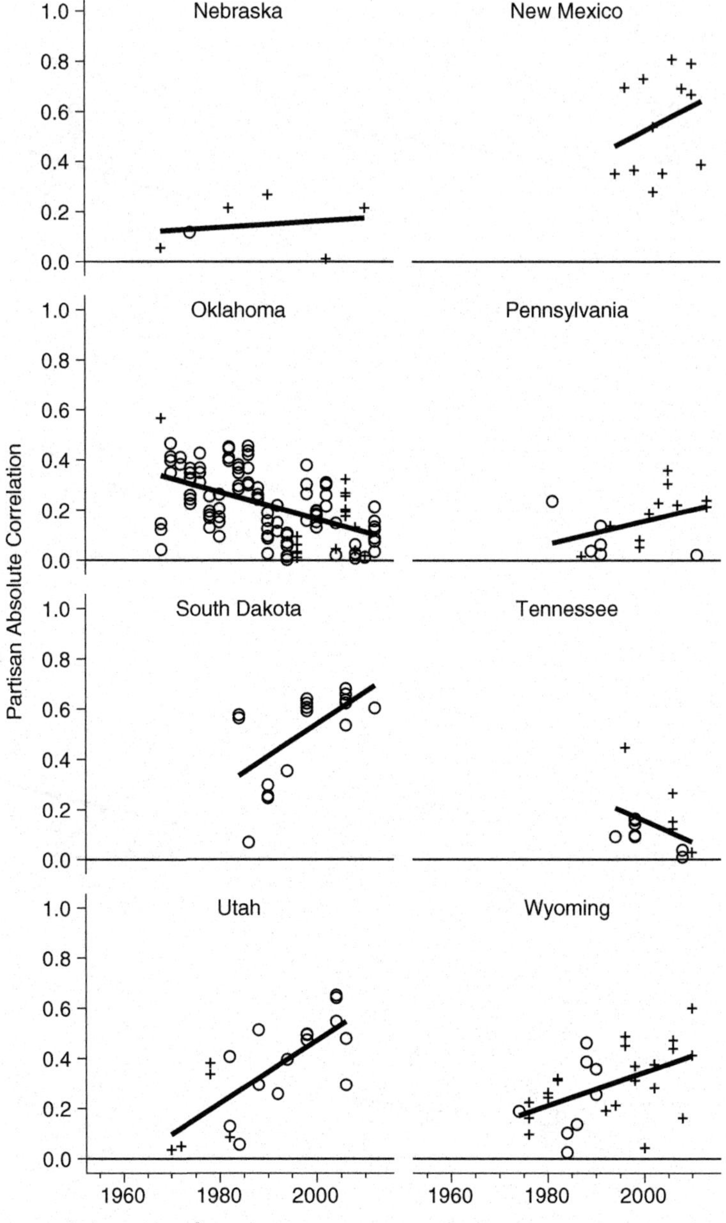

FIGURE 7.6. *(continued)*

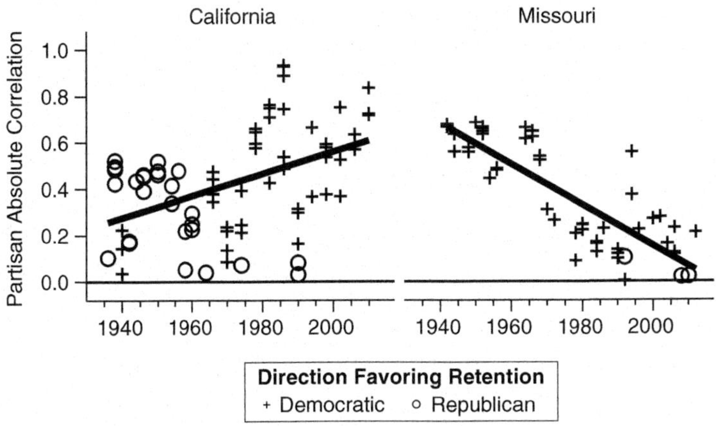

FIGURE 7.6. *(continued)*

This discussion has only considered whether the lines in Figures 7.5 and 7.6 appear to be sloping up or down. For some states, the scatter may be essentially random. To test this, I ran regressions predicting the partisan correlations and the partisan absolute correlations by year. Table 7.2 shows the simple regression slopes, the r^2s, and an indication of whether the slope differed from zero to a statistically significant degree. The table shows that neither of the two slopes for Alaska, Montana, Nebraska, New Mexico, or Tennessee differs statistically from zero. This is also true for the partisan absolute correlations for Pennsylvania and Arizona; the two Oklahoma courts require separate consideration, and as I will show, the significant results for Iowa are entirely a product of the response to the Iowa Supreme Court's same-sex marriage decision. What the table does make clear is that there is real change going on in most states, both with regard to the degree of the partisan pattern and the nature of that pattern.

The left panel in Figure 7.7 shows the pattern of partisan correlations in Iowa with lines plotted both including (solid line) and excluding (dashed line) the three 2010 elections, plus the one 2012 involving a justice who participated in the same-sex marriage decision. It is clear that the trend that appeared in Figure 7.5 for Iowa was generated in significant part by the contentious retention elections that occurred in response to the Iowa Supreme Court's same-sex marriage decision. Omitting those four elections, the trend line is less steep and the slope achieves statistical significance at the .05 level only if one assumes a one-tailed test (i.e., an advance hypothesis regarding the direction of change). The right panel shows the partisan absolute correlations. While including the four elections produces a positive trend line, without

TABLE 7.2. Time Trend Regressions for Partisan Correlations

State	Number	Partisan Correlations		Partisan Absolute Correlations	
		b	r^2	b	r^2
Alaska	24	0.0042	0.0436	0.0030	0.0327
Arizona	30	–0.0134*	0.1568	0.0056	0.0833
California	73	0.0161***	0.6249	0.0048***	0.1994
Colorado	33	0.0157***	0.5264	0.0110***	0.4739
Florida	42	0.0275***	0.7549	0.0091***	0.2427
Indiana	23	–0.0081**	0.3402	0.0049*	0.2228
Iowa	64	0.0069***	0.1899	0.0044**	0.1149
Kansas	60	0.0040*	0.0886	0.0027**	0.1193
Missouri	50	–0.0091***	0.6671	–0.0088***	0.6800
Montana	15	0.0017	0.0086	0.0037	0.1268
Nebraska (CJ only)	6	0.0037	0.1615	0.0012	0.0396
New Mexico	12	0.0099	0.0877	0.0099	0.0877
Oklahoma	111	0.0072***	0.2382	–0.0053***	0.2715
Supreme Court	78	0.0084***	0.3527	–0.0048***	0.2196
Criminal Appeals	33	0.0038	0.0593	–0.0065***	0.4033
Pennsylvania	17	0.0141***	0.5526	0.0046	0.1667
South Dakota	17	–0.0128**	0.3788	0.0127**	0.3788
Tennessee	13	0.0076	0.0519	–0.0084	0.1646
Utah	20	–0.0214***	0.6381	0.0125***	0.5477
Wyoming	29	0.0118*	0.2107	0.0066**	0.2589

*$p < .05$; **$p < .01$; ***$p < .001$.

those elections the slope of the line is actually negative, although it is effectively a flat line with a slope of zero. It may be that the elections in response to the same-sex marriage decision represent the beginning of a change in the partisan character of retention elections in Iowa, although partisanship did not appear to be a factor in the 2012 retention elections of the justices appointed to replace the three justices turned out of office in 2010. In any case, at this point there is no way to ascertain whether there will continue to be an increase in that partisanship in coming years.

As noted previously, Oklahoma is unique among states using retention elections for the state supreme court in having two courts of last resort, one for criminal cases and one for noncriminal matters. The information shown in Table 7.2 shows that there has been significant change in the partisan

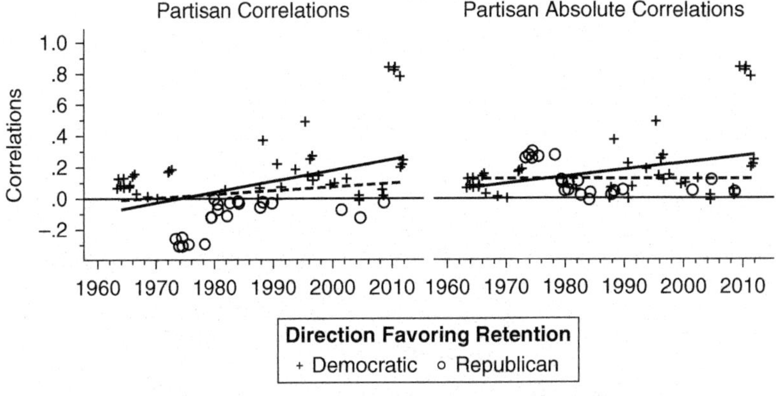

FIGURE 7.7. Partisan Correlations in Iowa, 1962–2012.

correlations in retention elections for the Oklahoma Supreme Court but not for the Oklahoma Court of Criminal Appeals (CCA). Figure 7.8 plots the partisan correlations for the two courts separately. The correlations for the Supreme Court are shown as either plus signs or open circles, with the trend line in black; the correlations for the CCA are shown as either X's or filled circles with the corresponding trend line shown as a solid gray line. Clearly, the line for the CCA is flatter than for the Supreme Court. However, that difference is entirely due to one outlier: the 1968 CCA retention election involving Judge Kirksey Nix.[25] When that election is omitted and the line is reestimated (shown as a dashed gray line), the lines for the two courts are very close, almost on top of one another; the slope for the CCA without the Nix election is .0079 compared to .0084 for the Supreme Court. The revised r^2 for the Court of Criminal Appeals (.368) is also actually slightly larger than the r^2 for the Supreme Court (.353). Omitting the outlier from the regression on the partisan absolute correlation has a lesser effect on the results showing a decline in the degree of partisanship over the forty-four years Oklahoma has used retention elections for its two courts of last resort.

[25] Nix barely kept his seat with 51.9 percent of the voters supporting his retention. He had originally won his seat on the Court of Criminal Appeals in a partisan election in 1958, winning both the primary (involving a runoff and defeating the incumbent) and the general election. He had previously served as a Democrat in both the state house and the state senate, and had lost a Democratic primary for the U.S. House. At the time of the 1968 election there was a lot of news coverage concerning his son and namesake, Kirksey Nix, Jr., who was linked to what was known as the "Dixie Mafia" and was facing a murder charge in Louisiana (he was convicted and is serving a life sentence at Angola Prison in Louisiana).

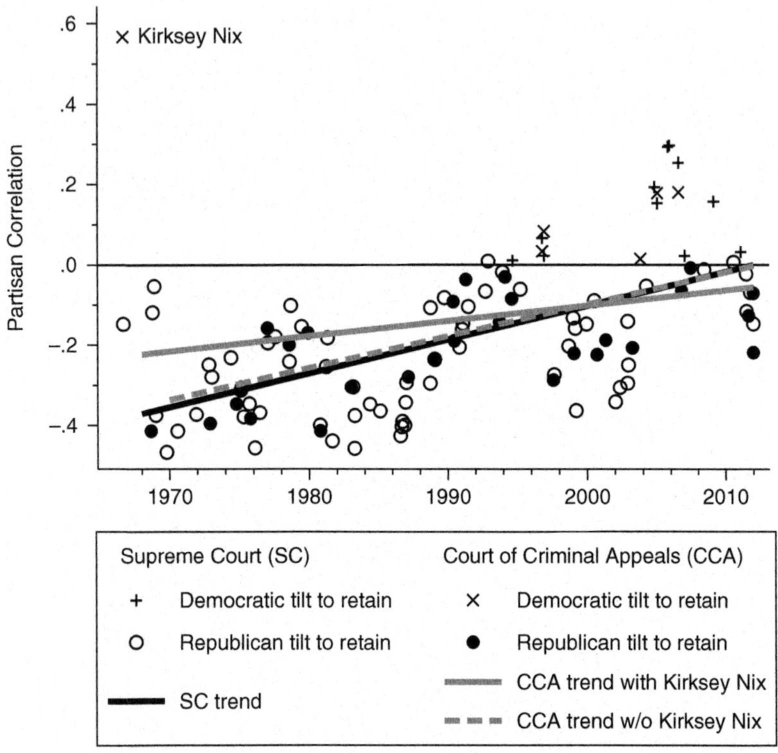

FIGURE 7.8. Partisan Correlations in Oklahoma, 1968–2012.

The results presented in this section show that the nature and/or degree of partisanship as reflected in the partisan correlations have changed over time in most states. The dominant pattern is an increase in the degree of partisanship and a shift toward Democratic-leaning counties voting more strongly for retention than do Republican-leaning counties. Importantly, these are by no means universal trends, with some states showing no change and others showing shifts in the opposite direction on degree and/or direction of partisanship. Equally important is that there remains in most states a lot of variation from one election to the next. For example, in Figure 7.8 for Oklahoma, elections in the first half of the 2000–2010 decade tended to have a Republican tilt toward retention, while the elections in the latter half had a Democratic tilt; throughout the decade, there were a number of elections in which the partisan correlations were effectively zero, and after 2010 the tilt shifted back to a Republican counties being more favorable of retention.[26] This leads to

[26] All four of the 2014 retention elections had a Republican tilt in favor of retention, although the correlations were modest, ranging from –.13 to –.28.

the question of whether it is possible to find systematic factors that explain the degree and direction of partisanship more broadly than simply looking at whether an incumbent was the target of a campaign for removal. The next section considers that question.

EXPLAINING PARTISANSHIP IN STATE SUPREME COURT RETENTION ELECTIONS

Partisan Correlations and Voting "Yes" to Retain

A first question to answer in seeking to explain both the degree and direction of partisanship in state supreme court elections is whether there is a relationship with the closeness of the election. Figure 7.9 shows the plot of partisan correlation by percentage voting yes for retention. The relationship is fairly clear in the figure: there is a moderate relationship ($r^2 = .108$, $b = -.0135$) with the correlation shifting from Democratic-leaning counties as the stronger supporters of retention to Republican-leaning counties being more likely to favor retention as the yes-vote increases. The broken line shown in Figure 7.9 was fitted using the lowess method (Cleveland 1979) which allows for nonlinearities; this line shows that there is a sharper drop-off in the correlation until the percentage voting to retain reaches about 55 percent.[27] While one might be tempted to interpret Figure 7.9 as showing that the relationship between partisanship and voting in favor of retention is largely a function of the close elections, the left panel of Table 7.3 makes it clear that this is not the case: there is a continuing decline in the mean partisan correlation as one goes from elections with a 60–69 percent yes-vote to an 80 percent or higher yes-vote.[28] Still, the relationship is at best modest, as indicated both by the r^2 and by the variation shown by the percentiles. There is much to explain beyond what can be accounted for by the election outcome.

While there is a clear relationship between the percentage voting to retain and the combination of the magnitude and direction of the partisan correlation, there is little relationship with the magnitude alone. What relationship there is, as shown in the right side of Table 7.3, is generated largely by the ten statewide elections in which the incumbent was not retained. Omitting those ten elections, the r^2 drops to .004, the slope drops by half, and the relationship no longer reaches the .05 level of statistical significance ($t = -1.08$, two-tailed $p = .109$).

27 Regressing the lowess fitted points to the correlations produces an r^2 of .1235, which is a slight improvement over the simple straight line.

28 If I use a finer set of categories (steps of .05 through .85), the means do not decline in a strictly monotonic fashion, but the overall trend remains.

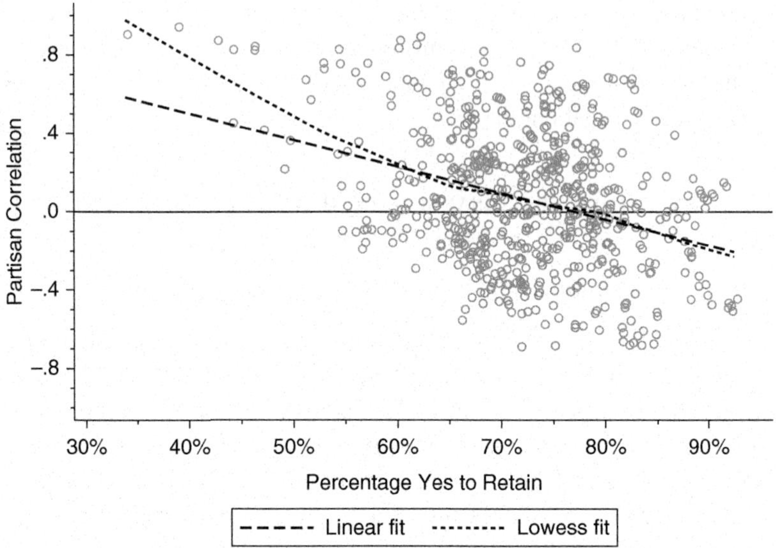

FIGURE 7.9. Partisan Correlation by Percent "Yes" to Retain.

A Multivariate Explanation of Partisan Correlations

What other factors might explain either the partisan correlation or the partisan absolute correlation? One obvious variable is whether a campaign opposing retention had occurred. Presumably any such campaign is likely to decrease the vote in favor of retention, and hence arguably this is effectively captured by the percentage voting in favor of retention. While I have identified some opposition campaigns (as described in the earlier section on close elections), I have not sought to identify systematically which elections did and did not involve a campaign in opposition. Looking beyond elections which prompted some level of organized opposition, the low visibility of retention elections might make newspaper (and possibly other) endorsements a factor that could increase the positive retention vote. Again, I have not sought to systematically count endorsements because doing so in any kind of systematic and comprehensive way would be extremely difficult, especially for the period before a large number of newspapers became available on Lexis-Nexis or Westlaw. Moreover, few newspapers have statewide circulation which means that one would need to look at a significant number of local papers, which would be a particularly difficult task. Finally, it is very unlikely that there were many cases of newspapers opposing retention outside of the small number of controversial elections previously discussed; rather the distinction would primarily be explicit endorsement versus silence.

TABLE 7.3. Partisan Correlations and Partisan Absolute Correlations by Percent "Yes" to Retain

Percentage "Yes" to Retain	N	Partisan Correlation					Partisan Absolute Correlation				
			Percentiles					Percentiles			
		Mean	10th	25th	75th	90th	Mean	10th	25th	75th	90th
Lost	10	0.67	0.27	0.42	0.89	0.93	0.67	0.28	0.42	0.89	0.93
50–59%	36	0.27	–0.11	–0.06	0.66	0.78	0.33	0.02	0.09	0.66	0.78
60–69%	203	0.11	–0.29	–0.16	0.35	0.60	0.29	0.04	0.14	0.405	0.60
70–79%	283	0.05	–0.38	–0.19	0.28	0.52	0.27	0.04	0.13	0408	0.54
80% and up	107	–0.12	–0.59	–0.41	0.08	0.31	0.28	0.03	0.08	0.48	0.64
All	639	0.06	–0.39	–0.19	0.29	0.58	0.29	0.04	0.12	0.43	0.62
		$r^2 = .108$		b = –.0135***			$r^2 = .024$		b = –.0038***		

***$p < .001$.

What then can be measured that might be relevant? First is the political context of the incumbent's original selection to the court. For most of the justices involved, this will be the result of appointment by a governor. This suggests the hypothesis that there is a directional relationship with appointees of Republican governors receiving greater support from Republican-leaning counties and appointees of Democratic governors receiving greater support from Democratic-leaning counties. Arguably this might also capture whether the incumbent had been politically active in the party of the governor on the assumption that the governor would be very reluctant to appoint someone to the state supreme court who had been active in the opposing party. For those justices who originally won their seat in a partisan election, one can use the party ticket they ran on as an indicator of party.[29] Similarly, for those justices who were initially appointed, and then ran for reelection on a partisan ballot,[30] one can use the party whose ballot the justice chose to run on in lieu of the party of the appointing governor.[31] For eight justices, neither piece of information is available because they were originally elected on a nonpartisan ballot before the selection system had changed to one of gubernatorial appointment or were in a state that only uses retention elections in lieu of a nonpartisan election when an incumbent is unopposed for reelection; for six of the eight, I was able to locate information indicating a party linkage (prior office holding or nominations, appointment to the federal courts, etc.). The remaining two were omitted from the analysis presented here.[32] I label this variable "party linkage," because it can reflect either the justice's prior partisan affiliation or the partisan identification of the governor who appointed the justice to the state supreme court.

A second variable that can be measured is how long the judge has been in office. One might hypothesize that a judge who has been in office only a very short time would have a high positive vote on the grounds that there would

[29] One Pennsylvania justice, Nicholas Papadakos, originally won his seat through election after capturing both parties' nomination. I have classified him as a Democrat because he was so described in some news reports of the time.

[30] This could arise if a state switched from partisan elections to a system using retention elections, or in one of the two states (Pennsylvania and New Mexico) that use statewide partisan elections for the initial election with retention through retention elections.

[31] While I have not checked every election, it would be the unusual justice who was appointed to fill a vacancy in a state using partisan elections who then chose to run on the ballot of the party opposed to that of the governor who appointed the justice. One exception occurred in Oklahoma where a Republican governor appointed a justice who subsequently ran in a partisan election (prior to the adoption of retention elections) as a Democrat, defeating a Republican opponent. I coded the judge as a Democrat for purposes of my analysis.

[32] The two omitted elections involved Fred B. Weber (Montana, 1988) and Robert E. Morgan (South Dakota, 1984).

be little basis for voting not to retain. This is particularly true in states where the first retention election for a judge comes very quickly (three years or less) after the judge's selection to the court. Conversely, one might expect either an increase or decrease in support for a long-serving justice, with an increase reflecting the buildup of respect or a decrease reflecting that the justice had served for a significant period of time during which the justice had participated in decisions that angered some sectors of the electorate. An alternative measure that might be used in place of time is whether the judge was running for retention for the first time, or had run for retention more than three times. This alternative measure is more problematic than the simple length of tenure due to the variation in length of terms in the states (ranging from 6 to 12 years).[33] Consequently, I rely on length of tenure.[34]

A final variable that needs to be considered is the political tendency in a state. That is, is the state politically liberal (leaning Democratic) or politically conservative (leaning Republican). This can be combined with the party of the appointing governor (or the party whose ballot the justice ran on initially) with the hypothesis that the partisan correlation would run against the candidate when there was an inconsistency between the state's political inclination and the partisan history of the judge's initial selection, and would run with it when the two were in sync. An appropriate measure to use for this is the state-level citizen ideology index devised by Berry et al. (1998; 2010). This measure was available on an annual basis for the period 1960–2010.[35] High values of this measure indicate citizen liberalism and low values, citizen conservatism. I also ran regressions using a folded version of the citizen ideology score (i.e., folded at the median) to provide a nondirectional measure of intensity of citizen ideology, the idea being that this might better explain the partisan absolute correlation than would the directional measure of state citizen ideology.

To examine the multivariate relationship, I applied ordinary least squares with robust standard errors clustered on the year and state to account for the fact that

33 In fact, length of tenure and number of prior retention elections are highly correlated ($r = .737$); thus, including both variables would introduce multicollinearity. A further complication is how to handle cases where a justice had previously stood for election under a contested model; this could happen if the system changed after the justice was on the court, if the state uses partisan elections for initial selection (Pennsylvania and New Mexico), or if the state uses nonpartisan elections which default to retention elections if the justice is unopposed (Montana and, for a time, Utah).

34 I compute the length of tenure as the year of the election minus the year the justice assumed office. For California justice Marvin Baxter, who stood for "confirmation" rather than retention, tenure was set to 0.

35 The indices were downloaded from http://rcfording.wordpress.com/state-ideology-data/ (last visited August 22, 2014).

TABLE 7.4. Summary Statistics for Regression Variables

Variable	Mean	Standard Deviation	Minimum	Maximum
Partisan correlation	0.064	0.344	−0.731	0.932
Partisan absolute correlation	0.280	0.210	0.001	0.932
Little z transformation	0.083	0.408	−0.931	1.677
Absolute little z transformation	0.313	0.275	0.001	1.677
Party linkage (1 = Democratic)	0.538	0.499	0	1
Citizen ideology	40.292	11.436	9.251	70.846
"Folded" citizen ideology	9.364	6.714	0.058	32.505
Percentage yes to retain	71.961	8.421	33.839	91.105
Percentage yes squared	5249	1175	1145	8300
Years on the court	7.610	7.033	0	37
Year of election	1989.5	13.274	1960	2010

opposition to one or more justices standing for retention might spill over to other justices up for retention the same year in the same state. One issue in using the correlation coefficient as the dependent variable in a regression analysis is that it has a constrained range of values (-1 to +1) and is not normally distributed. To adjust for this, I transformed the partisan correlations to Fisher's little z, a statistic that ranges from minus infinity to plus infinity and has an approximately normal sampling distribution (Kutner et al. 2004:85).[36] Finally, the patterns in Figure 7.3 and Table 7.3 suggest that the relationship between the partisan correlation and the percentage voting yes is not strictly linear, and preliminary analyses using the little z transformation of the partisan correlation show this is also true with that transformation; consequently, the model includes the square of the percentage voting yes to adjust for the nonlinear form. The analysis includes 573 observations due to the omission of observations outside the period 1960–2010 for which the Berry et al. measure of state ideology is available and the omission of the two justices for whom it was not possible to identify a partisan linkage.[37] Table 7.4 shows summary statistics for the variables included in the analysis.

Table 7.5 shows the regression results for the Fisher's little z transformation partisan correlation. Three models are shown: with no interaction between party linkage and citizen ideology (Model 1), with the standard multiplicative

[36] I have not included an additional adjustment for the heteroscedasticity that might be present given that the standard error of both r and little z are a function of the sample size. Presumably, the computation of robust standard errors due to clustering also accounts for any heteroscedasticity that might be present.

[37] The omission of the years before 1960 involves only two states, Missouri and California.

TABLE 7.5. Regression Results for Partisan Correlations

	Model 1		Model 2		Model 3	
	b	Robust Std. Err.	b	Robust Std. Err.	b	Robust Std. Err.
Party linkage	0.0880*	0.0378	–0.1338	0.1362	–0.1338	0.1362
Citizen ideology	0.0105***	0.0020	0.0072**	0.0027		
Republican linkage					0.0072**	0.0027
Democratic linkage					0.0126**	0.0025
Percentage yes to retain	–0.0823**	0.0268	–0.0804***	0.0268	–0.0804**	0.0268
Percentage yes squared	0.0005*	0.0002	0.0005*	0.0002	0.0005	0.0002
Years on the court	–0.0036#	0.0022	–0.0038#	0.0021	–0.0038#	0.0021
Year of election	0.0019	0.0021	0.0018	0.0021	0.0018	0.0021
Party x Ideology interaction			0.0054#	0.0033		
Constant	–0.7845		–0.4734		0.0018	
R^2	0.2723		0.2776		0.2776	

Note: Dependent variable is the (Fisher's) little z transformation of the correlation coefficient; N = 573.
#$p < .10$; *$p < .05$; **$p < .01$; ***$p < .001$; (all two-tailed).

interaction (Model 2), and with a reparameterization of the model that includes the interaction term (Model 3) which I will explain. The fit of the models is modest, explaining about a quarter of the variation in the partisan correlation. Not surprisingly, year of election is not significant in any of the models; this is consistent with the nature of the time trends shown in Figure 7.5, which makes it clear that the trends vary from one state to another.

Model 1 results show that the partisan correlation tends to be higher for justices linked to the Democratic Party and in states with liberal citizen ideology; this is as expected given the directionality of the partisan correlation, which is positive for higher votes to retain in counties trending Democratic in the gubernatorial election and negative for higher votes to retain in counties trending Republican in the gubernatorial election. As one would expect given the bivariate analysis shown in Table 7.3 and Figure 7.9, the partisan correlation is inversely related to the yes-vote percentage; the regression results suggest a shift downward in the partisan correlation of almost .75 as the yes-vote percentage goes from 44 percent (the mean yes-vote percentage for defeated justices) to 85 percent (the mean yes-vote percentage for the highest category in Table 7.3).[38] Model 2 introduces an interaction term between party linkage and citizen ideology. It is marginally significant statistically, and the terms not included in the interaction are essentially unchanged. Model 3 reparameterizes the interaction term as a conditional model (see Wright 1976), so that there are separate slope effects for elections in which the incumbent has a Democratic linkage and for elections in which the incumbent has a Republican linkage; mathematically this model represents the variation in exactly the same way as Model 2 using the traditional multiplicative interaction term, and the other terms and the R^2s are identical in Models 2 and 3. Model 3 makes it clear that citizen ideology has a stronger effect – about 75 percent higher – for justices with a Democratic linkage than for those with a Republican linkage. Figure 7.10 graphically estimates the impact of the different citizen ideology terms; in this figure, the little z dependent variable has been converted back to correlation; while useful for interpretation, these estimates are not at all precise, as indicated by the vertical lines which are confidence intervals for the estimates.[39] For justices with a Democratic linkage, the predicted partisan correlation increases from −.16 when the citizen ideology score is 10 to .57 when the ideology score is 75, a shift of .73;[40] for justices with a Republican linkage the overall shift is .45, from −.08 to .37. This indicates that the political climate has a greater impact for justices with a tie to the Democratic Party than is the case for justices with a tie to the Republican Party.

Table 7.6 displays selected regression results using the partisan absolute correlation (with little z transformation) as the dependent variable. The table shows that the overall fit for Models 4 and 5 is weaker than the overall fit for the corresponding models shown in Table 7.5 (Models 1 and 3), but there are nonetheless several statistically significant relationships. Note that I have omitted the model showing the multiplicative interaction term, which is not statistically significant ($t = 0.88$, $p = .380$), but I have included the conditional reparameterization because the sum of the interaction term and the citizen ideology term is statistically significant for reasons evident in Model 5. The effects of the variables other than party linkage and citizen ideology are essentially the same in Models 4 and 5: Consistent with the results in Table 7.3,

38 These mean percentages are for those elections included in the regression analysis (i.e., statewide elections between 1960 and 2010). This is calculated starting from the mean correlation for defeated justices, which is .668.

39 The estimation of the confidence intervals was done using the CLARIFY procedure described by King et al. (2000).

40 The values of 10 and 75 approximate the range observed for the states and years where retention elections took place.

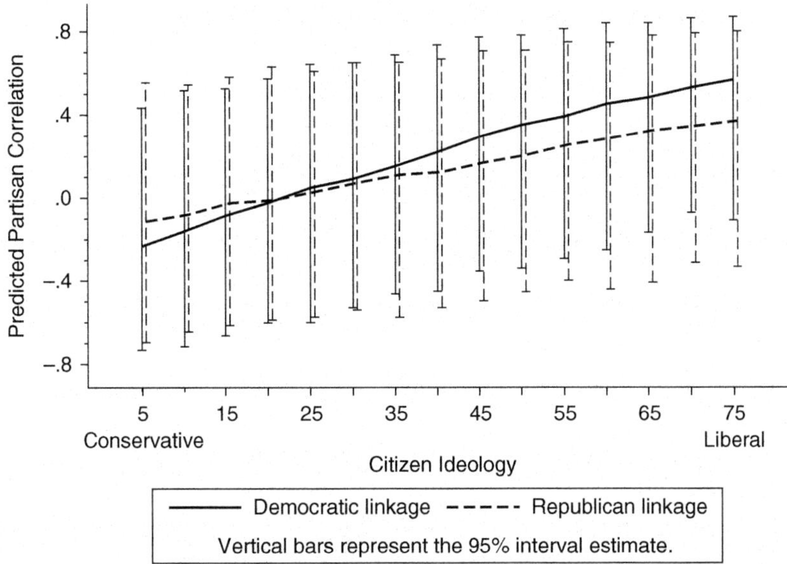

FIGURE 7.10. Effect of Citizen Ideology on the Partisan Correlation by Party Linkage.

the higher the percentage voting yes to retain, the lower the partisan absolute correlation. While there is no relationship with length of tenure, there is a relationship with the year of election, and this is noteworthy because the simple analysis of the partisan absolute correlation over time failed to reveal a significant change. With the control variables in place, it is now evident that there has been a gradual increase in the partisan absolute correlation, .01 every three years, or a total of about .18 over the fifty-year period covered by the model.[41]

Looking at the results for Model 4 one sees that the partisan absolute correlation is lower (by roughly .05 on average) for justices with ties to the Democratic Party and that the correlation tends to increase as citizen ideology moves in a liberal direction. Model 5 casts a different interpretation on the party linkage and ideology variables. Because there are now two different slopes for citizen ideology, one for justices linked to the Republican Party (.0024) and one for justices linked to the Democratic Party (.0043), the party linkage coefficient is now simply the gap between those two lines when citizen ideology is 0,

[41] If I divide the 50 years into 10 five-year periods (the last period has only four years), the mean partisan correlation for the first period is .181 compared to .394 for the last period. I note that looking at the means, there is a pattern of increase over time, but it is not strictly monotonic, and the largest increases occurred in the earliest and latest periods.

TABLE 7.6. Regression Results for Partisan Absolute Correlations

	Model 4		Model 5		Model 6	
	b	Robust Std. Err.	b	Robust Std. Err.	b	Robust Std. Err.
Party linkage	0.0565*	0.0256	–0.0231	0.0893	0.0326	0.0436
Citizen ideology	0.0036*	0.0015				
Republican linkage			0.0024	0.0020		
Democratic linkage			0.0043*	0.0018		
Folded Citizen Ideology					–0.0038	0.0031
Percentage yes to retain	–0.0829**	0.0284	–0.0822**	0.0283	–0.0896**	0.0283
Percentage yes squared	0.0005**	0.0002	0.0005**	0.0002	0.0006**	0.0002
Years on the court	0.0002	0.0015	0.0001	0.0015	–0.0002	0.0015
Year of election	0.0037**	0.0014	0.0037**	0.0014	0.0039**	0.0014
Party x Folded Citizen Ideology interaction					0.0018	0.0036
Constant	–4.1557		–4.0440		–4.0989	
R^2	0.1786		0.1801		0.1630	

Note: Dependent variable is the (Fisher's) little z transformation of the absolute value of correlation coefficient; N = 573.
#$p < .10$; *$p < .05$; **$p < .01$; ***$p < .001$; (all two-tailed).

which is not a particularly interesting piece of information.[42] Of greater interest are the two slope estimates: the influence of citizen ideology on the partisan absolute correlation does not differ significantly from 0 for justices linked to the Republican Party while the slope does differ from zero for justices with a Democratic linkage. Figure 7.11 is similar to Figure 7.10, but this time showing estimates for the partisan absolute correlation for a range of values of citizen ideology. While both slopes are positive, the slope for Republican-linked justice is much closer to being a flat line. The estimated partisan absolute

[42] Some simple calculations show that when citizen ideology is 10, which is essentially the lowest value among a set of retention elections between 1960 and 2010, the gap between the two lines is actually about +.02.

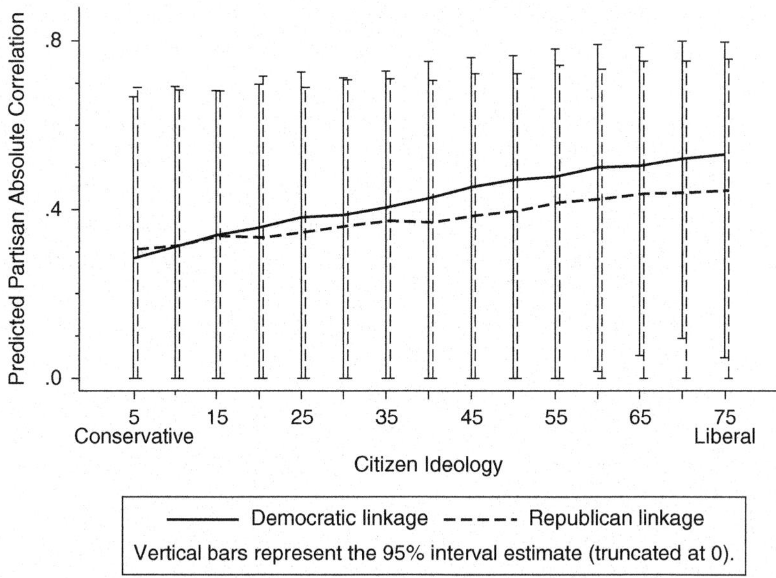

FIGURE 7.11. Effect of Citizen Ideology on the Partisan Absolute Correlations by Party Linkage.

correlation for justices with either linkage when citizen liberalism is at 10 is .31; for Democratic linked justices this rises to .53 when citizen liberalism is at .75, but increases to only .44 for Republican linked justices – again the slope does not differ significantly from zero.

CONCLUSION

The supporters of the Missouri Plan, which they prefer to describe as "merit selection," justify that method of selection as a means of removing ordinary politics from the process of selecting and retaining judges and justices (see, for example, O'Connor 2010). Retention elections are included as part of the Missouri Plan in no small part as a means of selling the plan to a public that strongly believes in the value of electing a very wide range of government officials. Proponents acknowledge that there have been some highly contentious retention elections, and the first part of this chapter shows that those elections have actually been strongly political in terms of partisanship. What the extended analysis in this chapter makes clear is that, while elections such as those in California in 1986 and Iowa in 2010 may be extreme examples of partisanship playing a role in such elections, there is a strong undercurrent of partisanship in a much larger number of state supreme court retention elections than previously assumed.

Of course the partisanship in retention elections is far less than one finds in the elections conducted on a partisan, even a semi-partisan (hybrid) basis. One might ask how the degree of partisanship in retention elections compares to what one finds in nonpartisan elections. Table 7.7 shows the distributions of partisan absolute correlations for both retention elections and nonpartisan elections; the left side shows the distributions for the full set of both types of elections (since the 1930s for retention elections and since 1946 for nonpartisan elections) and the right side shows the distributions limited to 1960 through 2013. Not surprisingly, retention elections are less likely to have high correlations (.7 or greater), 4.3 percent for retention elections versus 11.6 percent for nonpartisan elections since 1960. However, the percentage with a correlation in the range of .5 to .7 is fairly similar, 11.8 percent for retention elections and 13.1 percent for nonpartisan elections. Given the larger number of retention elections compared to contested nonpartisan elections, the number of retention elections since 1960 that have had partisan correlations exceeding .5 (97) is greater than the number of nonpartisan elections with partisan correlations exceeding .5 (64). Clearly, retention elections have a realized potential to involve significant partisanship just as is the case for ostensibly nonpartisan elections. The analysis in this chapter also makes clear that the nature of the partisanship in retention elections varies from state to state in a way that links to the broad political context of the individual state. Where there has been change over time in the pattern of partisan correlations in a state using retention elections, the nature of that change tends to reflect the changing political context of that state.

Elections are fundamentally political and voters seek out cues as to how to vote. Research has shown again and again that the most fundamental voting cue is political party. Party is far from a perfect piece of information, but lacking anything else voters will tend to turn to it. It should not be surprising that voters seek out cues in retention elections. In retention elections incumbency is a constant, so it provides guidance only for voters who have a basic preference for or against incumbents. Basic name recognition is another cue, and underscores what V. O. Key (1949:37) labeled friends-and-neighbors voting in his classic study of the politics of the southern states; there is some evidence of friends-and-neighbors voting in retention elections for appellate judges (Aspin and Hall 1989) – perhaps an increase of about 4 percentage points in the yes-vote. In retention elections partisanship works not through explicit labels but through other kinds of cues: prior office holding, prior office seeking, or the party of the appointing governor. It can also operate through votes that justices participate in on their courts when the issues in a case have strong partisan overtones.

Finally, this chapter once again brings home a point that has long been made about "merit" selection and the accompanying retention elections. Retention elections, and the so-called merit system of which it is often a part, do not remove politics from the judicial selection system. They at most change the nature of the politics.

TABLE 7.7. Comparing Partisan Correlations in Retention and Nonpartisan Elections

	All Retention		Nonpartisan since 1946		Retention since 1960		Nonpartisan since 1960	
Magnitude of Correlation[a]	Percentage	Cumulative Percentage	Percentage	Cumulative Percentage	Percentage	Cumulative Percentage	Percentage	Cumulative Percentage
≥0.9	0.3	0.3	1.8	1.8	0.3	0.3	2.3	2.3
0.8 to <0.9	1.7	2.0	3.7	5.5	1.8	2.2	4.6	6.9
0.7 to <0.8	2.0	4.1	4.0	9.5	2.2	4.3	4.6	11.6
0.6 to <0.7	6.4	10.5	6.7	16.2	5.5	9.8	6.6	18.1
0.5 to <0.6	6.7	17.2	6.4	22.6	6.3	16.1	6.6	24.7
0.4 to <0.5	10.3	27.5	14.0	36.6	8.6	24.8	14.7	39.4
0.3 to <0.4	11.9	39.4	12.5	49.1	12.3	37.0	12.4	51.7
0.2 to <0.3	18.9	58.4	17.4	66.5	19.8	56.8	16.2	68.0
0.1 to <0.2	20.2	78.6	15.2	81.7	20.8	77.6	16.2	84.2
<0.1	21.4	100.0	18.3	100.0	22.4	100.0	15.8	100.0
N's	639		328		602		259	

[a] For retention elections, this is the absolute value of the partisan correlation.

8

Judicial Elections in a Highly Partisan World

A BRIEF RECAP

The central focus of this book has been change, or the absence of change. The analysis in the preceding chapters shows that change has occurred since the 1940s. However, those changes are not necessarily the kind of change or the amount of change that many critics of judicial elections seem to believe.

- In the aggregate, competition and competitiveness in supreme court elections has increased since 1980, but that increase is concentrated in the southern states, and actually reflects a decline in the earlier years of the period followed by an increase as the South emerged for the era of overwhelming dominance by the Democratic Party.
- There has been an increase in expenditures on state supreme court elections, but that increase reflects broader changes in how American elections are conducted.
- Similarly, the role of television advertising in judicial elections has increased as it has generally in American elections; however, compared to elections for other offices and with exceptions for a small number of supreme court elections, that advertising has maintained an overall positive tone.
- Outside interest groups have been involved in some state supreme court elections in recent years, but this mirrors what has happened with elections more generally.
- In some states that use nonpartisan elections for their supreme courts, those elections have taken on a sharp partisan tone; in other nonpartisan states, the elections continue to be largely nonpartisan. In some states that use retention elections, those elections have shifted in the degree or nature of their partisan tone; however, while some states have seen increasing partisanship, others have seen a decrease.

Overall, the best description of the changes that have occurred in state supreme court elections is that they have tended to mirror the broader changes in politics and political campaigns in the United States, and that they are sometimes driven by the same divisions over highly salient policy issues that drive elections for the other branches of governments.

THE IMPORTANCE OF COURT AGENDAS

Chapter 1 contrasted the evolution of state supreme court elections in Wisconsin and Minnesota. In Wisconsin, which had a tradition of nonpartisanship dating back to the state's admission to the union in 1848, those elections have become highly partisan and sometimes bitter and nasty. In contrast, elections in Minnesota have remained relatively quiet and generally nonpartisan despite earlier periods of strong partisan patterns. My primary explanation for the differences between the two states is that the Minnesota court has not had to make decisions on the kinds of issues – death penalty, abortion, same-sex marriage,[1] and tort law – that mobilize interest groups and voters, while the Wisconsin court has made controversial decisions on questions related to tort law. One might be tempted to argue that this is because the Wisconsin legislature had adopted some tort reform measures while the Minnesota legislature had not; this does not explain all of the differences. The Wisconsin Supreme Court has made some tort-related decisions hat riled up conservative business interests that were not related to tort reform legislation; these included issues dealing with expert testimony[2] and market share liability for apportioning damages for products made by a wide range of manufacturers and where it is not possible to identify the particular source in a case.[3]

1 The Minnesota court actually did make a decision related to same-sex marriage, but this was back in 1971 (*Baker v. Nelson*, 191 N.W.2d 185).

2 As discussed in Chapter 1, the Wisconsin Supreme Court continued the use of its own fairly liberal relevancy standard (*State v. Walstad*, 351 N.W.2d 469 [Wis. 1984]) for the admission of expert testimony rather than adopting the *Daubert* standard preferred by defendants despite being asked on several occasions to change to the *Daubert* standard, most recently in *State v. Fischer*, 778 N.W.2d 629 (Wis. 2010). Well before the U.S. Supreme Court's decision in *Daubert v. Merrell Dow Pharmaceuticals* (509 U.S. 579 (1993)), the Minnesota Supreme Court had adopted what is known as the Frye-Mack standard which while not going as far as the *Daubert* standard incorporates some aspects of it (*State v. Mack*, 292 N.W.2d 764 (Minn. 1980).

3 This came in a case involving potential damages related to lead paint (*Thomas ex rel. Gramling v. Mallett*, 701 N.W.2d 523 (Wis. 2005)). Market-share liability is primarily associated with claims arising from the use of DES (*Sindell v. Abbott Lab.*, 607 P.2d 924 (Cal. 1980)), a drug prescribed in the 1950s to reduce the risk of miscarriage, and that was later found to cause vaginal and cervical cancer in the daughters of women who had taken the drug, which in fact did not reduce miscarriage risk. Market-share liability has not come before the Minnesota Supreme Court, although an appellate court rejected the theory in a case involving flammable clothing (*Bixler v. Avondale Mills*, 405 N.W.2d 428 [Minn. App. 1987]).

In Chapters 6 and 7 I examined voting patterns in statewide supreme court elections for states using partisan, nonpartisan, and retention elections. I found a mix of stability and change. As one would expect, in the small number of states that have continued to use partisan elections, voting patterns continue to be highly partisan. In the states using nonpartisan elections, some have followed Wisconsin's pattern into highly partisan voting patterns, while others have followed Minnesota's pattern of continuing a low level of partisanship. The detailed discussions of specific elections and candidates in those chapters supports the conclusion that the difference between these two groups of states is in significant part a function of the decisions the respective courts have been called on to make, with partisanship rising where courts have had to make decisions that align with partisan interests on highly salient issues. While one might be tempted to conclude that problems arise only when specific positions lose in the state supreme courts, this would be an oversimplification. Many of the more partisan voting patterns in ostensibly nonpartisan elections are for open seats and reflect an anticipation that an issue such as same-sex marriage, tort reform, or property-rights issues will come before the court. Chapter 7 makes it clear that opposition candidates are not needed in order for voters to respond in a partisan pattern after a court makes decisions on highly salient issues that reflect partisan alignments.

Given the dominant role of party in American voting patterns – the single best predictor of voting decisions from the president on down is the voter's sense of identification with one of the major political parties – it is curious that anyone should find it surprising for the public to respond in a partisan fashion when a branch of government becomes involved in issues that have strong partisan overtones. If courts make important decisions in cases that deal with issues that reflect partisan divisions, one should expect voters to respond accordingly. If citizens have the opportunity to vote directly for judges on the courts making such decisions, and citizens have information that allows them to identify the actual or likely positions of judges on the issues they care strongly about, the citizens tend to vote in line with their policy preferences. The idea that informed citizens would ignore their political preferences on highly salient issues and make decisions about candidates solely on the basis of some vague criteria such as "qualifications" or "judicial temperament" or "merit" is a fantasy. Moreover, as the selection of federal judges makes clear, leaving decisions regarding judicial selection and retention in the hands of elected officials in no way insulates the selection process from the preferences of the citizens; it only introduces one degree of separation, and adds the opportunity for the elected officials to introduce patronage considerations in addition to policy considerations.

While not central to my focus, one can ask whether we should approach judicial selection and retention of judges sitting on courts of last resort differently than we treat judges serving on trial courts or intermediate appellate courts handling many routine cases. Some of the discussion in Chapter 3 examined the influence of elections on trial judges handling criminal cases summarizing several studies that found that judicial decisions varied depending on where a judge was in his or her election cycle, with harsher sentences tending to be imposed when a judge's term was nearing an end. Some studies provide evidence that in capital cases elected judges sometimes use their ability to override a jury's leniency to impose the death penalty, a kind of decision that is hard to argue reflects a correction of a jury's erred judgment, particularly given the lesser inclination of those same judges to override a jury's decision to impose the death penalty; one study found that overrides that imposed the death penalty were more common when a judge would soon need to stand for reelection. Other than the American love affair with elections, it is difficult to find a benefit from making judges who are engaged almost entirely in routine decision-making subject to selection and/or retention by the voters. In fact, most trial-like proceedings in the states are overseen not by judges subject to election but by administrative law judges who, as discussed in the next section, come to their positions mostly through civil service-type selection processes (see Kritzer 2013:4733–36).

ALTERNATIVE SELECTION SYSTEMS: WHO CHOOSES THE CHOOSERS?

The system most often proposed to solve the perceived problems with judicial elections is what I have labeled the Missouri Plan but which proponents prefer to call "merit selection." Under this system, a nominating commission is chosen to screen potential appointees and present a list to the governor who then must make a choice from the list or reject the entire list. The appointee takes office and after a period of service stands in a retention election; at the end of each subsequent term the judge can stand again in a retention election unless the judge is barred from running by the mandatory retirement rules that exist in over half the states using elections to select or retain judges.

As discussed in Chapter 4, very few judges who stand in retention elections are actually defeated. This does not mean that judges do not worry about being defeated, and this worry can have effects on judicial behavior. Moreover, it does not mean that voters do not respond to decisions previously made by judges when those judges stand for retention, as evident in the retention election defeats of state supreme court justices in California, Tennessee, Nebraska, and, most recently, Iowa. It also does not mean that even in elections in which justices are easily retained there is no partisan tinge to voting patterns. At best the Missouri Plan system dampens some elements of politics. There is no evidence that it has broadly prevented governors from considering political issues in making their choices from among the nominees they receive from the nominating committee, particularly when the appointee is to assume a position on the state supreme court. In some states governors have effective control over who serves on the nominating commission, which in turn ensures that the nominees the governor receives will reflect the governor's political preferences (McLeod 2012). Thus, so-called merit selection does not eliminate potential problems with judicial elections, and at best moderates the influence of partisanship in the selection of persons to serve on state courts of last resort.

One possible advantage of the Missouri Plan over nonpartisan elections could be to discourage those who might want to unseat an incumbent because they could not be sure who would be appointed as the replacement if the incumbent were to be turned out of office (Sturdevant 2014). However, that would depend heavily on who would be making the replacement appointment. Recall, for example, the unsuccessful effort to remove three appointees of Jerry Brown in 1982 led in part by the Republican candidate for governor who was hoping to replace those judges with his own appointees. In 2014, conservatives mounted an unsuccessful campaign to reject three members of the Tennessee Supreme Court as "too liberal" and out of touch with "Tennessee values" (Blinder 2014a); the goal was to allow the conservative Republican governor to appoint conservatives to the court. A similar, also unsuccessful, attempt was made in Kansas that year; two justices appointed to the Kansas Supreme Court by former Democratic governor Kathleen Sebelius were targeted with the goal of allowing conservative Republican governor Sam Brownback, who endorsed the attempt, to name replacements (Biles 2014).

Proposals for reforms inevitably encounter the "who chooses the choosers" problem. American political culture places a strong emphasis on citizen control. This is reflected in the extensive use of elections to select even minor officials in the United States discussed briefly at the beginning of Chapter 2. The 1992 Census of Government found a total of almost 19,000 officials elected at the state level and close to half a million (493,830) persons elected to serve in general and special-purpose local governmental units (Bureau of the Census 1995:1).[4] While originally this attraction to elections probably reflected

[4] Until 1992, the periodic Census of Government included tables listing virtually all elected offices, and a table that provided a count of the number of elected officials. The information ceased to be included in the Census of Government after 1992.

a "no taxation without representation" perspective, it goes well beyond offices with taxing powers.

Citizens have been willing to remove some offices from those that they elect. Some, such as the Texas office of Inspector of Hides or the old New England office of Hog Reeve or the office of Fence Viewer in Belmont, Massachusetts, ceased to have any function in modern society. Other offices, such as the clerk of courts, ceased to be elected in some states once citizens became convinced that electing people to fill those offices served no real purpose, but those same offices continue to be elected in other states. Proposals to move positions from elected to appointed tend to evoke negative reactions. For example, in late July 2013 the Hampton Roads (Virginia) *Daily Press* published an editorial calling for eliminating elections for the offices of sheriff, commissioner of revenue, treasurer, and clerk of the Circuit Court. A follow-up story in another Virginia newspaper brought defenses of their elected status by persons holding the potentially affected positions; in the words of one person serving as the clerk of the local Circuit Court, "Elected officials have accountability to the public." A former elected official described her elected status as commissioner of revenue as guaranteeing "a system of checks and balances in assessments, determining the tax rate, and receipt, investment and disbursements of funds" (McCaffrey 2013). A letter to the editor in response to the original editorial concluded that elected "[c]onstitutional officers represent checks and balances in local government," and an online comment on the editorial argued that more positions should be elected, not fewer, "[w]e need more people ... that have to answer to the public, not ones appointed by their friends and family." The editorial's proposal prompted no evidence of support for eliminating any of the named elected positions.

The problem that arises in ending elections for an office that needs to continue to exist is deciding who will choose the person to fill the office which leads in turn to the question of who will choose the chooser. For some positions, such as clerk of courts, this is unlikely to raise significant concerns, but for others, such as judges, it can become a point of contention. Essentially, the questions are how many degrees of separation should there be between the electorate and a particular government official, and are there positions that should be fully insulated from the electorate, with regard to initial selection and/or retention? The traditional political patronage model placed all nonelected government positions only one degree of separation away from the electorate, and the development of the civil service model was intended to insulate covered positions from the electorate. For judicial positions, many states employ a range of alternatives, with some judicial positions subject to direct election, some a single degree away from the electorate (some types of specialized courts or adjudicatory bodies), and others insulated from the electorate (most administrative law judges); for some positions there may be two degrees of separation, with a political appointee in turn appointing judges.[5] Exactly where the line is drawn for a particular kind of court or adjudicatory body varies from state to state, almost certainly reflecting historical norms or specific events at the time a particular forum was created or the selection of its members was modified.

With regard to courts and judges, the American preference for elections as the means of selection and/or retention raises the question of whether Americans really want judges to be truly independent of the electorate. Recall that, as discussed in Chapter 1, the original move toward popular election of state judges was motivated at least in part to make judges independent of the political actors who had served as the appointers of judges during the first fifty years post-independence (Hall 1984a; Shugerman 2012). The citizenry almost certainly continues to support this dimension of independence, but that is not to say that they favor having judges who are fully independent of the electorate. Surveys show strong support for including elections in the selection and/or retention process (see Heagarty 2003:1300; Phillips 2003:145), even while indicating concerns about aspects of elections such as campaign contributions (Gibson 2012:28–29; Streb 2011:152). The strong preference for elections must either reflect a knee-jerk preference or a desire to maintain a check on the judiciary, and maintaining such a check is by definition a significant limitation on judicial independence. This does not mean that a person who wants to have a say in choosing and/or retaining judges wants to have judges who will ignore the facts of the case or ignore clearly settled law in order to decide cases the way the person would prefer; the preference is for judges who will look at cases without strong biases and make decisions consistent with the facts and the law. What people generally want are judges who are independent to a degree, but not too independent, and they want to be able to have a say in removing judges who cross the line between what the public sees as appropriate independence and too much independence.

RADICALLY DIFFERENT MODELS

Chapter 2 detailed the various ways elections are used to select and retain state supreme court justices in the United States. However, this is only part of the story of judicial selection and retention. The other part has to do with selection and retention through means other than popular election. In Chapter 2

[5] A good example here is the position of bankruptcy judge in the federal system; bankruptcy judges are appointed to 14-year terms by the judges of the Court of Appeals who are in turn appointed for life by the president, subject to confirmation by the Senate.

I discussed appointment processes in states that use elections, both those used in Missouri Plan states and in states where midterm vacancies are filled through appointment. There are also variations in selection and retention processes in the states that do not use popular elections to staff their supreme courts:

- In two of the states not relying on popular election, South Carolina and Virginia, the legislature chooses justices through a process described as election by the legislature, although in Virginia interim vacancies are initially filled by gubernatorial appointment.
- In the remaining eight states, the governor appoints all justices, and there is no election involved in the retention process; in some states a formal nominating/screening committee is used and in some states the governor's selection is subject to a confirmation or approval process by the legislature, except in Massachusetts where it is the Executive Council that must approve the governor's selection.
- In most states, not using elections retention is through the same process as initial appointment, although in Hawaii retention decisions are made by the Judicial Nominating Commission. In Massachusetts and New Hampshire there is no retention because justices serve until reaching the age of mandatory retirement; in Rhode Island justices serve until death or they choose to leave the bench.

Below the state supreme court, additional methods may be used to select at least some judges. For some lower level judicial officers, such as assistant judges or court commissioners, groups of judges or a single presiding judge may make the appointment.[6] Administrative law judges (ALJs) who staff a range of state adjudicatory bodies are typically selected through a competitive civil service hiring process involving formal application, references, interviews, and the like; in some states (and for those seeking to become a federal ALJ) a written examination is used to screen and rank candidates. Some number of years of prior practice experience is normally required in order to apply for one of these positions.

Despite the great variation in how judges are selected and retained in the United States, there are at least two additional models that would be radical departures from those current systems. Both of those systems substantially limit the role of elected officials in the selection process or even remove such officials from the decision process entirely. As I discuss these alternative models, it is important to keep in mind that the roles judges play vary from country

[6] Federal magistrate judges and federal bankruptcy judges are also appointed by other judges, as are associate judges in Illinois.

to country. Judges in the Unites States tend to have a more significant policy role than is true in most other countries, and this is particularly evident in their role in constitutional interpretation which in other countries is a function denied to judges of the ordinary courts. In some countries, such as the United Kingdom, there is a norm of parliamentary (legislative) supremacy, although this may increasingly be limited by international treaties or participation in transnational governmental bodies such as the European Union; however, at least in the UK judge-made common law continues to be vibrant, and the higher courts there are recognized to be lawmakers not just interpreters of the law (Darbyshire 2011:359). In some countries judges have a more extensive role in overseeing administrative decisions than do American judges.

The Career Model

Worldwide, the most common approach for staffing courts follows a bureaucratic model.[7] Under this model a person applies to become a judge upon completion of his or her basic legal education, which in almost all countries is a first degree roughly similar to the American bachelor's degree. Typically all candidates must take some type of competitive examination testing their legal knowledge, and only those achieving high scores are selected for training to become a judge (see Guarnieri 2012:202–13). In some systems, such as Japan, the examination is the same for those seeking to become legal professionals who advocate in court, prosecutors, and judges. In other systems those entering the system are deemed to be magistrates, some of whom serve as judges and others as prosecutors, with movement allowed between the two roles. The criteria for passing the exam may be set as achieving a certain score or alternatively there may be some set number who will be deemed to have passed. In some systems preparation for the exam often requires years of study beyond the basic legal education.

Those who pass the exam and survive any other required initial screening then enter a training program intended to prepare them for a career as a judge or magistrate. The length of this training program varies from country to country, as does the content. There may be some type of additional examination and/or evaluation at the end of this training. Those who successfully complete the training then start their careers, usually in a role handling minor cases or assisting a more senior judge. As the young judge gains experience, he or she will be evaluated periodically and, assuming positive evaluations, will progress

7 See Malleson and Russell (2006) for a treatment of judicial selection processes in a wide range of countries.

to higher level or more desirable courts; often a judge will have to make many moves during his or her career, with early positions in less desirable locations. Advancement thus flows from a combination of seniority and merit as ascertained by evaluations by senior members of the judiciary. Typically there will be a mandatory retirement age and a large proportion of those who enter the judiciary serve until reaching that age; some members of the judiciary will leave prior to reaching mandatory retirement either because they find they do not like the work or to take advantage of other opportunities.

A variant on this model requires that a law graduate first qualify as a legal practitioner and gain some number of years of practice experience before seeking to move into the judiciary. Selection to enter the judiciary will still be through a competitive process usually involving examinations, with entrants also progressing through a hierarchy of positions. Some systems may provide for a kind of lateral entry which might involve less or no post-entry training and allows the new judge to start higher in the judicial hierarchy than the normal entrant. Even with these variants, the basic design is best described as a hierarchical career model which is insulated from elected officials.

One important exception in many systems using a career model is appointment to the constitutional court, particularly in countries where the regular courts are not empowered to adjudicate issues dealing with the constitutionality of laws, regulations, or government actions. In many systems the process of selecting judges for the constitutional court is distinct from that for staffing the regular judiciary, and will typically directly involve elected officials. Some members of the constitutional court may have had careers in the judicial hierarchy, while others may come from the legal academy or be persons who had served in either elected or nonelected government positions outside the judiciary. Judges of these constitutional courts typically serve fixed-length terms and/or are subject to mandatory retirement at some specified age.

While a hierarchical, bureaucratic system may sound foreign to the American way of thinking about judges, it bears a lot of similarities to the systems used for selecting federal and state administrative law judges, particularly the variant where some period of experience is required before applying to become a judge. For at least some American ALJs there is a hierarchy among the positions they can assume. Movement upward in such roles would be at least partly a function of seniority and in some systems there may be evaluation mechanisms similar to those used in countries with a bureaucratic-style judiciary.

Even though this kind of system does exist to some degree in the United States, it is not likely to be acceptable as a replacement for current systems used to select judges of the regular trial and appellate courts. The countries relying on a bureaucratic-style judicial hierarchy have civil law systems where the role of the judge is deemed to be more limited than is true in common law countries such as the United States. Importantly, in civil law systems judges themselves tend to view their role more narrowly, although one can debate whether there is as much difference as is commonly presumed (see Shapiro 1981). One way in which there is a real difference is with regard to constitutional interpretation, something that American judges at essentially all levels may undertake, while in most systems with bureaucratic-style judiciaries, all constitutional issues must be decided by a separate constitutional tribunal.

The Appointments Commission Model

In common law countries, the norm is that judges are selected from among experienced legal practitioners. In England and Wales, where the legal profession is divided between barristers and solicitors, appointments to the higher level courts were until relatively recently restricted to barristers, and even today the judges from the highest courts come mostly from a small elite group of barristers who themselves come from a relatively elite segment of English society.[8] In England and Wales it is common for practitioners to serve in part-time positions while maintaining a private practice, and this is the usual path to full-time, higher level judicial positions, either as a circuit judge[9] or a high court judge (Darbyshire 2011:65, 124).[10]

In recent years the three primary constituent parts of the United Kingdom, which traditionally relied on appointment by a senior elected official, have adopted systems of screening and selection of judges which although formally maintaining the senior elected official as the appointing authority, have shifted the dominant role to an appointed Judicial Appointments

[8] One study found that as of 2005, 75 percent of the "senior judiciary" had attended private secondary schools, and 81 percent had attended Oxford or Cambridge (Darbyshire 2011:45). However, one should keep in mind that all current (as of 2014) members of the U.S. Supreme Court are graduates of either Harvard Law School or Yale Law School.

[9] "Circuit judges must be lawyers who have held a 'right of audience' (the right to appear in court as an advocate) for at least ten years, and should generally also have served either part-time as a recorder on criminal cases or full-time as district judges on civil cases before they can be appointed" (http://www.judiciary.gov.uk/about-the-judiciary/the-judiciary-in-detail/judicial+roles/judges/ciruit-judge, last visited August 16, 2013).

[10] Of the ten "senior" judges listed on the judiciary website (http://www.judiciary.gov.uk/about-the-judiciary/judges-magistrates-and-tribunal-judges/biographies, last visited August 16, 2013), six had served in part-time positions prior to becoming full-time judges. As of August 16, 2013, Wikipedia contained biographies for 67 of the then sitting 106 High Court judges; 54 of those biographies indicated service in some type of part-time judicial role (recorder, assistant recorder, deputy High Court judge) prior to appointment to a full-time position on the High Court.

Commission (JAC for England and Wales, JAC for Northern Ireland) or Judicial Appointments Board (JAB for Scotland).[11] With the exception of the highest judges who sit on what is now the UK Supreme Court, the heads of the central branches of some of the other higher courts, and the lay judges of the lowest level courts (the magistrates court), judges in the United Kingdom are now selected through a process whereby the main player is one of these bodies (Malleson 2007; Paterson 2007). Recommendations for appointments to the UK Supreme Court and the heads of the central branches of the higher courts are made by ad hoc commissions appointed by the lord chancellor; for the UK Supreme Court that ad hoc commission must include the president and deputy president of the Supreme Court along with one member each from the Judicial Appointments Commission of England and Wales, the Judicial Appointments Board of Scotland, and the Judicial Appointments Commission of Northern Ireland, with each of these designating which of its members should serve.[12] Applicants for positions as part-time, unpaid, lay magistrates are screened by local committees who make recommendations to the lord chancellor.[13]

Central to the JAC/JAB process is an open application process coupled with a rigorous system of screening and evaluation conducted with the assistance of a full-time, professional staff. The JAC/JAB process is used to staff both courts and the tribunals that deal with the kinds of issues handled by administrative law judges in the United States. The JAC for England and Wales deals with large numbers of appointments each year (almost 600 in 2012–13) while the JAB for Scotland and the JAC for Northern Ireland deal with many fewer (only eleven in 2012–13 in Scotland and only eighty-six including both new appointments and reappointments in Northern Ireland for 2011–12).[14] The professional staffs of these bodies number about seventy for England and Wales, eighteen for Northern Ireland, and four for Scotland.

[11] While originally the first minister was the appointing authority in Northern Ireland, this role shifted to the lord chancellor in 2004. Further changes in 2009 made the Judicial Appointments Commission for Northern Ireland itself the appointing authority for most positions.

[12] If the vacancy is for the president or deputy president of the Supreme Court, the most senior member of the court who is not a candidate to become president or deputy president must be appointed to the special commission.

[13] Most criminal matters plus a few noncriminal matters are dealt with by magistrates' courts (Darbyshire 2011:45). These courts are staffed either by a panel of three lay (nonlawyer), part-time magistrates assisted by a law-trained clerk, or by what is today called a district judge (previously called "stipendiary magistrates") who are full-time and have full legal qualifications. In 2011, Magistrates' Courts handled about 980,000 adult cases (about 40 percent of which were sufficiently serious that they could have been dealt with in the higher criminal court, the Crown Court) compared to about 150,000 handled by the Crown Court (https://www.gov.uk/government/statistics/judicial-and-court-statistics-annual, last visited July 31, 2014).

[14] All of these figures are from annual reports found on each of the JAC/JAB's websites.

The JAC for England and Wales describes its process as involving a series of stages that starts after the lord chancellor informs the JAC of a vacancy:[15]

1. Preparation of a tailored application form and the soliciting of applications through the JAC website.
2. Shortlisting, which is normally based *either* on anonymously marked qualifying tests, generally prepared and marked by experienced judges, that are designed to assess "the qualities and abilities required for judicial office," *or* reviews of the candidates' self assessments and references (both professional and personal) by a panel consisting of persons with a recruitment background who have been trained in the JAC process.
3. Shortlisted candidates then participate in a "selection day" which may consist of an interview and often some combination of a presentation, situational questioning, and/or a role play; the selection day is conducted and assessed by a panel of three persons. References are reviewed if that had not already been done, and the character of each candidate is assessed. Based on all of this information, the panel produces a summary report that is forwarded to the Commission.
4. As required by the Constitutional Reform Act (CRA), the summary reports for candidates deemed likely to move forward to the recommendation stage are forwarded for comment to the lord chief justice and one other person who has either held the position or has relevant experience.
5. Based on the summary reports and the responses from the consultation required by the CRA, the commissioners decide which single candidate to recommend to the lord chancellor.
6. The lord chancellor may accept the recommendation, ask the commission to reconsider its recommendation, or reject the recommendation. If the lord chancellor requests reconsideration or rejects the recommendation, he must provide in writing his reasons for doing so. If the lord chancellor rejects a recommendation, the commission may not recommend that person again for the same position but is not precluded from recommending the person for a future position.

Through the 2012/13 reporting period, the JAC had forwarded in excess of 3,300 recommendations to the lord chancellor, and through October 2012 the lord chancellor had rejected or requested reconsideration of only five recommendations for positions for the High Court or below (Gee 2012).

[15] This description is based on Appendix A from the 2012/13 JAC Annual Report. Note that the procedures for making recommendations for appointments to the Court of Appeal differ in some ways.

A key element in this process is the constraint placed on the lord chancellor (LC) after the LC has either rejected a recommendation or asked the JAC to reconsider the recommended candidate.[16] If the LC rejects the first name that the JAC forwarded, he may not reject the second name, although he can ask the JAC to reconsider the second recommendation. If the LC asks that a recommendation be reconsidered, he cannot ask that the name forwarded after reconsideration (which can be either the original name or a new name) be reconsidered, although he can reject the name forwarded. If the LC rejects or requests reconsideration after previously having rejected or requested reconsideration, his options on the third round are limited to accepting the third recommendation of the JAC or appointing the person who had been recommended at an earlier stage but not rejected. An example should make this clearer; consider a situation with three hypothetical candidates: Adams, Brown, and Clark.

1. The JAC recommends Adams; if the LC accepts Adams, the process ends. Alternatively, the LC may either reject Adams or ask the JAC to reconsider Adams.
2. If the LC rejects Adams, the JAC must send forward a new candidate, and this is Brown; if the LC accepts Brown, the process ends. The LC may not reject Brown, but can request that Brown be reconsidered.
   a. The LC asks that Brown be reconsidered: The JAC may send forward Clark or resend Brown.
      i. The JAC resends Brown; the LC **must** accept Brown.
      ii. The JAC sends Clark; the LC **must** accept Clark or accept Brown.
3. The LC asked that Adams be reconsidered.
   a. The JAC resends Adams; if the LC accepts Adams this time, the process ends. The LC may not ask that Adams be reconsidered again, but can reject Adams.
      i. The LC rejects Adams. The JAC sends forward Brown (it may not send Adams a third time); the LC **must** accept Brown.
   b. The JAC sends Brown; if LC accepts Brown the process ends. The LC may not ask that Brown be reconsidered but can reject Brown.
      i. The LC rejects Brown. The JAC resends Adams, who had been the JAC's initial recommendation that the LC had previously asked the JAC to reconsider; the LC **must** accept Adams.
      ii. The LC rejects Brown, the JAC sends forward Clark. The LC **must** accept either Clark or Adams.

[16] See Constitutional Reform Act 2005 (U.K.), §90.

What this boils down to is that the lord chancellor may reject one candidate and ask the JAC to reconsider one candidate, but once the LC has exercised both the right to reject and the right to request reconsideration, the LC is constrained to accept a candidate recommended by the JAC whom the LC has not previously rejected. Similar constraints exist on the lord chancellor in considering recommendations of the required ad hoc selection commission that is charged with identifying a candidate for appointment as a judge of the UK Supreme Court or a head of one of the major court branches.[17]

The nature of constraints in connection with the Judicial Appointments Board for Scotland and the Judicial Appointments Commission for Northern Ireland differ from those of the English JAC in opposite ways. In Scotland the appointing authority is the first minister, and there is no limit on the number of times the first minister can reject or request reconsideration of the JAB's recommendation in connection with an appointment.[18] In Northern Ireland starting in 2009 the JAC itself makes the appointments to most of the positions for which it previously made recommendations; for a small number of higher level positions it now makes recommendations directly to the lord chancellor with procedures similar to those of the JAC for England and Wales. The 2009 change probably reflected the realization that the recommendations of the JAC were effectively definitive, and it served no purpose for the appointing authority, which was the lord chancellor,[19] to devote any time or resources to reviewing recommendations that would always be accepted.

This system does raise some issues. It has been less successful than was hoped in recruiting highly qualified minorities to judicial positions in the UK (Advisory Panel on Judicial Diversity 2010; Bowcott 2012, 2014; Straw 2013), and there are also

17 For appointments to the Supreme Court, the lord chancellor notifies the rime minister of the outcome of the process, who then "recommends" to the Crown who should be appointed; the prime minister *must* recommend the person whose name he or she receives from the lord chancellor. See chapter 4, section 26 of the Constitutional Reform Act 2005 (available at http://www.legislation.gov.uk/ukpga/2005/4/pdfs/ukpga_20050004_en.pdf, last visited August 14, 2013).

18 See Paterson (2007) for a description of the Scottish JAB's process; also, as Paterson explains, more judicial appointments in Scotland lie outside the authority of the JAB than is true in England and Wales or in Northern Ireland.

19 Originally, under the provisions of the Justice (Northern Ireland) Act 2002 which created the JAC for Northern Ireland, the JAC forwarded its recommendations to the first minister of Northern Ireland who served as the appointing authority (except for a small number of higher level positions for which the lord chancellor was the appointing authority), and the first minister was constrained in the same manner as the lord chancellor was when the lord chancellor was dealing with recommendations from the JAC for England and Wales. The Justice (Northern Ireland) Act 2004 removed the first minister from the process and made the lord chancellor the appointing authority for all positions for which the JAC for Northern Ireland made recommendation (McCaffrey and O'Connell 2012:7–12).

concerns about the number of women being appointed (see Malleson 2014). How much of this is a function of who chooses to apply for judicial positions and how much it reflects who survives the screening process, either due to the structure of the process or unconscious bias on the part of the evaluators involved in the process, is not clear. Many of the positions to be filled do not pay especially well, and this may discourage minorities with successful practices, who are likely to be the best qualified in professional terms, from applying; even the more prestigious positions such as High Court Judge do not pay well in comparison to what most of the senior practitioners who would be prime candidates earn (see Genn 2008). It may also be that highly experienced and highly qualified candidates may not want to go through the rigorous screening process that is the core of the system, although to some degree this might be a generational issue, with the more senior candidates preferring the older approach that was often described as involving a "tap on the shoulder" (Genn 2008; Straw 2013). Particularly in connection with appointments to the UK Supreme Court, too great a role may have been given to sitting members of the judiciary creating a situation where the top elements of the judiciary may be "effectively self-perpetuating" (Paterson 2013:309).

This system has some parallels to the use of nominating commissions as part of the Missouri Plan system in the United States, although the differences are quite significant. Those differences include the use of a professionalized, standing body to manage the screening process; a more rigorous screening process that usually involves examinations and role playing to assess both knowledge and suitability; a dominant role for sitting members of the judiciary on the screening body (the JAC or the JAB); a single name is forwarded to the appointing authority; and substantial constraints on the decisions the appointing authority can make after receiving the recommendation. The structure of the process serves to give the screening body, which is designed to be nonpolitical, the dominant role, with the appointing authority having a limited ability to overrule the screening body. Also, and crucially, no popular elections are involved, although reappointments are possible for positions that involve fixed terms of service. There are elements of this system that could potentially be imported to the United States that would improve our systems of judicial selection, and that could be integrated with at least some direct role for the electorate.

WHAT REFORMS MIGHT BE POSSIBLE?

The Low Probability of Significant Change

Proposals to eliminate elections for appellate judges entirely, particularly those sitting on state supreme courts, are not likely to be successful given the American preference for elections. In fact, as noted in an earlier chapter, in the history of the United States, there are only two examples of states entirely eliminating elections for their courts of last resort. One of those was in Virginia, which adopted elections for all state judges in 1850, but abandoned elections in 1864 (when Virginia was part of the Confederacy), and then adopted election by the legislature during Reconstruction. The only other state to abandon elections entirely for its state supreme court was New York in the 1970s after a series of problematic elections (see Philip et al. 1976:107–32).

While there have been many changes to state supreme court selection/retention systems during the post–World War II period, other than New York they have all preserved a role for elections, although the nature of those elections often was changed. Between 1960 and 1982, sixteen states changed their election systems, with fifteen states adopting retention elections, two (Illinois and Pennsylvania) in combination with partisan elections for initial full terms, and only two states adopting nonpartisan elections, Kentucky in 1975 and Florida in 1971, although Florida quickly shifted to retention elections five years later (which is why there is a total of seventeen changes but only sixteen states that made changes). Between 1982 and 2014, only six states made changes, with two adopting retention elections, Tennessee in 1994 (by legislation rather than constitutional change – see Behm and Henri 2014) and New Mexico in 1988 (in combination with partisan elections for initial full terms), and four shifting to nonpartisan elections: Georgia in 1983, Mississippi in 1994, Arkansas starting in 2002, and North Carolina starting in 2004 (see Heagarty 2003). Thus, as this is written, only two states have made changes in the last twenty years, and no state has changed to retention elections.

Between 1978 and 2012, proposals to eliminate partisan or nonpartisan elections and move to a full Missouri Plan type system for some or all courts have failed in Florida (2000), Illinois (1996), Louisiana (multiple years), Michigan (2012), Nevada (2010), North Carolina (1999), Ohio (1987), Oregon (1978), Pennsylvania (1990), South Dakota (2004), Texas (multiple years), and Washington (2007) (Streb 2011),[20] and a similar effort in Minnesota is at a standsill as this is written in 2014 in part due to opposition from some conservative factions (Helgeson 2013; Sturdevant 2014).[21] Proposed changes in Florida, Nevada, Ohio, Oregon, and South Dakota were defeated by popular votes.

20 See also http://www.judicialselection.us/ (last visited August 14, 2013).

21 See http://www.impartialcourts.org/pdf/QuieReportCommissionRecommendations.pdf (last visited August 14, 2013). The lack of action on the Minnesota proposals was not only due to conservative opposition; beyond the legal profession, it is unclear that there were any strong bases of support. Even members of the judiciary were not necessarily supportive; some, perhaps many, judges who typically run unopposed for reelection see no benefit in a switch to retention elections because under the current system they know they are safe from opposition once the election filing date has passed while under the retention system they would have to be alert for potential opposition until the actual election day.

In recent years there have been a number of calls to move from Missouri Plan systems back to contested elections, to weaken the role of nominating commissions, or to modify the membership of the nominating commission in a way that would increase the influence of the governor (Angel 2008; Gibeaut 2012; Mannies 2007; "Missouri Compromised: Judicial Selection the Trial Lawyer Way" 2011; "Preserving Judicial Independence" 2012; Wiese 2008). For example, the Republican governor and legislature in Kansas eliminated nominating commissions and added state senate confirmation for appointments to the intermediate appellate court in Kansas, and 2013 saw efforts to do the same for the Kansas Supreme Court (Levy 2013);[22] however, the changes did not eliminate periodic retention elections. In 2014, the voters of Tennessee did adopt a change along these lines which eliminated the required screening commission, and will allow the legislature to reject the governor's nominee; retention elections will continue, but only at the end of a full or partial term (Boucher 2014). Most often the call for such changes has come from conservative or business groups that perceive that they can sway voters to elect judges favorable to the groups' preferred policies.[23] Ironically, it was many of these same groups that in the past sought to lessen the electorate's role in judicial selection because they feared that voters would favor populist judges who would be inclined to rule against business interests (Shugerman 2012:179–80).

What kinds of changes might potentially be doable that go beyond adopting one of the systems already in place? For this discussion, I ignore the political games played by ideological and interest groups seeking to manipulate the selection/election system for their own advantage – a long-standing practice in American politics. I do, however, accept that there must be at least some potential role for popular elections. With that in mind, I describe four changes that would be a step or more outside our current boxes.

Professionalize and Enhance the Screening Process

In all states, most judges come to their position through an appointment process, usually with the governor making the final decision for positions that

[22] Changing the method of selection of justices on the Kansas Supreme Court requires an amendment to the state constitution which in turn requires approval of the change by the voters. The legislature and governor together had the power to modify the selection system for the intermediate appellate court.

[23] The groups that supported the drive in Tennessee ranged from the Eagle Forum and Family Action of Tennessee to the Tennessee Business Roundtable and Tennessee Chamber of Business & Industry (see http://online.wsj.com/article/PR-CO-20130306-913195.html, last visited August 16, 2013). Members of the conservative Federalist Society have been active in at least some of the efforts around the country (Mannies 2007).

are formally part of the judicial system. By necessity there is usually some screening process required by law or implemented informally or by executive order. As already noted, for administrative law judges or equivalent positions a civil-service type screening process is typically used, but for other judicial positions the screening process tends to be ad hoc, carried out either by staff with no particular expertise related to evaluation or by volunteer committees typically composed of or dominated by some combination of lawyers and judges. These kinds of ad hoc screening mechanisms suffer from inconsistent procedures and limited institutional memory.

States could unify and professionalize the screening process used for all judge-like positions, including those in the judiciary, administrative law judges, and specialized hearing officers, by creating a Judicial Screening Commission (JSC) that combines a professional staff with a set of commissioners appointed for fixed terms. In principle, a person who seeks to run for judge in an open-seat election or as a challenger to a sitting judge could be required to submit to an evaluation by the screening commission as a condition for appearing on the ballot with the results of that evaluation made available to the voters.

The screening process could involve many or all of the elements used by the Judicial Appointments Commission for England and Wales. While the full-time professional staff would play a key role in conducting the screening, the commissioners would have the final say in the assessment of all candidates and in making actual recommendations. Depending on the level of position and other aspects of the appointment process, the JSC could be charged with forwarding some number of nominees to an appointing authority. Alternatively, it could be asked to assign ratings of some sort, either single ratings or ratings for a range of factors deemed relevant for a particular position.

A central question for such a system brings us back to the "who chooses the choosers" issue. That is, who would select the members of the Judicial Screening Commission? Presumably, the goal would be to limit political considerations, but it would be difficult to eliminate them entirely. One approach would be to ensure that there is an element of political balance on any such commission. This could be accomplished by having members designated through diverse mechanisms. The governor could name two, and the majority and minority leaders in the state legislature could name others; some members might be drawn from the bench; other members might be drawn from among deans of law schools within the state (or their designees); and still other members from the practicing bar. Nonlawyers should be included through some mechanism. The goal in designing the membership of the commission and how those commissioners would be selected should be insuring that it is difficult for one particular political perspective to capture control of the commission. One might give key political leaders the option to strike nominees to the commission as a means of trying to further dampen strong political ideologies from dominating the commission. Something along this line applies in California's Citizen Redistricting Commission, the nonpartisan body that is charged with drawing boundaries for California's legislative districts and for California's House of Representative districts (see Levitt 2011:534–35).

One other issue that would arise is whether any one state makes a sufficient number of judicial appointments that having a professionalized judicial appointments screening process is practical. No state is going to have the volume of appointments handled by the Judicial Appointments Commission for England and Wales; however, if the JSC handled appointments of administrative law judges and hearing officers as well as appointments to the judicial branch, many states would have at least as many positions to deal with as are handled by the JAC for Northern Ireland or the JAB for Scotland.[24] If the JSC also handled evaluations of sitting judges seeking reelection or reappointment, a proposal discussed later, JSCs in additional states would have sufficient work to support a professional staff. It is also in theory possible that two or more small states could share a professional staff that served several JSCs.

Part-Time Judgeships

Aside from local justices of the peace and some municipal and town courts, a number of state and local jurisdictions in the United States have positions for what are essentially part-time judges working in courts alongside and under the supervision of full-time judges. These positions exist under a variety of labels, including "assistant judge," "court commissioner," "magistrate," and "referee." These part-time judges handle a variety of matters including arraignments, bail hearings, pre-trial motions, small claims trials, various family law matters (child support, paternity, temporary divorce hearings, domestic abuse and harassment injunctions, and post-divorce matters), and in some jurisdictions these part-time judges can conduct trials, although usually limited to

[24] The population of Scotland is about 5 million and the population of Northern Ireland is less than 2 million; the population of England and Wales is about 62 million. The largest state, California, has a population of 38 million; 22 states have populations exceeding that of Scotland, and 36 exceed Northern Ireland.

misdemeanors or small civil cases. The pay for these part-time positions may be a salary if the judge works some set amount of time, or it may be on some type of per diem or per court session basis. Very often persons in these positions are selected by one or more of the judges in the court in which they will serve, and the terms of appointment may be as brief as one year, although normally the appointments are renewable.[25]

As discussed previously, in the UK a part-time judicial position frequently serves as a stepping stone into a full-time position as a District, Circuit, or High Court judge, and has been a virtual requirement for those who eventually become full-time judges.[26] Working as a judge part-time allows an experienced practitioner to try on the role of judge and determine whether the practitioner would like to give up his or her practice as a barrister or solicitor and become a full-time judge. More important, service as a part-time judge can provide information to the Judicial Appointments Commission when it is considering a candidate for a full-time position.[27] It also provides some flexibility to the officials who make assignments to hear cases or matters, allowing them to limit the number of assignments to a part-time judge who is deemed to be performing subpar in his or her work as a judge.

Recall that the vast majority of full-time state and local judges in the United States actually come to the bench initially through appointment. There is no indication that those making the appointments look on previous part-time experience as a judge as a significant consideration, nor is there any information on how, if at all, those screening candidates for full-time judicial appointments use a candidate's performance in a part-time position as part of the evaluation of the candidate. Expanding the use of part-time judicial appointments to handle more of the work of state trial courts, possibly including at least some types of administrative tribunals, could be functional for the courts (increased flexibility, possibly reduced costs, etc.), while providing information that could be very useful to those making full-time appointments. Even in situations in which someone initially seeks to obtain a full-time judgeship

25 In the federal district courts there are both full-time and part-time magistrate judges, with part-time magistrate judges appointed for four-year terms with full-time magistrates serving eight-year terms; 28 U.S.C. §631(e) (2012) (see http://uscode.house.gov/download/pls/28C43.txt, last visited August 16, 2013).

26 Darbyshire shadowed 77 English full-time judges over a period of years; every one of them "had been 'tested' as part-timers" (Darbyshire 2011:65).

27 Surprisingly, there does not appear to be any systematic process of assessing the performance of part-time judges in England and hence no way of systematically having such assessments serve as part of the screening for full-time appointments; however, the references that will be sought will probably include observations about the candidates' performance in their part-time roles.

by election, if there is a system in place for judicial evaluation, prior part-time judicial service could be an important element in evaluations that could be made available to the public just as is now done in some states in connection with judicial retention elections.

Constraining the Appointing Authority

A central element of the judicial appointments commission system in use in England and Wales is the constraints that have been placed on the ultimate appointing authority who is generally the lord chancellor. As previously detailed, in connection with any specific appointment, the appointing authority can once outright reject a proposed appointee and once ask that a proposed appointee be reconsidered. Essentially these constraints are such that the appointing authority must carefully weigh the strength of any objections to the initially proposed appointee. An appointing authority who rejects the first proposed appointee is limited with regard to a second proposed appointee to at most asking that proposed person be reconsidered, and if the JAC again forwards the second proposed appointee, the appointing authority must then appoint that person.

For most judicial appointments at the state level, the appointing authority is constrained only by the legal qualifications required for the position. Typically these are a license to practice law, a certain numbers of years of experience practicing law, and possibly location of residence; for some administrative law judgeships, tests required of applicants may limit the discretion of the appointing authority. In some states that use a formal nominating commission, the governor must either accept one of the persons forwarded by the nominating commission, or request the nominating commission to forward a new list, and in some states the governor's choice is subject to confirmation, usually by one or both houses of the state legislature. As discussed previously, the Missouri Plan system has come under attack, and one of the primary objections that critics have raised is to the modest constraint created by the requirement that the governor can only appoint someone forwarded by the nominating commission. Given that in many states, the governor effectively controls the nominating commission, it is not clear to what degree the nominating commission functions as a significant constraint. In states requiring legislative confirmation, that requirement is likely to be constraining only when the legislative body involved is not controlled by the governor's political party.

While imposing greater constraints on the appointing authority is likely to be controversial, it is a mechanism that would serve to reduce the partisan considerations in judicial appointments if combined with professionalized screening commissions that were designed to limit partisan considerations. A system similar to that in use in England and Wales still allows the appointing authority to veto an initial nomination to which he or she has strong objections, either on professional or political grounds. However, the kind of constraint that exists in England forces the appointing authority to be cautious in exercising his or her discretion. This kind of constraint in some ways resembles the constraint on lawyers in a number of systems in how they use peremptory challenges when choosing a jury. If the jury selection (*voir dire*) system operates such that a lawyer does not know who would be seated to replace a struck potential juror and the lawyer has only one remaining peremptory challenge, the lawyer will be very cautious in using that last challenge because the person who would replace the struck juror might be worse from the lawyer's perspective.[28]

Judicial Performance Evaluations and Eliminating Pointless Elections

Elections have value, but that does not mean that *all* elections have value. One possible modification to the current Missouri Plan system, or to a Missouri Plan system with the type of professionalized screening proposed in this chapter, would be to eliminate most retention elections, retaining such elections only under specific circumstances. A minuscule fraction of judges in systems relying on retention elections are ever defeated, substantially less than one percent (Aspin 2011). Why not reserve such elections for circumstances where they have meaning? Several states have adopted systems for evaluating judges in advance of retention elections (Esterling 1999; Gerkman 2012; Kourlis and Singer 2007; Elek et al. 2014), and the professionalized Judicial Selection Commissions described would provide a vehicle for improving and expanding evaluation systems, as well as possibly avoiding some of the potential pitfalls of such systems (Gill et al. 2011; Gill and Retzl 2014).[29]

With a strong evaluation system in place the default for retention could be automatic renewal, reserving retention elections for two situations. The first situation would be citizen initiated after the JSC or any other body responsible for evaluation found that a judge's performance merited renewal; if an organization or group of citizens strongly felt that a judge should not be

[28] At one time this was the most common system used in the *voir dire* process. However, today many jurisdictions have moved to a system where the number of jurors seated after challenges for cause is equal to the jury size plus the number of alternates plus the total number of peremptory challenges to be exercised by the two sides; the two sides then proceed to alternate in using their peremptory challenges. Thus, the lawyers know at the end who will be left when they use their final peremptory challenge.

[29] See Contini et al. (2014) for a broad set of perspectives on the issue and process of evaluating judicial performance in the United States and elsewhere.

retained despite the results of the performance evaluation, that group could collect some required number of signatures to force a retention vote. Under this arrangement one would want to set the number of signatures required such that it was neither a trivial requirement nor a requirement that was so demanding as to make it effectively impossible to meet. The second situation would be when the evaluation commission found that a judge should not be retained; under that circumstance, the judge would have the right to stand in a retention election and make his or her case for retention. It seems highly unlikely that a judge that had been so poorly evaluated would seek retention, but that option should be available as a minimal check on the evaluation process. In either of these two situations where a retention election did actually occur, the election would serve something more than a symbolic purpose, and the voters would have a reasonable chance of having available the information needed to cast a meaningful vote.

THE LOW LIKELIHOOD OF INNOVATIVE CHANGE AND THE POSSIBLE ADVANTAGES OF PARTISAN ELECTIONS

While I view the kinds of changes I described in the previous section as providing some real, practical alternatives to the existing systems for judicial selection and retention, I am not so naïve as to think any of them, with the possible exception of some increased use of formal judicial performance evaluations, are likely to be adopted any time in the foreseeable future. This partly reflects that the proposals remove key points of influence in the selection and retention process, either influence by elected officials or influence by voters and organized interests. The citizens of the United States do value judicial independence, but at the same time want that independence to be limited, and elections serve to impose some limits. Organized interests want judges sympathetic to groups' preferences and want to have as much influence as possible in judicial selection, and many groups see judicial elections as an important vehicle for that influence. Moreover, as previously discussed, groups will seek change that serves their goals and resist any change that they think might make it more difficult to achieve those goals.

One interesting finding in the study of group influences in state supreme court elections is that they appear to be dampened when those elections are conducted on a partisan basis. The results suggest that ideological and interest groups have more influence in nonpartisan and retention elections because of the absence of partisan cues that are so important to voters. That is, without the information provided by party labels, voters can be more easily influenced by advertising that may be misleading or that might make false claims.

While historically there has been a movement away from partisan judicial elections and there continues to be hostility to involving parties in judicial elections (see, e.g., "Editorial: Keep Parties Out of Judicial Elections" 2014), it might be time to rethink whether partisan elections would be better, at least at the state supreme court level, than are either nonpartisan or retention elections. In the southern states, the drive to eliminate partisan elections was in significant part a last-ditch effort of the flagging southern state Democratic parties to hang on to some influence which they rightly feared would be lost to the rising southern Republicans. Outside the South, a central concern that helped the drive away from partisan elections was the desire of reformers to eliminate the influence that party leaders exercised over the nomination of candidates in the period before primary elections became the main mechanism for nominating a party's candidates. With the rise of the primary system, the role of party leaders in most states is minimal (Gill 2013:284).

This does not mean that the electorate is captivated by political parties or partisan elections, although surveys of Wisconsin residents in 2011 and 2012 found that almost 60 percent of respondents favored partisan elections for the Wisconsin Supreme Court, with only about 40 percent favoring nonpartisan elections and elements of the Missouri Plan (Jacobs et al. 2013).[30] Nonetheless, research has consistently shown that voters depend very heavily on the information provided by party labels on the ballot, and many of the bizarre election results that occur in down-ballot elections, a sampling of which were discussed in prior chapters, reflect the voter confusion that arises in the absence of the cues party labels provide. While the proponents of the nonpartisan ballot envisioned an electorate that would do what was needed to make informed decisions in the absence of party labels, we now know that that simply does not happen. Modern advertising has empowered interest groups and candidates to broadly disseminate information that can be deceptive or downright false. While such information can also be provided in the context of partisan elections, it is likely to be less effective because voters have the partisan cue on the ballot which can at least partially counterbalance biased, misleading, and false advertising.

Importantly, partisan cues are only likely to matter in states where the political parties are competitive. In states where one party is overwhelmingly

[30] The element of the Missouri Plan described to respondents was "have a nonpartisan commission nominate qualified candidates and then have the governor select one of those nominees to serve on the court." Less than 20 percent of respondents would favor having the governor or state legislature appoint justices (presumably in the more traditional way without any nonpartisan nominating commission).

dominant, such as contemporary Texas, party cues are likely to have little effect in statewide elections, regardless of whether the minority party chooses to field a candidate. The meaningful elections that do happen in those states take place in the primary of the dominant party, and in those elections there is no party cue. One of the most striking examples of name confusion, that involving Don Yarbrough discussed in Chapter 2, occurred in a primary election. In states such as Texas, the system for statewide elections is for all intents and purposes nonpartisan, as was true for the South for much of the twentieth century (Key 1949). In those states it probably makes little difference if the system is partisan or nonpartisan. Although I would favor partisan elections for state supreme courts in states that choose to use elections, I would not include the state supreme court as part of a straight-party ticket voting option in the states that have that option. To do so might make state supreme courts subject to partisan swings that have nothing to do with the actions of state supreme courts.[31]

Finally, partisan elections for the lower courts raise issues that need to be considered before deciding whether such elections would be better than other election alternatives. For example, while Texas is effectively a one-party state for statewide elections, that is not true for local elections, particularly in some of the larger cities. This has created some problems at the trial court level in cities such as Houston and Dallas when there have been major swings, problems that were greatly amplified by the inclusion of the local trial court candidates on the straight-party ticket option (Tolson 2012; Ramsey 2012). The result in some elections has been the wholesale ouster of large numbers of trial judges of one party who were replaced by new judges affiliated with the other party. This has meant that judges who might have been handling a complex, ongoing case were suddenly replaced by a new judge who had limited familiarity with what had been happening in the case; these changes create significant costs and delays for the parties. Moreover, trial judges do not make broadly applicable decisions that create binding precedent on other judges. This is not to say that trial judges do not on occasion make decisions that have broad impact, such as rulings on evidentiary matters and the like in large cases. However, judges at this level would be the most obvious place to seriously consider the kind of judicial selection commission combined with a judicial performance evaluations and limited use of retention elections that I described earlier.

[31] Where a straight-ticket option is offered, omitting some offices from the straight-ticket does raise a potential problem. Specifically, some voters may select the straight-ticket option and believe that they have voted for all offices and thus not cast votes for the offices not on the straight ticket (see Bonneau and Loepp 2014:123).

Whether a move back toward partisan elections would be desirable for judges at the intermediate appellate level is less clear. The research that has been done on elections for the intermediate appellate court does not reveal evidence of the kinds of changes that have occurred for state supreme courts (Frederick and Streb 2008, 2011; Streb et al. 2007). However, as discussed, in Kansas the selection model for intermediate appellate courts was recently changed to eliminate the nominating commission and to make appointees subject to confirmation by the state senate while keeping retention elections as the retention mechanism. While states do vary regarding the precedential value of the decisions of their intermediate appellate court, there is little evidence that decisions by courts at that level have created substantial outcries from either interest groups or the public. At this time the elections for intermediate appellate courts, whether of the contested variety or retention variety, have not involved the kind of advertising that has been used in state supreme court elections that suggest the advantages of partisan elections.[32] While I would advocate moving toward the kind of judicial selection commission model described in this chapter, it probably would make little difference whether elections for intermediate appellate courts in states currently using either nonpartisan or retention elections once again became partisan or remain as they are.

[32] Salamone et al. (2014:15) report that less than 3 percent (6 of 224) of television ads for state appellate courts other than state supreme court broadcast between 2006 and 2013 were attack ads, compared to about 16 percent of ads in state supreme court elections, and all six of the attack ads were sponsored by a candidate's campaign. Note that in their analysis the Courts of Criminal Appeals in Texas and Oklahoma were included in their category of appellate courts excluding state supreme courts; it is likely that some, if not all, of the attack ads involved these contests for these courts. More than 96 percent of the ads in these elections were candidate-sponsored. Note that these figures refer to distinct ads, not ad airings.

References

Abramowitz, Alan I. (1988) "Explaining Senate Election Outcomes." 82 *Political Science Review* 385–403.

Abrams, Burton A. and Russell F. Settle (1976) "The Effect of Broadcasting on Political Campaign Spending: An Empirical Investigation." 84 *Journal of Political Economy* 1095–1107.

Adamany, David (1969) "The Party Variable in Judges' Voting: Conceptual Notes and a Case Study." 63 *American Political Science Review* 57–73.

Adamany, David and Philip Dubois (1976) "Electing State Judges." *Wisconsin Law Review* 731–79.

Advisory Panel on Judicial Diversity (2010) "The Report of the Advisory Panel on Judicial Diversity." London: Ministry of Justice; http://www.justice.gov.uk/publications/docs/advisory-panel-judicial-diversity-2010.pdf.

"Advocates Do Battle as Court Candidates Keep Low Profile." (1998) *Grand Rapids Press,* November 1, p. 10.

Allen, Mike, Edward Mabry, and Drue-Marie McKelton (1998) "Impact of Juror Attitudes about the Death Penalty on Juror Evaluations of Guilt and Punishment." 22 *Law and Human Behavior* 715–31.

Alozie, Nicholas O. (1988) "Black Representation on State Judiciaries." 69 *Social Science Quarterly* 979–86.

(1990) "Distribution of Women and Minority Judges: The Effects of Judicial Selection Methods." 71 *Social Science Quarterly* 315–25.

(1996) "Selection Methods and the Recruitment of Women to State Courts of Last Resort." 77 *Social Science Quarterly* 110–26.

American Bar Association (2003) "*Commission on the 21st Century Judiciary: Justice in Jeopardy*." Chicago: American Bar Association.

Anderson, David A. (2007) "Judicial Tort Reform in Texas." 26 *Review of Litigation* 1–46.

Anderson, Paul H. and G. Barry Anderson (2011) "Judicial Selection – A Minnesota Update." 95 *Judicature* 45.

Angel, Marina (2008) "'Merit Selection' Means Stealing My Vote." *Philadelphia Inquirer,* March 24.

Ansolabehere, Stephen and Shanto Iyengar (1995) *Going Negative: How Political Advertisements Shrink and Polarize the Electorate*. New York: Free Press.

Arbour, Brian K. and Mark J. McKenzie (2010) "Has the 'New Style' of Judicial Campaigning Reached Lower Court Elections?" 93 *Judicature* 150–60.

Arrington, Theodore S. (1996) "When Money Doesn't Matter: Campaign Spending for Minor Statewide Judicial and Executive Offices in North Carolina." 18 *Justice System Journal* 257–66.

Aspin, Larry (2011) "The 2010 Judicial Retention Elections in Perspective: Continuity and Change from 1964 to 2010." 94 *Judicature* 218–32.

Aspin, Larry and William F. Hall (1989) "Friends and Neighbors Voting in Judicial Retention Elections: A Research Note Comparing Trial and Appellate Court Elections." 42 *Western Political Quarterly* 587–96.

Atkins, Burton M. and Henry R. Glick (1974) "Formal Judicial Recruitment and State Supreme Court Decisions." 2 *American Politics Quarterly* 427–49.

Ayres, Ian (2000) "Disclosure Versus Anonymity," pp. 19–54 in Ian Shapiro and Stephen Macedo, eds., *Designing Democratic Institution*. New York: Oxford University Press.

Bannon, Alicia, Eric Velasco, Linda Casey, and Lianna Reagan (2013) "*The New Politics of Judicial Elections 2011–12: How New Waves of Special Interest Spending Raised the Stakes for Fair Courts*." New York: Brennan Center for Justice, New York University School of Law; http://www.brennancenter.org/sites/default/files/publications/New%20Politics%20of%20Judicial%20Elections%202012.pdf.

Barber, Kathleen L. (1971) "Ohio Judicial Elections – Non Partisan Premises with Partisan Results." 32 *Ohio State Law Journal* 762–89.

(1982) "Nonpartisan Ballots and Voter Confusion in Judicial Elections" paper presented at Annual Meeting of the Midwest Political Science Association. Milwaukee, Wisconsin, April 28–May 1.

Barclay, Scott and Andrew Flores (2014) "State Courts and Public Support for Marriage Equality." Los Angeles: UCLA School of Law.

Bartels, Larry M. (1991) "Instrumental and 'Quasi-Instrumental' Variables." 35 *American Journal of Political Science* 777–800.

Basting, Thomas J., Sr. (2008) "Gutter Politics and the Wisconsin Supreme Court." *Wisconsin Lawyer*, May, pp. 5, 52.

Baum, Lawrence (1987) "Explaining the Vote in Judicial Elections: The 1984 Ohio Supreme Court Elections." 40 *Western Political Quarterly* 361–71.

Baum, Lawrence and David Klein (2007) "Voter Responses to High-Visibility Judicial Campaigns," pp. 140–64 in Matthew J. Streb, ed., *Running for Judge: The Rising Political Financial, and Legal Stakes of Judicial Elections*. New York: New York University Press.

Baumgartner, Frank R. and Beth L. Leech (1998) *Basic Interests: The Importance of Groups in Politics and in Political Science*. Princeton, NJ: Princeton University Press.

Becker, Daniel and Malia Reddick (2003) "Judicial Selection Reform: Examples from Six States." Des Moines, IA: American Judicature Society; http://www.judicialselection.com/uploads/documents/jsreform_1185395742450.pdf.

Bedford, Sybille (1961) *The Faces of Justice: A Traveller's Report*. New York: Simon & Schuster.

Behm, Margaret L. and Candi Henri (2014) "Judicial Selection in Tennessee: Deciding 'The Decider'." 1 *Belmont Law Review* 143–79.

Beiser, Edward N. and Jonathan J. Silberman (1969) "The Political Variable: Workmen's Compensation Cases in the New York Court of Appeals." 3 *Polity* 521–31.

Benesh, Sara C. (2006) "Understanding Public Confidence in American Courts." 68 *Journal of Politics* 697–707.
Berdejó, Carlos and Noam Yuchtman (2013) "Crime, Punishment, and Politics: An Analysis of Political Cycles in Criminal Sentencing." 95 *Review of Economcs and Statistics* 741–56.
Berry, William D., Richard C. Fording, Evan J. Ringquist, Russell L. Hanson, and Carl Klarner (2010) "Measuring Citizen and Government Ideology in the American States: A Re-appraisal." 10 *State Politics & Policy Quarterly* 117–35.
Berry, William D., Evan J. Ringquist, Richard C. Fording, and Russell L. Hanson (1998) "Measuring Citizen and Government Ideology in the American States, 1960–93." 41 *American Journal of Political Science* 327–48.
Biles, Jan (2014) "State Supreme Court Justices Stave Off Ousting Campaign." *Topeka Capital-Journal*, November 4.
Bills, Bronson D. (2008) "A Penny for the Court's Thoughts? The High Price of Judicial Elections." 3 *Northwestern Journal of Law and Social Policy* 29–61.
Black, Merle (2004) "The Transformation of the Southern Democratic Party." 66 *Journal of Politics* 1001–17.
Blinder, Alan (2014a) "Conservatives See Potential in Tennesssee Judical Race." *New York Times*, August 5.
(2014b) "Despite Failure, Campaign to Oust Tennessee Justices Keeps Conservatives Hopeful." *New York Times*, August 9.
Bonneau, Chris W. (2004) "Patterns of Campaign Spending and Electoral Competition in State Supreme Court Elections." 25 *Justice System Journal* 21–28.
(2005) "What Price Justice(s): Understanding Campaign Spending in State Supreme Court Elections." 5 *State Politics & Policy Quarterly* 107–25.
(2006) "Vacancies on the Bench: Open-Seat Elections for State Supreme Courts." 27 *Justice System Journal* 143–59.
(2007a) "Campaign Fundraising in State Supreme Court Elections." 88 *Social Science Quarterly* 68–85.
(2007b) "The Dynamics of Campaign Spending in State Supreme Court Elections," pp. 59–72 in Matthew J. Streb, ed., *Running for Judge: The Rising Political Financial, and Legal Stakes of Judicial Elections*. New York: New York University Press.
(2007c) "The Effects of Campaign Spending in State Supreme Court Elections." 60 *Political Research Quarterly* 489–99.
Bonneau, Chris W. and Damon M. Cann (2009) "The Effect of Campaign Contributions on Judicial Decisions." Unpublished paper available on SSRN; http://ssrn.com/abstract=1337668.
(2011) "Campaign Spending, Diminishing Marginal Returns, and Campaign Finance Restrictions in Judicial Elections." 73 *Journal of Politics* 1267–80.
(2015) *Voters' Verdicts: Citizens, Campaigns, and Institutions in State Supreme Court Elections*. Charlottesville: Virginia University Press.
Bonneau, Chris W. and Melinda Gann Hall (2004) "The Wisconsin Judiciary," pp. 171–96 in Ronald E. Weber, ed., *Wisconsin Government and Politics*. Boston: McGraw-Hill.
(2009) *In Defense of Judicial Elections*. New York: Routledge.
Bonneau, Chris W. and Eric Loepp (2014) "Getting Things Straight: The Effects of Ballot Design and Electoral Structure on Voter Participation." 34 *Electoral Studies* 119–30.

Boucher, Dave (2014) "Amendment 2 to Change Judicial Selection Passes." *Tennessean*, November 4.

Bowcott, Owen (2012) "More Female Judges Appointed – But Ethnic Minority Candidates Making Slower Progress." *Guardian*, 14 June.

(2014) "Judiciary Needs Fast-track Scheme to Boost Diversity, Says Top Judge." *Guardian*, September 17.

Brace, Paul and Brent D. Boyea (2007) "Judicial Selection Methods and Capital Punishment in the American States," pp. 186-203 in Matthew J. Streb, ed., *Running for Judge: The Rising Political, Financial, and Legal Stakes of Judicial Elections*. New York: New York University Press.

(2008) "State Public Opinion, the Death Penalty, and the Practice of Electing Judges." 52 *American Journal of Political Science* 360–72.

Brace, Paul and Melinda Gann Hall (1997) "The Interplay of Preferences, Case Facts, Context and Rules in the Politics of Judicial Choice." 59 *Journal of Politics* 1206–31.

(2000) "Comparing Courts Using the American States." 83 *Judicature* 250–66.

(2001) "State Supreme Court Data Project." Houston, TX: Rice University; http://www.ruf.rice.edu/~pbrace/statecourt.

Brace, Paul, Melinda Gann Hall, and Laura Langer (1999) "Judicial Choice and the Politics of Abortion: Institutions, Context, and the Autonomy of Courts." 62 *Albany Law Review* 1265–1300.

Brace, Paul, Laura Langer, and Melinda Gann Hall (2000) "Measuring the Preferences of State Supreme Court Judges." 62 *Journal of Politics* 387–413.

Brace, Paul, Jeff Yates, and Brent D. Boyea (2012) "Judges, Litigants, and the Design of Courts." 46 *Law & Society Review* 497–522.

Brandenburg, Bert and Rachel Paine Caufield (2009) "Ardent Advocates [Review of Bonneau and Hall's, *In Defense of Judicial Elections*]." 93 *Judicature* 79–81.

Brandenburg, Bert and Roy A. Schotland (2008) "Justice in Peril: The Endangered Balance Between Impartial Courts and Judicial Election Campaigns." 21 *Georgetown Journal of Legal Ethics* 1229–58.

Bratton, Kathleen A. and Rorie L. Spill (2002) "Existing Diversity and Judicial Selection: The Role of the Appointment Method in Establishing Gender Diversity in State Supreme Courts." 83 *Social Science Quarterly* 504–18.

Brodie, Mollyann (2001) "Impact of Issue Advertisements and the Legacy of Harry and Louise." 26 *Journal of Health Politics, Policy and Law* 1353–60.

Bronner, Ethan (1989) *Battle for Justice: How the Bork Nomination Shook America*. New York: W.W. Norton.

Brooks, Richard R. W. and Steven Raphael (2002) "Life Terms or Death Sentences: The Uneasy Relationship Between Judicial Elections and Capital Punishment." 92 *Journal of Criminal Law and Criminology* 609–39.

Bureau of the Census (1995) "1992 Census of Governments; Volume 1: Government Organization; Number 2: Popularly Elected Officials." Washington, DC: Bureau of the Census; http://www.census.gov/prod/2/gov/gc/gc92_1_2.pdf.

Burnside, Fred B. (1999) "Dying to Get Elected: A Challenge to the Jury Override." 1999 *Wisconsin Law Review* 1017–49.

Caldarone, Richard P., Brandice Canes-Wrone, and Tom S. Clark (2009) "Partisan Labels and Democratic Accountability: An Analysis of State Supreme Court Abortion Decisions." 71 *Journal of Politics* 560–73.

Canes-Wrone, Brandice and Tom Clark (2009) "Judicial Independence and Nonpartisan Selections." 2009 *Wisconsin Law Review* 21–65.

Canes-Wrone, Brandice, Tom S. Clark, and Jason P. Kelly (2014) "Judicial Selection and Death Penalty Decisions." 108 *American Political Science Review* 23–39.

Canes-Wrone, Brandice, Tom S. Clark, and Jee-Kwang Park (2012) "Judicial Independence and Retention Elections." 28 *Journal of Law, Economics, and Organization* 211–34.

Cann, Damon M. (2002) "Campaign Contributions and Judicial Behavior." 23 *American Review of Politics* 261–74.

(2007) "Justice for Sale? Campaign Contributions and Judicial Decisionmaking." 7 *State Politics and Policy Quarterly* 281–97.

Cann, Damon M., Chris W. Bonneau, and Brent D. Boyea (2012) "Campaign Contributions and Judicial Decisions in Partisan and Nonpartisan Elections," pp. 38–52 in Kevin T. McGuire, ed., *New Directions in Judicial Politics*. New York: Routledge.

Cann, Damon M. and Jeff Yates (2008) "Homegrown Institutional Legitimacy: Assessing Citizens' Diffuse Support for State Courts." 36 *American Politics Research* 297–329.

Canon, Bradley C. (1972) "The Impact of Formal Selection Processes on the Characteristics of Judges–Reconsidered." 6 *Law & Society Review* 579–93.

Caplan, Lincoln (2012) "Justice for Sale." *American Scholar*, Summer.

Carbon, Susan B. and Larry C. Berkson (1980) "*Judicial Retention Elections in the United States*." Chicago: American Judicature Society.

Cardona, Felisa (2010a) "Four Supreme Court Justices Face a Tough Vote in Elections." *Denver Post*, February 15.

(2010b) "Three Colorado High Court Justices Face Stiff Opposition." *Denver Post*, October 3.

Carter, Terry (2006) "Tort Reform Texas Style." 92(10) *ABA Journal* 30–36.

Cassie, William E. and David A. Breaux (1998) "Expenditures and Election Results," pp. 99–114 in Joel A. Thompson and Gary F. Moncrief, eds., *Campaign Finance in State Legislative Elections*. Washington, DC: CQ Press.

Caufield, Rachel P. (2007) "The Changing Tone of Judicial Election Campaigns as a Result of *White*," pp. 38–54 in Matthew J. Streb, ed., *Running for Judge: The Rising Political Financial, and Legal Stakes of Judicial Elections*. New York: New York University Press.

Cauthen, James N. G. and C. Scott Peters (2003) "Courting Constituents: District Elections and Judicial Behavior on the Louisiana Supreme Court." 24 *Justice System Journal* 265–82.

Champagne, Anthony (2001) "Interest Groups and Judicial Elections." 34 *Loyola of Los Angeles Law Review* 1391–1408.

(2002) "Television Ads in Judicial Campaigns." 35 *Indiana Law Review* 669–89.

(2006) "Judicial Reform in Texas: A Look Back After Two Decades." 43 *Court Review* 68–79.

Champagne, Anthony and Kyle Cheek (2002) "The Cycle of Judicial Elections: Texas as a Case Study." 29 *Fordham Urban Law Journal* 907–40.

Cheek, Kyle and Anthony Champagne (2004) *Judicial Politics in Texas: Partisanship, Money and Politics in State Courts*. New York: Peter Lang.

Cleveland, William S. (1979) "Robust Locally-Weighted Regression and Smoothing Scatterplots." 74 *Journal of the American Statistical Association* 829–36.

Cohn, Nate (2014) "Demise of the Southern Democrat Is Now Nearly Complete." *New York Times*, December 4.

Contini, Francesco, Sharyn Roach Anleu, and David Rottman, eds. (2014) "Evaluating Judicial Performance." 4(5) *Oñati Sociol-Legal Series* [electronic] 843–1116 [table of contents at http://opo.iisj.net/index.php/osls/issue/view/36; all articles available on SSRN].

Cook, Herb, Jr. and Sharon Crook West (1983) "Ohio Lawyers Ask: Is This Any Way to Run the Supreme Court? Frank Celebrezze Answers: Damn Right!" *Columbus Monthly*, pp. 50–56, 121–24.

Corriher, Billy (2012) "Big Business Taking over State Supreme Courts: How Campaign Contributions to Judges Tip the Scales Against Individuals." Washington, DC: Center for American Progress; http://www.americanprogress.org/wp-content/uploads/2012/08/StateCourtsReport.pdf.

(2013) "Fixing Wisconsin's Dysfunctional Supreme Court Elections." Washington, DC: Center for American Progress; http://cdn.americanprogress.org/wp-content/uploads/2013/07/CorriherWisconsinSupremeCourt-2.pdf.

Culver, John H. and John T. Wold (1986) "Rose Bird and the Politics of Judicial Accountability in California." 70(2) *Judicature* 81–89.

(1993) "Judicial Reform in California," in pp. 139–62 Anthony Champagne and Judith Haydel, eds., *Judicial Reform in the States*. Lanham, MD: University Press of America.

Curran, Barbara A (1977) *The Legal Needs of the Public: The Final Report of a National Survey*. Chicago: American Bar Foundation.

Dao, James (2005) "In a Rare Battle, Justices Are Fighting for Their Seats " *New York Times*, November 5.

Darbyshire, Penny (2011) *Sitting in Judgment: The Working Lives of Judges*. Oxford, UK: Hart Publishing.

Davey, Monica (2011a) "Wisconsin Court Reinstates Law on Union Rights." *New York Times*, June 14.

(2011b) "Wisconsin Judge Said to Have Attacked Colleague." *New York Times*, June 25.

Davis, Claude J. (1959) *Judicial Selection in West Virginia*. Morgantown: Bureau for Government Research, West Virginia University.

DeFour, Matthew (2011) "Supreme Court Justices' Schism Not Unusual." *Wisconsin State Journal*, June 19.

Demer, Lisa (2010) "Allies Defend Fabe as Justice Fights Campaign to Oust Her." *Anchorage Daily News*, October 29.

Devins, Neal (2010) "How State Supreme Courts Take Consequences into Account: Toward a State-Centered Understanding of State Constitutionalism." 62 *Stanford Law Review* 1629–94.

Devins, Neal and Nicole Mansker (2010) "Public Opinion and State Supreme Courts." 13 *University of Pennsylvania Journal of Constitutional Law* 455–509.

"Dispute Injects Politics into Judicial Races in Ohio." (1984) *New York Times*, October 14.

Driscoll, Amanda and Michael J. Nelson (2012) "The 2011 Judicial Elections in Bolivia." 31 *Electoral Studies* 628–32.

(2013) "The Political Origins of Judicial Elections: Evidence from the United States and Bolivia." 96 *Judicature* 151–60.

Dubois, Philip L. (1978) "Judicial Elections in the States: Patterns and Consequences." PhD Dissertation, Political Science, University of Wisconsin – Madison.

(1979) "The Significance of Voting Cues in State Supreme Court Elections." 13 *Law & Society Review* 757–79.

(1980) *From Bench to Ballot: Judicial Elections and the Quest for Accountability*. Austin: University of Texas Press.

(1983) "The Influence of Selection System and Region on the Characteristics of a Trial Court Bench." 8 *Justice System Journal* 59–87.

Dudley, Robert L. (1997) "Turnover and Tenure on State High Courts: Does Method of Selection Make a Difference?" 19 *Justice System Journal* 1–16.

Duquette, Christopher, Steven Caudill, and Franklin Mixon Jr. (2008) "The Impact of Money on Elections: Evidence from Open Seat Races in the United States House of Representatives, 1990–2004." 4 *Economics Bulletin* 1–12.

Echeverria, John D. (2000) "Changing the Rules by Changing the Players: The Environmental Issue in State Judicial Elections." 9 *New York University Environmental Law Journal* 217–303.

(2015) "State Judicial Elections and Environmental Law: Case Studies of Montana, North Carolina, Washington and Wisconsin." 16 *Vermont Journal of Environmental Law* 363–483.

"Editorial: Keep Parties Out of Judicial Elections." (2014) *Minneapolis Star Tribune*, August 27, A8.

"Editorial: Money and Judges, a Bad Mix." (2014) *New York Times*, November 2.

"Editorial: Voters Can Judge for Themselves." (1996) *Wisconsin State Journal*, March 7, 13A.

Elazar, Daniel J. (1966) *American Federalism: A View from the States*. New York: Thomas Y. Crowell.

"Elect Judge Jack Landau to Oregon Supreme Court." (2010) *Oregonian*, April 20.

Elek, Jennifer K., David B. Rottman, and Brian L. Cutter (2014) "Judicial Performance Evaluation in the States: A Re-examination." 98 *Judicature* 12–19.

Emmert, Craig F. and Henry R. Glick (1988) "The Selection of State Supreme Court Justices." 16 *American Politics Quarterly* 445–65.

"The Encouragement of Ugliness." (1982) *Los Angeles Times*, November 5, E10.

Endicott, William (1978a) "Drives to Oust Justice Bird Lag." *Los Angeles Times*, October 17, pp. 3, 22.

(1978b) "Rose Bird Sees Positive Results: Says Voters Don't Want Decisions Based on Threats." *Los Angeles Times*, November 9, pp. B3, B22.

(1978c) "Rose Bird on Ballot, Judiciary on Trial: Vote on Chief Justice Viewed as Test of Public Discontent with System." *Los Angeles Times*, November 5, pp. B1, B7.

Endicott, William and Robert Fairbanks (1978) "Supreme Court Decision to Reverse Gun Law Reported." *Los Angeles Times*, November 7, pp. A6, A22.

Epstein, Lee (2013) "Electoral Benefits: The Assault on the Assaulters of Judicial Elections." 96 *Judicature* 218–22.

Equal Justice Initiative (2011) "Death Penalty in Alabama: Judge Override " Montgomery, AL: Equal Justice Initiative; http://media.al.com/live/other/death-penalty-alabama-override-report.pdf.

Esterling, Kevin M. (1999) "Judicial Accountability the Right Way: Official Performance Evaluations Help the Electorate As Well As the Bench." 82 *Judicature* 206–15.

Esterling, Kevin M. and Seth S. Andersen (2000) "Diversity and the Judicial Merit Selection Process: A Statistical Report," pp. 1–39 in Kevin M. Esterling, ed., *Research on Judicial Selection, 1999*. Chicago: American Judicature Society.

Farrell, Peter (2000a) "Judicial Race Blurs Traditional Rules on Campaigning." *Oregonian*, October 11.

(2000b) "Longtime Appellate Judge Competes for Spot on State Supreme Court." *Oregonian*, October 25.

(2000c) "Sizemore Alliance Haunts Candidate for Seat on Oregon Supreme Court." *Oregonian*, October 24.

Fedor, Liz (1996) "Different Paths Lead Maring, Vogel to Supreme Court Contest." *Grand Forks Herald*, September 9, p. A1.

Feeley, Malcolm M. (1971) "Another Look At the 'Party Variable' in Judicial Decisionmaking: An Analysis of the Michigan Supreme Court." 4 *Polity* 91–104.

Finch, Susan (2008) "Tulane Law School Issues Apology to Louisiana Supreme Court." *Times-Picayune*, September 16.

Fitzpatrick, Brian T. (2009) "The Politics of Merit Selection." 74 *Missouri Law Review* 675–708.

Flango, Victor E. and Craig R. Ducat (1979) "What Difference Does Method of Judicial Selection Make? Selection Procedures in State Courts of Last Resort." 5 *Justice System Journal* 25–44.

Flesher, John (1998) "Campaigns for Michigan Supreme Court ..." [Associated Press news item]. Westlaw, 1998 WL 7451488.

"Foes Want Voters to Fire Judge; Battle Rages in Wyoming, Spurred by Claim that Supreme Court Justice Is Too Easy on Criminals." (1992) *Rocky Mountain News*, October 29, p. 7.

Folwell, William Watts (1969) *A History of Minnesota*, Vol. III. St. Paul: Minnesota Historical Society.

Fosmire, M. Sean, Roger A. Smith, and Beth Andrews (2013) "Tort Reform in Michigan, 2013 Edition." Garan Lucow Miller P.C.; http://www.garanlucow.com/wp-content/uploads/2013/02/TRIM-20131.pdf.

Fowler, Erika Franklin and Travis N. Ridout (2013) "Negative, Angry, and Ubiquitous: Political Advertising in 2012." 10 *Forum* 51–61.

Franz, Michael M., Paul D. Freedman, Kenneth M. Goldstein, and Travis N. Ridout (2008) *Campaign Advertising and American Democracy*. Philadelpha: Temple University Press.

Frederick, Brian and Matthew J. Streb (2008) "Paying the Price for a Seat on the Bench: Campaign Spending in Contested State Intermediate Appellate Court Elections." 8 *State Politics & Policy Quarterly* 410–29.

(2011) "The Cost of Going for the Gavel: Individual Candidate Spending in Intermediate Appellate Court Elections." 32 *Justice System Journal* 25–43.

Friedman, Lawrence M. (1973) *A History of American Law*. New York: Simon & Schuster.

Gaddie, Ronald Keith and Charles S. Bullock, III (2000) *Elections to Open Seats in the U.S. House*. Lanham, MD: Rowman & Littlefield.

Galante, Mary Ann (1986) "California Justices Face Own 'Executions': Bitter Campaign Focuses on Death Penalty." *National Law Journal*, November 3, pp. 1, 9–10.

Galloway, Angela (2002) "Builders Backing Top-Court Candidate: Johnson Campaign Got $180,000 from Industry, But He Vows to Be Independent." *Seattle Post-Intelligencer*, October 28, p. B1.

Gee, Graham (2012) "The Crime and Courts Bill and the JAC," in *UK Constitutional Law Blog*; http://ukconstitutionallaw.org/tag/lord-chancellor/.

Geer, John G. (2006) *In Defense of Negativity: Attack Ads in Presidential Election Campaigns*. Chicago: University of Chicago Press.

(2012) "The News Media and the Rise of Negativity in Presidential Campaigns." 45 *PS: Political Science & Politics* 422–27.

Genn, Hazel (2008) "The Attractiveness of Senior Judicial Appointment to Highly Qualified Practitioners." London: Directorate of Judicial Offices for England and Wales; http://www.ucl.ac.uk/laws/academics/profiles/docs/Hazel/The%20Attractiveness%20of%20Senior%20Judicial%20Appointment%20Research%20Report.pdf.

Gerkman, Alli (2012) "Judicial Performance Evaluation Results Released as Voter Tool in Judicial Reaces." Denver, CO: Institute for the Advancement of the American Legal System; http://online.iaals.du.edu/2012/10/16/press-release-judicial-performance-evaluation-results-released-as-voter-tool-in-judicial-races/.

Geyh, Charles G. (2007) "Preserving Public Confidence in the Courts in an Age of Individual Rights and Public Skepticism," pp. 21–51 in Keith Bybee, ed., *Bench Press: The Collision of the Courts, Politics and the Media*. Stanford, CA: Stanford University Press.

(2008) "The Endless Judicial Selection Debate and its Implications for the Future of an Independent Judiciary." 21 *Georgetown Journal of Legal Ethics* 1259–81.

Geyh, Charles Gardner (2003) "Why Judicial Elections Stink." 64 *Ohio State Law Journal* 43–79.

Gibeaut, John (2012) "Co-Equal Opportunity: Legislators Are Out to Take Over Their State Judiciary Systems, While Critics Say It's an Attack on Separation of Powers." 98(1) *ABA Journal* 45–49, 55.

Gibson, James L. (2008a) "Campaigning for the Bench: The Corrosive Effects of Campaign Speech?" 42 *Law & Society Review* 899–928.

(2008b) "Challenges to the Impartiality of State Supreme Courts: Legitimacy Theory and 'New-Style' Judicial Campaigns." 102 *American Political Science Review* 59–75.

(2009) " 'New-Style' Judicial Campaigns and the Legitimacy of State High Courts." 71 *Journal of Politics* 1285–1304.

(2012) *Electing Judges: The Surprising Effects of Campaigning on Judicial Legitimacy*. Chicago: University of Chicago Press.

(2013) "*Electing Judges*: Future Research and the Normative Debate about Judicial Elections." 96 *Judicature* 223–31.

Gibson, James L., Jeffrey A. Gottfried, Michael X. Delli Carpini, and Kathleen Hall Jamieson (2011) "The Effects of Judicial Campaign Activity on the Legitimacy of Courts." 64 *Political Research Quarterly* 545–58.

Gill, Rebecca D. (2013) "Beyond High Hopes and Unmet Expectations: Judicial Selection Reform in the States." 96 *Judicature* 278–93.

Gill, Rebecca D. and Kenneth J. Retzl (2014) "The JPE Commission: Toward a More Transparent and Informative Evaluation." 98 *Judicature* 26–34.

Gill, Rebecca D., Sylvia R. Lazos, and Mallory M. Waters (2011) "Are Judicial Performance Evaluations Fair to Women and Minorities? A Cautionary Tale from Clark County, Nevada." 45 *Law & Society Review* 731–59.

Glaberson, William (1999) "Ohio Supreme Court Voids Legal Limits on Damage Suits." *New York Times*, August 17.

(2000a) "Chief Justices to Meet on Abuses in Judicial Races." *New York Times*, September 8, 2000, p. A12.

(2000b) "A Spirited Campaign for Ohio Court Puts Judges on New Terrain." *New York Times*, July 7.

Glick, Henry R. and Craig F. Emmert (1987) "Selection Systems and Judicial Characteristics: The Recruitment of State Supreme Court Judges." 70 *Judicature* 228–35.

Glick, Henry R. and George W. Pruet, Jr. (1986) "Dissent in State Supreme Courts: Patterns and Correlates of Conflict," pp. 199–214 in Sheldon Goldman and Charles M. Lamb, eds., *Judicial Conflict and Consensus: Behavioral Studies of American Appellate Courts*. Lexington: University Press of Kentucky.

Goldberg, Deborah (2007) "Interest Group Participation in Judicial Elections," pp. 73–95 in Matthew J. Streb, ed., *Running for Judge: The Rising Political Financial, and Legal Stakes of Judicial Elections*. New York: New York University Press.

Goldberg, Deborah, Craig Holman, and Samantha Sanchez (2000) "The New Politics of Judicial Elections: How 2000 Was a Watershed Year for Big Money, Special Interest Pressure, and TV Advertising in State Supreme Court Campaigns." New York: Brennan Center for Justice, New York University School of Law; http://www.justiceatstake.org/media/cms/JASMoneyReport_E7C1343619C9F.pdf.

Goldberg, Deborah, Sarah Samis, Edwin Bender, and Rachel Weiss (2004) "The New Politics of Judicial Elections 2004: How Special Interest Pressure on Our Courts Has Reached a 'Tipping Point'–and How to Keep Our Courts Fair and Impartial." New York: Brennan Center for Justice, New York University School of Law; http://brennan.3cdn.net/dd00e9b682e3ca2f17_xdm6i068k.pdf.

Goldberg, Deborah and Samantha Sanchez (2004) "The New Politics of Judicial Elections 2002: How the Threat to Fair and Impartial Courts Spread to More States in 2002." New York: Brennan Center for Justice, New York University School of Law; http://brennan.3cdn.net/3e06222f06bc229762_yom6bgubs.pdf.

Goldman, Darren (2009) "Mandatory Retirement: A Comprehensive Analysis Exploring Key Differences Between Trial & Appellate Level Judges." http://www.socialaw.com/slbook/judgeyoung09/05Goldman-Paper.pdf.

Goldstein, Ken and Paul Freedman (2002) "Campaign Advertising and Voter Turnout: New Evidence for a Stimulation Effect." 64 *Journal of Politics* 721–40.

Goodman, Shira J. and Lynn A. Marks (2006) "Lessons from an Unusual Retention Election." 42 *Court Review* 6–14.

(2007) "A View from the Ground: A Reform Group's Perspective on the Ongoing Effort to Achieve Merit Selection of Judges." 34 *Fordham Urban Law Journal* 425–52.

Gordon, Sanford C. and Gregory A. Huber (2007) "The Effect of Electoral Competitiveness on Incumbent Behavior." 2 *Quarterly Journal of Political Science* 107–38.

Graham, Barbara Luck (1990) "Do Judicial Selection Systems Matter? A Study of Black Representation on State Courts." 18 *American Politics Quarterly* 316–36.

Green, Ashbel S. (2006) "Linder Leads Roberts in Pricey Fight for High Court." *Oregonian*, November 8, p. C1.

Green, Donald Philip and Jonathan S. Krasno (1988) "Salvation for the Spendthrift Incumbent: Reestimating the Effects of Campaign Spending in House Elections." 32 *American Journal of Political Science* 884–907.

Greenhill, Joe R. and John W. Odam, Jr. (1971) "Judicial Reform of Our Texas Courts – A Re-Examination of Three Important Aspects." 23 *Baylor Law Review* 204–26.

Grodin, Joseph R. (1989) *In Pursuit of Justice: Reflections of a State Supreme Court Justice*. Berkeley: University of California Press.

Guarnieri, Carlo (2012) "Judges, Their Careers, and Independence," pp. 193–215 in David S. Clark, ed., *Comparative Law and Society*. Cheltenham, UK: Edward Elgar Publishing.

Hager, Philip (1982a) "Campaign Against 3 Justices Stepped Up." *Los Angeles Times*, October 23, 1982, p. B5.

(1982b) "Four Justices on Top Bench Face Review." *Los Angeles Times*, September 20, pp. F1, F3.

(1986) "Reynoso Uses Media Campaign in Effort to Retain Judgeship." *Los Angeles Times*, October 19, pp. A3, A36, A38.

Hall, Kermit L. (1983) "The Judiciary on Trial: State Constitutional Reform and the Rise of an Elected Judiciary, 1846–1860." 45 *Historian* 337–54.

(1984a) "Progressive Reform and the Decline of Democratic Accountability: The Popular Election of State Supreme Court Judges, 1850–1920." 1984 *American Bar Foundation Research Journal* 345–69.

(1984b) "The 'Route to Hell' Retraced: The Impact of Popular Election on the Southern Appellate Judiciary, 1832–1920," pp. 229–55 in David J. Bodenhamer and James W. Ely, Jr., eds., *Ambivalent Legacy: A Legal History of the South*. Jackson: University Press of Mississippi.

Hall, Melinda Gann (1992) "Electoral Politics and Strategic Voting in State Supreme Courts." 54 *Journal of Politics* 427–46.

(1995) "Justices as Representatives: Elections and Judicial Politics in the American States." 23 *American Politics Quarterly* 485–503.

(2001) "State Supreme Courts in American Democracy: Probing the Myths of Judicial Reform." 95 *American Political Science Review* 315–30.

(2007) "Competition as Accountability in State Supreme Court Elections," pp. 165–85 in Matthew J. Streb, ed., *Running for Judge: The Rising Political Financial, and Legal Stakes of Judicial Elections*. New York: New York University Press.

(2011) "On the Cataclysm of Judicial Elections and Other Popular Antidemocratic Myths," pp. 223–47 in Charles G. Geyh, ed., *What's Law Got to Do With It? What Judges Do, Why They Do It, and What's at Stake?* Stanford, CA: Stanford University Press.

(2012) "Representation in State Supreme Courts: Evidence from the Terminal Term." Paper presented at State Politics and Policy Conference. Houston, TX, February 16–18.

(2014a) *Attacking Judges: How Campaign Advertising Influences State Supreme Court Elections*. Stanford, CA: Stanford University Press.

(2014b) "Televised Attacks and Incumbency Advantage in State Supreme Court Elections." 30 *Journal of Law, Economics & Organization* 138–64.

Hall, Melinda Gann and Chris W. Bonneau (2008) "Mobiling Interest: The Effects of Money on Citizen Participation in State Supreme Court Elections." 52 *American Journal of Political Science* 457–70.

(2013) "Attack Advertising, the White Decision, and Voter Participation in State Supreme Court Elections." 66 *Political Research Quarterly* 115–26.

Hall, Melinda Gann and Paul Brace (1992) "Toward an Integrated Model of Judicial Voting Behavior." 20 *American Politics Quarterly* 147–68.

Hansen, Mark (1998) "A Run for the Bench." 84(10) *ABA Journal* 68–72.

Hanssen, F. Andrew (1999) "The Effect of Judicial Institutions on Uncertainty and the Rate of Litigation: the Election Versus Appointment of State Judges." 28 *Journal of Legal Studies* 205–32.

Hare, Christopher and Keith T. Poole (2014) "The Polarization of Contemporary American Politics," 46 *Polity* 411–29.

Haughney, Kathleen (2010) "Central Florida Group Seeks Ouster of 2 High-Court Judges." *Miami Herald*, September 29.

Heagarty, J. Christopher (2003) "Judicial Campaigns and Voters' Experience." 39 *Williamette Law Review* 1287–1311.

Hearn, Lorie (1986) "TV Ad Aims at Court Opposition; Says Big Business Is Behind Attacks on Bird, 2 Others." *San Diego Union-Tribune*, October 21, p. A3.

Hedin, Douglas A. (2010) "Results of the Elections of Justices to the Minnesota Supreme Court"; http://www.minnesotalegalhistoryproject.org/assets/Election%20Results%201858–2010.pdf.

Helgeson, Baird (2013) "Politcs Snags Judicial Vote Plan." *Minneapolis Star Tribune*, September 23, pp. A1, A9.

Helland, Eric and Alexander Tabarrok (2002) "The Efrfect of Electoral Institutions on Tort Awards." 4 *American Law and Economics Review* 341–70.

Heller, Emily (2000) "Mixed Results for C of C: Fails to Oust Ohio Justice But Backs Some Winners." *National Law Journal*, November 20, pp. A1, A11.

Heller, Emily and Mark Ballard (2000) "Hard-fought, Big-money Judical Races: U.S. Chamber of Commerce Enters Fray with Ad Money." *National Law Journal*, November 6, pp. A1, A8.

Herrington, Gregg (2002) "Fire District Levy Falls Five Votes Short of 60 Percent." *Columbian*, November 21, p. C1.

Herrnson, Paul S. and Owen G. Abbe (2002) "Campaigning for Judge: Noisier, Nastier," pp. 156–57 in Thad Beyle, ed., *State and Local Government 2002–2003*. Washington, DC: CQ Press.

Holder, Paul (1980) "That's Yarborough – Spelled with One "O": A Study of Judicial Misbehavior in Texas," pp. 185–93 in Eugene W. Jones et al., eds., *Practicing Texas Politics*. Boston, MA: Houghton Mifflin.

Hollihan, Thomas A. (2009) *Uncivil Wars: Political Campaigns in a Media Age*. Boston, MA: Bedford/St. Martin's.

Huber, Gregory A. and Sanford C. Gordon (2004) "Accountability and Coercion: Is Justice Blind when It Runs for Office?" 48 *American Journal of Political Science* 247–63.

Hurst, James Willard (1950) *The Growth of American Law: The Law Makers*. Boston, MA: Little, Brown.

Hurwitz, Mark S. and Drew Noble Lanier (2003) "Explaining Judicial Diversity: The Differential Ability of Women and Minorities to Attain Seats on State Supreme and Appellate Courts." 3 *State Politics & Policy Quarterly* 329–52.

Ireland, Dough (2013) "Danvile Animal Control Officer Race Heats Up." *North Andover (Massachusetts) Eagle Tribune*, February 5.

Jackson, Donald W. and James W. Riddlesperger, Jr. (1991) "Money and Politics in Judicial Elections: The 1988 Election of the the Chief Justice of the Texas Supreme Court." 74 *Judicature* 184–89.

Jacob, Herbert (1964) "The Effect of Institutional Differences in the Recruitment Process, Case of State Judges." 13 *Journal of Public Law* 104–19.

Jacobs, Charles F., Wendy Scattergood, and Dave Wegge (2013) "Judicial Elections and State Court Accountability: A Survey of Wisconsin Voters." Paper presented at Annual Meeting of the Western Political Science Association. Hollywood, CA, March 28–30.

Jacobson, Gary C. (1978) "The Effects of Campaign Spending in Congressional Elections." 72 *American Political Science Review* 469–91.

(1980) *Money in Congressional Elections*. New Haven, CT: Yale University Press.

(1985) "Money and Votes Reconsidered: Congressional Elections, 1972–1982." 47 *Public Choice* 7–62.

(1990) "The Effects of Campaign Spending in House Elections: New Evidence for Old Arguments." 34 *American Journal of Political Science* 334–62.

Jamieson, Kathleen Hall and Michael Hennessy (2007) "Public Understanding of and Support for the Courts." 95 *Georgetown Law Journal* 899–902.

Jefferson, Wallace B. and Rebeccas Love Kourlis (2010) "An Analysis of Accountability in Judicial Selection: Recounting the Period of Straight Party Voting." 53 *Advocate* 8–11.

Johnson, Gene (2010) "Justice Sanders in Tight Re-election Fight." *KOMO News*; http://www.komonews.com/news/local/106583294.html.

Jones, Richard P. (1995) "Little Interest, Big Bucks Put into State Judicial Race." *Milwaukee Journal*, February 5, p. 1.

"Judge, Lawyer Battle for Seat on High Court; the Challenger and Incumbent Avoid Discussing Sexual Orientation." (2004) *Statesman Journal*, May 3, p. C1.

Justice at Stake (2013) "20/20 Insight Public Opinion Poll (campaign financing)." http://www.justiceatstake.org/file.cfm/media/news/toplines337_B2D51323DC5D0.pdf

Kales, Albert (1914) *Upopular Government in the United States*. Chicago: University of Chicago Press.

Kang, Michael S. and Joanna M. Shepherd (2011) "The Partisan Price of Justice: An Empirical Analysis of Campaign Contributions and Judicial Decisions." 86 *NYU Law Review* 69–130.

Kaplan, Sheila (1987) "Justice for Sale." *Common Cause Magazine*, pp. 29–32.

Kaplan, Sheila and Zoe Davidson (1998) "The Buying of the Bench." *Nation*, January 26, pp. 11–17.

Kelleher, Christine A. and Jennifer Wolak (2007) "Explaining Public Confidence in the Branches of State Government." 60 *Political Research Quarterly* 707–21.

Kelleher, Susan (2006) "Owens Wins Another Term After Unusually Costly Race." *Seattle Times*, November 8, p. B5.

Key, V. O., Jr. (1949) *Southern Politics*. New York: Knopf.

Keyes, E. W. (1895) "State Supreme Court: An Historical Sketch; Judicial Elections in Wisconsin for Forty Years." *Milwaukee Sentinel*, April 15.

King, Gary (1997) *A Solution to the Ecological Inference Problem: Reconstructing Individual Behavior from Aggregate Data*. Princeton, NJ: Princeton University Press.

King, Gary, Michael Tomz, and Jason Wittenberg (2000) "Making the Most of Statistical Analyses: Improving Interpretation and Presentation." 44 *American Journal of Political Science* 341–55.

Klarman, Michael (2013) *From the Closet to the Altar: Courts, Backlash, and the Struggle for Same-Sex Marriage*. New York: Oxford University Press.

Klein, David and Lawrence Baum (2001) "Ballot Information and Voting Decisions in Judicial Elections." 54 *Political Research Quarterly* 709–28.

Koehler, Michael (2001) "Baseball, Apple Pie and Judicial Elections: An Analysis of the 1967 Wisconsin Supreme Court Race." 85 *Marquette Law Review* 223–50.

Kolbert, Elizabeth (1995) "Special Interests' Special Weapon." *New York Times*, March 26.

Kourlis, Rebecca Love and Jordan M. Singer (2007) "Using Judicial Performance Evaluations to Promote Judicial Accountability." 90 *Judicature* 200–07.

Kritzer, Herbert M. (2011) "Competitiveness in State Supreme Court Elections, 1946–2009." 8 *Journal of Empirical Legal Studies* 237–59.

(2013) "The Trials and Tribulations of Counting Trials." 63 *DePaul Law Review* 415–41.

Kritzer, Herbert M. and Darryn C. Beckstrom (2007) "Daubert in the States: Diffusion of a New Approach to Expert Evidence in the Courts." 4 *Journal of Empirical Legal Studies* 983–1006.

Kutner, Michael H., Christopher J. Nachtsheim, and John Neter (2004) *Applied Linear Regression Models*. Boston: McGraw-Hill Irwin.

LaBrant, Robert S. (2004) "What Does *McConnell v. F.E.C.* Mean for Michigan Judicial Elections?" Pp. 43–46 in *Perspectives on Michigan Judicial Elections*. Detroit: Wayne State University Law School; http://www.mcfn.org/pdfs/reports/CFNSymposium.pdf.

Ladinsky, Jack and Jack Silver (1967) "Popular Democracy and Judicial Independence." 1967 *Wisconsin Law Review* 128–69.

Lau, Richard R., Lee Sigelman, and Ivy Brown Rovner (2007) "The Effects of Negative Political Campaigns: A Meta-Analytic Reassessment." 69 *Journal of Politics* 1176–1209.

Lau, Richard, Lee Sigelman, Caroline Heldman, and Paul Battit (1999) "The Effects of Negative Political Advertisements: A Meta-Analytical Assessment." 93 *American Political Science Review* 851–76.

Lax, Jeffrey R. and Justice H. Phillips (2014) "Gay Rights in the States: Public Opinion and Policy Responsiveness," 103 *American Political Science Review* 367–86.

Leamer, Laurence (2013) *The Price of Justice*. New York: Times Books.

Lee, Stephen E. (1973) "Judicial Selection and Tenure in Arizona." 1973 *Law and the Social Order* 51–80.

Lemennicier, Bertrand Claude and Nikolai Wenzel (2014) "The Judge and His Hangman: Judicial Selection and the Accountability of Judges." Unpublished paper available at http://ssrn.com/abstract=2485878.

Leonard, Meghan E. (2014) "Elections and Decision Making on State High Courts: Examining Legitimacy and Judicial Review." 35 *Justice System Journal* 45–61.

Leonhart, David (2014) "The Supreme Court Blunder That Liberals Tend to Make." *New York Times*, June 3, p. A3.

LeRoy, Michael H. (2010) "Do Partisan Elections of Judges Produce Unequal Justice When Courts Review Employment Arbitrations?" 95 *Iowa Law Review* 1569–1620.

Levitt, Justin (2011) "Weighing the Potential of Citizen Redistricting." 44 *Loyola of Los Angeles Law Review* 513–43.

Levy, Collin (2013) "Judicial Showdown In Kansas." *Wall Street Journal*, August 2.

Lim, Claire S. H. (2008) "Turnover and Accountability of Appointed and Elected Judges." Stanford, CA: Stanford University; http://www.economicdynamics.org/meetpapers/2009/paper_190.pdf.

Liptak, Adam (2013) "Alabama Judges Retain the Right to Override Juries in Capital Sentencing." *New York Times*, November 18.

Liptak, Adam and Janet Roberts (2006) "Campaign Cash Mirrors a High Court's Rulings." *New York Times*, October 1.

Liptak, Adam and Timothy Egan (2006) "A Sharply Divided Washington Supreme Court Upholds State's Ban on Same-Sex Marriage." *New York Times*, July 27, p. A18.

London, Robb (1990) "For Want of Recognition, Chief Justice Is Ousted." *New York Times*, September 28.

Mahtesian, Charles (1998) "Bench Press." *Governing*, August, pp. 18–23.

Malleson, Kate (2007) "The New Judicial Appointments Commission in England and Wales: New Wine in New Bottles?" pp. 39–55 in Kate Malleson and Peter H. Russell, eds., *Appointing Judges in an Age of Judicial Power: Critical Perspectives from Around the World*. Toronto: University of Toronto Press.

(2013) "Gender Quotas for the Judiciary in England and Wales," pp. 481–99 in Ulrike Schultz and Gisela Shaw, eds., *Gender and Judging*. Oxford: Hart Publishing.

Malleson, Kate and Peter Russell, eds. (2006) *Appointing Judges in the Age of Judicial Power: Critical Perspectives*. Toronto: University of Toronto Press.

Mannies, Jo (2007) "Conservatives Rev Up Effort to Revamp Missour's Judicial-Selection System." *St. Louis Post-Dispatch*, May 1.

Mark, David (2009) *Going Dirty: The Art of Negative Campaigning*. Lanham, MD: Rowman & Littlefield.

Marley, Patrick (2011) "Supreme Court Tensions Boil Over: Prosser Says He Was Goaded Into Insulting Chief Justice." *Milwaukee Journal Sentinel*, March 19.

Marshall, Thomas R. (1988) *Public Opinion and the Supreme Court*. Winchester, MA: Unwin.

(2005) "American Public Opinion and the Rehnquist Court." 89 *Judicature* 177–80.

Martin, Edward M. (1936a) *The Role of the Bar in Electing the Bench in Chicago*. Chicago: University of Chicago Press.

(1936b) "The Selection of Judges in Chicago and the Role of the Local Bar Therein." 30 *American Political Science Review* 315–23.

Martin, Jonathan (2010) "Sharp Ideological Contrasts in State Supreme Court Race." *Seattle Times*, August 1.

McCaffrey, Ray and Fiona O'Connell (2012) "Judicial Appointments in Northern Ireland." Northern Ireland Assembly; http://www.niassembly.gov.uk/Documents/RaISe/Publications/2012/justice/1912.pdf.

McCaffrey, Scott (2013) "Proposal to Combine, Abolish Constitutional Offices Draws Little Interest." *Arlington Sun Gazette*, August 7.

McCall, Madhavi (2001) "Campaign Contributions and Judicial Decisions: Can Justice Be Bought?" 22 *American Review of Politics* 349–73.

(2003) "The Politics of Judicial Elections: The Influence of Campaign Contributions on the Voting Patterns of Texas Supreme Court Justices, 1994–1997." 31 *Politics and Policy* 314–43.

McCall, Madhavi M. and Michael A. McCall (2007) "Campaign Contributions, Judicial Decisions, and the Texas Supreme Court: Assessing the Appearance of Impropriety." 90 *Judicature* 214–25.

McKenzie, Mark Jonathan and Michael A. Unger (2011) "'New Style' Campaigning, Citizen Knowledge, and Sources of Legitimacy for State Courts: A Case Study in Texas." 39 *Politics & Policy* 813–34.

McLeod, Aman (2008) "Bidding for Justice: A Case Study about the Effect of Campaign Contributions on Judicial Decision-Making." 85 *University of Detroit Mercy Law Review* 385–405.

(2012) "The Party on the Bench: Partisanship, Judicial Selection Commissions, and State High-Court Appointments" 33 *Justice System Journal* 262–74.

Medvic, Stephen K., ed. (2011) *New Directions in Campaigns and Elections*. New York: Routledge.

Mezey, Susan Gluck (2009) *Gay Families and the Courts: The Quest for Equal Rights*. Lanham, MD: Rowman & Littlefield.

Miletich, Steve (2010) "Justice Richard Sanders, as Usual, Draws Fire from Two Election Opponents." *Seattle Times*, July 28.

Mintz, Howard (2014). "California Supreme Court and State Appeals Court Justices Face Easy Election Road." *San Jose Mercury News*, October 15.

"Missouri Compromised: Judicial Selection the Trial Lawyer Way." (2011) *Wall Street Journal*, September 15.

Modie, Neil (2002) "Spearman Backs Fairhurst for State High Court." *Seattle Post-Intelligencer*, September 19, p. B7.

Moos, Malcolm (1941) "Judicial Elections and Partisan Endorsements of Judicial Candidates in Minnesota." 35 *American Political Science Review* 69–75.

Moyer, Bill (2010) "Bill Moyer's Journal: Justice for Sale Revisited (Transcript)"; http://www.pbs.org/moyers/journal/02192010/transcript1.html.

Murphy, Daniel J. (1994) "When State Judges Are Elected." *Invester's Business Daily*, November 7, 1994, p. A1.

Nagel, Stuart S. (1973) "Comparing Elected and Appointed Judicial Systems." 1(4) *Sage Professional Papers in American Politics* [entire issue].

National Center for State Courts (1999) "How the Public Views the State Courts: A 1999 National Survey." Williamsburg, VA: National Institute for State Courts; http://digitalcommons.unl.edu/cgi/viewcontent.cgi?article=1016&context=publicpolicypublications.

(2002) *Call to Action: Statement of the National Summit on Improving Judicial Selection*" Williamsburg, VA: National Center for State Courts.

Neff, Erin (2004) "Political Notebook: Candidate Runs Afoul of Veterans." *Las Vegas Review-Journal*, October 25.

Nelson, Michael (2011) "Uncontested and Unaccountable? Rates of Contestation and the Quest for Accountability in General Jurisdiction Trial Courts." 94 *Judicature* 208–17.

Nelson, Michael J., Rachel Paine Caulfield, and Andrew D. Martin (2013) "OH, MI: A Note on Empirical Examinations of Judicial Elections." 13 *State Politics & Policy Quarterly* 495–511.

O'Brien, David M (2006) "The Politics of Judicial Selection and Appointments in Japan and Ten South and Southeast Asian Countries," pp. 355–74 in Kate Malleson and Peter Russell, eds., *Appointing Judges in the Age of Judicial Power: Critical Perspectives*. Toronto: University of Toronto Press.

O'Connor, Sandra Day (2007) "Justice for Sale: How Special-Interest Money Threatens the Integrity of Our Courts." *Wall Street Journal*, November 15.

(2010) "Take Justice Off the Ballot." *New York Times*, May 22.

O'Hagan, Maureen (2004) " Supreme Court Races Lack Usual Mystery." *Seattle Times*, October 23, p. B1.

"Ohio Justices Say School System Is Legal but Must End Disparities." (2001) *New York Times*, September 7.

Olsen, Randy M. (2005) "Alaska Bar Controversy Claims First Judge." 29 *Alaska Bar Rag* 1, 18–19.

Palmer, Vernon V. (2010) *The Recusal of American Judges in the Post-Caperton Era: An Empirical Assessment of the Risk of Actual Bias in Decisions Involving Campaign Contributors*. New Orleans, LA: Tulane Law School; http://ssrn.com/paper=1721665.

Palmer, Vernon V. and John Levendis (2008) "The Louisiana Supreme Court in Question: An Empirical and Statistical Study of the Effects of Campaign Money on the Judicial Function." 82 *Tulane Law Review* 1291–1314.

Partin, Randall W. (2002) "Assessing the Impact of Campaign Spending in Governors' Races." 55 *Political Research Quarterly* 213–33.

Paterson, Alan (2007) "Scottish Judicial Appointments Board: New Wine in Old Bottles?" pp. 13–38 in Kate Malleson and Peter H. Russell, eds., *Appointing Judges in an Age of Judicial Power: Critical Perspectives from Around the World*. Toronto: University of Toronto Press.

(2013) *Final Judgment: The Last Law Lords and the Supreme Court*. Oxford, UK: Hart Publishing.

Peltason, Jack W. (1945) "The Missouri Plan for the Selection of Judges." 20 *University of Missouri Studies* [entire issue].

Pettys, Todd E. (2013) "Retention Reux: Iowa 2012." 14 *Journal of Appellate Practice and Process* 47–79.

Philip, Cynthia O., Paul Nejelski, and Aric Press (1976) *Where Do Judges Come From*. New York: Institute of Judicial Administration.

Phillips, Thomas R. (2003) "Electoral Accountability and Judicial Independence." 64 *Ohio State Law Journal* 137–47.

Pinello, Daniel R. (1995) *The Impact of Judicial Selection Method on State Supreme Court Policy Innovation, Reaction, and Atrophy*. Westport, CT: Greenwood Publishing Group.

Pommer, Matt (1997) "Thompson's Fortunes Could Hinge on Judicial Race." *Madison Capital Times*, March 29–30, p. 6A.

Pozen, David E. (2008) "The Irony of Judicial Elections." 108 *Columbia Law Review* 265–330.

"Preserving Judicial Independence." (2012) 95 *Judicature* 249–50.

Princeton Survey Research Associates International (2009) "Separate Branches, Shared Responsibilities: A National Survey of Public Expectations on Solving Justice Issues"; http://cdm16501.contentdm.oclc.org/cdm/ref/collection/ctcomm/id/118.

Radelet, Michael L. (2011) "Overriding Jury Sentencing Recommendations in Florida Capital Cases: An Update and Possible Half Requiem." 2011 *Michigan State Law Review* 793–822.

Ramsey, Ross (2012) "Straight-ticket Voting Takes a Trusting Soul." *New York Times*, October 13.

Reid, Traciel V. (1999) "The Politicization of Retention Elections: Lessons from the Defeat of Justices Lanphier and White." 83 *Judicature* 68–77.

Rice, Douglas (2014) "On Courts and Pocketbooks: Macroeconomic Judicial Behavior across Methods of Judicial Selection." 2 *Journal of Law and Courts* 327–47.

Ridout, Travis N., Michael Franz, Kenneth Goldstein, and Paul Freedman (n.d.) "Measuring Exposure to Campaign Advertising." Madison: University of Wisconsin; http://wiscadproject.wisc.edu/pdf/MeasuringExposureToCampaignAdvertising.pdf.

Robinson, William S. (1950) "Ecological Correlations and the Behavior of Individuals." 15 *American Sociological Review* 351–57.

Rock, Emily and Lawrence Baum (2010) "The Impact of High-Visibility Contests for U.S. State Court Judgeships: Partisan Voting in Nonpartisan Elections." 10 *State Politics & Policy Quarterly* 368–96.

Romenesko, James (1990) "Wisconsin Court Race Gets Nasty." *National Law Journal*, April 2, pp. 3, 32.

Romero, Francine Sanders, David W. Romero, and Victoria Ford (2002) "The Influence of Selection Method on Racial Discrimination Cases: A Longitudinal State Supreme Court Analysis." 2 *Research on Judicial Selection* 17–31.

Rood, W. R. (1978) "Justice Bird's Opponents Gearing Up for TV Blitz." *Los Angeles Times*, September 30, pp. 1, 16.

Roscoe, Douglas D. and Shannon Jenkins (2005) "A Meta-Analysis of Campaign Contributions Impact on Roll Call Voting." 86 *Social Science Quarterly* 52–68.

Rosenbaum, Jason (2009) "Bill Altering Missouri's Plan Fails: Plan Opponents Look to Initiation Process Next." *Missouri Lawyers Media*, April 30.

Ross, J. R. (2005) "Crooks to Seek Re-election to High Court." *Madison Capital Times*, July 23–24, p. 3A.

Rottman, David N. and Sauna M. Strickland (2006) "State Court Organization 2004." Washington, DC: Bureau of Justice Statistics; http://bjs.gov/content/pub/pdf/sco04.pdf.

Russakoff, Dale (1996) "Legal War Conquests State's Politics: In Tort Reform Fight, Alabama Court Race Cost $5 Million." *Washington Post*, December 1, p. A1.

Russell, Katheryn K. (1994) "The Constitutionality of Jury Override in Alabama Death Penalty Cases." 46 *Alabama Law Review* 5–45.

Salamone, Michael F., Orion A. Yoesle, and Travis N. Ridout (2014) "Campaigning for the Bench: The Content of Political Advertising in Judicial Races." Paper presented at the Annual Meeting of the American Political Science Association. Washington, DC, August 28–31.

Sample, James, Charles Hall, and Linda Casey (2010a) "The New Politics of Judicial Elections." 94 *Judicature* 50–58.

Sample, James, Lauren Jones, and Rachel Weiss (2007) "The New Politics of Judicial Elections 2006: How 2006 Was the Most Threatening Year Yet to the Fairness and Impartiality of Our Courts–and How Americans Are Fighting Back." New York: Brennan Center for Justice, New York University School of Law; http://brennan.3cdn.net/49c18b6cb18960b2f9_z6m62gwji.pdf.

Sample, James, Adam Skaggs, Jonathan Blitzer, and Linda Casey (2010b) *The New Politics of Judicial Elections 2000–2009: Decade of Change*. New York: Brennan Center for Justice, New York University School of Law.

Savchak, Elisha Carol and A. J. Barghothi (2007) "The Influence of Appointment and Retention Constituencies: Testing Strategies of Judicial Decisionmaking." 7 *State Politics & Policy Quarterly* 394–415.

Schlesinger, Joseph (1966) *Ambition and Politics: Political Careers in the United States*. Chicago: Rand McNally.

Schotland, Roy A. (1985) "Elective Judges' Campaign Financing: Are State Judges' Robes the Emperor's Clothes of American Democracy?" 2 *Journal of Law & Politics* 57–167.

(2011) "Iowa's 2010 Judicial Election: Appropriate Accountability or Rampant Passion?" 46 *Court Review* 118–28.

Schubert, Glendon (1959a) "The 'Packing' of the Michigan Supreme Court," pp. 129–41 in Glendon Schubert, ed., *Quantitative Analysis of Judicial Behavior*. New York: Free Press.

Schubert, Glendon A. (1959b) *Quantitative Analysis of Judicial Behavior*. Glencoe, IL: Free Press.

Schwartz, John (2009) "Effort Begun to End Voting for Judges." *New York Times*, December 24, 2009.

Segall, Cary (1996) "High Court Race Pits Flamboyant Fine, Conservative Crooks." *Wisconsin State Journal*, pp. 1A, 9A.

(1997) "Court Defends 'Family Values'." *Wisconsin State Journal*, March 9, p. 1C.

Selzer, Renata Olafson (2006) "The Future of Judicial Elections in North Dakota." 82 *North Dakota Law Review* 197–234.

Shapiro, Martin (1981) *Courts*. Chicago: University of Chicago Press.

Sharkey, Mary Anne and W. Stevens Ricks (1984) "Frank Celebrezze: A Law Unto Himself." *Cleveland Plain Dealer*, pp. 1-A, 20-A, 21-A.

Sheldon, Charles H. and Linda S. Maule (1997) *Choosing Justice: The Recruitment of State and Federal Judges*. Pullman: Washington State University Press.

Shepherd, Joanna M. (2009a) "Are Appointed Judges Strategic Too?" 58 *Duke Law Journal* 1589–1626.

(2009b) "Money, Politics, and Impartial Justice." 58 *Duke Law Journal* 623–85.

(2009c) "The Influence of Retention Politics on Judges' Voting." 38 *Journal of Legal Studies* 169–206.

(2013) "Justice at Risk: An Empirical Analysis of Campaign Contributions and Judicial Decisions." Washington, DC: American Constitution Society for Law and Policy; http://www.acslaw.org/ACS%20Justice%20at%20Risk%20(FINAL)%206_10_13.pdf.

Shepherd, Joanna M. and Michael S. Kang (2014) "Skewed Justice: *Citizens United*, Television Advertising and State Supreme Court Justices' Decisions in Criminal Cases." Washington, DC: American Constitution Society for Law and Policy; http://skewedjustice.org.

Shugerman, Joel H. (2012) *The People's Courts: Pursuing Judicial Independence in America*. Cambridge, MA: Harvard University Press.

Simons, Abby (2014a) "Will Michelle MacDonald's GOP Drama Be a Boon to Her Campaign?" *Star Tribune*, August 31.

(2014b) "Embattled Supreme Court Candidate Michelle MacDonald Files GOP Complaint." *Star Tribune*, September 4.

(2014c) "Jury Convicts Supreme Court Candidate of Resisting Arrest, Refusing Breath Test." *Star Tribune*, September 18.

Sisk, Chas (2009) "Election of Judges in Tennessee Is Rejected: Commission Will Get New Name, Members." *Tennessean*, May 29.

Skaggs, Adam, Maria da Silva, Linda Casey, and Charles Hall (2011) *The New Politics of Judicial Elections, 2009–10*. New York: Brennan Center For Justice, New York University School of Law.

Slater, Jesse (2013) "The History of Minnesota's Judicial Elections: A Description and Analysis of the Changes in Judicial Election Laws and Their Effect on the Competitiveness of Minnesota's Judicial Elections." 10 *University of St. Thomas Law Journal* 367–91.

Smith, Malcolm (1951) "The California Method of Selecting Judges." 3 *Stanford Law Review* 571–600.

Souders, Ryan L. (2006) "A Gorilla at the Dinner Table: Partisan Judicial Elections in the United States." 25 *Review of Litigation* 519–74.

Southworth, Ann (2008) *Lawyers of the Right: Professionalizing the Conservative Coalition*. Chicago: University of Chicago Press.

Squire, Peverill (1995) "Candidates, Money, and Voters – Assessing the State of Congressional Elections Research." 48 *Political Research Quarterly* 891–917.

Squire, Peverill and Eric R.A.N. Smith (1988) "The Effect of Partisan Information on Voters in Nonpartisan Elections." 50 *Journal of Politics* 169–79.

Stason, E. Blythe (1958) "Judicial Selection Around the World." 41 *Journal of the American Judicature Society* 134–41.

Stassen-Berger, Rachel E. and Glenn Howatt (2013) "Spending on State Legislative Races Has Doubled in 10 Years." *Minneapolis Star-Tribune*, September 1, pp. A1, A9.

Stephenson, Crocker, Cary Spivak, and Patrick Marley (2011) "Justices' Feud Gets Physical: Prosser, Bradley Clashed on Eve of Union Ruling." *Milwaukee Journal Sentinel*, June 25.

Straw, Jack (2013) *Aspects of Law Reform: An Insider's Perspective*. Cambridge, UK: Cambridge University Press.

Streb, Matthew J. (2011) "Judicial Elections and Public Perception of the Courts," pp. 147–67 in Bruce Peabody, ed., *The Politics of Judicial Independence: Courts, Politics, and the Public*. Baltimore, MD: Johns Hopkins University Press.

Streb, Matthew J. and Brian Frederick (2009) "Conditions for Competition in Low-Information Judicial Elections." 62 *Political Research Quarterly* 523–37.

Streb, Matthew J., Brian Frederick, and Case LaFrance (2007) "Contestation, Competition, and the Potential for Accountability in Intermediate Appellate Court Elections." 91 *Judicature* 70–79.

Streb, Matthew J., Brian Frederick, and Casey LaFrance (2009) "Voter Rolloff in a Low-Information Context: Evidence From Intermediate Appellate Court Elections." 37 *American Politics Research* 644–69.

Sturdevant, Lori (2014) "The Right-Wing Litmus Test, Part Two: Judges." *Minneapolis Star Tribune*, March 2, pp. OP1, OP3.

Stutzman, Rene (2014) "Tallahassee Federal Judge Throws Out Florida's Ban on Same-sex Marriage " *Orlando Sentinel*, August 21.

"Supreme Court Runoff Is a Low-Key Race." (2006) *Statesman Journal*, October 17, p. C1.

Tabarrok, Alexander and Eric Helland (1999) "Court Politics: The Political Economy of Tort Awards." 42 *Journal of Law and Economics* 157–88.

Talbot, Stephen, Sheila Kaplan, and Bill Moyers (1999) "Frontline: Justice for Sale [Transcript]"; http://www.pbs.org/wgbh/pages/frontline/shows/justice/etc/script.html.

Tarr, G. Alan (2003) "State Judicial Selection and Judicial Independence," Appendix D in *Justice in Jeopardy: Report of the ABA Commission on the 21st Century Judiciary*. Chicago: American Bar Association.

(2012) *Without Fear or Favor: Judicial Independence and Accountability in the States*. Stanford, CA: Stanford University Press.

Teles, Steven M. (2008) *The Rise of the Conservative Legal Movement: The Battle for Control of the Law*. Princeton, NJ: Princeton University Press.

Thomas, Ralph (2006a) "Alexander Prevails in Bitter Court Race." *Seattle Times*, September 21, 2006, p. B1.

(2006b) "Interest Groups Targeting State Supreme Court Races." *Seattle Times*, May 23, p. B1.

Thompson, Robert S. (1988) "Judicial Retention Elections and Judicial Method: A Retrospective on the California Retention Election of 1986." 61 *Southern California Law Review* 2007–64.

Tolson, Mike (2012) "Divided Electorate Flusters Harris County Judges." *Houston Chronicle*, November 26.

Toomey, Sheila (2000) "Judges under Attack: Gay, Abortion Rulings Rile Foes." *Anchorage Daily News*, October 29, p. B1.

Tully, Kevin R. and E. Phelps Gay (2010) "Rebuttal of Vernon Palmer's Thesis, Take Two"; http://www.lasc.org/press_room/press_releases/2012/Rebuttal.pdf.

"Two Face Off for Oregon Supreme Court Seat." (2010) *Statesman Journal*, May 4, p. C1.

Uelmen, Gerald F. (1988) "Supreme Court Retention Elections in California." 28 *Santa Clara Law Review* 333–55.

Ulmer, S. Sidney (1962) "The Party Variable in the Michigan Supreme Court." 11 *Journal of Public Law* 352–62.

(1966) "Politics and Procdures in the Michigan Supreme Court." 46 *Southwestern Social Science Quarterly* 373–84.

"Voting in the Dark." (2006) *Register-Guard*, October 31, p. A6.

Waltenburg, Eric N. and Charles S. Lopeman (2000) "Tort Decisions and Campaign Dollars." 28 *Southeastern Political Review* 241–63.

Ware, Stephen J. (1999) "Money, Politics and Judicial Decisions: A Case Study of Arbitration Law in Alabama." 15 *Journal of Law & Politics* 645–86.

Wasmann, Erik, Nicholas P. Lovrich, and Charles H. Sheldon (1986) "Perceptions of State and Local Courts: A Comparison Across Selection Systems." 11 *Justice System Journal* 168–95.

Watson, Richard A. and Rondal G. Downing (1969) *The Politics of the Bench and Bar: Judicial Selection Under the Missouri Nonpartisan Court Plan*. New York: John Wiley & Sons.

Wattenberg, Martin P. and Craig Leonard Brians (1999) "Negative Campaign Advertising: Demobilizer or Mobilizer?" 93 *American Political Science Review* 891–99.

West, Darrell M. (1996) "Harry and Louise Go to Washington: Political Advertising and Health Care Policy." 21 *Journal of Health Politics, Policy and Law* 35–68.

(2014) *Air Wars: Television Advertising and Social Media in Election Campaigns, 1952–2012*, 6th ed]. Thousand Oaks, CA: Sage/CQ Press.

Wiese, Kelly (2008) "Proposed Changes to Missouri Plan Gather Steam at Capital." *Daily Record and Kansas City Daily News-Press*, March 12.

Williams, Margaret S. and Corey Dislear (2007) "Bidding for Justice: The Influence of Attorneys' Contributions on State Supreme Courts." 28 *Justice System Journal* 135–56.

Wilson, Betty (1990) "Perpich on Hot Seat Over Court Vacancy." *Minneapolis Star Tribune*, July 4, p. 1A.

Winslow, John Bradley (1912) *The Story of a Great Court*. Chicago: T.H. Flood & Company.

Winters, Glenn R. (1968) "The Merit Plan for Judicial Selecton and Tenure – Its Historical Development." 7 *Duquesne Law Review* 61–78.

Wipf, Thomas (2002) "Swiss Cantons," pp. 1567–69 in Herbert M. Kritzer, ed., *Legal Systems of the World*. Santa Barbara, CA: ABC-CLIO.

Wold, John T. and John H. Culver (1987) "The Defeat of the California Justices: The Campaign, the Electorate, and the Issue of Judicial Accountability." 70 *Judicature* 348–55.

Wright, Gerald C. (1976) "Linear Models for Evaluating Conditional Relationships." 20 *American Journal of Political Science* 349–73.

Wright, Gerald, Robert S. Erikson, and John McIver (1985) "Measuring State Partisanship and Ideology with Survey Data." 47 *Journal of Politics* 469–89.

Yankelovich, Skelly & White (1978) *The Public Image of the Courts*. Williamsburg, VA: National Center for State Courts.

Yates, Jeff, Holley Tankersley, and Paul Brace (2010) "Assessing the Impact of State Judicial Structures on Citizen Litigiousness." 63 *Political Research Quarterly* 796–810.

Yoachum, Susan (1986) "Embattled Justices Wage TV War." *San Jose Mercury News*, November 2, p. 2H.

Zimmerman, Bill (1986) "The Campaign That Could't Win: When Rose Bird Ran Her Own Defeat." *Los Angeles Times*, November 9.

Zorn, Christopher (2001) "Generalized Estimating Equation Models for Correlated Data: A Review with Applications." 45 *American Journal of Political Science* 470–90.

CASES CITED

American Tradition Partnership, Inc. v. Bullock, 567 U.S. ___ (2012)

Andersen v. King County, 138 P.3d 963 (Wash. 2006)

Baker v. Nelson, 191 N.W.2d 185 (Minn. 1971)

Bixler v. Avondale Mills, 405 N.W.2d 428 (Minn. App. 1987)

Buckley v. Valeo, 424 U.S. 1 (1976)

Caperton v. A.T. Massey Coal Co., 556 U.S. 868 (2009)

Citizens United v. Federal Election Commission, 558 U.S. 50 (2010)

Daubert v. Merrell Dow Pharmaceuticals, Inc., 509 U.S. 579 (1993)

Ferdon v. Wisconsin Patients Compensation Fund, 701 N.W.2d 440 (Wis. 2005)

Frye v. United States, 293 F. 1013 (D.C. Cir. 1923)

Godoy v. E.I. DuPont, 768 N.W.2d 674 (Wis. 2009)

Goodridge v. Department of Public Health, 798 N.E.2d 941 (2003)

Guinn v. Legislature of the State, 71 P.3d 1269 (Nev. 2003) *Harris v. Alabama*, 513 U.S. 504 (1995)

In the Matter of the Marriage of J.B and H.B [which consolidated with *State of Texas v. Angelique Naylor and Sabrina Dal*] argued November 5, 2013 (as of March 1, 2015, the Texas Supreme Court had not rendered a decision).

Madison Teachers, Inc., et al. v. Scott Walker et al., 2014 WI 99

Page v. Carlson, 488 N.W.2d 274 (Minn. 1992)

Republican Party of Minnesota v. White, 536 U. S. 765 (2002)

Sindell v. Abbott Lab., 607 P.2d 924 (Cal. 1980)

State of Texas v. Angelique Naylor and Sabrina Dal [consolidated with *In the Matter of the Marriage of J.B and H.B*] argued November 5, 2013 (as of March 1, 2015, the Texas Supreme Court had not rendered a decision).

State of Wisconsin ex rel. Ismael R. Ozanne v. Jeff Fitzgerald et al., 798 N.W.2d 436 (Wis. 2011)

State v. Fischer, 778 N.W.2d 629 (Wis. 2010)

State v. Mack, 292 N.W.2d 764 (Minn. 1980)

State v. Walstad, 351 N.W.2d 469 (Wis. 1984)

Thomas ex rel. Gramling v. Mallet, 701 N.W.2d 523 (Wis. 2005)
Varnum v. Brien, 763 N.W.2d 862 (Iowa 2010)
U.S. v. Windsor, 570 U.S. ___ (2013)
Williams – Yulee v. The Florida Bar (U.S. Supreme Court case no. 13-1499) [decision expected 2015].
Wisconsin v. Milwaukee Braves, Inc., 144 N.W.2d 1 (Wis. 1966)

LAWS AND STATUTES CITED

Ark. Const., Amend. 29, §2
Constitutional Reform Act 2005 (U.K.)
Justice (Northern Ireland) Act 2002
Laws of Minnesota 1997, chapter 203, article 10
Minn. Const., Art. VI §9
Wis. Stat. Ch. 5, §38, 1911
1913 Wis. Sess. Laws 558
2011 Wisconsin Act 10 ("Act 10")

Index

CPSIA information can be obtained
at www.ICGtesting.com
Printed in the USA
LVOW01*2104241115
464010LV00010B/165/P